JUVENILE JUSTICE TODAY

4TH EDITION

JUVENILE JUSTICE TODAY

GENNARO F. VITO, PH.D.
University of Louisville

CLIFFORD E. SIMONSEN, PH.D.

PEARSON
Prentice
Hall

Upper Saddle River, New Jersey 07458

Library of Congress Cataloging-in-Publication Data

Vito, Gennaro F.
  Juvenile justice today / Gennaro F. Vito, Clifford E. Simonsen.— 4th ed.
      p. cm.
  Previous edition: Juvenile justice in America / Clifford E. Simonsen. 3rd
  ed. New York: Macmillan Pub. Co., 1991.
    ISBN 0-13-011993-8
  1. Juvenile justice, Administration of—United States. 2. Juvenile
  delinquency—United States. 3. Juvenile
  delinquents—Rehabilitation—United States. I. Simonsen, Clifford E.
  Juvenile justice in America. II. Simonsen, Clifford E. III. Title.
    HV9104 .S55 2004
    364.36'0973—dc22

                                                          2003015909

Publisher: Stephen Helba
Executive Editor: Frank Mortimer, Jr.
Assistant Editor: Sarah Holle
Production Editor: Nicholas P. Angelides, Pine Tree Composition
Production Liaison: Barbara Marttine Cappuccio
Director of Manufacturing and Production: Bruce Johnson
Managing Editor: Mary Carnis
Manufacturing Buyer: Cathleen Petersen
Creative Director: Cheryl Asherman
Cover Design Coordinator: Miguel Ortiz
Cover Designer: Cheryl Asherman
Cover Image: Andrew Liechtenstein/Corbis Sygma
Editorial Assistant: Barbara Rosenberg
Marketing Manager: Tim Peyton
Formatting and Interior Design: Pine Tree Composition
Printing and Binding: Phoenix Book Tech Park

Part Photo Credits		
I:	p. 1	*CORBIS*
II:	p. 79	Chris Takagi
III:	p. 315	Spencer Grant/ *PhotoEdit*
IV:	p. 321	*Photo Researchers Inc.*

Pearson Prentice Hall™ is a trademark of Pearson Education, Inc.
Pearson® is a registered trademark of Pearson plc
Prentice® Hall is a registered trademark of Pearson Education, Inc.

Pearson Education LTD.
Pearson Education Singapore, Pte. Ltd.
Pearson Education Canada, Ltd.
Pearson Education—Japan
Pearson Education Australia PTY, Limited
Pearson Education North Asia Ltd.
Pearson Educacíon de Mexico, S.A. de C.V.
Pearson Education Malaysia, Pte. Ltd.

10 9 8 7 6 5 4 3
ISBN 0-13-011993-8

This book is dedicated to:

Anthony, Gina, and Mary Vito
Kris, Kory, and Fran Simonsen.

CONTENTS

3

JUVENILE CRIME: MEASUREMENT AND ANALYSIS   56

PART II

THE JUVENILE JUSTICE SYSTEM   79

4

THE JUVENILE JUSTICE PROCESS   81

5

JUVENILES AND THE POLICE: WHERE THE SYSTEM STARTS   98

6

THE JUVENILE COURT   127

7

JUVENILE'S LEGAL RIGHTS   162

8

JUVENILE PROBATION—CHEAPER OR BETTER?   184

9

JUVENILE INSTITUTIONS: THE SUCCESS OF FAILURE   217

10

JUVENILE PAROLE: USEFUL OR HARMFUL?   254

11

GROUP HOMES, FOSTER CARE AND ADOPTION   272

12

JUVENILE JUSTICE ASSESSMENT AND CLASSIFICATION   295

PART III

JUVENILE JUSTICE IN THE TWENTY-FIRST CENTURY   315

13

DEALING WITH DELINQUENCY: THEORIES, ISSUES, AND PRACTICE   317

14

THE FUTURE OF JUVENILE JUSTICE   355

INDEX   367

PREFACE

Juvenile Justice Today is written for the student beginning to develop an interest in the juvenile area of the criminal justice system. It focuses on the system itself, the processes within it, and the young people who become involved in it. We also present an historical view of the juvenile justice system and how it relates to the entire criminal justice system.

This text is based on a specific model emphasizing concise chapters that logically build upon each other. It is designed to keep the reader's attention and interest by presenting each chapter in self-contained, yet interrelated parts that can be easily read in short sessions without excessive effort. References are contained at the end of each chapter.

Aside from covering the practical and theoretical elements of the juvenile justice system and process, the text makes use of current literature and research, including timely materials available on the World Wide Web.

ORGANIZATION OF THIS EDITION

This fourth edition is divided into three major sections and fourteen chapters. Part I presents the history of juvenile justice. It examines the handling of juveniles by justice systems from ancient times up to the present, along with the slow emergence of a separate system of juvenile justice. Chapter 1 traces the development of juvenile justice from Babylon to the United States in the early part of the twentieth century. Chapter 2 focuses upon changes in the treatment of juveniles from 1900 through the establishment of and changes in the operations of the juvenile court in the twentieth century. Chapter 3 examines statistics on juvenile justice and crime today that provides a basis for the examination of issues covered in the remainder of the text.

Part II is an extensive coverage of the entire juvenile justice process. It examines the parts of the juvenile justice system that are both similar to and different from the adult criminal justice system. Chapter 4 reviews the process model of juvenile justice and the specialized language and terminology used to handle juvenile cases. A handy lexicon of related phrases is provided to help the student understand the differences between the adult and juvenile justice models. Chapter 5 deals with the relationships that exist with the juvenile in trouble and his or her first point of contact—the police. The development of police organizations to deal with juveniles is reviewed with special attention given to community and problem-oriented policing. Chapter 6 traces the development of the juvenile court and the modern pressures for change, primarily to make it more like the adult system in regard to both due process and accountability. Chapter 7 provides a review of the legal rights of juveniles, tracing the significant legal decisions that have begun to shape and change the juvenile justice process.

Chapter 8 examines the problems and hopes that lie in juvenile probation, a system that is splintered into so many jurisdictions that it seems to be no system at all. Special attention is given to innovations in juvenile probation, such as electronic monitoring and school probation. Chapter 9 traces the dismal history of juvenile institutions as a response to delinquency. In particular, the serious issues of disproportionate minority confinement and the holding of juveniles in adult jails and prisons are examined. Chapter 10 examines juvenile parole and its less-than-fulfilled promise to successfully return the juvenile to the community. A new model, the Intensive Aftercare Program, is also presented. Chapter 11 looks a group homes, foster care, and adoption as potential ways to place juveniles in productive environments rather than the formal juvenile justice process. Chapter 12 examines the systems of classification and assessment that are designed to put juveniles into groups to facilitate custody and treatment plans in both the institution and the community.

Part III considers the future of juvenile justice. Chapter 13 examines the connection between theory, issues, and juvenile justice practice. Here, theory is integrated with a serious problem presented by juveniles and a practice that is proposed to deal with them. The death penalty for juveniles, gangs, violence, and status offenses are covered in this chapter. Chapter 14 is the conclusion of the text. It presents an overview of the problems faced by the juvenile justice system in the opening years of the twenty-first century.

OUTSTANDING FEATURES OF THIS EDITION

The true purpose of any textbook is to transmit and clarify ideas and information to students. It is essential, therefore, that the writing style be clear and understandable. Readability is a key feature of this edition. We have taken steps to make this text easier for the instructor to use and to make it a more pleasant and worthwhile learning experience for the reader.

This edition has been revised and rearranged for student understanding. Material presented is as current and timely as possible. Where appropriate, references are made to web sites that will allow students to check statistics and information as they use the text. Important information appears in boxes throughout the text to present current issues while not interrupting the flow of thought.

Along with readability, the reorganization of the text makes this edition clearer to the reader. The subject matter flows in a more logical and planned fashion following the system as a whole and the process that juveniles are subjected to.

Also available for the busy instructor is a revised *Instructor's Manual* prepared by Dr. Julie Kunselman of the University of West Florida. The manual contains test questions for quizzes and examinations as well as PowerPoint slides for lectures.

ACKNOWLEDGMENTS

We are indebted to many people for the preparation and production of this fourth edition. First of all, Jennifer Dunn at the University of Louisville conducted extensive research to locate current research on juvenile justice programs and operations that served as the basis for the revision of the text. Also, the fourth edition was reviewed by several of our colleagues around the country. Their thoroughness, attention to detail, and expertise in juvenile justice was a tremendous help.

Our thanks go to Michael Leiber, University of Northern Iowa, Cedar Falls, IA; Marty Gruher, Rogue Community College, Grant Pass, OR; Kimberly Tobin, Westfield State College, Westfield, MA; Richard Lawrence, St. Cloud University, St. Cloud, MN; Gary Keveles, University of Wisconsin–Superior, Superior, WI; Thomas Phelps, California State University, Sacramento, CA; and Shaun Gabbidon, Penn State University, Harrisburg, PA.

The Kentucky Department of Juvenile Justice provided many of the illustrations in the text and is the hope of juveniles in the commonwealth. Our Prentice Hall editors changed during the preparation of the fourth edition. Both Kim Davies and her successor, Frank Mortimer, have our sincere appreciation for their encouragement and patience. Our assistant editor, Sarah Holle, took our coal and turned it into a diamond.

Of course, our wives deserve a special note of thanks. Mary and Fran put up with our absences and gave us the time away from our chores and families to do the work necessary to complete the work. We hope that this text helps children in trouble and those persons who work so hard in the juvenile justice system and elsewhere on their behalf.

G.F.V.

C.E.S.

JUVENILE JUSTICE TODAY

PART ONE

THE HISTORY OF JUVENILE JUSTICE

chapter 1

CHILDREN IN TROUBLE (2000 B.C. TO THE TWENTIETH CENTURY)

The failure or inability of children and youth to live up to standards set by adults is age-old. The forbidden behavior of children and youth, along with the severe punishments dealt out, is included in the general criminal laws of different countries in different periods.

— Ruth Shonle Cavan

CHAPTER OVERVIEW

The history of the way society has cared for, treated, and punished its young people would provide material for a shelf of books (and has). In Chapters 1 and 2 we will attempt to provide the student a glimpse of the variety and inventiveness of the treatment that has prevailed from ancient times up to the present day. Much of the later history is derived from our English antecedents, a system from which much of the American system of justice—and the foundations for juvenile justice—have been built.

Is the concept of juvenile justice as a system something new? How did this concept evolve to the juvenile justice system we have today? Have children always received more lenient treatment than adults from those who make and enforce the law? How did early societies control the child who got outside the boundaries of their folkways, mores, and laws? In this brief overview, these and many other questions will be explored.

Box 1.1 Juvenile

A person subject to juvenile court proceedings because a statutorily defined event was alleged to have occurred while his or her age was below the statutorily defined limit of original jurisdiction of a juvenile court. Typically, a juvenile delinquent has been adjudicated by a juvenile court for a crime - law violations that would be crimes even if an adult had committed them.

Prologue

In this chapter we will look at the ancient as well as the more recent antecedents of juvenile justice, from 2000 B.C. to the end of the nineteenth century. It should be noted that this is not a history text; but, as the writer Studs Terkel said, "A society that doesn't know its past cannot understand its future." It is important for students of juvenile justice and juvenile crime to be familiar with the rich history of this segment of the criminal justice system. Chapter 1 contains some long quotes and features some strange, old language. But the content of these examples of the earliest forms of juvenile justice are most important. They demonstrate the timelessness of the problems both presented and caused by juveniles and their behavior. We will try to show how the complaints of adults in ancient times mirror those made about juveniles today. We sincerely hope this survey will stimulate the student to seek other volumes to fill in the blanks of the brief history presented herein. We shall start with development of the concept of laws to control the order and structures of early societies.

PRIMITIVE LAWS

Behaviors can be viewed as points on a continuum, as shown in Figure 1.1. From the earliest times, certain acts have been universally forbidden, or **proscribed.** Some examples are rape, incest, murder, treason, kidnapping, and rebellion. These acts fall at the forbidden end of the behavioral continuum. Approved or prescribed acts, such as getting married, having children, or having a job fall at the opposite, or approved, end. Most socially acceptable behavior falls somewhere near the middle and were generally referred to as **folkways. Mores** were generally enforced through the use of strong social *disapproval,* such as ostracism, exile, punishment, and even death. Mores were also reinforced through the use of rewards such as strong social approval, such as money and lands, dowries, and fertility rites.

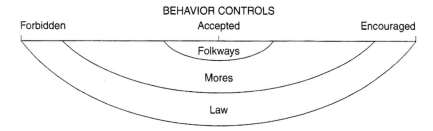

FIGURE 1.1 Continuum of behavior. (*Source:* Simonsen, Clifford E., *Juvenile Justice in America,* 3rd ed.)

As societies progressed, their loosely structured sanctions became codified and referred to as **law.** However, enforcement was gradually taken out of the hands of the general citizenry and given to special law enforcement groups ranging from witch hunters to the Magistrates Court of England.

The Old Testament concept of an "eye for an eye" (Exodus 21:24) best describes how ancient humans dealt with wrongs committed against themselves or their property. While this concept of revenge cannot be considered to have been "law," it has had a strong influence on the development of most legal systems throughout history.

As early societies developed language and writing skills, they began to record their laws. The **Hammurabic Code,** which dates from c. 2270 B.C., is considered by many historians to be the first comprehensive attempt at codifying such laws. This code recorded the laws of Babylon. It attempted to regulate business transactions, property rights, rights of master and slave, and family relationships.[1]

In the period of the Code of Hammurabi, the husband and father was decidedly in charge of the family. A part of that code was written as follows:

If a son strike his father, one shall cut off his hands.[2]

Compared with such early bloody forms of punishment of children by their parents, today's practice of referring the juvenile to court for rebellion or misconduct (status offenses) seems very mild.

The code also provided for the adoption of children. However, in return for a home, adopted children were expected to be loyal to their adoptive parents. If such an adopted child were to deny the parentage of his adoptive family, he could have his tongue cut out, and if he were to return to his natural father's or mother's home, he could have an eye plucked out.[3]

The code also had many regulations regarding the care of children by parents and marital arrangements. However, these laws were concerned with behavior within the family unit; public offenses were not mentioned. This would lead one to believe that the family was the primary agent in the supervision or punishment of its youth. Outside the home, it is reasonable to assume that children suffered the same punishments as adults.

At that time, boys attended school twelve hours a day all year long from the time they were very young through early manhood. Liberal use of corporal punishment helped to encourage their industriousness. Fathers wanted their sons to stay in school, do their homework, respect their elders, and use their spare time constructively. In other words, the father admonished his son to do just what most parents today still want their children to do—get a good education.

Peoples influenced by ancient Chinese civilizations had effective methods of dealing with families in which the children—and even the parents—become troublesome. For example, if a man murdered six members of another family, then he and five of his male children (irrespective of age) were executed to atone for the murders. Likewise, if a son were to commit a crime, the father could be flogged one hundred times or more in punishment, even if he knew nothing of the crime committed by his child. In the Old Testament, such acts were described as "visiting the sins of the fathers upon the children," and vice versa. However, the Hebrew codes sought to change this approach and make each person (or child) punishable for only his or her own offenses.

The Babylonian code is just one example of numerous codes of justice developed before Anglo-Saxon times. Another example is the sixth-century Byzantine Code of Justinian, which attempted to balance the punishment received with the crime committed. Thus there evolved the concept and symbol of the scales of justice.[4]

Eventually, societies began to move away from vengeance and blood feuds in dealing with criminal or deviant behavior. The public good and the protection of the social order became more important than personal injury or revenge. For example, we see the Code of Draco, an early criminal code of ancient Greece. Although extremely harsh, it was the first to allow any citizen to prosecute an offender in the name of the injured party. The word *Draconian* still is used to refer to some extremely severe form of punishment.

Little has been recorded about crime that may have been committed by youths in early human history. Our knowledge of the time consists primarily of examples of some of the punishments. The types of court systems employed, what jails or prisons were like, and how the policing of juveniles was conducted remain on the whole an historical mystery. What we do know is that discipline and control of children was generally considered the responsibility of parents. Since there was no juvenile court, a royal court or a local magistrate dealt with juveniles outside their family. Persons, including children, were not generally imprisoned in early history as a form of punishment. They were normally detained only until their punishment was determined and applied.

In fact, one of the first prisons in the world was designed to incarcerate juveniles. In 1704, Pope Clement XI built the **Hospice at San Michele** in Rome to rehabilitate wayward youth. Of course, the Holy Father was interested in saving youthful souls and having them atone for their sins. This early institution housed the two sets of juvenile clients that remain with us today: those sentenced for actual crimes and "incorrigible" boys who could not be controlled by their parents. Barnes and Teeters describe the conditions at the Hospice:

> The young offenders worked in association in a central hall at tasks in spinning and weaving. Chained by one foot and under a strict rule of silence, they listened to the brothers of a religious order while they droned through the Scripture of religious tracts. The incorrigible boys were kept separated, day and night, in little cubicles or cells. Large signs, hung throughout the institution, admonished "Silence." Floggings were resorted to as penalties for "past mistakes" as well as for the infraction of rules.[5]

Thus, the desire to "save the children" was evident from the very beginning of juvenile institutions.

THE ENGLISH EXPERIENCE (A.D. 600 TO 1825)

In the Middle Ages, social disorder and chaos was widespread. The Catholic Church exercised vast influence in Europe and acted as the prime determinate of justice. Those who transgressed civil or canon law were forced to pay debts to both society and God. To determine innocence or guilt, the **ordeal** was the Church's method of trial. The ordeal consisted of subjecting a person to painful and oftentimes fatal tests. One such ordeal consisted of binding a person's arms and legs and throwing him or her into a lake. If the person eventually floated to the surface, the verdict was innocent. If the person remained submerged, the verdict was guilty. In either case, the person would probably end up dead. Needless to say, the brutality of most trails by ordeal ensured a high rate of conviction.

Sexual activities also came under the purview of the Church, with those convicted of public or unnatural sexual acts receiving horrible punishments. Extreme punishment was also meted out for crimes involving witchcraft or heresy. Often the mere suspicion of such acts resulted in death after severe punishment.

Laws for Juvenile Offenses in the Middle Ages

As in the twenty-first century, there was delinquency in medieval Europe, and laws provided specific penalties for offenses committed by children. The following are typical examples of English versions of a "juvenile justice system" in the Middle Ages.

THE LAWS OF KING AETHELSTAN, A.D. 924

Of Thieves
First: that no thief be spared who may be taken "handhaebbende" [i.e., with the goods in his hand] above XII years, and above eight pence. And if any one so do, let him pay for the thief according to his "wer" [*pretium nativitatis*], and let it not be the more settled for the thief, or that he clear himself thereby. But if he will defend himself, or flees away, then let him not be spared.[6]

The City of London Chamberlain's Court, or the City Custom of Apprenticeship, 1299
. . . The City Chamberlain's Court for dealing with offences of masters and apprentices was in existence in 1299 . . .

 Next year the procedure was regulated, two Aldermen being associated with the Chamberlain for the purpose of ensuring that all indentures were registered at Guildhall, and for taking fines from apprentices. More serious cases were brought before the Mayor's Court by bill or petition.[7]

By 1300 there was a considerable body of law regulating apprenticeships, laws that affected many freeborn English children of the time. An apprentice had to be at least 12 years old; he was expected to be obedient, industrious, orderly, and not wasteful of the goods of his master. If an apprentice got out of line, the child could be sued in the Mayor's Court.[8]

 The following is an illustrative example of the case of a delinquent child in sixteenth-century England:

This yeare, the 29 of Januarie [1537/8] was arreigned at Westminster in the afternoone a boye of Mr. Culpepers, Gentleman of the King's Privie Chamber, which had stolne his maisters purse and pd.11 of money, with a jewell of the Kinges which was in the same purse, and there condemned to death; but the morrowe after when he was brought to the place of execution, which was at the ende of the tylt yeard afore the Kinges Pallace at Westminster, and that the hangman was takinge the ladder from the gallowes, the Kinge sent his pardon for the sayde boye, and so he was saved from death, to the great comforte of all the people there present, &c . . . .[9]

The Chamberlain's Court (Gentlemen of the King's Prince Chamber) is considered to be the forerunner of our modern juvenile courts. This court handled matters between a master and an apprentice only, however. Other courts handled offenses committed by an apprentice outside the purview of his master.

Examples of Penalties for Juvenile Crime

The Christian church continued to play an important role in regulating the behavior of disobedient children. As frequently as not, punishment for crimes in the Middle Ages was the same for children as for adults. For example, children convicted of *"petie treason"* or willful murder, could be drowned, hanged, or burned alive, depending on their background. However, there were exceptions for severe punishments based on the age of the child. For example, children fourteen years of age and under could not be convicted of burglary[10] or larceny[11] in England.

In addition to the Chamberlain's Court already mentioned, children were also tried in the central court in London, which was commonly called the **Old Bailey.** Court records reveal that the numbers of children tried in this court were miniscule when compared with the number of adults. And, although court records indicate that many children were sentenced to death, it cannot be ascertained whether these death penalties were ever carried out. Many sentences were commuted or the judge pardoned the offender, and such events often went unrecorded.

The examples of punishment of children in this period are many. In 1682, Quaker children in Bristol were put in the **stocks** and whipped for misbehavior. In Halifax, in 1691, children were thrown into debtors' prison; to avoid their rotting in jail and dying of starvation, these children were compelled to work for their creditors until the debt was paid. Many were less than 14 years of age. In 1716, in England, a mother and her 11-year-old daughter were executed for witchcraft.

Other juvenile issues dealt with during this period parallel the problems of the present day, including dealing with children in need due to homelessness and poverty.

The Mayor of London Orders Constables to Take Up Vagrant Children, 1732.
Mayors Proclamation, November 28, 1732.
This Court taking Notice, that divers Poor Vagrant Children are suffered to skulk in the Night-time, and lie upon Bulks, Stalls, and other Places in the Public Streets of this City, whereby many of them perish by the Extremity of the Weather, and other Inconveniences ensue. Therefore to prevent the same for the Future, This Court doth desire the several Aldermen of this City to call before them the several Constables and Beadles within their respective Wards, and to give them

strictly in charge, that if they or any of them shall find any poor Vagrant-Child, or Children, or others, lurking in the Publick Streets of this City in the Night-time, that they immediately apprehend such, and secure him, her or them, in their Watch-house, or some other convenient Place, until they convey them before some Justice of the Peace for this City and Liberty thereof, that they may be examined and sent to the Places of their Legal Settlements, or otherwise disposed of according to Law. And if any Constable, Beadle, or other Officer, shall be found negligent or remiss in his Duty, and shall suffer such poor Child, or Children, or others, to be vagrant, or lie in the said Streets, without obeying this Order as aforesaid, such Constable, Beadle, or other Officer, shall be punished for such his or their Neglect with the utmost Severity of the Law. . . .[12]

Later in the same century, other methods of dealing with delinquent or vagrant youth were tried. One of them, as explained here, could well be an early forerunner for our present trade or industrial school.

The Marine Society Apprentices Vagrant and Delinquent Boys to Sea Service on Warships, 1756.
Jonas Hanway, An Account of the Marine Society . . . from the Commencement of July 1756, to September 30, 1759.
One of the earliest private agencies in London to become interested in reclaiming delinquent boys was the Marine Society, established in 1756. No single individual can claim the undisputed honor of founding this Society, but Jonas Hanway, an eccentric London philanthropist, and Sir John Fielding, blind magistrate, both contributed substantially of their services in getting the infant Society started and in smooth working order.

England at this time was at war with France and Spain, and needed greatly to increase its naval forces. At this juncture the Marine Society was organized with the primary object of encouraging recruits for the Royal Navy, first by outfitting landmen with suitable clothing for sea service (the navy had no regular uniform at this time), and second, by sending stout, active boys, properly clothed, between the ages of thirteen and fifteen, to serve on board the King's ships, as servants to the captains and the other officers. It was expected that these boys after getting a taste of sea life would remain in the service as active sailors. The Society announced it would take no runaway apprentices, nor boys running away from home without their parents' knowledge. Since three thousand boys were needed however, the Society could not be too rigid in its requirements, as regards social status and conduct record. Young vagabonds from the city streets, who were not "defective in sight, or lame, dwarfish, or laboring under any chronical distemper" were regarded as fair subjects for recruiting. Magistrates were encouraged also to commit delinquent boys to the Marine Society, rather than send them to prison. Even after boys were committed to prison they sometimes were released to the Society, which was proud to claim that by checking these young vagabonds "in the dawnings of iniquity, Tyburn might be left a desert."[13]

In 1758, construction was begun in London on a prototype of what has come to be known today as a "group home." It was established by Sir John Fielding and was called the "**House of Refuge** for Orphan Girls." The purpose of this home was to rescue vagrant girls from almost certain lives of prostitution.

Public asylums for the children of convicts and other destitute or neglected children, such as that founded by the Philanthropic Society in London, were proposed in 1786. Records from the Report of the Select Committee Appointed by the House of Commons, show that between 1787 and 1797, ninety-three delinquent children were transported for crimes from England to Australia. This practice continued into the early 1800s. During transportation, the children were kept in confinement upon the various decrepit ships that took them from their native land.

Boys on Board the Hulks
On board the Leviathan [out of a total of 500 convicts] were 35 convicts under 20 years of age, a boy of 13 was the youngest. . . .

On board the Retribution, the wards were better ventilated than in the other ships—they contained in the whole 552 prisoners, and the following is a list of their respective ages and sentences:

Boys under 15 years of age for life 8
Ditto, for 14 years 6
Ditto, for 7 years 23
Total 37

On board this ship were 37 boys confined . . . and not working on shore [with the men]:—they are employed as tailors, shoemakers, coopers, carpenters, bookbinders, etc. . . Among these boys were two little infants from Newgate of nine years of age.[14]

By 1829, transportation[15] for life was the recommended punishment for the growing number of juvenile delinquents.

Imprisonment of children, while frowned upon by early social reformers, did exist, although the social reformers had a hand in changing some of the more deplorable conditions of the time, including the treatment and confinement of young criminals. The Warwick County Asylum, instituted in 1818, was the result of the united endeavors and generous contributions of concerned, benevolent citizens. The proposed object of the asylum was to make available to the criminal boy a place where he could escape the ways of vice and corruption. As is the case today, early efforts at reform suffered from the lack of sufficient funds. The public soon lost interest in the asylum, and the only way it survived was by showing the franchised public that it could save them money.

Box 1.2 Transportation

One of the earliest forms of social vengeance was banishment. In primitive societies the offender was cast out into the wilderness, usually to be eaten by wild beasts. Much later, in the period following the breakup of feudalism, the wandering and jobless lower classes were concentrated mostly in high-crime slums in the major cities. As economic conditions worsened, the number of imprisonable crimes was increased to the point that the available prisons were filled. In England, from 1596 to 1776, the pressure was partly relieved by deporting or "transporting" malefactors to the colonies in America. Estimates vary greatly of how many American settlers arrived in chains. Some authorities put the number at between three and four hundred annually; others put the figure as high as two thousand a year. The use of convict labor was widespread before the adoption of slavery in the colonies—both in America and Australia. And, even though the entering flow of dangerous felons was somewhat slowed by the introduction of slavery, the poor and the misdemeanant continued to come in great numbers.

In 1776, transportation to America was brought to an abrupt halt by the Revolution. But England still needed to send the criminals overloading their crowded institutions somewhere. Fortunately, Captain James Cook had discovered Australia in 1770, and soon the system of transportation was transferred to that continent. It was planned that the criminals would help tame that new and wild land. Over 135,000 felons were sent to Australia between 1787 and 1875, when the British finally abandoned the system.

The ships in which felons were transported have been described as "floating hells"—an understatement. The conditions below decks were worse than those of the jails. Many died on the long voyages, but enough survived to make it a profitable venture for the ship owners, who fitted out ships specifically for this purpose. Other nations turned to the use of transportation in the nineteenth century.

CLASSIFYING JUVENILE DELINQUENTS DURING THE EIGHTEENTH AND NINETEENTH CENTURIES

The age at which a child should be held responsible for his or her actions has been debated for centuries. Sir William Blackstone stated that no child under the age of discretion should be punished for any crime.[16] However, just what the age of discretion actually was seemed unclear; it varied from nation to nation. Today, it still varies from state to state.

Early attempts were made at a classification system for delinquent children. Civil law separated minors (those persons under the age of 25) into three classes:

1. Infants, from birth to 7 years,
2. Pueritia, from 7 to 14, and
3. Puberta, from 14 to 25.

The period of *pueritia,* or childhood, was divided further into two subcategories:

1. *Aetas pueritia proxima,* ages 7 to 10½, and;
2. *Aetas pubertati proxima,* ages 10½ to 14.

Generally, children in the first stage of life and the first half of the second stage, or from birth through 10½ years, were not punishable for any crime. Delinquent children from 10½ to 14 years of age were punishable only if the prosecution could prove intent, and persons 14 to 25 could receive capital and other punishments as readily as adults.

By 1815, juvenile crime in London had reached serious proportions, and inquiries were conducted to discover the causes. One of the earliest recorded surveys of juvenile delinquency took place in London between 1815 and 1816. According to the survey, juvenile delinquency in metropolitan London was epidemic. Organized gangs of homeless boys survived life on the streets by picking pockets and stealing. Actual figures on the number of delinquents in metropolitan London at the time of the survey are not available. However, the committee had reason to believe that there were thousands of boys under the age of 17 who engaged daily in criminal activities.

The group formed to conduct the survey realized that inquiry alone would serve no purpose, so they also set out to find ways of providing help so that these wayward youths might turn their paths from vice to virtue. In this effort, they often ran into problems similar to those encountered today. They had to find funding sources for suggested reforms. They had to convince the parents or guardians of a delinquent youth that leaving him in the community and not putting him in prison might serve the best interests of the juvenile. Having a child or children put in jail was cheaper for the parents—and many of them would then have extra money for alcohol or gambling.

Parens Patriae

Like most of America's criminal justice system, our juvenile justice system derives from the common law of England. In it, the king was considered the father of his country (*parens patriae*), who assumed responsibility for protecting all orphans and otherwise dependent children. In England, this responsibility was fulfilled by the chancery courts, in which the needful child became a ward of the state under the protection of *parens patriae*. The chancery court was designed to act more flexibly than the more rigid criminal courts. The main concern was for the welfare of the child, and legal procedures that might hamper the court in its beneficial actions were either circumvented or ignored. Thus, there were two concepts under the common law: (1) that children from birth to age 7 were not responsible for their actions, and (2) that a certain category of children was in need of protection by the state. It was not until the ages of possible responsibility were raised to 16 and 18 that these two concepts merged into the idea of juvenile delinquency.

From the ages of 8 through 14, offenders were not held responsible unless the state could prove that they could clearly distinguish between right and wrong. Last, when offenders were over the age of 14, they were assumed to be responsible for their acts and therefore deserving of punishment. In this last case, the burden rested with the defendants to prove that they were not legally responsible.

EARLY CAUSAL THEORIES OF DELINQUENCY

Theory about the causes of behavior of human beings abound. Theories about *why* people act the way they do help us devise ways to prevent or change behavior. In nineteenth-century England there were several popular theories about the causes of delinquency. Not too surprisingly, many causal theories of delinquency have changed little over the centuries. The following passage, taken from *A Treatise on the Police and Crimes of the Metropolis* by John Wade, is an example of one such theory.

> There are probably 70,000 persons in the Metropolis [London] who regularly live by theft and fraud; most of these have women, with whom they cohabit, and their offspring, as a matter of course, follow the example of their parents, and recruit the general mass of mendicancy, prostitution, and delinquency. This is the chief source of juvenile delinquents, who are also augmented by children, abandoned by the profligate among the working classes, by those of poor debtors confined, of paupers without settlement, and by a few wayward spirits from reputable families, who leave their homes without cause, either from the neglect or misfortune of their natural protectors. Children of this description are found in every part of the metropolis, especially in the vicinity of the theatres, the marketplaces, the parks, fields, and outskirts of the town. Many of them belong to organized gangs of depredators, and are in the regular employ and training of older thieves; others obtain a precarious subsistence by begging, running errands, selling playbills, picking pockets, and pilfering from

shops and stalls. Some of them never knew what it is to be in a bed, taking refuge in sheds, under stalls, piazzas, and about brick-kilns; they have no homes; others have homes, either with their parents, or in obscure lodging-houses, but to which they cannot return unless the day's industry of crime has produced a stipulated sum.[17]

According to this report, some chief causes, if not the chief causes, of delinquency were poverty, lack of education, and poor parental guidance. Not too surprisingly, studies in the mid-1990s show that children from low-income families who are poor, do not get an education and from bad or broken homes are much more likely to get into trouble with the law by the age of 18 than are youths from middle- or high-income families.[18]

In addition to the mentioned causes noted, the public was also blamed for the failure of the "Poor Laws" of the time to provide adequate homes and care for destitute children. However, poor children did not make up the entire population of England's delinquents. As in the present day, reforms are made and public interest aroused only when the problem of crime and delinquency creeps out of the ghettos of poverty and racism and begins to affect the middle-class, rich, or wealthy.[19]

Up through the Age of Enlightenment, the treatment for children in trouble seemed to be corporal punishment and tough discipline. Children during that long period were treated more as property than as small human beings with their own rights. Of course, this era also provided little but severe punishment as the primary response to adults in trouble. The prevailing method of treatment for adults and juveniles alike seemed to be to try to "beat the devil" out of the offender. Often this resulted in a death sentence for the person being "treated," if the devil was reluctant to leave. In the eighteenth century, as Old World practices were imported to the New World, problems with children began to gain at least some attention from the criminal justice systems of the colonies and then from the fledgling United States of America.

THE EARLY AMERICAN EXPERIENCE

Thus far, the origins of juvenile justice systems have been described, as they existed in Europe, particularly in England. Your authors hope that this brief history gives the reader a background to better understand the source of America's juvenile justice system and the major influences on that system.

Colonial youth did not escape the wrath of secular law or of strict Puritanical thinking and preaching, nor was their treatment much different from that of the youth of "Jolly Old England." Punishment being dealt out to delinquent children in the early era of the New England colonies (1641–1672) is described in the following passages:

Tryals

Also Children, Ideots, Distracted persons, and all that are Strangers or new comers to our Plantation, shall have such allowances, and dispensations in any case, whether Criminal or others, as Religion and Reason require [1641].exts.

The Laws and Liberties of Massachusetts, reprinted from the copy of the 1648 edition.

Burglarie and Theft

For the prevention of Pilfring and Theft, it is ordered by this Court and Authoritie therof; that if any person shal be taken or known to rob any orchard or garden, that shall hurt, or steal away any grafts or fruit trees, fruits, linnen, woollen, or any other goods left out in orchards, gardens, backsides; or any other place in house or fields; or shall steal any wood or other goods from the water-side, from mens doors, or yards; he shall forfeit treble damage to the owners therof. And if they be children, or servants that shall trespasse heerin, if their parents or masters will not pay the penaltie before expressed, they shal be openly whipped . . .

Capital Lawes

If any child, or children, above sixteen years old, and of sufficient understanding, shall CURSE, or SMITE their natural FATHER, or MOTHER: he or they shall be put to death: unles it can be sufficiently testified that the Parents have been very unchristianly negligent in the education of such children; or so provoked them by extream, and cruel correction; that they have been forced therunto to preserve themselves from death or maiming. Exod. 21. 17. Lev. 20. 9. Exod. 21. 15.

Children

[The selectmen of every town are required to keep a vigilant eye on the inhabitants to the end that the fathers shall teach their children knowledge of the English tongue and of the capital laws, and knowledge of the catechism, and shall instruct them in some honest lawful calling, labor or employment. If parents do not do this, the children shall be taken away and placed (boys until twenty-one, girls until eighteen) with masters who will so teach and instruct them.]

The Code of 1650, Being a Compilation of the Earliest Laws and Orders of the General Court of Connecticut . . . (Hartford, 1822).[20]

The American Colonies were quick to catch up with and even surpass the English at incarcerating criminals, including juveniles. In Philadelphia in 1790, the Quakers were instrumental in founding the nation's first true correctional institution in a section of the Walnut Street Jail. Al-

A jail in Walnut Street, Philadelphia, Pennsylvania. (Getty Images, Inc.—Hulton Archive Photos)

though the present method of using a separate court for juveniles had not yet been implemented at that time, juvenile delinquents did come before Colonial Courts and early American Courts. It seems that court judges faced the perplexing problem of what to do with these children then, just as we do now.

America, too, had its reform movements. Several citizen groups tried to deal with the problem of the rising number of juvenile delinquents. *Dunlap's American Daily Advertiser,* August 5, 1791, carried the following editorial concerning teenage gangs in Philadelphia:

The custom of permitting boys to ramble about the streets by night, is productive of the most serious and alarming consequences to their morals. Assembled in corners, and concealed from every eye, they can securely indulge themselves in mischief of every kind. The older ones train up the younger, in the same path, which they themselves pursue; and here produce in miniature, that mischief, which is produced, on a larger scale, by permitting prisoners to associate together in crowds within the walls of a jail. What avails it to spend the public money in erecting solitary cells to keep a few prisoners from being corrupted by evil communication, whilst we hourly expose hundreds of our children to corruption from the same cause; and this too, at an age, when the mind is much more susceptible of every impression, whether good or evil? But, tell it not in New-York, neither publish it in the streets of Baltimore, that the citizens of Philadelphia thus strain at gnats, while they swallow camels,—as it were hurtle-berries!

A few nights ago, a number of boys assembled in Fifth-street, between Market and Chestnut-streets, to divert themselves with firing squibs. A gentleman on horse-back, and a servant driving a carriage, with a pair of horses, happened to pass by at the same instant; and also several persons on foot, who might have had their limbs shattered, if the horses had broken loose. The boys thought this a fine opportunity for sport and mischief, and eagerly seized the moment, to light a squib, and fling it towards the horses. Luckily, indeed, the beasts were in good hands, and, though frighted, were yet, by dextrous management, prevented from taking head. Had not this been the case, the newspapers might, before now, have given us a list of five or six persons killed or wounded. This may be sport to *boys*, but 'tis death to *us* men.[21]

It is obvious that the editor of this early American newspaper was not at all happy about the differential treatment afforded youths, even in 1791.

In 1823, the New York Society proposed a house of refuge for juvenile delinquents for the Prevention of Pauperism. To plead for their cause, the society obtained statistics on persons brought before the police magistrates during 1822: There were 450 persons, all under the age of 25, and a considerable percentage of these were both boys and girls from ages 9 to 16. None of these children had actually been charged with a crime other than vagrancy; they had no homes and were forced to fend for themselves.

The Age of Reform and Reform Schools: 1825 to the Early 1900s

As the Industrial Revolution began, many secular and Puritanical laws against truancy and vagrancy were conveniently forgotten in order to take advantage of cheap child labor and to make way for the urban sweatshops that lay just around the corner. Unfortunately for adults as well as for children, the expanding, exploitative economy of young America provided less protection for the individual. In an attempt to keep pace with the newly emerging economy and its needs, the prison movement's search for the causes of delinquency soon gave way to merely dealing with the physical manifestations of delinquency and to exploiting the child labor potential.

In the first decade of the nineteenth century, legislatures began to delegate the *parens patriae* role to the legal structure, which for a while served to mask the vast differences between the Puritan-like "reformer" and the "child saver" outcomes expected for children and families. The reformers used tradition and the concept of social order as a basis for reducing state intervention at the expense of child-saving efforts. The child-savers expounded the Protestant work ethic, were primarily philanthropic, and supported the rehabilitation model. They had little real interest in the law or legal issues. Any overreach of the legal rights of the children was excused under the concept of *parens patriae*.

The Elmira Reformatory for youthful offenders. (American
Correction Association)

By 1828 the first institution for juvenile delinquents in the United
States came into existence. It had taken over five years of careful planning and maneuvering for public support on the part of the Society for the
Prevention of Pauperism, which went on to become the Society for the Reformation of Juvenile Delinquents in the City of New York. The concept of
this early institution was sound; it provided juveniles with a place of imprisonment or punishment that separated them from adults. However,
what it did not provide was separate kinds of punishments. Children were
still bound and fettered as adults with such things as handcuffs, the ball
and chain, leg irons, and the "barrel."[22]

A routine day in the house of refuge in 1828 was not unlike a child's
routine day in one of our modern youth prisons.

> The Refuge movement spread north to Boston and south to Balti-
> more and became the public-private merger solution to the growing
> number of homeless and troublesome street kids. As it spread, cruel
> and archaic practices spread with it. What started as a good idea
> based on real and pressing needs became, in the hands of people in-
> terested more in their jobs and an image of order, very much like
> what it was designed to replace.[23]

Sporadic attempts were made to expose the deplorable conditions in those
"houses of refuge" to the public and the press. Some reforms were brought
about by the efforts of such men as Elijah Devoe, the assistant superintendent of the New York House of Refuge; William Sawyer, a magistrate in
Massachusetts who decried sending children to places that turned them
out in worse condition than when they were put in; and Edward Everett

Hale, whose 1855 essays on juvenile delinquency offered the suggestion of guilt and stigma-free alternatives to the "criminal rules" of the day.

The depression of 1837 rekindled the flame of "nativism." Again, foreign-born paupers were victims of abuse and neglect at the hands of the politicians—and victims of worse at the hands of refuge house managers. Refuge houses went so far as to publish the names and native citizenship of juveniles and their parents. In the beginning, blacks were barred from admittance to houses of refuge or, if admitted, were treated badly. Philadelphia's house of refuge chief stated that it would be degrading to the white children to associate them with "the offending offspring of the poorest, most ignorant, most degraded and suffering members of our community." Eventually separate houses were opened for black youths.

The goal of refuge managers was to indoctrinate the poor unfortunates who passed through their doors with "good solid middle-class values." Those who were slow to get the point in the beginning soon learned to play the game. The transformation of institutionalized young people into streetwise youth is nothing new.

Offending juveniles were often apprenticed to farmers or to others offering an honest trade in return for hard work. The idea then, just as it remains today, was to get a child a job and keep him busy; after all, "idle hands are the devil's workshop." In fact, about 90 percent of the children released from houses of refuge each year entered into apprenticeships. By the mid-1800s, houses of refuge were enthusiastically declared a great success. Managers even advertised their houses in juvenile magazines such as the *Youths Casket* (1851). Managers took great pride in seemingly turning total misfits into productive, hard-working members of society. Redeemed children even wrote managers letters of testimony: "I seem plucked as a brand from the burning. I am a guilty rebel, saved by grace,"[24] stated one lad.

However, these exaggerated claims of success were disputed from both without and within. Managers and administrators often disagreed over methods of discipline. By the 1850s, there was a proliferation of reform schools in most Eastern seaboard states. The houses of refuge had failed to prevent the growth of juvenile delinquency by reforming delinquents, and there arose a need to identify certain children as a special class of deviants known as juvenile delinquents.

PREVENTIVE AGENCIES AND REFORM SCHOOLS

In 1849, George Matsell, the New York City police chief, publicly warned that the numbers of vicious and vagrant youth were increasing and that something must be done. And done it was. America moved from a time of houses of refuge into a time of preventive agencies and reform schools.

Philanthropists and others viewed the causes of delinquency differently behind this new movement. Refuge house managers had viewed children as inherently wicked and sought to change them. In the new system, children were thought most likely to be corrupted by their environments. Reformers of the day wanted to give children a break, a fresh start, and not condemn them for coming from the "wrong side of the tracks."

The church also took a strong hand in trying to deal with the problem of delinquency. The Methodist Episcopal Church, for example, opened a mission in New York City, (called the Five Points Mission), to give vagrant and destitute children a basic education. The mission's director, Reverend Lewis Pease, even moved his wife and family into Five Points, which was in one of the poorest areas of New York City, and gave out clothing, food, and jobs to the poor. Child-saving societies employed agents to take groups of delinquent or vagrant children west by train. The children were then parceled out in towns along the way. Unlike the apprenticeships associated with the houses of refuge, there were no binding agreements between the child or the child placers and the families with whom they were to begin new lives.

Thus, agrarian work ethic emerges as the panacea of delinquency. Reformers sought to empty the streets of the slum children and put them all on farms. No one epitomized this movement more than Charles Loring Brace (1826–1890), the founder of the Children's Aid Society in 1853. In one of his many speeches, Brace told of the speech of one of his "westernized" newsboys to fellow "newsies": "Do you want to be newsboys always, and show blacks, and timber merchants in a small way selling matches? If ye do you'll stay in New York, but if you don't you'll go out West, and begin to be farmers, for the beginning of a farmer, my boys, is the making of a Congressman, and a President."[25]

Placing-out encountered strong opposition, even though, as Brace claimed, a survey of Western prisons and almshouses in 1875 proved that his "children" had gotten into very little trouble in their new environments. The opposition came from the institutions that were deprived of the labor of children in training. Others argued that it was senseless to send a child all the way out West when there were adequate facilities for them in the East.

Beginning in the mid-1800s, municipal and state governments became interested in founding and administering juvenile institutions. They were called "reform schools," and they emphasized formal training. States and municipalities initially sought private support for their reform schools, but eventually the majority of the costs were paid out of state or city revenues.

Box 1.3 Charles Loring Brace (1826–1890)

A reformer of the nineteenth century, Charles Loring Brace founded the Children's Aid Society in New York City. He worked tirelessly for juvenile justice reform throughout his long life.

Also in the mid-1800s, cottage reform schools emerged that divided children into classes based on their criminal profiles. However, the majority of school operators did not use this method, stating for example, "You may divide these boys into classes, and the vicious will grow more vicious, . . . but when mixed with the rest, and when they see a public opinion in favor of reform, they will reflect, improve, and in the end be reformed."[26] The proponents of the cottage reform schools contended that mixing different classes of delinquents would simply multiply the crime problem and not solve it.

During the Civil War, penitentiaries and jails were practically empty, while reform schools were filled beyond capacity. This latter situation was attributable to the absence of parental authority when fathers were called into the service. Many of the reform schools made room for younger boys by releasing the older ones to the military.

Post–Civil War economic conditions forced institutions for juvenile delinquents to curb many of their non-basic activities. During the late nineteenth and early twentieth centuries, governments of Western and Northern states were given the responsibility for the control and care of many additional categories of indigent persons, including children in orphanages, almshouses, insane asylums, and mental hospitals. This shift in responsibility forced the juvenile institutions into competition with these other agencies for the funds they needed. As a result, many of the juvenile correctional facilities were forced to operate on deficit budgets that reduced them to nothing more than delinquent warehouses.

Although the number and variety of institutions for delinquents did recover from this economic setback and resumed their growth, the severity of the problems that they faced also grew. As a result of poor management and lack of adequate resources both during and following institutionalization, the state institutions founded after the turn of the twentieth century offered very little in the way of adequate treatment and subsequent planned reentry for youths into the community once it was determined that they were ready to be discharged. All too often, youths were forced out of institutions for lack of space and without any other alternative than to turn them loose unsupervised and back on the streets.

SUMMARY

In the dark history of the treatment of juveniles in trouble, up through the Age of Enlightenment, the answer seemed to be punishment and tough discipline. Children through that huge span of history were treated as property, rather than as small humans with the rights and privileges of adults. It should be noted, however, that this long period also delivered harsh and cruel punishment to adults. It seems that a prevailing philosophy for adults and juveniles was to "beat the devil out of them." As was shown, this method usually resulted in the demise of the offending person if the devil was reluctant to depart. It was not until the eighteenth century that children with problems began to gain at least some attention from the new nation called the United States in regard to some separation of juvenile and adult miscreants.

The early efforts at a juvenile court system in 1899 began the movement toward a truly separate system for juvenile justice. Before the start of the modern era, several circumstances molded the future of the juvenile justice system in America. Among them was the practice of dealing with delinquent and dependent youth that has come to be known as the **mother image,** in which women crusaded for children's rights and for treatment of children different from that accorded adult criminals. These social activists became known as "the **child savers.**" Modern practices of social work with neglected and dependent youths owe much to this movement, which was strictly a female domain. These women, including Jane Addams, Louise Bower, Ellen Herotin, and Julia Lathrop, were usually well traveled and well educated, and they had access to financial and political resources.

However, scholars have questioned the motives of these activists. Platt (1969) was one of the first to suggest that their humanitarian efforts disguised the paternalistic and severely punitive system of correction for juveniles.[27] Eventually, their reforms created a number of policies that thwarted juvenile rehabilitation.

Another practice that began before the start of the modern era but that has carried over into our present-day juvenile justice system was that of providing alternatives (resources and conditions permitting) to institutionalization for dependent and neglected juveniles. However, despite the existence of houses of refuge, reform schools, special institutions, and the practice of placing-out children into apprenticeships, children were still jailed or imprisoned with little or no consideration of whether they had committed a crime. The incarceration of dependent and neglected youths (status offenders) today is comparable to the practice in the late 1800s and early 1900s.

In Chapter 2 we will examine the great impacts in dealing with juveniles in the twentieth century and the efforts of society to adapt. Such things as changes from two world wars, (with the Great Depression in between), the Korean War, and Vietnam, Woodstock, drugs and gangs affected the way Juveniles and Juvenile Justice tried to adjust to the rapidly changing times.

TERMS TO REMEMBER

Child savers	Hammurabic Code
Draconian	Hospice at San Michel
Folkways	House of Refuge

Laws	*Parens patriae*
Mores	Proscribed
Mother image	Reform school
Old Bailey	Stocks
Ordeal	Transportation

REVIEW QUESTIONS

1. What is meant by the term *parens patriae?* Where does it come from?
2. Name some of the social reformers of the nineteenth century. What was their motivation to seek changes in the system?
3. List some of the major reasons for the juvenile court movement.
4. Were the problems of delinquency in early societies different from those faced today? If so, how?
5. Describe the concept of a "continuum of behavior" and tell how it applies to the juvenile justice system.
6. Who were the "child savers?" What were they trying to accomplish?
7. How did the penalties for juvenile misbehaviors and delinquency differ from those used today?
8. What was the aim of transportation? How does it compare to the punishments of today?
9. Define the aims and purposes of the reform schools.
10. Do you think the doctrine of *parens patriae* should guide the operations of the juvenile justice system? Why or why not?

NOTES

[1]For a thorough and comprehensive look at the Code of Hammurabi and other early laws, see Albert Kocaurek and John H. Wigmore, *Source of Ancient and Primitive Law, Evolution of Law, Select Readings on the Origin and Development of Legal Institutions, Volume 1* (Boston: Little, Brown, 1951).

[2]Code of Hammurabi, item 195. Richard R. Cherry, Barrister-at-law, Reid Professor of Constitutional and Criminal Law in the University of Dublin. Reprinted from *Lectures: Growth of Criminal Law in Ancient Communities* (London: Macmillan & Co., 1890).

[3]Ibid., pp. 192–193.

[4]Although the Code of Emperor Justinian did not survive the fall of the Byzantine Empire, it did form the basis of most of the Western law.

[5]Harry Elmer Barnes and Negley K. Teeters, *New Horizons in Criminology*, 3rd ed. (Englewood Cliffs, N.J.: Prentice Hall, 1959), p. 334.

[6]Benjamin Thorpe, ed., *Ancient Laws and Institutes of England* (London, 1840), pp. 47, 85, 103.

[7]A. H. Thomas, ed., *Calendar of Plea and Memoranda Rolls, Preserved Among the Archives of the Corporation of the City of London at the Guild-hall, a.d. 1364–1381* (Cambridge: Cambridge University Press, 1929), pp. 16, xl, xlvi.

[8]For further discussion on the subject of apprenticeships see Evans Austin, *The Law Relating to Apprentices, Including Those Bound According to the Custom of the City of London* (London, 1890), pp. 110–111.

[9]Charles Wriothesley (Windsor Herald), "A Chronicle of England During the Reigns of the Tudors, from a.d. 1485 to 1559," in William Douglas Hamilton, ed., *Volume I, M.S. 11* (Printed for the Camden Society, 1875), pp. 73, 134–135; and *Volume II*, p. 129.

[10]Wiley B. Sanders, ed., *Juvenile Offenders for a Thousand Years* (Chapel Hill: University of North Carolina Press, 1970), p. 11.

[11]Ibid., p. 14.

[12]Sanders, *Juvenile Offenders for a Thousand Years.*

[13]Ibid., pp. 52–53.

[14]Ibid., p. 70.

[15]For a thorough and insightful history of transportation, see Robert Hughes, *The Fatal Shore* (New York: Knopf, 1987).

[16]Sir William Blackstone ed. Thomas M. Cooley, *Commentaries on the Laws of England, Volume 1* (Chicago: Callaghan, 1899), p. 1230.

[17]Sanders, *Juvenile Offenders for a Thousand Years*, p. 135.

[18]See, for example, Scott H. Decker and Barik Van Winkle, *Life in the Gang: Family, Friends, and Violence* (London: Cambridge University Press, 1996).

[19]Barry Krisberg and James F. Austin, *Reinventing Juvenile Justice* (Newbury Park, CA: Sage, 1993), pp. 112–139.

[20]Sanders, *Juvenile Offenders for a Thousand Years*, p. 46.

[21]Ibid., pp. 330–331.

[22]The child was tied with arms and legs around a barrel, thus exposing his or her backside quite readily to the whip.

[23]Larry Cole, *Our Children's Keepers* (New York: Grossman, 1972), p. xviii.

[24]Robert M. Mennel, *Thorns and Thistles* (Hanover: University of New Hampshire Press, 1973), p. 24.

[25]Compare this practice with the program of sending ghetto children to summer camps once a year.

[26]Mennel, *Thorns and Thistles*, pp. 56–57.

[27]Anthony M. Platt, *The Child Savers: The Invention of Delinquency* (Chicago: University of Chicago Press, 1969).

THE TWENTIETH CENTURY AND JUVENILE JUSTICE

When you're a Jet . . . You're a Jet all the way . . .

— West Side Story

CHAPTER OVERVIEW

The child savers sought to help juveniles by setting up a system entirely separate from those institutions designed to serve adults. While admirable, this system also had some undesirable side effects; particularly, it failed to hold juveniles accountable for serious criminal behavior. The contradiction between saving the child and protecting the public from violent crime has always caused problems for the juvenile justice system. In this chapter, we follow the evolution of the juvenile justice system by continuing our historical review of its development in the modern era.

DELINQUENCY AND DELINQUENTS: THE LATE 1890s AND THE EARLY 1900s

The years preceding and following the turn of the century did see some basic though often crude attempts to explain delinquency and the emergence of various treatments for changing human behavior patterns. These attempts accompanied the introduction of the social science approach in the field of juvenile corrections. Granville Stanley Hall (1846–1924), for example, developed an evolutionary explanation of delinquent behavior based on the notion that childhood years are a period of savagery in which the forces of good and evil constantly do battle with one another for the possession of the child's soul. Hall categorized juveniles in trouble as victims of circumstances who deserved pity, understanding, and love. When forces of good had won the child, he was considered "born again." Thus, this theory came to be known as the "recapitulation theory": namely, through proper guidance and influence, social reformers could transform evil youths into "angels of virtue." Again, we encounter the "child savers." As mentioned in Chapter 1, these reformers were primarily females who crusaded for children's rights and for treating them differently from adult criminals.

As a prime example, Jane Addams (1860–1935) was a noted child saver and founder of a famous social settlement in Chicago known as Hull House. Influenced by recapitulation theory, Addams believed that juveniles had naturally free spirits in quest of joy and happiness. She felt that the urban environment that placed commercial interests above creative fun and recreation stifled this quest. Addams viewed delinquents as actually being good children who were turned bad by the urban environment and poverty. Unfortunately, her belief could not explain why some juveniles were incarcerated and why others from similar backgrounds were not. This quandary led to a search for other explanations for delinquent behavior.

For example, one of Addams' contemporaries, William Forbush, believed that juveniles who were struggling with the forces of good and evil became stuck in what he called **psychic arrest.** Psychic arrests were considered periods of continued tendencies toward crime. It was believed by Forbush that, if the period of his or her psychic arrest did not pass, a juvenile could be permanently locked into a life of crime. However, this theory, like those before it, lacked empirical verification and was based almost entirely upon speculation.

Despite their humanitarian intentions, the child savers have been criticized for imposing their class, ethnic, and racial biases on the poor, immigrants, and minorities.[1] For example, Kasinsky states that minority mothers were labeled "unfit" because their style of care did not conform to those of the child savers. Thus, these mothers were the objects of state control and their children were often removed from their homes.[2]

Box 2.1 Jane Addams (1860–1935)

Born in Illinois, Jane Addams was a person who always concerned herself with social issues and social reform. She became deeply involved of the problems of youths and founded Hull House, a theater for young people. She was a settlement founder, suffragette for women's rights, and a peace worker in World War I.

Scientific explanations of delinquency advanced very little toward proof during this period. There were some attempts to apply scientific principles of study to delinquents, but these were conducted more as laboratory experimentation than as scientific attempts to explain delinquent behavior. For example, in the early 1900s special institutions for defective delinquents offered scientists and behaviorists a captive population for their experimental use. In Indiana, in 1907, the first sterilization statute in America was passed; other states followed suit, and by 1936 twenty-five states had similar laws allowing for the sterilization of defective delinquents.[3]

Sound scientific explanations for delinquent behavior failed to permeate the institutional atmospheres of the day. According to Mennel:

> The difficulty remained learning how to teach morality—the supposed foundation of social and individual lawfulness. Organized care of juvenile delinquents continued to be challenged by crises and changes most of which originated quite apart from the constructs of scientists and pedagogues. Similarly, proposed solutions to institutional problems were often derived from nonscientific ideas and attitudes.[4]

Often the result of economic pressures, contemporary views of morality, and political manipulations, these nonscientific ideas and attitudes brought the advancement of significant, scientifically based, causal theories of delinquency to a standstill.

THE JUVENILE COURT MOVEMENT BEGINS

Despite concern for their children's welfare, most communities have a tolerance point for the disruptive behavior of juveniles. When children go beyond this point, they can be taken into custody and recorded as delinquents and placed in institutions. The mixing of juvenile offenders and adult felons was a practice that had existed for centuries but in America's early history was looked on as repugnant. However, it was not until 1899 that the delinquent juvenile began to receive differential attention in the courts. The first **juvenile court** was established in that year in Cook County (Chicago, Illinois). The delinquent then joined the dependent and neglected child as a ward of the state.[5]

When the juvenile delinquent was thus placed under the cloak of *parens patriae,* he or she was removed entirely from the formal criminal justice system of adults. A new set of terms was developed to describe juvenile court processing. Here is an outline of the general procedures for the handling of juvenile delinquents today from the National Juvenile Clearinghouse:

Arrest

The juvenile justice process often begins with an investigation by a police officer either because he or she observes a law violation or because a violation is reported to the police.

The police officer may decide to release the child to his or her parent with a warning or reprimand, or the officer may release to the parents on condition that the juvenile enroll in a community diversion program.

Or, the officer may take the juvenile into custody and refer the matter to the Juvenile Court's intake officer for further processing.

Intake

The intake officer is responsible for determining whether or not a case should move ahead for further court processing.

The intake officer may decide to release the juvenile to the parents with a warning or reprimand or may release the child on condition that the child enroll in a community diversion or submit to informal probation (supervision by a Juvenile Court officer).

If not, the intake officer will recommend that a petition be filed, equivalent to filing a charge, and will refer the case to the Juvenile Court prosecutor. The intake officer also makes the initial decision as to whether the child shall be detained pending further court action or released to the parents pending hearing. If the juvenile is detained, a judge or a court administrator at a Juvenile Court detention hearing reviews the decision.

Adjudication

The Juvenile Court judge must review all the evidence presented at a hearing and determine whether to sustain or reject the allegations made on the petition.

The Juvenile Court judge may reject the allegations made in the petition; then the juvenile is released. In some cases the judge may believe that the allegations are true but withhold adjudication on condition the child agrees to enroll in a community program that the court feels will help resolve the problem. By withholding adjudication, many of the problems identified by labeling theorists are avoided or, at least, lessened.

Disposition

At a hearing, the Juvenile Court judge reviews the recommendations of all concerned parties as to what should happen to the child.

Even now, the judge may decide that a severe form of treatment is not to the advantage of the youth or the community. In this case, the disposition may be probation, a warning or reprimand, some form of community service, a fine, or "home detention," in which the juvenile continues to live at home but receives rigorous daily counseling.

Other dispositions are more stringent. They may be such nonsecure custodial treatment as foster care or group home placement—but they may range up to incarceration in a secure juvenile correctional facility. The judge's disposition will depend on the seriousness of the offense and the child's previous court history.

Aftercare
Whatever disposition is made of the case, the court may make the termination of that disposition contingent upon the juvenile's acceptance of aftercare—probation, counseling, enrollment in a community program, or any of a number of other forms of treatment designed to lessen the chance that the youth will get in trouble again.[6]

Juvenile courts spread rapidly across the nation. By 1919, juvenile court legislation was a reality in all but three states. By 1932, there were estimated to be over 600 independent juvenile courts in the United States. By 1945, there were juvenile courts in every state in the Union.

The early juvenile court system was part of a general movement toward the separation of juvenile offenders from adult felons. It was regarded as one of the greatest advances in the crusade to protect children's welfare and to revolutionize the treatment of delinquent and neglected youths. But the juvenile court system, although revolutionary in theory, was not the hoped-for panacea that it was at first thought to be. Eventually, major problems developed as a result of this combination of delinquent, dependent and neglected children as wards of the state (*parens patriae*) under the same rubric. From the 1920s through the 1970s, the emphasis in dealing with juveniles had shifted from punishment and imprisonment to an attempt to understand the delinquent as a member of society.

Categories of Juveniles

The juvenile court system represents a significant event in the lives of the three categories of children who come into contact with it. They are:

- Dependent children;
- Neglected children and incorrigible children, and;
- Delinquent juveniles.

In the first two categories, children have committed no offense. In fact, if they were adults, they would not be in court. Their *status* as juveniles brings them to court. Thus, they are referred to today as **status offenders.** They are either **dependent** (without family or support) or **neglected** (with a family situation that is harmful to them). The only category that involves an offense is the delinquent juvenile.

Dependent children need the protection of the state to meet their basic life needs. Usually their parents have died, and they have no other adult relatives who can take care of them. In the early days of America, other families took in these unfortunates. Later, when their numbers increased, orphans and other dependent children gravitated to the growing cities, and various types of institutions were opened to handle them. Orphanages, common in the nineteenth century, are seldom found in America today. Some of the dependent children were kept in almshouses and other institutions, public and private, to give them food and shelter.

Neglected children become wards of the state, subject to at least some control by the courts. Whenever possible, these children are placed in foster homes. Neglected children have problems similar to those of dependent children. However, they often need the protection of the state not because their parents are dead, but because their parents either abuse, mistreat or ignore them. Often these children are the victims of a tragic circumstance known as the **battered child syndrome,** in which the parents' emotional problems lead them to lose control and hurt their offspring. The child who is physically abused by a parent or guardian usually comes to the attention of the authorities through reports from neighbors, friends, or relatives. Even when badly abused, children are usually very loyal to their parents, and seldom report their neglect to the authorities. The young victims also seldom report sexual abuse by parents (incest) to anyone in authority.

The care of neglected and dependent children is important but the juvenile courts were originally established primarily to deal with delinquent juveniles. For judicial purposes, delinquents are divided into three categories. The first category is composed of children who have allegedly committed an offense that would be a crime if an adult had committed it. This group makes up about 75 percent of the population of the state institutions for delinquent juveniles.

The second category of delinquent juveniles consists of those who have allegedly violated regulations that apply only to juveniles: curfew restrictions, required school attendance, and similar rules and ordinances. The third group is labeled the incorrigible juveniles (those who have been declared unmanageable by their parents and the court). The second and third groups are often referred to as **PINS (persons in need of supervision)** or **MINS (minors in need of supervision).** Most concerned juvenile correctional officials would like to remove these children as well as status offenders from the facilities designed primarily for the first category of delinquent juveniles.[7]

In addition to handling the three major categories of juveniles, the court may also have to deal with other children's problems such as adoption, termination of parents' rights, appointment of guardians, custody in divorce, nonsupport, and related situations. It is this broad overreach of the juvenile court and the resultant conglomeration in juvenile detention and correctional facilities that generates most of the attacks on the system. Juvenile facilities, although generally much more humane than the adult systems, have had and still have many drawbacks.

A Whole New Vocabulary

Even after the juvenile delinquent was officially removed from the criminal justice system and juvenile courts had been established in every state, administrators continued to practice many aspects of the adult criminal system in dealing with juveniles. It became apparent that different terms used by the states, even by neighboring counties, were applied to the same old things and were compounding the problem of a clear separation of the two systems. Therefore, various terms used in the criminal courts were changed to apply solely to juvenile justice and, although the meanings essentially remained the same, the new vocabulary helped to emphasize the difference between the criminal and the juvenile courts.

It is essential to understanding the juvenile justice process to recognize how the new terms relate to the old. For example, petition replaces complaint, summons replaces warrant, finding of involvement replaces conviction, and disposition replaces sentencing. Table 2.1 covers most of the significant terms used in the juvenile system.

TABLE 2.1   Glossary of Terms Used in the Juvenile Justice System

Juvenile Term	Adult Term
Adjudication A decision by the judge that the child has committed delinquent acts.	**Conviction of guilt**
Adjudicatory hearing A hearing to determine whether the allegations of a petition are supported by the evidence beyond a reasonable doubt or by a preponderance of evidence.	**Trial**
Adjustment A reference to matters that are settled or brought to a satisfactory state so that the parties can agree without the official intervention of the court.	**Plea bargaining**
Aftercare The supervision given to a child for a limited period of time after he/she is released from the training school but still under the control of the school or the juvenile court.	**Parole**
Commitment A decision by the judge that the child should be sent to a training school.	**Sentence to Imprisonment**
Court The court having jurisdiction over children who are alleged to be or found to be delinquent. Juvenile delinquency procedures should not be used for neglected children or those needing supervision.	**Court of record**
Delinquent act An act that if committed by an adult would be called a crime. The term *delinquent acts* does not include such ambiguities as *being ungovernable, truancy, incorrigibility,* and *disobedience.*	**Crime**

(continued)

TABLE 2.1   Glossary of Terms Used in the Juvenile Justice System (continued)

Juvenile Term	Adult Term
Delinquent child A child who is found to have committed an act that would be considered a crime if committed by an adult.	**Criminal**
Detention The temporary care of a child alleged to be delinquent who requires secure custody in physically restricting facilities pending court disposition or execution of a court order.	**Holding in jail**
Dispositional hearing A hearing held after the adjudicatory hearing in order to determine what order of disposition should be made concerning a child adjudicated as delinquent.	**Sentencing**
Hearing The presentation of evidence to the juvenile court judge, his consideration of it, and his decision on disposition of the case.	**Trial**
Petition An application for an order of court for some other judicial action. Hence, a "delinquency petition" is an application for the court to act in the matter of a juvenile apprehended for a delinquent act.	**Accusation or indictment**
Probation The supervision of a delinquent child after the court hearing but without commitment to a training school.	**Probation (with meaning)**
Residential child-care facility A dwelling other than a detention or shelter-care facility, which provides living accommodations, care, treatment, and maintenance for children and youth and is licensed to provide such care. Such facilities include foster family homes, and halfway houses.	**Halfway house**
Shelter The temporary care of a child in physically unrestricting facilities pending court disposition or execution of a court order for placement. Shelter care is used for dependent and neglected children and minors in need of supervision. Separate shelter-care facilities are also used for children apprehended for delinquency who need temporary shelter but not secure detention.	**Jail**
Take into custody The act of the police in securing the physical custody of a child engaged in delinquency; avoids the stigma of the word *arrest*.	**Arrest**

The words *child, youth,* and *youngster* are used synonymously and denote a person of juvenile court age. Juvenile court laws define a *child* as any person under the specified age, no matter how mature or sophisticated he or she may seem. Juvenile jurisdictions in at least two-thirds of the states include children under 18; the others also include youngsters between the ages of 18 and 21.
Source: National Advisory Commission on Criminal Justice and Goals, *Corrections* (Washington, D.C.: U.S. Government Printing Office, 1973), p. 248; Ruth S. Cavan, *Juvenile Delinquency,* 2nd ed. (New York: Lippincott, 1969), p. 367.

Treatment of Juveniles in the 1800s

With the creation of the juvenile justice system, these new institutions became the central instrument to discipline and control children. Strict laws regulated behavior and the penalties juvenile offenders were severe. The first of the early juvenile reform schools was the New York House of Refuge that opened in 1825. Their numbers grew during the nineteenth century, and their creation was overtaken by the state. The first state juvenile reform school opened in 1846, and by 1876 the country had fifty-one reform schools. Facility administrators determined the length of stay and had broad discretion in transferring disruptive youths to adult prisons.[8] During the first half of the twentieth century, separate facilities for girls were created. The schools emphasized deference to authority with an emphasis upon physical labor that remained central to reform schools throughout their history.[9] In fact, administrators built juvenile facilities in rural areas, assuming that farm work would aid the reform process. When conditions of confinement deteriorated sharply after the Civil War, many states established boards to oversee their facilities.

The goal of these institutions was to provide "a good dose of institutionalization" to "benefit" the juvenile offender, the wandering street arab, the willfully disobedient child, and the orphan to "shield them from the temptations of a sinful world."[10] For example, the Philadelphia House of Refuge sought to expose its youthful charges to "a course of rigid but not cruel or ignominious discipline" including "unrelenting supervision, mild but certain punishments for any infraction of the rules, and habits of quiet and good order at all times."[11] The hope was that institutionalization would repair the damage caused by the outside environment.

Juvenile Justice During the Depression: A Bleak Era

The 1930s—the period of the Great Depression—brought a disruption in the progress and development of the juvenile justice system. As a result of the Depression, institutional and reform school budgets were cut back, and skilled and knowledgeable administrators were let go when staffs were reduced. Once again the philosophy of control and repression, accompanied at times by cruel and unnecessary punishment, became dominant.

During the Great Depression, new explanations of juvenile delinquency were proposed. One of these was the causal theory championed by Virginia P. Robinson and Jesse Taft, two maverick social workers. They believed that delinquency was the result of family disintegration and conflict: because of conflict and maladaptation within the family unit, the child does not develop the ability to differentiate between right and wrong and therefore exhibits unacceptable social behavior. Psychiatric treatment became the cure of the day. From this approach, many forms of psychoanalytic treatment, including those developed by Freud, were used.

Yet it was still a generally accepted belief that the family alone was responsible for delinquency, and this led to demands that parents of delinquents be punished for failure to control the behavior of their children. For about ten years (1937–1946) the systematic punishment of parents was tried. Parents were fined heavily and even jailed for the acts of their offspring. However, the social effects of punishing parents were often disastrous, with the mother or father in prison and the home broken up.

Children were placed in institutions or foster homes, or often left to shift for themselves.

It was also found that judges began to rely on punishing the parents instead of attempting to deal with the rehabilitation of the children. It became evident that blaming delinquency entirely on the family and punishing the parents for the "sins" of their children was not the answer to the problem. It was simply one of the many serious attempts to find a single, simple cause of delinquency.

Courts did continue a tendency toward treatment of children that was lenient compared with the punishment of adults for similar offenses. Unfortunately, courts and law enforcement agencies across the country varied widely in their treatment or punishment of juveniles who had committed like offenses. Punishment ranged from horsewhipping to prison terms. The following article appeared on January 8, 1930:

Boy Burglar is Sentenced
With his mother standing at his side, Eugene Wheeler, 19-year-old burglar, was sentenced yesterday to serve from one to four years at Monroe reformatory by Superior Judge Malcolm Douglas Wheeler. With three other youths, he broke into the plant of the Currin-Green Shoe Manufacturing Company, 2715 Western Avenue, December 1. Arthur King, one of the gang, was sentenced last month to the Monroe reformatory. The other two were turned over to the juvenile court.[12]

The next article appeared on December 24, 1930, concerning a case in Lapeer, Michigan:

Fathers Thrash Sons by Order
By order of the court, seven boys were severely horsewhipped by their fathers today as their mothers looked on approvingly. Circuit Judge Henry H. Smith prescribed the unusual sentence after the youths had pleaded guilty to a store theft.[13]

The Depression era was also plagued by many of our current problems. For example, a very large number of juveniles are arrested today on drug charges. In the 1930s, juveniles were arrested with equal zeal for drinking—a violation of the prohibition of alcoholic beverages.[14] Not unlike the casualties of today's drug culture, Prohibition had its own casualties.

It is interesting to note that the parents of the juveniles involved bemoaned the fact that their children could not acquire "innocuous light wines and beer" instead of the "vile bootleg whisky." One wonders how many parents of juveniles spaced out on crack, angel dust, crystal methamphetamine, ecstasy, or heroin today might bemoan the fact that their children could not legally acquire "innocuous supplies of marijuana" instead of "vile" and potentially fatal doses of the "hard" drugs.

The Postdepression Era: The 1940s and 1950s

Although the Illinois Court Act of 1899 did much to lead the way toward individualized treatment of the juvenile delinquent and dependent child, its practicality and efficacy came into question in the post-Depression era of the 1940s and 1950s. It became apparent that the juvenile was confronted with a **"Catch 22."**[15] For although the courts in fact gave the youths treatment, the informality of proceedings under *parens patriae* deprived the juvenile of the same legal rights provided to adults who committed similar acts.

Deprived of equal protection under the Constitution, juveniles were subject to the discretionary authority of the courts, the police, and child service agencies. The courts, therefore, did what they could to process the ever-increasing number of juvenile cases coming before them.

The post-Depression era also spawned large detention facilities for juvenile offenders. The Youth House, a "kid Big House for big and little kids" in New York City, was typical of large juvenile detention facilities of this era. It soon acquired the reputation of being a poorly equipped, understaffed dumping ground for delinquent and dependent children. All the cruelties and brutalities that could be imagined in a "kid prison" took place in the original Youth House and its equally notorious successor. It has been claimed that Youth House and detention facilities and institutions like it destroyed more children each year than any known disease. Youth House processed thousands of children in New York each year, and although conditions there periodically become a public issue, it continued to operate with the same destructive force as in the past.

In the 1940s and 1950s, with a growing number of crimes committed by juveniles, police forces began to set up specialized juvenile units made up of specially assigned officers. For example, in 1944 the Chicago Police Department's Crime Prevention Bureau provided increased educational opportunities for juvenile officers. Juvenile personnel, especially policewomen, were given a special twelve-week course of instruction on the treatment of juveniles, including the subject of their referral to social agencies.[16]

The growing number of crimes committed by juveniles in this period meant a growing institutional population. Although an effort was made to provide juveniles with facilities to keep them separated from adult criminals, in most large cities these new juvenile detention facilities became little more than juvenile jails. And, when they became filled, dependent delinquents and status offenders were often moved to adult jails, which defeated the purpose of separate facilities.

In the post-Depression era, belief that the disintegration of the family was the prime cause of delinquency faded, and environmental factors and individual personalities were seen as its main cause. Many authorities of the day believed that "official" delinquency was primarily a lower-class phenomenon. However, the findings of several studies conducted during the 1950s indicated that there was not a universal causal relationship between social class and law-violating behavior.

Some current attempts to cope with and/or prevent delinquency are not so different in scope and design from those of the 1940s and 1950s. For example, the concept of a youth authority such as that in California and several other states had its beginnings in 1940 with the development of the American Law Institute's Model Youth Correction Authority Act. The major concern was for the treatment of those juvenile offenders who fell outside the age of most juvenile court jurisdictions and who, as a result, were often tried in adult criminal courts and sentenced to adult prisons. The model act was published in an attempt to urge various states to adopt a similar body of procedures and guidelines:

1. Name: Youth Correction Authority.
2. Administrative organization: board of three persons with staggered nine-year terms, appointed by the governor, the board to select its chairman.
3. Age of jurisdiction: 16 to 21, from criminal or juvenile court.
4. Type of commitment: mandatory commitment to the Youth Authority by the court for all persons under 21 at the time of apprehension, convicted of a crime punishable by imprisonment for less than life; children aged 16 and over might be committed by the juvenile court. The Authority, not the judge, would make the decision whether to grant probation or commit to an institution.
5. Type of commitment: the commitment to the Authority would be for an indeterminate period; the Authority would make the decision when to terminate commitment, release on parole, and so on; however, persons might not be held after age 25 and those under 18 committed by the juvenile courts not after the age of 21. If release would be dangerous, the court might approve of continued control.
6. Administration of facilities for diagnosis and retraining: the function of the Authority was to be mainly diagnostic, but it was also permitted to administer training schools and similar facilities.[17]

California adopted this concept for both adults and juveniles; Wisconsin and Minnesota followed suit, as did a number of other states, although they made several modifications. To date, although many such modifications have been made, states have been reluctant to implement the full provisions of the youth authority movement; however, the concept of parole release and aftercare supervision of children (see Chapter 10, "Juvenile Parole") did get a tremendous boost in the 1940s and 1950s from the youth authority model.

Other similarities between present-day trends and the 1940s and 1950s are reflected in the following description of an unusual project in

1946 to prevent youths' troubles; the chairperson of a special subcommittee of the District Health Committee of New York City made this description.

> The committee confronted two questions. First, can we identify at an early state symptomatic difficulty that later may develop into serious behavior trouble? Secondly, in these cases, by mustering and coordinating the skills of the psychiatrist, psychologist, social worker, physician, vocation worker, and others, can we successfully diagnose the underlying difficulty in the child and his family, and offer a planned treatment service which will remove or modify that difficulty? The answer to both was an emphatic yes.
>
> The committee has a six-step procedure that consists of, first, the principal of the school selecting those students whose personality deviations indicate serious social or health problems. The case was then cleared with the social services exchange. Data about the student was gathered by either a committee member or a social worker and assembled and presented for clinical discussion. The fifth step is the formulation of a plan of action for the student and finally periodic reports were made to the committee on the child's progress. Basically the plan was an attempt to manipulate the environment of a child under stress, or stated in somewhat different terminology, to bring together all the resources of the community to aid the child.[18]

It is often assumed that the idea of community-based treatment, diagnosis, and planning in the field of juvenile delinquency is the brainchild of the 1960s and early 1970s. As the passage cited indicates, community involvement in juvenile justice is far from new.

The post-Depression era gave rise to many studies and causal theories including a book by Sheldon and Eleanor Glueck, *Unraveling Juvenile Delinquency,* about which one reviewer said:

> The book is the result of a 10-year study by the Gluecks and others on their team to ascertain the causes of youthful criminality. It appears that up to this time most people were in agreement that some-

---

Box 2.2 Sheldon (1896–1980) and Eleanor (1898–1972) Glueck

A husband and wife team at Harvard University who worked together on a large number of privately funded research projects in an eclectic fashion. He held the Roscoe Pound Chair at Harvard Law School, and she was a trained social worker. Their work exerted great influence on the study of crime, especially juvenile delinquency. They authored 258 items in their forty years of work.

thing should be done about the youthful offender but no one had identified the problems except to state that they in fact did exist. The Gluecks found three factors prevalent among their 500 delinquents studied:

- The boys generally had poor family relations. Their fathers were needlessly harsh or completely lax in maintaining discipline, seldom firm but kindly. They received little parental love.
- They clashed with other people; were highly assertive, defiant, suspicious, destructive, and impulsive.
- They had turbulent personalities, were adventurous, extroverted, suggestible, stubborn, and emotionally unstable.

Two conclusions were made in the article. First, that detecting delinquency in its earliest stages is a job for specialists. It cannot be done, the Gluecks admit, by any simple, easily interpreted pencil and paper test. Secondly, the husband and wife team felt that in delinquency, society is faced not with predestination, but with destination. And probably destination can often be modified by intelligent early intervention.[19]

The literature of the 1940s and early 1950s was filled with reports of **intervention strategy,** in which there was introduced into the life of a juvenile some outside intervening factor, such as intensive counseling. The influence of this intervening factor on the juvenile's future delinquent behavior was then evaluated. Dr. Edwin Powers described an experiment that utilized one such intervention strategy in an attempt to prevent delinquent behavior among a population of 650 boys.

This particular 10-year study called for 650 boys to be divided among 10 counselors. (The essence of the relationship between the boy and his counselor was personal intimacy and friendship.) Treatment consisted of the application of whatever skills each counselor was capable of supplying. Dr. Powers states, "In brief, it can be said that the treatment program, utilizing some of the best professional advice obtainable, comprised an unusually wide diversity of special services to boys and their families, from removing nits from boys' heads to preparing them for higher education."

The conclusion of the study was somewhat vague in that the counselors were unable to stop the rapid advance of young boys into delinquency with any greater success than the usual deterrent forces in the community. Some of the boys were evidently deflected from delinquent careers that, without the counselors' help, might have resulted in continued or more serious violations. The researchers felt that although they were not completely successful in the first stage of delinquency prevention that in working with boys ages 8–11 later and more serious stages were to some degree curtailed.[20]

In the 1950s, a number of intervention strategy programs for youths were set up, providing job training and creating jobs. In 1956, for example, the Citizens Union of New York for the Prevention and Cure of Delinquency recommended the establishment of work camps for delinquent boys. The basic idea behind these camps and similar programs was to divert juveniles from exhibiting delinquent behavior by providing them opportunities for good jobs. This idea was expanded upon in the early 1960s and thereafter through the establishment of such programs as (1) the Job Corps under Title 1-A of the Federal Poverty Program, (2) the Neighborhood Youth Corps under Title 1-B of the same program, and (3) the work-study program for college students under the same program. Through these programs, underprivileged youths are given an opportunity to upgrade their education and to learn a trade or a skill that might lead to a decent, steady job. It should be noted that, although the primary goal of these programs is to provide opportunities to juveniles in need, the prevention of delinquency is often a secondary objective and result. This differs somewhat from the concept of the work camps of the 1950s, whose primary objective was the prevention of recurrent delinquent behavior in juveniles who had already exhibited such behavior before coming into the programs.

The 1960s and 1970s: Chaos and Construction

In the 1960s and 1970s there were revolutionary legal, social, and procedural changes in the development and scope of the juvenile justice system. At the end of these two decades, the United States had disengaged from the unpopular war in Vietnam; seen confrontations, riots, and killings on

Institutional education program. (Kentucky Department of Juvenile Justice)

college campuses; witnessed major political assassinations; and gone through radical changes in all areas of social intercourse and activity.

During this era, men had been put on the moon, planes had been perfected that travel faster than sound, surgeons had transplanted human organs and performed other almost unbelievable feats in medicine. Humanity had advanced technically and scientifically beyond our great-grandparents' wildest dreams.

But had these technical and social advances solved the problem of juvenile delinquency in this country? Had scholars, writers, and researchers found any revolutionary new theories regarding the cause, cure, or prevention of this major problem? Unfortunately, the answer to both questions is "no."

The ethical issues that face the juvenile justice system are essentially the same as those faced by the general society. Because of the highlighting of this system, however, the ethical dilemmas are exacerbated by observers and participants alike. If members of the healing professions (e.g., psychologists and psychiatrists) find that certain treatments have promise, they are again faced with an ethical kind of Catch 22. Is it ethical to treat those in the juvenile justice system, or is it preferable to divert them from the system completely?

The importance of delinquency prevention was reflected by the growing concern of the federal government during the 1960s. In 1961, the President's Commission on Juvenile Delinquency and Youth Crime was established. This committee recommended the enactment of the Juvenile Delinquency and Youth Offenses Control Act of 1961. Originally authorized for three years, the act was later extended through fiscal year 1967. In 1967, the President's Commission on Law Enforcement and the Administration of Justice highlighted the importance of prevention in dealing with crime and delinquency in a report. It stated that:

> In the last analysis, the most promising and so the most important method of dealing with crime is by preventing it—by ameliorating the conditions of life that drive people to commit crimes and that undermine the restraining rules and institutions created by society against antisocial conduct.[21]

In the following year (1968), Congress enacted both the Juvenile Delinquency Prevention and Control Act and the Omnibus Crime Control and Safe Streets Act. In 1972, the Juvenile Delinquency Prevention Control Act of 1972 was passed with funding remaining under the auspices of the U.S. Department of Health, Education, and Welfare. Two years later, Congress enacted the Juvenile Justice and Delinquency Prevention Act of 1974. It established the Office of Juvenile Justice and Delinquency Prevention (OJJDP) within the Law Enforcement Assistance Administration of the Department of Justice. The concern of the federal government regarding delinquency and the importance of prevention is evidenced not only in the title of the 1974 act, but in the attention given to prevention as an important strategy of forestalling the antisocial behavior among adolescents and young adults. In pointing to the major objectives of the act, Congress noted that its declared policy was:

> to provide the necessary resources, leadership, and coordination (1) to develop and implement effective methods of preventing and reducing juvenile delinquency; (2) to develop and conduct effective programs to prevent delinquency, to divert juveniles from the traditional juvenile justice system and to provide critically needed alternatives to institutionalization; (3) to improve the quality of juvenile justice in the United States; and (4) to increase the capacity of State and local governments and public and private agencies to conduct effective juvenile justice and delinquency prevention and rehabilitation programs and to provide research, evaluation, and training services in the field of juvenile delinquency prevention.[22]

Despite such attempts at reform, however, the rights of juveniles within the process were still in question.

THE DUE PROCESS REVOLUTION

We have indicated that adults are getting more protection under the law than are juveniles. The courts have attempted to rectify this situation by concentrating on bringing about reforms in the treatment given to both delinquent and nondelinquent juveniles. It should be pointed out, however, that the question of children's rights is multidimensional and complex. It involves not just procedural rights in juvenile courts and the applicability of constitutional rights to juveniles, but extends to the complex issues of the political, economic, and social position of minors in our society. This subject is made even more complex by the ever-changing status of youth and the resulting confusion reflected in adult attitudes toward them. The key issue here is the previously discussed doctrine of *parens patriae*. While this doctrine called for the protection and treatment of children differently from adults, it also meant that children would not have the basic rights of adults held in criminal proceedings.

The basic principle that juveniles should be treated differently from adults, primarily for the purpose of prevention rather than punishment, was the case of the *Duke of Beaufort v. Berry* (England, 1721). This viewpoint did not receive immediate acceptance, but it is considered to be fundamental element of juvenile law. The tenet of individualized justice for youth came with the decision *Rex v. Delaval* (England, 1763). *Parens pariae*, the concept that allows the state to assume parental responsibility for any child under its purview, evolved from the case of *Ellesley v. Ellesley* (England, 1828).

As we have noted, early American practices did not reflect such a parental concern for juveniles. In colonial times, children who committed crimes were often punished more severely than adults. However, by the nineteenth century, several champions had surfaced to lead the crusade for children's rights. Americans were recognizing that children might not be as responsible for their criminal behavior as adults. By 1858, in California, a youth industrial school was established as an institution for children under the age of 18 who were leading "idle or immoral" lives. In 1887, California held that it was unlawful to confine children under the age of 16 to jails.

However, under *parens patriae,* confinement was also different for children that adults sentenced to institutions. For example, in 1870, boys could be sent to the Chicago Reform School under an indeterminate sentence and be held until they were 21. Boys could be committed for an offense or be sent by their parents or guardians for their own protection and benefit. Such an extended sentence, of course, is not possible for adults. The nature of this type of a commitment became the basis for the case of *People v. Turner* (55 Ill. 280, 1870). The Illinois Supreme Court declared that the petitioner had been denied basic due process of law and declared the commitment to an "infant penitentiary" unconstitutional. Protection could easily become punishment under *parens patriae.*[23]

Nevertheless, the juvenile court movement pressed forward. The nation's first juvenile court was established in Cook County, Chicago, in 1899. *Mill v. Brown* (Utah, 1907) highlights the significance of the laws establishing early juvenile courts: "The juvenile court law is of such vast importance to the state and society that, it seems to us, it should be administered by those who are learned in the law and versed in the roles of procedure, effective and individual rights respected. Care must be exercised in both the selection of a judge and in the administration of the law."

In 1923, the National Probation Association's Annual Conference proposed a Standard Juvenile Court Act. The last state to adopt this act was Wyoming, in 1945. Between 1925 and 1945, various states defined their own juvenile code.

The "new" court system, which was over one hundred years in coming, defined all procedures of the juvenile courts as civil rather than criminal. (*Civil* suits relate to and affect only individual wrongs, whereas *criminal* prosecutions involve public wrongs.) It is evident, therefore, that the greatest effort in the juvenile justice system has been aimed at creating a separate court system for youths and delinquents. This separate system and the perpetuation of the doctrine of *parens patriae* have resulted in a system that largely ignored the legal rights of juveniles. Those rights accorded to adults, such as the right to speedy trial, the right to trial by jury, the right to bail, the right to confront one's accusers, and the right to protection from self-incrimination, were seen as unnecessary for juveniles.

However, due process rights for juveniles were not clearly established until the rulings of the U.S. Supreme Court under the leadership of Chief Justice Earl Warren. Landmark cases of the Warren Court, such as in *Miranda v. Arizona,* were decisions that did have a bearing on both adult and juvenile rights. The decision in *Gideon v. Wainwright,* 372 U.S. 335 (1963), set the stage for legislation regarding legal representation in the criminal process. Although concerned with the right of legal counsel in adult, non-capital felony cases, several states have required that indigent children who request counsel be so provided and at public expense. *Gault* established this right for juveniles.

Some Landmark Cases

In some landmark opinions in *Kent v. United States,* 383 U.S. 541 (1966) and *In re Gault,* 387 U.S. 1 (1967), the Supreme Court at long last evaluated juvenile court proceedings and children's constitutionally guaranteed rights. In *Kent v. United States,* the Court noted that the child involved in certain juvenile court proceedings was deprived of constitutional rights and at the same time not given the rehabilitation promised under earlier juvenile court philosophy and statutes. It pointed out that "there may be grounds for concern that the child receives the worst of both worlds."[24]

In the *Kent* case, the Court did not have occasion to pass directly on the right to counsel and the notice of this right because the juvenile involved had been given counsel within twenty-four hours of his arrest. The next year, however, the Supreme Court did have occasion to render a decision on these rights in *In re Gault.* On May 15, 1967, the Supreme Court rendered its first decision in the area of juvenile delinquency procedure. Gerald Gault allegedly made a telephone call to a woman living in the neighborhood, during which he used some obscene words and phrases. The use of a telephone for such purpose violated an Arizona statute, and hence Gerald, aged 16, was subject to adjudication as a juvenile delinquent. The adjudication was in fact made after a proceeding in which he was not offered the basic procedural protections to which he would have been entitled had he been charged in a criminal court. In this decision, Justice Abraham Fortas ruled that a child alleged to be a juvenile delinquent had at least the following rights:

1. Right to notice of the charges in time to prepare for trial.
2. Right to counsel.
3. Right to confrontation and cross-examination of his or her accusers.
4. Privilege against self-incrimination, at least in court.

The *Gault* decision ended the presumption that the juvenile courts were beyond the scope or purview of due process protection. The primary lesson learned here was that juvenile courts would have to become courts of law and follow standard procedures concerning the constitutional rights of those on whom they passed judgment. *In re Gault* did, however, fail to answer one question: whether a juvenile must be advised of his or her rights at some point in the prejudicial stages of a case. When serious offenses are involved and the juvenile might be transferred to an adult criminal court, some police forces are giving such warnings.[25]

Some states like California as a rule apply *Miranda* restrictions to juvenile interrogations. In another case related to the *Gault* decision, *In re Winship,* 397 U.S. 358 (1970) the Supreme Court held that to justify a court finding of delinquency against a juvenile, the proof must be beyond a reasonable doubt that the juvenile committed the alleged delinquent act.[26] Before this case, the requirement seemed to be that the judge be influenced only by a preponderance of evidence against the accused delinquent.

Finally, the Supreme Court agreed to hear arguments about whether juveniles had a constitutional right to a jury trial. In *McKeiver v. Pennsylvania,* 403 U.S. 528 (1971), implying that the due process standard of "fundamental fairness" applied, the Court rejected the concept of trial by jury for juveniles. The Court contended that the "juvenile proceeding has not yet been held to be a 'criminal prosecution' within the meaning and reach of the Sixth Amendment.[27] The Supreme Court stated that it was as yet unwilling to "remake the juvenile proceeding into a full adversary process" and put "an effective end to what has been the idealistic prospect of an intimate, informal protective proceeding."[28] The Court concluded by encouraging the states to "seek in new and different ways the elusive answers to the young."

The Supreme Court has not been the only source of change in the area of juvenile rights, Federal acts and legislation have also played an important role. For example, until the Uniform Juvenile Court Act of 1968, police or others could still take a child into custody in a situation in which the Fourth Amendment would have exempted an adult. This act also set some limits on nondiscriminatory home removals of children. It provided for the removal of a child from his or her home only if there are reasonable grounds to believe that the child is suffering from illness or injury or is in immediate danger from the environment and that removal from that environment is therefore necessary.

In 1974, the U.S. Congress passed the Juvenile Justice and Delinquency Prevention Act (Public Law 93-415). It requires:

> a comprehensive assessment regarding the effectiveness of the existing juvenile justice system. This legislation also provides the impetus for developing and implementing innovative alternatives to prevent juvenile delinquency and to divert status offenders from the juvenile justice system. The intent of the Act is to clearly identify those youth who are victimized or otherwise troubled but have not committed criminal offenses and to divert such youth from institutionalization.

Simultaneously this will promote the utilization of resources within the juvenile justice system to more effectively deal with youthful criminal offenders.[29]

When juvenile courts were first established at the turn of the century they were seen as a positive response to the demand for social justice. The objective was "not so much to punish as to reform, not to degrade but to uplift, not to crush but to develop, not to make him a criminal but a worthy citizen."[30] The doctrine of *parens patriae* was used to justify the relaxation of traditional criminal law procedures. While this doctrine allowed the courts to assume parental responsibility for the child and thus to look out for his or her welfare, it had unforeseen consequences. Because the state was proceeding in the "best" interests of the child, some courts believed that rights such as entitlement to bail, indictment by grand jury, speedy trial, trial by jury, immunity against self-incrimination, confrontation of accusers, and the right to counsel could be denied.

These landmark cases attempted to bridge the gap between the ideal and reality in juvenile court proceedings and recognize the rights of juveniles charged with criminal or delinquent acts. Other rights governing the operations of the juvenile justice process will be referred to in later chapters on the system.

Institutions in the 1960s, 1970s, and 1980s

The institutionalization of delinquent children continued in the 1980s. Are these institutions any more effective in treating delinquency or rehabilitating juvenile delinquents than in the past? Did locking these youths away solve any of the delinquency problems that society must face? Charles Mangel, in an article entitled "How to Make a Criminal Out of a Child," offered some sobering answers to these questions in 1971:

As I write this, some 100,000 children are sitting in jails and jail-like institutions throughout the country. They are as young as six. Most, perhaps 60 percent are not delinquents. They have committed no criminal acts. Yet we pass all this by as if it does not exist. "Why are we so willing to give up on the child in trouble?" asks Lois Forer in *No One Will Listen.* "There are two possible reasons. The first is that we don't want to help; the second, that we don't believe we can help. We know that the children who suffer from lack of facilities are primarily poor children—black, Puerto Rican, Indian, deprived—in short, not our children."

Few people feel any sense of outrage. I met in Chicago with a group of lawyers, judges, and social workers who spend their days working with children in court. They impressed me as decent men and women. They uttered all the right words. But they spoke with a curious hollowness of feeling. As the evening wore on, I found myself being grateful that the future of my children did not depend on their concern.

"The way things are now, it is probably better for all concerned if young delinquents were not detected," says Milton Luger, former director of the New York State Division for Youth. "Too many of them get worse in our care." Not one state in this country, adds the National Council, is doing a proper job of rehabilitating kids in trouble.

We are a slipshod people. We tend to do nothing unless a crisis is at hand, and then we seek simplistic, temporary measures. We wrap ourselves in our comforts, tend to think the universe is where we are and blink at those who are cold, hungry, sick, in trouble. It appears the time of slippage may be ending. The time may be beginning when, compassion and purity of purpose aside, we are going to be hurt significantly if we don't reach out to those aliens who dare not to be self-sufficient. "If you are among brigands and you are silent, you are a brigand yourself," a folk saying goes. Civilization is not a matter of museums and global communications. It derives from a quality of mind and of concern. And by that definition, we, of course, are not a civilized nation at all, rather a self-centered, stupid one. And the soothing words of all our politicians, all our churchmen, all our "important" people matter not. We are incompetent.[31]

Only excerpted here in part, the entire article is a harsh criticism of the way in which juveniles are treated in this country by the courts, the institutions, or whomever. While there are fine programs and many good staff people doing excellent work throughout the country with delinquents, they are dealing with only a small percentage of our youths. For the majority, what Mangel has described is reality. Unfortunately, this

---

Box 2.3 Jerome Miller

The Commissioner of the Department of Youth Services, Jerome Miller, a pioneer in deinstitutionalization, convinced the Governor of Massachusetts to approve the closing of all but one juvenile correctional institution (the Shirley Training School, which served a few remaining girls) and placing all other adjudicated juveniles into community-based programs. This bold move, supported by the media and politicians, has been copied in many states since that time and proved that the large majority of adjudicated juveniles could be better dealt with in the community.

reality remained a fairly true picture in the 1980s and probably will remain so.

The Massachusetts Experiment

In 1969, Dr. Jerome Miller took over as youth commissioner for Massachusetts and made some revolutionary changes in that state's juvenile justice system. Juvenile corrections in the United States has not been the same since.

One of the more radical actions was closing the Lyman School for Boys in January 1972. The Lyman School for Boys was opened in 1846 and was the first institution of its kind in the nation. The closing of Lyman School was the finale of an intense drama that had been going on in Massachusetts for more than two years. The era of confining children in large correctional institutions was dead, declared Dr. Jerome Miller, commissioner of the Department of Youth Services (DYS), and a new age of decent, humane, community-based care for delinquent youngsters was beginning.

The idealistic young reformers who had worked so hard to close down the institutions cheered. But juvenile justice professionals, both in Massachusetts and other states, were stunned, and in many cases, horrified, at what Jerome Miller had done.

Miller is not without his critics. As a matter of fact, most juvenile corrections administrators outside of Massachusetts, when queried in the mid-1970s, were generally in disagreement with the closing of institutions. Several very important figures in the field were interviewed by Corrections Magazine in 1975 and had mostly criticism for the actions of Miller. These ranged from "Very tragic and I'd hate to see other states imitate it" to "[Only] when you've got training schools that are brutalizing kids, then you should close them."[32] Whether from this lack of support from his peers or from the somewhat inclusive results from the early years of the experiment in Massachusetts, Jerome Miller was finally a victim of his own turbulent actions and left the state in 1973. What were the results of this "crusade" in Massachusetts? Did closing down the larger juvenile correctional institutions make a difference? Miller had contended that training schools were not only ineffective at reforming juvenile lawbreakers, but that they were profoundly destructive, and that those children who went through them were more likely to commit new crimes when they left than when they were admitted.[33]

A team of researchers from Harvard University found, after eight years of intensive examination of youngsters released from institutions and youngsters released from community programs that the experiment was successful. They examined the recidivism rates of boys released from the traditional institutions in 1968 with a sample of boys placed under community supervision in 1974. The rates for both reappearance in court

(74 versus 66 percent) and for either probation or commitment (55 versus 47 percent) were slightly higher for the boys who were released from the institutions. Girls also had a lower rate of reappearance (37 versus 24 percent) and probation/commitment (25 versus 10 percent).[34]

Some of the researchers' conclusions were that the community programs did not go far enough and in many cases merely replaced institutionalization with a similar condition in small group homes.

> Instead of having "institution kids" we now have a new group of "agency kids." They are generally treated better, but their experience in these agencies is still quite foreign to the worlds in which they live. If these private agencies are to prevent recidivism better than the training school model, they must take the risk of becoming involved in the community to a more significant degree than simply retaining a "community board."[35]

Services were often lacking and support systems weak. Because of these findings and the fact that the community group was probably older and tougher, the researchers warned against quick conclusions that the community approach does not work. On the contrary, they cautioned those who still used institutions extensively to look in depth at the extent of services and the results (favorable) that were obtained when services were not available. Miller feels that the harsh institutional approach is at least as ineffective as the community programs that provide no services and that both should be avoided in favor of community programs that address the full range of client needs.[36]

Yet, there are those in the field of juvenile corrections who feel that simply closing an institution is not enough. They feel that as institutions are closed, they should also be torn down. For example, there are many old prisons that have been "abandoned" for new ones, only to be reopened in a short while. Americans are great at finding a use for vacant buildings. If not used as prisons, they are used as facilities for the mentally ill or other social misfits.

However, the aims of Miller's deinstitutionalization reforms had far reaching effects. Deinstitutionalization was the basis of the 1974 Juvenile Justice and Delinquency Prevention Act. This movement was not overcome until conservative political rhetoric led to punitive legislative reforms in the 1980s.[37]

The 1990s and Beyond

The provisions of the Federal Anti-Gang and Youth Violence Act of 1997 outline the problems both presented and faced by juveniles during this decade. The Act was intended to deter and punish serious gang and violent crime, promote accountability in the juvenile justice system, prevent juvenile and youth crime, and to protect juveniles from various forms of abuse. Its provisions include:

- Targeting violent gang, gun, and drug crimes (includes targeting illicit gun markets and protecting children from guns and drugs)
- Protecting witnesses to help prosecute gangs and other violent criminals (includes penalties for obstruction of justice offenses involving victims, witnesses and informants)
- Protecting victims' rights (includes the extension of the Victims of Child Abuse Act)
- Federal prosecution of serious and violent juvenile offenders
- Rules governing the incarceration of juveniles in the adult Federal system
- The creation of the Office of Juvenile Crime Control and Prevention (including Juvenile Crime Assistance, and Missing and Exploited Children).

The Act reflects the dichotomy present in the juvenile justice system since its inception. We have the desire to protect children from harm but also to hold them accountable for serious crimes.

During this decade, the rehabilitative nature of juvenile justice was called into question. The **"Get Tough" movement** featured stricter penalties for youths including the sentencing of juveniles as adults and the death penalty. This new model focuses on such issues as punishment, justice, and accountability. This terminology reflects the view that juveniles must bear individual responsibility for their crimes, particularly serious crimes, as adults do. It represents a movement away from the original doctrines of the child savers and the juvenile court. Traditionally, the juvenile justice system should not punish youths because they are not responsible actors. The "Get Tough" viewpoint holds the opposite view that juveniles should be punished to make them more responsible. Thus, this movement represents a revolution in the philosophy and operations of the juvenile justice system.[38]

While the juvenile offenders of the past were considered wayward youth rather than hardened criminals, juvenile offenders are considered ruthless and unconcerned about the consequences of their actions. The "Get Tough" movement focuses on the crimes committed rather than the underlying causes of delinquency. As a result, more youths are being tried in criminal courts and sent to adult prisons. Juvenile facilities were also made more secure. In addition, budget cutbacks in the 1980s resulted in a reduction of programs for juveniles. Special education programs were developed, but crowding became a problem, increasing pressure to sentence juveniles as adults. Yet, many juvenile justice experts emphasize the need to work with families and communities to reduce problems before they are out of hand and to put more emphasis on treatment programs.[39]

SUMMARY

From the era of the Depression and Prohibition through the post-Depression era and into the 1960s, 1970s, and 1980s, U.S. society has been faced with social, moral, and economic problems caused by juveniles. They commit crimes, run away from home, or simply refuse to be treated as children any longer.

Drugs, alcohol, and the pressures of a thermonuclear society all pressed in on the juvenile of the 1980s. What are they really?

Researchers and experts in the field of juvenile corrections continuously debate typologies and treatment modalities. Institutions and prisons for juveniles are seen as ineffective by such as Jerry Miller and his followers. Still, others see them as worthwhile and appropriate by some and as necessary evils. Police forces have become "specialized" in attempting to deal with delinquents. Some are trying to prevent juvenile crime by working closely with the community in developing diversions for children who might otherwise get into trouble.

Supreme Court decisions such as *In re Gault* have brought some constitutional protection and redress from legal wrongs to our young people, but many other court actions are still in progress.

It seems that the definition of delinquency and standardization of semantic, meanings for other terms commonly used in the field of juvenile justice still need to be resolved. Also, we have seen that the procedures of a juvenile court in one county in a state may differ significantly from those of a neighboring county in the same state.

Lest we become too depressed by the situation at the end of the 1980s, it is important to note that the percentages of persons under age 18 involved in crimes cleared by arrest has been coming down steadily since their peak in the mid-1970s. Most young people are not juvenile delinquents and not all of them are involved in drugs, sex, and rock and roll. The juvenile justice system, however, is set up to deal with those that deviate from societal standards of conduct. Not all deviant behavior is criminal or delinquent, but all criminal and delinquent behavior is deviant. It is this latter behavior that we shall discuss for the remainder of this text, now that we have a broad overview of the history of how we got to where we are today and where we seem to be going in the new century.

Increasing caseloads and restricted budgets have now produced deteriorating conditions of confinement. Although the current situation has many similarities to that of 100 years ago, the Office of Juvenile Justice and Delinquency Prevention is exercising a national leadership role in blending treatment and public safety concerns. Renewed interest also exists in upgrading professional standards, professional associations are speaking out against punitive rhetoric, and private philanthropy is supporting progressive juvenile justice reform.[40]

We have presented this review to consider the impact of history upon the future. Bernard has identified an historical "cycle of juvenile justice" that has been repeated throughout American history. This cycle begins with the official and public perception that juvenile crime is exceptionally high. This perception is coupled with the belief that punishments are too harsh and that more lenient treatment is in order for juveniles. In turn, such changes fuel the next cycle where officials and the public blame these lenient treatments for the latest increase in juvenile delinquency. The predictable reaction is that punishments are increased and juveniles are subjected to the same penalties as adults.[41] It appears that we are in the midst of a punitive cycle at the present time. Time will tell if Bernard's prediction for the next turn in juvenile justice policy will be toward treatment over punishment.[42]

Another noted historian, Randall Sheldon, worries that the juvenile justice system is returning to its more punitive past. Sheldon notes that juvenile justice initially emphasized institutionalization as the solution to delinquency. One of the problems with this approach is what Sheldon terms the "Field of Dreams Syndrome"—the construction of institutions that are filled soon after they are built. The result is that institutions become cemented into the system, even in the face of the optimistic evidence from the Massachusetts experiment that institutions are unnecessary.[43]

Several experts have called for continuing reform in the system to adapt to changing times. For example, Watkins has suggested that juvenile court, as a separate entity, is still valuable. However, it must adapt to both the nature and the problems faced by today's youths. He calls for a reinvigoration of the juvenile court to offer methods of child saving relevant to twenty-first century children.[44] He concludes by documenting the jurisprudential shift in sentencing policy from treating delinquent offenders to punishing them. For example, Feld outlines three alternatives to the current juvenile justice system: restructuring juvenile courts to fit their original therapeutic purpose, combining appropriate punishment with criminal procedural safeguards, and abolishing juvenile co-jurisdiction over criminal conduct and trying young offenders in criminal courts after making certain substantive and procedural changes.[45]

The "Get Tough" movement appears to be the norm of the day. It is important to examine recent crime statistics to examine trends in juvenile crime. Is getting tough warranted? Are things getting worse? These questions will be considered in Chapter 3.

TERMS TO REMEMBER

Battered child syndrome

"Catch 22"

Dependent

"Get Tough" movement

Intervention strategy

Juvenile Court

MINS (Minors In Need of
Supervision)

Neglected

PINS (Persons In Need of
Supervision)

Psychic arrest

Status offenders

REVIEW QUESTIONS

1. How did the "due process revolution" affect the rights of juveniles?
2. How did "child savers" like Jane Addams view the problem of juvenile delinquency?
3. What were the aims of the first juvenile court? How do the procedures for handling juveniles under *parens patriae* compare to how adults are treated in the criminal justice system?
4. What are the distinguishing features of status offenders, dependent and neglected children, PINS, and MINS? How should they be treated?
5. In what ways are the delinquents of today different from those of fifty years ago?
6. What was juvenile delinquency like during the Great Depression?
7. How did the Juvenile Justice and Delinquency Prevention Act of 1974 propose to change the operations of the juvenile justice system?
8. How did the doctrine of *parens patriae* affect the legal rights of juveniles?
9. How did the landmark cases of the due process revolution change this situation?
10. Did the "Massachusetts Experiment" work?
11. What did the Federal Anti-Gang and Youth Violence Act of 1997 attempt to do?
12. What are the elements of the "Get Tough" movement? How do they represent a change in operations of the juvenile justice system?
13. What is the meaning of Bernard's "cycle of juvenile justice"?
14. What is the "Field of Dreams" syndrome and what does it mean to the juvenile justice system?
15. What juvenile justice reforms do Watkins and Feld call for?

NOTES

[1]Anthony M. Platt, *The Child Savers: The Invention of Delinquency* (Chicago: University of Chicago Press, 1969).

[2]Renee G. Kasinsky, "Child Neglect and 'Unfit' Mothers: Child Savers in the Progressive Era," *Women and Criminal Justice*, Vol. 6 (1994), pp. 97–129.

[3]See Alexander W. Pisciotta, *Benevolent Repression: Social Control and the American Reformatory–Prison Movement* (New York: New York University Press, 1994).

[4]Robert M. Mennel, *Thorns and Thistles* (Hanover: University of New Hampshire Press, 1973), p. 101.

[5]John C. Watkins, *Juvenile Justice Century: A Sociological Commentary on American Juvenile Courts* (Durham, NC: Carolina Academic Press, 1998).

[6]National Juvenile Justice Clearinghouse, *Facts about Youth and Delinquency: A Citizen's Guide to Juvenile Justice* (Washington, D.C.: U.S. Department of Justice, Office of Juvenile Justice and Delinquency Prevention, 1982), pp. 7–10.

[7]Marc LeBlanc and Louise Biron, "Status Offenses: A Legal Term Without Meaning," *Journal of Research in Crime and Delinquency*, Vol. 17 (January 1980), pp. 114–125.

[8]Barry Krisberg, "The Legacy of Juvenile Corrections," *Corrections Today*, Vol. 57 (5) (August, 1995), p. 122.

[9]S. Schlossman, "Delinquent Children: The Juvenile Reform School," in Norval Morris and David J. Rothman, eds. *The Oxford History of the Prison: The Practice of Punishment in Western Society*, (Oxford: Oxford University Press, 1995) pp. 363–389.

[10]David J. Rothman, *The Discovery of the Asylum* (Boston: Little, Brown, 1971), p. 215.

[11]Ibid.

[12]*Seattle Post Intelligencer*, January 8, 1930. p. 1.

[13]*Seattle Post Intelligencer*, December 24, 1930. p. 1B.

[14]The Prohibition Act, or the Eighteenth Amendment (ratified January 16, 1920), banned the sale of alcoholic beverages. *U.S. Statutes at Large, Volume 41*, p. 305.

[15]"Catch 22" means that you can escape from an unpleasant situation only by meeting certain conditions. But if you meet those conditions, you cannot escape. This expression was popularized by Joseph Heller in his novel of the same name. The novel is about an army pilot constantly required to fly suicide missions. He knew it was crazy to fly the missions, but according to the army, because he knew it was crazy he was perfectly sane. And since he was sane, he could continue to fly the missions.

[16]Eliot Ness of Chicago's Police Department Crime Prevention Bureau, and later of television fame, advocated that instead of apprehending young delinquents as offenders, police or juvenile officers should be trained to make referrals to proper social agencies for guidance and treatment. See Eliot Ness, "New Role of the Police," *Survey* (March 1944), p. 77.

[17]See Clifford Shaw and Henry D. McKay, *Juvenile Delinquency in Urban Areas* (Chicago: University of Chicago Press, 1942); Cletus Dirksen, *Economic Factors in Delinquency* (Milwaukee: Bruce, 1948); William W. Wattenburg and J. J. Balistrieri, "Gang Membership and Juvenile Delinquency," *American Sociological Review*, Vol. 18 (1950), pp. 631–635; Ernest W. Burgess, "The Economic Factor in Juvenile Delinquency," *Journal of Criminal Law, Criminology, and Police Science* (May–June, 1952), pp. 29–42; Albert K. Cohen, *Delinquent Boys: The Culture of the Delinquent Gang* (New York: Free Press, 1955); and Sol Rubin, "Changing Youth Correction Authority Concepts," *Focus*, Vol. 29 (1950), pp. 77–82.

[18]Elizabeth Fajen, "Curing Delinquency at the Source," *Survey* (October 1946), pp. 261–262.

[19]Adams, ed., *Juvenile Justice Management*, pp. 323–324.

[20]Edwin Powers, "An Experiment in the Prevention of Delinquency," *The Annals of the American Academy*, (January 1949), p. 81.

[21]President's Commission on Law Enforcement and Administration of Justice, *The Challenge of Crime in a Free Society* (Washington, D.C.: U.S. Government Printing Office, 1967), p. 58.

[22]*Juvenile Justice and Delinquency Prevention Act of 1974*, Public Law 93-415, 93rd Cong. S. 821, September 7, 1974, p. 2.

[23]Platt, *The Child Savers*, pp. 103–104.

[24]*Kent v. United States*, 383 U.S. 541 (1966).

[25]*In re Gault*, 387 U.S. 1 (1967). See also Barry C. Feld, "Transformation of the Juvenile Court," *Minnesota Law Review*, Vol. 75 (1991), pp. 691–726.

[26]*In re Winship,* 397 U.S. 358, 365–66 (1970). See also *Debacher v. Bainard,* 396 U.S. 28, 6Crl 3001 (1970).

[27]See for example *In re Richard S.,* 27 N.Y. 2d 802, 264 N.E. 2d 353, 315 N.Y.S. 2d 861 (1970).

[28]The doubt expressed must be one that a reasonable man or woman would express when presented with all of the evidence.

[29]J. Senna and L. Siegel, *Juvenile Law: Cases and Comments* (St. Paul, MN: West, 1976), p. 344.

[30]Mildred L. Midonick, *Children, Parents, and the Courts: Juvenile Delinquency, Ungovernability, and Neglect* (New York: Practicing Law Institute, 1972), p. 1.

[31]Charles Mangel, "How to Make a Criminal Out of a Child," *Look,* June 29, 1971.

[32]"Moving the Kids Out: A Unique Experiment," *Corrections Magazine* (November–December 6, 1975): 29.

[33]Robert B. Coates, A. D. Miller, and Lloyd E. Ohlin, *Diversity in a Youth Correctional System: Handling Delinquents in Massachusetts,* (Cambridge, MA: Ballinger, 1978), pp. 149–154.

[34]Ibid.

[35]Ibid., p. 173.

[36]"Moving the Kids Out," p. 30.

[37]Krisberg, "Legacy," p. 152.

[38]H.R. 810, the Anti-Gang and Youth Violence Act of 1997.

[39]M. E. Blomquist and M. L. Forst, "Punishment, Accountability, and the New Juvenile Justice," in Barry W Hancock and Paul M. Sharp, eds. *Criminal Justice in America: Theory, Practice, and Policy* (Upper Saddle River, N.J.: Prentice Hall, 1996), pp. 356–369.

[40]S. Gluck, "Wayward Youth, Super Predator: An Evolutionary Tale of Juvenile Delinquency From the 1950s to the Present," *Corrections Today,* Vol. 59 (June, 1997), pp. 62–64, 66.

[41]Krisberg, "Legacy," p. 154.

[42]Thomas J. Bernard, *The Cycle of Juvenile Justice* (Oxford: Oxford University Press, 1992).

[43]Randall G. Shelden, *Juvenile Justice in Historical Perspective: Confronting the Edifice Complex and Field of Dreams Syndrome* (From Dan Macallair and Vincent Schiraldi, *Reforming Juvenile Justice: Reasons and Strategies for the 21st Century* (Dubuque, IA: Kendall/Hunt Publishing Co., 1998), pp. 7–28.

[44]Watkins, *Juvenile Justice Century.*

[45]Barry C. Feld, "Criminalizing the American Juvenile Court," in Michael Tonry, ed. *Crime and Justice: A Review of Research* (Chicago: University of Chicago Press, 1993), pp. 197–280. See also Jerome G. Miller, *Last One Over the Wall: The Massachusetts Experiment in Closing Reform Schools* (1998).

chapter *3*

JUVENILE CRIME:
MEASUREMENT AND ANALYSIS

Perhaps at no other time in history has the need for the "cool light of reason" been more necessary in planning for juvenile justice than today, when there is so much of the "heat of emotion" directed toward the behavior of youth and the need for society to control it within acceptable boundaries.

— Paul H. Hahn

MEASURING DELINQUENCY

The measurement of the extent of juvenile crime (generally that committed by persons under the age of 18) is a problem that has vexed researchers from the beginning of their attempts to determine the extent of it. Since juvenile crime has been the domain of a highly splintered system, the only valid data have tended to deal with crime on a local area only. Most tools now used to measure juvenile crime are, of course, from either official or unofficial sources. Variance in the numbers is great, depending on the source, the timeframe, and the scope of the database. Most official figures come from the FBI's **Uniform Crime Report (UCR),** reports from the National Criminal Justice Reference Service (NCJRS), reports of the Office of Juvenile Justice and Delinquency Prevention (OJJDP), juvenile court statistics, institutional and aftercare records, and cohort studies. Unofficial figures come from self-report studies, victimization surveys, and various academic studies conducted by universities and research organizations.

Statistics: The Baseline for the Analysis of Juvenile Crime

Statistics provide information. Information is needed to deal with juvenile crime and delinquency in an effective way. Analysis of the data presented in this chapter will give us a picture of the extent and nature of juvenile crime. However, students should keep in mind that statistics, although important, do not always accurately represent the amount of delinquency and the nature of the delinquents. The data are imperfect and limited and must be considered with this in mind.

THE UNIFORM CRIME REPORT

The Uniform Crime Reporting program (UCR) is a cooperative statistical effort of among city, county, and state law enforcement agencies. They voluntarily report data on crimes that witnesses and victims bring to their attention or that are uncovered by the police themselves. Thus, they collectively represent the amount of *crimes known to the police* in a given year and they are presented in their annual report, *Crime in the United States.*

Historical Background

Recognizing the need for national crime statistics, the International Association of Chiefs of Police (IACP) formed the Committee on Uniform Crime Records in the 1920s to develop a system of accurate police statistics. Establishing offenses known to law enforcement as the appropriate measure, the committee evaluated various crimes on the basis of their seriousness, frequency, pervasiveness in all geographic areas of the country, and their likelihood of being reported to the police. After studying state criminal codes and evaluating record keeping practices in use, the committee completed a plan for crime reporting that became the foundation of the UCR program.

Seven offenses were chosen to serve as an index for gauging fluctuations in the overall volume and rate of crime. Known collectively as the **Crime Index,** these offenses included the violent crimes of murder and non-negligent manslaughter, forcible rape, robbery, and aggravated assault and the property crimes of burglary, larceny-theft, and motor vehicle theft. By congressional mandate, arson was added as the eighth index offense in 1979.

During the early stages of the program, it was recognized that the differences among criminal codes precluded a mere aggregation of state statistics to arrive at a national total. Further, because of the variances in punishment for the same offenses in different state codes, no distinction between felony and misdemeanor crimes was possible. To avoid these problems and provide nationwide uniformity in crime reporting standardized (or "uniform") offense definitions by which law enforcement agencies were to submit data were formulated.

In January 1930, 400 cities representing 20 million inhabitants in 43 states began participating in the UCR program. Congress enacted Title 28, Section 534, of the United States Code, authorizing the attorney general to gather crime information. The attorney general, in turn, designated the FBI to serve as the national clearinghouse for the data collected. Since that time, data based on the uniform classifications and procedures for reporting have been obtained from law enforcement agencies across the nation.

Beginning in 1991, the UCR program began moving toward a system of crime data collection that should increase the ability to conduct crime analysis. This new system, the National Incident Based Reporting System (NIBRS), is designed to collect more detailed information on crimes. NIBRS will report both crimes and arrests. It will eventually replace the UCR as the source of official FBI counts of crimes reported to law enforcement agencies.

The Juvenile Crime Problem

In its Web-based "Statistical Briefing Book," the Office of Juvenile Justice and Delinquency Prevention compiles and presents information on juvenile crime and juvenile justice system processing that is compiled from several sources, including the Uniform Crime Report.[1] The following statistics are presented from the briefing book.

First, we shall examine juvenile arrest trends for the period 1980–1999 for violent index offenses:

- **The juvenile arrest rate for all offenses reached its highest level in the last two decades in 1996, and then declined 16 percent by 1999.** The overall juvenile arrest rate was still seven percent higher in 1999 than in 1980.[2]
- **The juvenile Violent Index Crime arrest rate in 1999 was at its lowest level since 1988—36 percent below the peak year of 1994.** About one-third of one percent of the juveniles' aged 10-17 was arrested for a violent crime in 1999. In fact, even at the 1994 peak, the proportion of arrests for violent crimes that involved juveniles (20 percent) was about the same as it was in 1965.[3]
- **Of all the Violent Index Crime Offenses, the juvenile arrest rate for murder registered both the greatest increase and the greatest decline between 1980 and 1999.** The juvenile arrest rate

for murder more than doubled between 1987 and 1993. However, between 1993 and 1999, it dropped 68 percent—the lowest level since the 1960s.[4] The peak in homicides by juveniles between 1987 and 1993 was firearm related. Interestingly, the decline between 1993 and 1998 was also entirely attributable to a drop in firearm related homicides committed by juveniles.[5]

- **The juvenile arrest rate for forcible rape in 1999 was at its lowest level since 1980.** It was 31 percent below the peak year of 1991.[6]
- **The juvenile arrest rate for robbery in 1999 was lower than any point since at least 1980.** Between 1994 and 1999, it fell dramatically—53 percent.[7]
- **For aggravated assault, the juvenile arrest rate in 1999 was 69% above its low point in 1983.** It more than doubled between 1983 and 1994.[8]

The following pattern was present for juvenile arrests for Property Index Crimes during the time period:

- **The juvenile arrest rate for Property Index offenses in 1999 was at its lowest level since at least 1980.** This rate peaked in 1991 but, between 1997 and 1999, it dropped 23 percent to its lowest level in a generation.[9]
- **The juvenile arrest rate for burglary declined consistently and substantially (60 percent) between 1980 and 1999.** The 1999 rate was less than half than that of 1980.[10]
- **The juvenile arrest rate for larceny-theft remained relatively constant between 1980 and 1997 then declined 23 percent by 1999.** The 1999 rate was the lowest since at least 1980.[11]
- **Between 1990 and 1999, the juvenile arrest rate for motor vehicle theft was almost cut in half.** The 1999 rate was the lowest level since 1984.[12]
- **Following a peak in 1994, the juvenile arrest rate for arson declined 25 percent.**

Compared to other property crimes, the arrest rate for arson is very small.[13] For substance abuse violations during the time period, the following patterns were evident:

- **For drug abuse violations, the juvenile arrest rate peaked in 1997.** It was more than double than the average rate of the 1980s. By

1999, it has dropped 13 percent. Between 1990 and 1999, the increase in juvenile drug abuse violation arrests was greater for females (190 percent) than for males (124 percent).[14]

- **The juvenile arrest rate for driving under the influence increased 58% between 1993 and 1999.** However, the 1999 rate was still 36 percent below that of 1980.[15]
- **For drunkenness, the juvenile arrest rate rose 43 percent between 1993 and 1998 and then dropped 13 percent in 1999.** These trends are similar to those for driving under the influence.[16]

Overall, these statistics reveal that juvenile crime is declining. However, the OJJDP research report reaches the following conclusions:

> **Even with recent declines, juvenile crime remains too high.** Despite decreases in recent years, juvenile arrests in 1999 were 11 percent higher than in 1990. For violent crimes committed by juveniles, 1999 arrests were 5 percent higher than in 1990. Such increases confirm that juvenile crime and delinquency remain serious problems in the nation. **Communities should place special focus on young offenders and female offenders.**[17]

This was the great debate of the 1990s—the supposed worsening of juvenile crime and what to do about it. Bernard examined juvenile crime statistics for roughly the same time period and concluded that there is no crime wave and thus, no reason to make radical changes in juvenile justice policy.[18] The statistics are not wrong but as always, they are open to interpretation. However, there are other sources of statistics to consider as we attempt to find out whether juvenile crime is getting worse.

NATIONAL CRIME VICTIMS SURVEY

Another source of crime information is the **National Crime Victims Survey (NCVS).** The Bureau of Justice Statistics has conducted this survey since 1972. Its aim is to uncover unreported crime by going directly to the victim. The NCVS is a scientifically designed survey of U.S. households. It is designed to represent the nation. Approximately 60,000 households respond to the survey each year. Information in this report is also presented as a population rate: the number of victims per 1,000 households.

As an estimate of the risk of crime victimization, it is an improvement over UCR for two reasons. First, the survey presents information taken directly from victims whether they report the crime to the police or not. Second, it collects background information on victims, making it possible to decide which groups have the highest rates of victimization for particular types of crime.

Analysis of victimization survey data from 1973 to 1997 reveals that:

- **Violent crime victimization among juveniles dropped by 33 percent between 1993 and 1997.** For example, robbery victimization rose in 1981 and 1983 but, by 1997, it dropped to the low rates recorded in the 1970s.[19]
- **On average, juveniles were involved in one-quarter of the serious violent victimizations annually over the past 25 years.** Aggravated assault victimizations among juveniles peaked at 31 percent in 1994 but declined to 27 percent by 1997.[20]
- **Juvenile violence peaks in the after-school hours on school days and in the evenings on non-school days.** Aggravated assaults among juveniles are most common around 3 P.M., while the number of juvenile robberies peaks around 9 P.M. Sexual assaults peak in the hours after school. It appears that after school programs have more crime prevention potential than curfews.[21]
- **Juveniles injure more victims during the hours after school than at any other time.** A high proportion of firearm-involved crime among juveniles occurs at this time.[22]
- **School crime was not uncommon.** Almost four in ten high school students were involved in a physical fight. Four in 100 were injured but both of these rates were higher for minority group males. One-third of high school students had property stolen or vandalized at school. Yet, the fear of crime at school kept only 4 percent of high school students at home during the past month.[23]
- **Nine percent of high school students carried a weapon on school grounds during the past month.** During one year, 7 percent of high school students said that they were threatened or injured with a weapon at school.[24]

Lifestyle choices by juveniles are also a risk factor in delinquency. The *Juvenile Offenders and Victims* report also compiles information on this subject from a variety of sources. The findings include:

- **More than half of high school students surveyed in 1998 admitted using an illicit drug at least once.** Fifty-two percent said they had used alcohol in the past month, while about 23 percent had used marijuana.[25]
- **Drug use was more common among males than females and among whites than blacks.** Males were more likely than females

to drink alcohol and to use drugs. Blacks had lower drug, alcohol, and tobacco use rates than whites.[26]

- **Thirty-two percent of the students had been offered, sold, or given an illegal drug on school property in the past year.** These percentages were highest for Hispanic males (47 percent) and lowest for black females (17 percent).[27]
- **Illicit drug use by juveniles declined during the 1980s but has increased since 1992.**[28]
- **The percentage of seniors who admitted breaking the law was greater among the drug users than the nonusers.**[29]
- **Among youth 14 and older, black males and females were more likely to have had sex in the past year than either white or Hispanic males and females.**[30]

Such trends must be considered when attempting to design policies and programs for juveniles. Risk factors must be addressed within the target population that you are trying to serve.

COHORT STUDIES: ANOTHER WAY TO MEASURE DELINQUENCY

A cohort study examines a selected group (cohort) of individuals who share a common experience in time. Delinquency research has featured the use of *birth cohorts*—persons born at the same time and living in the same place over a long period of time. Since World War II, there have been major cohort studies on delinquency conducted in several different locations. These studies give us some interesting insights into the delinquency of a large group of juveniles in their specific settings, and some tentative generalizations to the larger population of juveniles.

The Philadelphia Birth Cohorts

In this massive effort to describe delinquency in Philadelphia, renowned criminologist Marvin Wolfgang and his colleagues studied two birth cohorts.[31] The first birth cohort was comprised of all males born in 1945 in Philadelphia from age 10 to 18. The second birth cohort consisted of all males and females born in 1958 that lived in Philadelphia from age 10 to 18. The two studies were designed to determine the effects of growing up in the 1960s and 1970s. The first cohort included almost 10,000 subjects, while the second included almost 30,000 subjects. This latter group reflects the rapid expansion of the "baby boom" generation after World War II. These are known as the **Philadelphia Birth Cohorts.**

The first cohort study revealed the existence of a group of 627 chronic offenders who were responsible for the majority of the crimes committed by the entire cohort. Their criminal histories were related to the age at which they first committed a crime. The earlier a juvenile committed their first offense, the greater the number of offenses they committed by age 17. Race and family income also figured heavily in chronic delinquency. Over two-thirds of the chronic offenders were black. Yet, family income had more of an impact than race. Nonwhites of low socioeconomic status were three times more likely to be chronic offenders than whites of the same status.[32] Chronic offending was also related to intelligence and educational performance. The chronic offenders had lower mean IQ scores, below-average school achievement, and a higher incidence of retardation.

The 1958 cohort had a higher rate of offending per 1,000 subjects. In addition, the members of this cohort committed almost twice as many index offenses and three times as many violent crimes as the 1945 cohort. Moreover, the 1958 cohort had an offense rate that was five times higher for robbery, three times higher for homicide, twice as high for assault, and almost twice as high for rape. Finally, injurious offenses were much more prevalent and harmful in the 1958 cohort. In sum, the 1958 cohort members committed more, and more serious offenses than the 1945 cohort.

Like the 1945 cohort, the 1958 cohort contained a group of chronic offenders. The chronic offenders in the 1958 cohort were a larger group and they committed a higher percentage of the total number of offenses (61 versus 52 percent of all the crimes committed by the cohort). The chronics of 1958 accounted for the majority of the serious violent crime committed by the group.

Once again, race and socioeconomic status had an effect upon the rate of crime committed by the 1958 chronics. Among whites, chronics committed 50 percent of the offenses. Among nonwhites, they accounted for 65 percent of the crime. Chronics of high socioeconomic status committed 51 percent of the offenses for their subgroup, while chronics of low socioeconomic status committed 65 percent of the offenses in their subgroup. The chronics in the 1958 cohort evidenced the same social problems as those in the 1945 cohort. They moved more often, had lower achievement scores, had less schooling, and were more likely to have disciplinary problems at school.

The 1958 birth cohort study was designed to replicate the first with one significant difference. More than half of the cohort were female. Their offending patterns were substantially different than those of males. The number of boys who had their first police contact before age 18 was two and a half times higher than that for females. Females were primarily one-time offenders (60 percent) who were less likely to commit serious crimes that involved injury and stolen money. Only 7 percent of the females were chronic offenders.

The relationship between race and socioeconomic status among the chronic offenders was similar for both males and females. Nonwhites and offenders with low socioeconomic status, both male and female, were most likely to be chronic delinquents. However, the size and impact of the female chronic delinquents was much smaller than that of males.

A comparison of the research findings from both cohorts leads to several generalizations. Evidently, delinquency was prevalent among non-whites and subjects with low socioeconomic status. Delinquency was also related to residential instability, poor school achievement, and failure to graduate from high school.[33] The offenders in the 1958 cohort committed a greater number of crimes, and their crimes were more serious. Finally, in both cohorts, a core of chronic offenders was responsible for the bulk of serious crime.

A recent study examined the rates of adult offending within the 1958 cohort. Overall, the violent and chronic juvenile offenders had the highest rates of adult offending. Sixty-three percent of this subgroup committed an adult offense. However, comparisons between rates of offending among males and females could be made within this cohort. 612 males were classified as both violent and chronic offenders. They represented over 62 percent of the chronics and 54 percent of the serious male delinquents. This group was smaller among females—for each serious and chronic female delinquent there were seven such males. Yet, females in this subgroup committed a more disproportionate share of adult crime than the males.

Socioeconomic status also had an impact that overshadowed the effect of race and ethnicity on the rates of adult offending. Disadvantaged living conditions heightened the risk of future crime. The authors concluded that the risk factors associated with delinquency and adult crime must be identified in order to develop effective ways to treat juveniles and prevent crime.

Socioeconomic status also had an impact that overshadowed the effect of race and ethnicity on the rates of adult offending. Disadvantaged living conditions heightened the risk of future crime. The authors concluded that the risk factors associated with delinquency and adult crime must be identified in order to develop effective ways to treat juveniles and prevent crime.[34]

These studies became a model for several other efforts to determine the extent of delinquency through the use of official records, community studies, self-reporting data, and other sources to measure any large birth cohort.

The Columbus Cohort

The records of all juveniles born between 1956 and 1960 in Columbus, Ohio, who had been arrested for a violent crime were examined. Hamparian and her colleagues compared the backgrounds of 1,138 arrestees with various personal and social characteristics to try to determine who was most likely to commit serious crimes. They found that males outnumbered females by about six to one (85 percent to 15 percent). Blacks outnumbered whites. 85 percent of the offenders fell below the median income level. Yet, a very small percentage of the cohort (2.5 percent) were involved in violent crimes. Among this group, a significant number (12.2 percent) had siblings who had also committed violent offenses. Finally, institutional treatment seemed to have a negative effect upon the offenders.[35]

Unlike the Philadelphia findings, the **Columbus Cohort** did not progress from lesser to more serious types of crime, nor did they specialize in any specific type of crime. The researchers also followed the cohort members into adulthood. They found that:

1. The frequency of arrests declines with age.
2. Most adult crimes committed by juvenile violent offenders were not violent.
3. Four out of ten adult offenders were arrested for at least one index violent crime.
4. Almost half of the arrested cohort members were imprisoned as adults. More than 80 percent were released, and half went back a second time.

These findings did not identically match those from Philadelphia. It appears that juvenile offenders do not get a "clean slate" as adults. The adult system does not accord them the leniency usually given to real first offenders.

Following the cohort into adulthood also gave the Hamparian research team the opportunity to explore some key policy issues. The findings are summarized for three categories: one-time only offenders, juvenile assaulters, and chronic offenders.

1. One-time only offenders:
   - More likely to be white.
   - Disproportionately female.
   - Usually not committed to training schools.
   - Usually arrested for non-index violent offenses (55.6 percent).
   - Frequently charged with an assault occurring while police attempted an arrest for another, less serious crime.

2. Juvenile Assaulters:
   - The most serious juvenile violent offense arrest for nearly three-quarters of all female cohort members.
   - Over 51 percent were white while only 42 percent of the index violent offenders were white.
   - One-time-only offenders were less likely to be chronic offenders.
   - Both violent and nonviolent offenders were probably arrested for the first time before age 13.

3. Chronic Offenders:
   - Disproportionately male; first arrested by age 13, had been incarcerated in juvenile training schools.
   - Three-quarters of juvenile chronic offenders were also adult offenders.
   - Over 50 percent of adult offenders were also chronic juvenile offenders.
   - Juvenile chronic offenders (8 percent) were also repeat adult index violent offenders. They accounted for one third of all adult arrests for index violence.
   - Most juvenile chronic offenders had been incarcerated. 54 percent were committed at least once to training schools. Almost 64 percent had at least one adult imprisonment.[36]

It is interesting to note that the removal of chronic offenders from the cohort would have reduced the number of cohort arrests by 50 percent. This study demonstrated that the continuity between juvenile and adult crime is a reality and that policy decisions that affect these offenders *before* they become adults could have a drastic impact upon future adult crime.

The Racine Cohort

Lyle Shannon and his colleagues conducted a longitudinal study that examined the criminal careers of 6,127 persons born in Racine, Wisconsin in 1942, 1949, and 1959. The study examined the development of criminal careers within the three birth cohorts. Data on reported police contacts were collected through 1974. As in the Philadelphia studies, the goal was to identify those individuals who were more likely to engage in delinquency, who stopped committing crimes, and who continued their criminal careers into adulthood. However, from analyzing the **Racine Cohorts,** the findings were different from those in Philadelphia.

Shannon reported that the rates for serious felonies more than doubled from 1942 to 1955 for the age group 6–17. The rate more than tripled for the 18–20 age group. Crime rates were highest in the inner city areas where unemployment and underemployment were commonplace. Offenders with a juvenile record were more likely to commit crime as adults. Yet, it was impossible to predict which juveniles would become adult offenders.[37]

Lab and Dorner (1987) compared female delinquency patterns to that of the males in the three Racine (WI) birth cohorts. They reported that, over time, female delinquency rose for status, victimless, and minor property offenses. Yet, in terms of major property and personal offenses, the female rates did not match those of their male counterparts.[38]

The Cambridge (UK) Study of Delinquent Development

The **Cambridge (UK) Study of Delinquent Development** followed 411 London (UK) working-class males from age 8 to 32, beginning in 1961–62. Data were obtained from (1) tests and interviews conducted at ages 8, 10 and 14; (2) interviews conducted at ages 16, 18, 21, 25, and 32; (3) parental interviews; (4) questionnaires completed by the subjects' teachers; and (5) statistics compiled by the Criminal Record Office in London. These data were analyzed to identify predictors of: (1) participation (prevalence) in officially recorded offending between ages 10 and 20 years; (2) early onset (between ages 10 and 13) versus later onset (ages 14 to 20) of offending; and (3) persistence versus desistance of offending in adulthood (ages 21 to 32).

Here, Farrington found that the peak age for the annual prevalence of convictions is 17 (11.2 males per 100 convicted). The best childhood predictors (at age 10) of prevalence were childhood antisocial behavior, convicted parents, impulsivity and daring, low intelligence and attainment, low income and poor housing, and poor child rearing practices (including separation from parents). The number of offenses committed per year peaked at age 17 (16.8 per 100 males). The peak age of onset was 14 (4.6 first convictions per 100 males) with a secondary peak at 17. The *age of desistance*—when the last offense is typically committed—was 23.3. Farrington also determined that violent offenders committed their crimes frequently. Therefore, measures designed to reduce future violence might as well be targeted on frequent as well as currently violent offenders.[39]

In particular, the early onset of offending was predicted by low paternal involvement with the boy in leisure activities. The same factor led to persistence in crime between ages 21 and 32, together with a low degree of commitment to school and low verbal IQ at ages 8–10.[40] A long-term follow-up study of the cohort found that nearly all subjects had been sent to prison. Most of the subjects thought imprisonment had no effect upon them, though some believed it had made them less likely to reoffend. Generally, chronic offenders led more dysfunctional lives in adulthood than other offenders. The most important childhood risk factors for chronic offending were troublesomeness, daring, and having a delinquent sibling or a convicted parent. On the basis of such features, Farrington and West believed that most of the chronic offenders might have been predicted at age 10 and that treatment could have been identified.[41] Another study of the life course of these offenders revealed that several social variables (work history, relations with spouses) distinguished between chronic and other types of offenders.[42]

The results of the Cambridge study emphasize the need to consider the different stages and elements of a criminal career as separate entities. It also seems that the most promising methods of preventing offending appear to be behavioral parent training and preschool intellectual enrichment programs.[43]

In reaction to the findings of the cohort studies, experts have suggested that juvenile courts adopt a policy of close, intensive supervision perhaps for first-time and certainly for second-time juvenile, Index offenders. After a third Index offense, incapacitation should become "the rule rather than the exception. . . . Juveniles can and should receive severe penalties in juvenile court when their most current offense and prior record warrant such action."[44] In addition, policies should be established to better identify the chronic offender and an enhanced system of record keeping should ease identification of them.[45] Hamparian and her colleagues recommended that chronic violent offenders be dealt with severely, not just with punishment, but with a graduated series of programs. These programs should range from incarceration to work readiness projects providing sheltered employment in the form of a "Community Conservation Corps" for young adults. They stressed the importance of not waiting for chronic juvenile offenders to become adult criminals.

SERIOUS JUVENILE OFFENDER PROGRAMS

In 1984, the federal government concluded that it was necessary to focus on the serious juvenile offender. In particular, programs that had the potential to decrease the probability that serious juvenile offenders would spend their "adult lives in prison" were encouraged (National Advisory Committee, 1984: 11).[46] As a result, the **Violent Juvenile Offender (VJO) Program** was established. It places chronically violent juvenile offenders in an intervention program that features four elements: reintegration, case management, social learning processes, and a phased re-entry from secure facilities to intensive supervision in the community. This program is now in operation in Detroit, Memphis, Newark, and Boston; the experimental and control groups have permitted a test of its effectiveness.

One study found that the average juvenile in a VJO Program has been involved in over ten crimes that resulted in over five formal juvenile court adjudications per offender. Violence predominated: Almost 60 percent of the youths were charged with and 40 percent adjudicated for three or more violent crimes.[47] Self-reports showed an even more intense involvement in violent crime. These youths averaged approximately one violent, one property, and one drug offense per week. These youths did not specialize in violent crime alone, however, and did not progress from a less serious offense to violent crime. They tended to commit violent acts early in their delinquent careers.

The life experiences of these youths contained several elements that encouraged delinquency. Their families were typically single-parent households headed by the mother. Since over 70 percent of the mothers were unemployed, the juveniles lived in poverty. Family life was marked by violence, particularly wife battering. There also was a high rate of criminal justice system involvement among family members, particularly among fathers and siblings. Over a quarter of the youths were not enrolled in school at the time of the most recent offense. Eighteen percent of the juveniles were employed during this period.

Although a high degree of gang involvement was not noted in this study, friends of these youths were also engaging regularly in delinquent behavior. Over 22 percent of the youths admitted to substance abuse problems (either drugs or alcohol). They also believed that drugs and alcohol contributed to their violent behavior.

Elliot studied serious violent offending in data from the National Youth Survey (NYS)—a national probability sample of 1,725 youths aged 11–17 in 1976. His group has been continuously interviewed. In the eighth wave of data (1993), the respondents were aged 27–33. The data set contains both self-report and official record data for respondents and official record data for parents or primary caretakers. His findings also illuminate the concept of a violent juvenile offender. His focus was upon serious violent offending (SVO). In 50 percent of these events, a weapon was used. In about two-thirds of these, a gun or knife was used and some medical treatment was required.

At the peak age of 17, 36 percent of African-American males and 25 percent of white males report one or more SVOs. Regarding sex, Elliot reported three significant differences in the age curve: (1) the peak age in prevalence is earlier for females; (2) the decline (maturation effect) is steeper for females; (3) the gender differential becomes greater over time; and (4) nearly one black female in five and one white female in ten report involvement in serious violent offending.

Serious violent offending begins between ages 12 and 20. The risk of initiation is close to zero after age 20. By age 18, nearly 40 percent of black males have become involved, compared to 30 percent of white males. However, when socioeconomic status is taken into account, the difference between races was insignificant. Over 60 percent of all males who would ever be involved (by age 27) in serious violent offending were actively involved by age 17. Elliot noted that the rates of serious violent offending in this study were three to four times greater than those studies based upon official records alone.

Unlike the previous studies on this subject, Elliot reported that the activity of serious violent offenders followed a progression. The "typical sequence" was from assault to robbery to rape. The overall pattern suggested "a clear escalation in the seriousness of criminal behavior over time in a criminal career." Similar to the chronic group from the birth cohort studies, the serious violent offenders were less than five percent of the National Youth Survey sample but they accounted for 83 percent of the Index offenses and half of all offenses reported.

Elliot's study on serious violent offenders had several different conclusions: their prevalence is much higher; onset of violent offending occurred much earlier; the demographic correlates were much weaker; evidence for escalation in seriousness, frequency, and variety of offenses over the career was much stronger; evidence for the sequencing of serious forms of violent behavior was stronger; and the continuity of SVO from the juvenile to the adult years was similar for males and for females. Blacks were more likely to continue their violent offending into their adult years. Once they begin their career of violence, theft, and substance use, persons from disadvantaged families and neighborhoods are trapped. They have fewer opportunities for conventional adult roles, and they are more deeply embedded in and dependent upon the gangs and the illicit economy that flourish in their neighborhoods. However, if they were able to make the transition to a conventional lifestyle of work and family, they dropped their involvement in violent crime. Therefore, policies and programs should target youths for work and conventional adult roles.[48]

Fagan has reported on the development of VJO programs in four cities (Boston, MA; Detroit, MI; Memphis, TN; and Newark, NJ). He tracked the experiences of 227 males who had been adjudicated for an Index felony (e.g., homicide, rape, robbery, assault). The program was based upon an intervention model stressing early childhood socialization factors.[49]

Recidivism outcomes were clearly related to the therapeutic intervention. Experimental youths in Boston consistently had lower recidivism scores than controls. The differences for the experimental youths in all four cities suggested positive impacts from intervention. The VJO program and similar projects can advance crime control and rehabilitative policies. Fagan concluded that policies to reallocate resources and reorganize juvenile corrections systems should emphasize reintegratration efforts to sustain institutional treatment through the process of community re-entry. He concluded that the VJO Program should continue to focus upon reintegration of these offenders.[50]

Another program that targets chronic juveniles is the **Serious Habitual Offender/Drug Involved (SHODI) Program,** which provides a structured, coordinated focus on serious, habitual juvenile crime and seeks to improve the law enforcement system's response to drug-related juvenile crimes.[51] The National Council of Juvenile and Family Court Judges has established guidelines for the SHODI Program. Acknowledging the seriousness of the problem, the judges caution that these juveniles must be properly and carefully identified. Then, the system can take the appropriate response and hold them accountable for their crimes. Juvenile records should be made available to adult courts so that habitual juvenile offenders do not appear to be first offenders. Records should also be shared across law enforcement and social agencies to provide a full picture of the nature of the juvenile's criminal involvement and home life.

Treatment and rehabilitation should not be abandoned. Substance abuse programs for these juveniles should be readily provided, and other appropriate community resources should be developed as well. The judges emphasize that SHODIs are only a small part of the juvenile justice system and should not become the court's sole focus.

Program of Research on the Causes and Correlates of Delinquency

The Office of Juvenile Justice and Delinquency Prevention (OJJDP) has sponsored an extensive program of research since 1986. Studies were conducted in three cities (Denver, CO; Pittsburgh, PA; and Rochester, NY) to examine the delinquent careers of sampled juveniles. Interviews were conducted with juveniles every six to twelve months during their developmental years. The studies involved more than 4,000 inner city children and youth who were aged from 7 to 15 years at the beginning of the research.[52]

Analysis of the first three years of data from the program has yielded several conclusions about the risk factors for delinquency.

- **Multiple family transitions are a risk factor for delinquency.** There was a consistent relationship between family instability and their involvement with drugs and delinquency.
- **Among males, early involvement with drug use and delinquency is highly correlated with teen fatherhood.** In Rochester, nearly one-half of the high-rate delinquents (top 25 percent) later became teen-age fathers. Only 23 percent of the nondelinquent and low-rate delinquents became fathers as teenagers.
- **Teen fatherhood does not make young males more responsible and law-abiding.** In fact, the added responsibility increases the social pressures upon these young males, may further isolate them from more positive peer groups and lead to drinking, drug use, and poor school performance.

For these reasons, the authors recommend that programs that target at-risk juveniles need to include their families. The family structure and situation of delinquent youth must be examined and problems addressed. In addition, teen pregnancy programs must focus on both boys and girls to achieve better results.[53]

Research on Very Young Offenders

Also sponsored by OJJDP, current research by Loeber and Farrington examine the early involvement of very young children in delinquency. This research was spurred by the previously cited findings that most chronic and violent juvenile offenders begin their delinquency careers by ages 10–12. These studies have revealed some significant conclusions:

- **Young offending is serious business.** Very young delinquents engage in serious crime at high rates of involvement. In this study, they were responsible for one in three juvenile arrests for arson, one in five juvenile arrests for sex offenses and vandalism, and one in twelve juvenile arrests for violent crime.
- **There is no evidence that a new and more serious "breed" of child delinquent and young murderer exists.** Crime statistics do not indicate a dramatic shift in juvenile offending. Between 1980 and 1997, the number of murders committed by offenders age 12 or younger remained fairly constant (about thirty per year).
- **These young offenders will not "grow out" of delinquency.** Child delinquents are twice as likely to engage in serious violent behavior and chronic offending. They have longer delinquent careers and are more likely to become gang members and engage in substance abuse.
- **Incarceration appears to be ineffective and may even make things worse.** There is no evidence that incarceration slows the development of a violent delinquent career. In fact, their early exposure to older, serious offenders may aggravate the situation.[54]

Researchers have also identified some "early warning signs" of serious delinquent behavior:

- **Disruptive behavior that is apparent during the preschool and certainly the elementary school years.** This is significant especially if this behavior is more disruptive and severe than that of other children.
- **Physical fighting.**
- **Cruelty to people or animals.**
- **Covert acts such as frequently lying, theft, and fire setting.**
- **Inability to get along with others.**
- **Low school motivation during elementary school.**
- **Substance abuse.**
- **Repeated victimization (e.g., child abuse or peer bullying).**[55]

In order to prevent the development of delinquency, programs should focus on "risk and protective factors" such as: birth complications, hyperactivity, impulsivity, parental substance abuse, or poor child rearing practices are at highest risk of becoming serious, violent, and chronic offenders.[56] Communities should engage in early intervention programs that encourage conflict resolution and violence prevention,[57] featuring partnerships between appropriate social agencies and the juvenile justice system.

SUMMARY

Determining the level of juvenile crime and delinquency is a difficult task. In this chapter, we presented data from a number of sources in order to obtain a complete picture. Each of the sources has their own strengths and weaknesses in terms of their ability to measure crime. The Uniform Crime Reports are the only true national measure of crime. Unfortunately, they consist of crimes known to the police. Naturally, they cannot include crimes that go unreported or unseen. Therefore, to a certain extent, they reflect police operations. If the police are concentrating on a certain type of crime or targeting juveniles in one area, then the UCR statistics will reflect that emphasis. In other words, the UCR often represents what the police are doing rather than how much crime there actually is.

The National Crime Victims Survey attempts to get around this problem by interviewing victims directly. But this source does not present data by state, county, or city. Although some breakdowns are provided by region of the county and level of urbanization, its findings are representative of the nation as a whole.

The cohort studies are limited to the area in which they were conducted and by their reliance upon official statistics. However, they do provide a long-term view of how juvenile delinquency develops over time and who is responsible for most of it.

Given these limitations, there are several conclusions that can be reached in our review of recent juvenile crime statistics and studies:

1. Juvenile crime does not appear to be worsening. Although there were some increases in the 1990s, the levels of juvenile crime are declining or leveling off. This is true for both violent and property crime.

2. The present levels of substance abuse (including alcohol) are troubling. Special emphasis must be given to prevention and treatment of substance abuse among adolescents.

3. Most juvenile victimizations occur during after school hours. The need for supervision and structure during this period is apparent.

4. The findings of the cohort and young offenders studies reveals that parents, teachers, church officials, family members, and all concerned citizens must be aware of the warning signs of delinquent behavior and attempt an appropriate intervention. Punishment after the fact

is not as effective as prevention. Risk factors, like substance abuse and teen fatherhood, must be attended to.

Recent studies have emphasized the need for an effectiveness of treatment for chronic juvenile offenders. An Orange County (CA) study defined chronic offenders as juveniles referred to the Department of Juvenile Probation four or more times over a three-year period. They found that this group of 8 percent of all referrals accounted for over 55 percent of future referrals. These youths tended to be 15 or younger, have school behavior and performance problems and family problems, engage in substance abuse and either stealing, running away, or gangs. A program was developed to help such juveniles and their families that focused on parental involvement and victim/offender mediation. Their research revealed that juveniles who were treated under this program were significantly less likely to commit new crimes or to have petitions filed in juvenile court.[58]

This study was replicated in Philadelphia among over 15,000 cases referred to juvenile court. However, the juvenile chronics represented a different proportion and were identified through different characteristics than in California. For example, chronic offenders with more than four arrests were 17 percent of the total. In terms of attributes, different rates of offending were revealed for early (15 or less) and later (16 or older) offenders. They also found that Latinos, males, and the offenders who entered the system at a young age were likely to become chronic offenders. Risk factors that were identified included: poor school attendance record, family related measures (lack of intimacy and communication, lack of instrumental communication), and a history of substance abuse. Some treatment programs for these offenders appeared to be more effective than others, including: community based programs, mixed (family, individual, and group) counseling, and school-based programs. In addition, neighborhoods identified as "service wastelands" had higher proportions of high-risk juveniles who became chronic offenders. Overall, these studies demonstrate that treatment can be effective in the prevention of long term offending by chronic juvenile delinquents.[59]

Statistics themselves do not offer solutions to problems. What they do provide is direction—where to concentrate efforts and what to work on. Since juvenile delinquency, victimization, and other behaviors are always subject to change, it is important to continue research. Information is the key to effective program and policy development.

TERMS TO REMEMBER

Cambridge (UK) Study of
  Delinquent Development
Columbus Cohort
Crime Index

National Crime Victims Survey
  (NCVS)
Philadelphia Birth Cohorts
Racine Cohorts

Serious Habitual Offender/Drug
  Involved (SHODI) Program
Uniform Crime Report (UCR)

Violent Juvenile Offender (VJO)
  Program

REVIEW QUESTIONS

1. What is the pattern of violent crime by juveniles presented from the UCR?

2. What is the pattern of property crime by juveniles presented from the UCR?

3. Compare your answers to Questions 1 and 2. Is there an overall trend for juvenile crime?

4. Among the data, what are the most common characteristics of juvenile offending?

5. What is the victimization pattern presented concerning school crime?

6. How do the findings of the cohort studies compare? Do they have anything in common?

7. Do you think the Violent Juvenile Offender Program has been effective? Why or why not?

8. Do you think the SHODI Program has been effective? Why or why not?

9. What do results on the correlates and causes of delinquency mean? What interventions should be developed?

10. In your opinion, what is the most significant risk factor revealed by the very young offender research?

NOTES

[1]The OJJDP Statistical Briefing Book can be accessed at the following website: www.ojjdp.ncjrs.org/ojstatbb/index.html.

[2]*OJJDP Statistical Briefing Book.* December, 2000. Online. Available: http://ojjdp.ncjrs.org/ojstatbb/qa255.html.

[3]Ibid. Online. Available: http://ojjdp.ncjrs.org/ojstatbb/qa256.html.

[4]Ibid. Online. Available: http://ojjdp.ncjrs.org/ojstatbb/qa257.html. See also John H. Laub and Phillip J. Cook, "The Unprecedented Epidemic in Youth Violence," in Michael Tonry and Mark H. Moore, eds., *Youth Violence* (Chicago, IL: University of Chicago Press, 1998), pp. 27–64.

[5]Office of Juvenile Justice and Delinquency Prevention, *Juvenile Offenders and Victims* (Washington, D.C.: U.S. Department of Justice, 1999), p. 54.

[6]*OJJDP Statistical Briefing Book.* Online. Available: http://ojjdp.ncjrs.org/ojstatbb/qa258.html.

[7]Ibid. Online. Available: http://ojjdp.ncjrs.org/ojstatbb/qa259.html.

[8]Ibid. Online. Available: http://ojjdp.ncjrs.org/ojstatbb/qa260.html.

[9]Ibid. Online. Available: http://ojjdp.ncjrs.org/ojstatbb/qa261.html.

[10]Ibid. Online. Available: http://ojjdp.ncjrs.org/ojstatbb/qa262.html.

[11]Ibid. Online. Available: http://ojjdp.ncjrs.org/ojstatbb/qa263.html.

[12]Ibid. Online. Available: http://ojjdp.ncjrs.org/ojstatbb/qa264.html.

[13]Ibid. Online. Available: http://ojjdp.ncjrs.org/ojstatbb/qa265.html.

[14]Ibid. Online. Available: http://ojjdp.ncjrs.org/ojstatbb/qa269.html.

[15]Ibid. Online. Available: http://ojjdp.ncjrs.org/ojstatbb/qa270.html.

[16]Ibid. Online. Available: http://ojjdp.ncjrs.org/ojstatbb/qa272.html.

[17]Office of Juvenile Justice and Delinquency Prevention, *OJJDP Research 2000: Report* (Washington, D.C.: U.S. Department of Justice, 2001), p. 23.

[18]Thomas J. Bernard, "Juvenile Crime and the Transformation of Juvenile Justice: Is There a Juvenile Crime Wave?" *Justice Quarterly,* Vol. 16, No. 2, (1999), pp. 337–356.

[19]*Juvenile Offenders and Victims,* p. 62. Note that this report also compiles information about juvenile victimization from other official sources.

[20]Ibid., p. 63.

[21]Ibid., pp. 64–65.

[22]Ibid., p. 66.

[23]Ibid., p. 67.

[24]Ibid., p. 68.

[25]Ibid., p. 70.

[26]Ibid., p. 71.

[27]Ibid., p. 72.

[28]Ibid., p. 74.

[29]Ibid., p. 75.

[30]Ibid., p. 76.

[31]Marvin Wolfgang, Robert Figlio, and Thorsten Sellin, *Delinquency in a Birth Cohort* (Chicago: University of Chicago Press, 1972), pp. 65–131.

[32]Ibid., p. 192.

[33]Paul Tracy, Marvin Wolfgang, and Robert Figlio, *Delinquency Careers in Two Birth Cohorts* (New York: Plenum Press, 1990), p. 292.

[34]Kimberly Kempf-Leonard, Paul E. Tracy, and James C. Howell, "Serious, Violent, and Chronic Juvenile Offender: The Relationship of Delinquency Career Types to Adult Criminality," *Justice Quarterly,* Vol. 18 (2001), pp. 449–478.

Donna M. Hamparian, Richard Schuster, Simon Dinitz, and John P. Conrad, (1978). *The Violent Few: A Study of Violent Juvenile Offenders* (Lexington, MA: Heath, 1978) pp. 38–40.

[35]Donna M. Hamparian, J. M. Davis, J. M. Jacobson, and R. E. McGraw, *The Young Criminal Years of the Violent Few* (Washington, DC: U.S. Department of Justice, 1985), pp. 14–15.

[36]Ibid., pp. 19–20.

[37]Lyle W. Shannon, *Criminal Career Continuity: Its Social Context.* (New York: Human Sciences Press, 1988).

[38]Steven P. Lab and William G. Doerner, "Changing Female Delinquency in Three Birth Cohorts," *Journal of Crime and Justice,* Vol. 10 (1987), pp. 101–116.

[39]David P. Farrington, "Criminal Career Research in the United Kingdom," *British Journal of Criminology,* Vol. 32 (1992), pp. 521–536.

[40]David P. Farrington and J. David Hawkins, "Predicting Participation, Early Onset and Later Persistence in Officially Recorded Offending." *Criminal Behaviour and Mental Health,* Vol.1 (1991), pp. 1–33.

[41]David P. Farrington and David J. West, "Criminal, Penal and Life Histories of Chronic Offenders: Risk and Protective Factors and Early Identification," *Criminal Behaviour and Mental Health,* Vol. 3 (1993), pp. 492–523.

[42]Daniel S. Nagin, David P. Farrington, and Terrance E. Moffitt, "Life-Course Trajectories of Different Types of Offenders." *Criminology,* Vol. 33 (1995), pp. 111–139.

[43]David P. Farrington, "Implications of Criminal Career Research for the Prevention of Offending." *Journal of Adolescence,* Vol. 13 (1990), pp. 93–113.

[44]Tracy, Wolfgang, and Figlio, *Delinquency Careers,* pp. 295, 297.

[45]Kimberly L. Kempf, "Career Criminals in the 1958 Philadelphia Birth Cohort: A Follow-up of the Early Adult Years." *Criminal Justice Review,* Vol. 15 (1990), pp. 151–172.

[46]National Advisory Committee for Juvenile Justice and Delinquency Prevention, *Serious Juvenile Crime: A Redirected Federal Effort.* (Washington, DC: Office of Juvenile Justice and Delinquency Prevention, 1984).

[47]E. Hartstone and K.V. Hansen, "The Violent Juvenile Offender: An Empirical Portrait" in R.A. Mathias, P. DeMuro, and R.S. Allinson, eds. *Violent Juvenile Offenders: An Anthology* (San Francisco, CA: National Council on Crime and Delinquency. 1984), pp. 83–112.

[48]Delbert S. Elliot, "Serious Violent Offenders: Onset, Developmental Course, and Termination - The American Society of Criminology 1993 Presidential Address. *Criminology,* Vol. 32 (1994), pp. 1–21.

[49]Jeffrey Fagan, "Social and Legal Policy Dimensions of Violent Juvenile Crime. *Criminal Justice and Behavior,* Vol.17 (1990), pp. 93–133.

[50]Jeffrey Fagan, "Treatment and Reintegration of Violent Juvenile Offenders: Experimental Results." *Justice Quarterly,* Vol. 7(1990), pp. 233–263.

[51]R.O. Heck, W. Pindur, and D.K. Wells, "The Juvenile Serious Habitual Offender/Drug Involved Program: A Means to Implement Recommendations of the National Council of Juvenile and Family Court Judges." *Juvenile and Family Court Journal,* Summer (1985), p. 28.

[52]David Huizinga, Rolf Loeber, Terence P. Thornberry, and Lynn Cothern, "Co-occurrence of Delinquency and Other Problem Behaviors." *OJJDP Juvenile Justice Bulletin* (Washington, D.C.: U.S. Department of Justice, November, 2000), p. 2. For current information on these studies, check the web site: www.ojjdp.ncjrs.org/ccd/.

[53]*OJJDP Research 2000: Report,* pp. 6–8.

[54]Ibid., pp. 3–4.

[55]Ibid., p. 5.

[56]See Stanton E. Samenow, *Before It's Too Late: Why Some Kids Get into Trouble and What Parents Can Do About It* (New York: Times Books, 1998).

[57]See Jan Arnow, *Teaching Peace: How to Raise Children to Live in Harmony—Without Fear, Without Prejudice, Without Violence* (New York: Perigee, 1995).

[58]M. Schumacher and G.A. Kurz, *The 8% Solution: Preventing Serious Repeat Juvenile Crime* (Thousand Oaks, CA: Sage, 2000).

[59]Peter R. Jones, Phillip W. Harris, Jamie Fader, and Lori Grubstein, "Identifying Chronic Juvenile Offenders," *Justice Quarterly,* Vol. 18 (2001), pp. 479–508.

PART TWO

THE JUVENILE JUSTICE SYSTEM

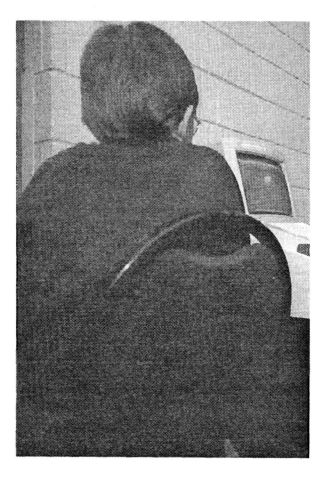

chapter

THE JUVENILE JUSTICE PROCESS

According to the labeling and stigmatization process, at least part of the responsibility for the development of an identity and subsequent career as a "juvenile delinquent" appears to rest with the handling of the juvenile by the police and the courts. Ambiguity in the laws governing juvenile conduct places a great deal of emphasis upon the exercise of discretionary powers.

— Harold J. Vetter

CHAPTER OVERVIEW

This chapter provides the reader with an overview of the three components of the juvenile justice system: police, courts, and corrections. One of the major problems faced by the administrators of these components is lack of control resulting from the fragmentation of the juvenile justice "system." In terms of actual coordination between all of its parts, the juvenile justice system does not automatically operate in an integrated fashion. All three of the elements of the criminal justice system have developed special ways for dealing with children and young people in trouble—as they should. Because of the need to protect information regarding juveniles and because of conflicting purposes and missions within these subsystems, the fragmentation problem is even more exacerbated in the juvenile system than in the adult system.

Police departments have responded to the problems of juvenile crime in a number of different ways, usually through specialized units for juvenile control. The juvenile courts, sharing their duties with other tribunals, have also developed special philosophies and procedures to deal with their wards, but the recent movement away from the philosophy of *parens patriae* to one that stresses due process and constitutional safeguards for juveniles has placed the courts in need of change. Juvenile and adult institutions developed independently and have in large part remained autonomous in the United States until the past few decades. Several states have now recognized the practical, economic value of combining the services and institutions of the adult and juvenile justice systems of corrections, although the use of probation as an alternative to incarceration has been more accepted in the juvenile than in the adult system. As a result, juvenile corrections have moved in the direction of community-based programs at a faster rate than has adult corrections.

The basic problem with the juvenile justice process is the clear presence of **goal conflict**.[1] This conflict operates at two levels. First, it must deal with juveniles who have committed crimes—the delinquents. Under the doctrine of *parens patriae,* the juvenile justice system (especially juvenile court) was designed to be a place of redemption and rehabilitation—saving the child from the rigors of the adult system. The belief was that exposure to adult institutions could not only harm the juvenile, but could also spur the delinquent on the way to the development of a criminal career. Second, the juvenile justice system was structured for **dual beneficiaries**[2]—it is designed to serve both delinquents and **children in need of services (CHINS)**—the abused and neglected. These can be different populations or delinquency can be the result of unmet needs and adverse environmental influences—broken homes, drug, sexual, and/or physical abuse.

Thus, the basic issue is the conflict between guardianship (under *parens patriae*) and accountability (notably, punishment). As we shall see, the balance between the two ideals is moving toward punishment. Most states have abandoned rehabilitation and *parens patriae* in favor of holding delinquents responsible, punishing them as if they were adults. The growing emphasis toward punishment has led the Supreme Court to also depart from *parens patriae* and provide procedural safeguards to protect the rights of juveniles. This chapter will examine some of the problems in various parts of the juvenile justice "system."

Figure 4.1 presents a case flow diagram of the Juvenile Justice Process from the Office of Juvenile Justice and Delinquency Prevention. Since case processing varies from state to state and jurisdiction-to-jurisdiction, this chart provides a general overview of juvenile practices and outlines a series of decision points. Refer to this chart as we review the various decision points in the juvenile justice process.

THE POLICE: FIRST POINT OF CONTACT

The restrictive procedures by which the law protects juveniles tend to create many administrative problems for the police—who are charged with a mandate to enforce all laws. A youth's age, for instance, is a major factor in

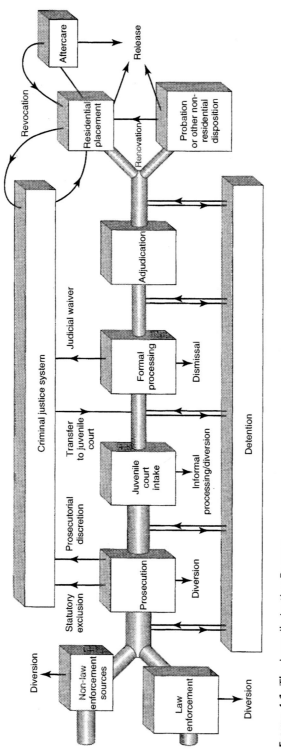

FIGURE 4.1 The Juvenile Justice Process.

determining criminal responsibility. Below the age of 7 years, children are normally considered free of criminal responsibility. Between the ages of 7 and 16 or 18, (depending upon the jurisdiction), the offender is considered a juvenile delinquent rather than criminal. The problem is clouded further by the fact that about half of all juveniles who come in contact with the police are "status offenders" whose conduct would violate no criminal statute if they were adults (e.g., runaways, dependent children).

The police officer (in this case, the administrator of juvenile justice) that comes into contact with a juvenile offender has a number of discretionary choices to make. The officer can ignore the delinquent behavior altogether and go on his or her way. The contact could be very casual, with light conversation and inquiry to identify participants in the offense. The police may then escalate from questioning to search, an order for dispersal, or other more "official" action. Even after deciding to intervene, the officer can still decide to take the offenders home, warn them or their parents, or some other form of "street corner justice." Only when informal alternatives seem to be inadequate to the task at hand will most police officers take formal and official action that will start the juvenile through the justice system. The decision as to how to proceed with these alternatives is often determined by departmental policy, whether explicit or implicit. Of course, the response is also determined by the seriousness of the offense. The effect of policy varies greatly among departments and rigid enforcement of policy within a department is difficult in the environment that allows the freedom of action and the range of discretion enjoyed by most juvenile officers.

In Figure 4.1, beginning with arrest, the police decide between sending the case further into the juvenile justice system and diverting the juvenile into some type of alternative program. Typically, the decision is made after the police officer talks to the victim, the juvenile, and the parents. The record of the juvenile's prior contacts with the system is also routinely reviewed. According to federal regulations, juveniles should not be held in jail or in adult lockups following an arrest. If detained, juveniles cannot be held for longer than six hours and in an area that is not within the sight and sound of adult inmates.[3]

Juvenile crime should concern *all* personnel in a modern police department. Although it is important to have available the specialized skills required for many juvenile problems, separate sections should be set up only if a demonstrated need has been established. Separate juvenile units are needed to deal with special investigation techniques for the processing of juveniles, disposition requirements, and coordination with family and community. Since juvenile offenders react to the criminal justice process different from adult offenders, special interrogation skills and handling techniques are needed to help expedite cases. The delinquency specialist is attuned to the community and to the needs of the juvenile in a way that the "regular" police officer usually is not.

The juvenile specialist is *supplemental* to the operations of the patrol division in most agencies, so the patrol field unit is usually responsible for all preliminary investigation procedures. The initial report of a crime seldom identifies the perpetrator as juvenile or adult, and juvenile investigators do not generally become involved until after the initial contacts have been made and an initial investigation has been completed.

A number of names have been used in the past for juvenile units in police organizations. Crime Prevention Bureau, Juvenile Bureau, Youth Aid Bureau, and Juvenile Control Bureau are but a few. Logically, the functions of a juvenile unit seem to be as follows:

1. Discovery of delinquents, potential delinquents, and conditions including delinquency.
2. Investigation of delinquency and causes of delinquency.
3. Disposition or referral of cases.
4. Protection of children and youth.
5. Community organization.

Although these functions are general in nature, they provide the basis for the operation of the juvenile unit. When viewed in terms of overall departmental objectives for juvenile control as discussed in the previous chapters, they provide the basis for the juvenile control unit's operation.[4]

Smaller departments have less of a problem with organization and administration. In agencies with from one to fifteen persons, every officer must be prepared to assume *all* the police functions; specialization for juvenile cases would be an impractical and expensive use of limited resources. One person in the department, often the chief, may be assigned as the juvenile case coordinator. Because the juvenile problem often impacts on the community in a different manner from adult crime, the small department chief tends to follow it closely.

In departments larger than fifteen officers, the assignment of a juvenile bureau, even if it is composed of only one officer, seems to be the most common practice. This bureau is often assigned a number of duties, such as bicycle patrol, school safety patrol, "Officer Friendly" programs, and others aimed at the juvenile population. It has often been the practice to assign a capable *policewoman* to the juvenile bureau, even the one-person bureau. Until all police roles were opened to women, juvenile duty was likely to be considered one of a number of female-oriented roles within the agency.

As police organizations adjust to meet the changes in the juvenile control mission, the problems of the police administrator are magnified. The administrator, working in an environment that is changing from protective to punitive, must try to upgrade juvenile bureau personnel while cracking down on juvenile crime. He or she must justify some of the progressive changes in the police sector while social attitudes toward juvenile crime are hardening. Continuing to protect the *rights* of juveniles and protecting the juveniles *themselves* from the harsh realities of the enforcement sector of the adult system remains another continuing headache for the police administrator. It is recommended that the juvenile division *solely* conduct the investigation of juvenile crime. Care must be exercised to ensure that the rights of juveniles are protected during investigations.

THE JUVENILE COURT: THE HEART OF THE SYSTEM

The Role of the Prosecutor

Returning to Figure 4.1, the court intake function is the responsibility of the juvenile probation department, and/or the prosecutor's office. Many states require that prosecutors file serious cases involving juveniles in the adult criminal justice system. Here, the legislature has determined that juvenile offender should be treated as an adult. A growing number of states have decided that both the juvenile and adult courts have original jurisdiction over these cases. The prosecutor selects the court that will handle the matter. The growth of **prosecutorial discretion** in juvenile cases reflects the shift toward punishment as a key element in the juvenile process. The general feeling is that juveniles should be treated as adults when they commit serious crimes such as murder. Such cases, although they involve juvenile offenders have been **statutorily excluded** from the juvenile justice system.[5]

Juvenile Court Intake

At juvenile court intake, the decision is made to either (1) dismiss the case, (2) handle the matter informally, or (3) send it on to juvenile court. The intake officer makes this decision by reviewing the facts of the case to determine if there is sufficient evidence to prove the allegation.

About half of all cases referred to juvenile court intake are handled informally. Most informally processed cases are dismissed. In the other informally processed cases, the juvenile voluntarily agrees to specific conditions for a specific time period. These conditions are often outlined in a written agreement, generally called a "consent decree." Conditions may include such items as victim restitution, school attendance, drug counseling, or a curfew. In most jurisdictions, a juvenile may be offered an informal disposition only if he or she admits to committing the act. A probation officer often monitors the juvenile's compliance with the informal agreement. Consequently, this process is sometimes labeled "informal probation."

If the juvenile successfully complies with the informal disposition, the case is dismissed. If, however, the juvenile fails to meet the conditions, the intake decision may be to formally prosecute the case. Then, the case will proceed just as if it would have if the initial decision had been to refer the case for an adjudicatory hearing.[6]

If the juvenile court judge believes that it is in the best interests of the child, juveniles can be held in a secure detention facility. Either juvenile probation officers or detention workers to determine whether the juvenile should be held pending a judicial hearing then review the case.

In every state, the detention hearing must be held within the time period defined by statute (usually twenty-four hours). At this hearing, the judge reviews the case and determines if the youth should be released or continues to be detained. Detention may extend beyond the adjudicatory and dispositional hearings.[7]

Formal Processing

If the case is handled in juvenile court, two types of petitions may be filed—**delinquency petition** or **waiver petition.** The delinquency petition states the charges against the juvenile. It seeks to have the juvenile **adjudicated** delinquent. The juvenile then becomes a ward of the court. Note the difference in tone from the adult criminal justice system where the offender is *convicted* and *sentenced.*

In response to the delinquency petition, an **adjudicatory hearing** is scheduled. During the hearing, witnesses are called and facts of the case are presented. Typically, a judge makes the final decision about the case.

If the prosecutor or the intake officer feels that the case belongs in the adult rather than juvenile justice system, a waiver petition is filed. Here, the juvenile court judge determines if there is probable cause that the juvenile in question committed the act. If this determination is positive, then the court decides whether the case should be waived to adult court. The judge's final decision typically centers on whether the juvenile is amenable to treatment in the juvenile justice system. In its arguments, the prosecution may present the previous record of the juvenile and note that past treatment failed to prevent recidivism. The prosecutor may also argue that the crime is so serious that the court cannot meet the time period necessary to rehabilitate the youth.

If the judge transfers the case to adult criminal court, juvenile jurisdiction is waived. The case is filed in adult court. If the waiver is not approved, the case remains in juvenile court and an adjudicatory hearing is scheduled.[8]

The Disposition Hearing

If adjudicated delinquent, a disposition plan is developed for the juvenile. Probation staff develops the plan, examining the background of the youth, family, school, church, and other relevant social support systems. Recommendations are made following a detailed assessment of the juvenile: psychological examinations and other diagnoses (i.e., drug tests, IQ tests) can be ordered by the court.

These recommendations are presented at the hearing. The prosecutor and the juvenile can make other dispositional recommendations. The judge considers all this information and orders a final disposition for the case. It can include

- A probation order with special conditions like drug counseling, weekend confinement in local juvenile detention center, community and/or victim restitution.
- A period of probation that is either specified (limited) or open-ended. Review hearings are conducted to monitor the performance of the juvenile client. If the conditions of probation are successfully met, the judge terminates the case.
- Residential commitment for a specific or indeterminate specified time period.[9] Juvenile facilities are operated by private corporations as well as the government.

Some facilities have very secure environments, whereas others have an open setting. If sent to the state department of juvenile corrections, department officials determine the placement of the juvenile and when the youth will be released. Review hearings are held to assess the progress of the juveniles in custody.

Juvenile Aftercare

Like the adult system of parole, juveniles released from an institution are often ordered to follow a period of aftercare. During this period, the youth is under the supervision of the court or the department of juvenile corrections. If the conditions of release are not followed, the youth can be recommitted to a juvenile facility.

Status Offense Cases

Status offenses are acts committed by juveniles that would not be considered crimes if committed by adults. They include such offenses as running away from home, truancy, juveniles who are beyond the control of their parents or guardians ("ungovernable" or "incorrigible"), curfew violations, and underage drinking. The issue with status offenders is how to treat them—like delinquents or like dependents? Some experts believe that treating status offenders like delinquents will lead them to become delinquent and/or criminal in the future. In effect, juvenile justice processing will make them worse. For example, Schur condemns status offenses as moral judgments that make a bad situation worse. A runaway placed in a juvenile institution can become a serious criminal as a result of incarceration. Schur advocates a policy of **radical nonintervention:** Leave the kids alone whenever possible.[10]

Three procedures involve removing juveniles from formal processing. Decriminalization makes the act committed by the juvenile no longer a crime that is subject to sanction. Its primary aim is to remove certain types of behaviors from the scope of law that are not dangerous to society. Typically, these acts are seen as deviant rather than illegal and are "not the law's business."[11] To handle such things as status offenses, **deinstitutionalization** has been implemented. For example, the Institute of Juvenile Administration of the American Bar Association recommended the following:

1. A juvenile's acts of misbehavior, ungovernability, or unruliness, which do not violate the criminal law should not constitute a ground for asserting juvenile court jurisdiction over the juvenile committing them.
2. Any law enforcement officer who reasonably determines that a juvenile is in circumstances which constitute a substantial and immediate danger to the juvenile's physical safety requires such action, take the juvenile into limited custody (subject to the limitations of this part).[12]

Finally, **decarceration** removes as many juveniles as possible from custody and treats them in an open environment. Given the violent nature of many of the incarcerated juveniles, this option has been questioned. It seems more appropriate for the juveniles who should be diverted from the system because they have committed either status or nondangerous offenses.

Due Process Rights of Juveniles

The establishment of protections for juveniles against unjustified punishment were put in place as a result of several well-known cases. *In re Gault* [387 U.S. 1 (1967)] established that proceedings that determine delinquency "must measure up to the essentials of due process and fair hearing." Juveniles must be given adequate notice of the specific charges against them, the assistance of counsel, the right to confront and cross-examine witnesses against them, and the privilege against self-incrimination. *In re*

Winship [397 U.S. 358 (1970)] stated that the Supreme Court held that due process required that every fact presented to prove delinquency must meet the "beyond a reasonable doubt" standard.

However, it is clear that the U.S. Constitution does not require that all aspects of adult criminal procedure be applied in juvenile court. In *McKeiver v. Pennsylvania,* 403 U.S. 528 (1971), the court held that due process did not require that an alleged delinquent be extended the right to trial by jury. The court's language indicated that it retained hope for the preservation of the juvenile court as a separate and distinguishable process:

> The juvenile concept held high promise. We are reluctant to say that despite disappointments of grave dimensions, it still does not hold promise, and we are particularly reluctant to say . . . that the system cannot accomplish its rehabilitative goals. So much depends on the availability of resources, on the interest and commitment of the public, on willingness to learn, and on understanding as to cause and effect and cure.[13]

After all screening or diversionary actions have been taken or all nonjudicial alternatives exhausted, the juvenile who is still a problem will finally be referred to the juvenile court for disposition.

When considering the nature and future of juvenile court, there are two central concerns that persist. The first is the place of the juvenile court in the criminal justice system, including the breadth of its jurisdiction over juveniles, its location within the judicial system to hear such cases, and its relationship to other agencies. The second area of concern is its procedures, including those used during the formal hearing as well as the methods by which the decision is made to detain a juvenile prior to the formal hearing itself.

The appropriate administrative approach to the processing of delinquency cases is the formal court procedure. It should vary little from that of adult criminal prosecutions. The processing of juvenile cases should differ from that of adult cases primarily in a greater willingness to use informal, nonpunitive measures. If, however, formal court action is sought and the juvenile contests the facts upon which court jurisdiction is sought, the procedure for resolving the dispute should not differ substantially from that used in adult cases. Such an approach can preserve the value of the juvenile justice process as a means of dealing with young offenders without unduly sacrificing the right of alleged offenders to a full and fair determination of whether official action is justified.

The juvenile court judge is in a position of real conflict in today's justice environment. He or she is pressed from one sector for more humane sentencing practices, more diversion, and differential decision-making despite limited information. From another sector, there is pressure to "get tough"—to inflict more punishment, impose longer institutional confinement, and exhibit less interest in the juvenile's rights. Not surprisingly, the juvenile justice process as a means of dealing with young offenders is not without the problems of overcrowding and repeat offenders.

JUVENILE CORRECTIONS

Juvenile corrections seem to be at a crossroads. Partly because of the emphasis on juvenile rights and partly because of the failure of past models, juvenile correctional administrators are looking for new answers to old questions. Obstacles to juvenile corrections reform are the fragmentation of corrections, the variety of governmental authorities involved, and, most of all, a lack of overall correctional planning that assigns each segment of the system specific involvement and accountability. Detention and incarceration may be overused for some crimes. An additional obstacle is the ambivalence of community members: they want treatment but they also want punishment; they want good programs but they do not want to pay the price for them; they want offenders incarcerated but they do not want juvenile delinquents back in the community upon release. Lack of sufficient information upon which to base good planning is one more serious deficiency.

The focus on diversion, particularly for status offenders, often causes some legal problems. For example, if a child referred to a social agency has caused *social* but not *legal* problems, should he or she be processed through the courts for the same offense? If so, a case could be made for double jeopardy.[14] Status offender cases—for example, drunkenness, truancy, incorrigibility—might well be treated in a separate system. However, most jurisdictions cannot afford even one juvenile correctional system. There is little probability of setting up a separate status offender system. Another major issue is the amount of discretion that exists in the system. Juvenile court judges, the police, the correctional programs, and the district attorney have a wide discretion in the decisions they make. The system lacks consistent standards to govern this discretion.

In corrections, treatment and justice are intertwined and almost inseparable. Corrections is committed to both. The juvenile correctional administrator has no choice about whom the court commits to his or her care but has had the choice of determining how long they are kept. Their ability to alter or change the direction of juvenile justice is very difficult to determine. The administrator has little choice but to continue to follow the direction of court decisions and legislatures.

The juvenile justice administrator comes in several different forms: police officers with great discretion, probation officers who must respond to several constituencies, judges faced with many problems in protecting both the juvenile and the public. The juvenile correctional administrator has the most clearly defined role, but even it suffers from fragmentation of jurisdictional control among cities, counties, and states. Only a few states have seen fit to consolidate juvenile and adult corrections under a single authority. The lingering fear of the "terrible" adult institutions still inhibits the vast majority from taking that difficult but seemingly logical step. The management muddle of our juvenile justice "nonsystem" can be cleared up only when American society decides whether it wants to *punish, protect,* or *treat* its miscreant youth. That prospect seems dim, so we struggle on, trying to make programs work in an environment of administrative uncertainty whose by-product is uncertain administrators.

THE DIRECTION OF JUVENILE JUSTICE

Disenchantment with and criticisms of the juvenile court and its *parens patriae* procedures have been voiced across the board. Here, we introduce several problems facing the juvenile justice system that will be closely examined in later chapters.

For example, criticisms have led to alterations in the juvenile justice funnel and in the handling of juveniles; specifically, both **diversion** and the **transfer of juveniles to adult court** have been introduced. Although these alternatives share the goal of getting juveniles out of the system, they do so for remarkably different reasons. Whereas diversion looks to the welfare of the juvenile and to use the system only when necessary, transfer to adult court holds that the seriousness of the behavior of delinquents and the nature of the acts they commit merit more severe punishment than the juvenile justice system is designed to mete out.

Diversion

The due process model for juveniles was derived from the *Gault, Winship,* and *Kent* decisions. They defined the constitutionally guaranteed rights that must be accorded to every citizen, both adults and juveniles. The diversion of juveniles involves the official halting or suspension of formal juvenile justice proceedings against an alleged offender at any legally prescribed processing point after a recorded justice system entry, and referral of that person to a treatment program (administered by a public or private agency)—or to no program at all.

Diversion programs are designed to take youths (especially status offenders) out of the juvenile justice system. Diversion can occur at any point in the system. The aim is to avoid formal contact with the court and correctional agencies. Instead, it encourages the use of alternative programs including remedial education programs, foster homes, group homes, and local counseling facilities and centers.

Diversion has a number of different policy aims. First, it can be designed to relieve pressure and the caseload burden upon the juvenile justice system—especially in court and in detention facilities. Once less serious and more promising juveniles are diverted, the system can concentrate upon the more serious offenses and offenders.

It is also hoped that diversion will alleviate issues of discrimination throughout the juvenile justice system. Minorities are far more likely to face serious outcomes throughout the juvenile justice process. For example, minorities are more likely to be detained and sentenced to a detention facility than Caucasians regardless of the seriousness of the charge against them.[15] Diversion could help reduce bias in processing by removing minorities from the system where it is appropriate to do so.

Another expectation with diversion is that rehabilitation is more likely to occur outside of the formal system. Juveniles and their families are matched with services that meet their needs and reduce the risk of delinquency. However, the effectiveness of such programs has been questioned. In particular, studies of diversion programs have found that they often result in a **widening of the net.** This means that diversion has extended the jurisdiction of the juvenile justice system. Instead of taking juveniles out of the system, diversion programs often bring in juveniles that were normally not subject to the system. Then, the programs divert these formally untargeted youths, rather than taking out juveniles who were in the system. In this way, the scope and power of the juvenile justice system is expanded and strengthened. The previously listed benefits of diversion are wiped out. Diversion is an example of an idea gone haywire.

To prevent such problems, Ezell has recommended that diversion programs should feature the following elements:

- More sound criteria to determine which youth are diverted so that net-widening is prevented.
- Greater attention to due process rights to juveniles accused of delinquent acts that are considered for diversion.
- Improved ability to match diverted youth to appropriate interventions and services.
- Avoidance of stigmatization of youths who are diverted.[16]

One example of a diversion program designed to accomplish such objectives is the Detention Diversion Advocacy Program (DDAP).

DDAP features a case management system that is designed to integrate services provided to the juvenile by a number of different agencies and service providers and to develop the skills of the client. It also features the use of laypersons acting on behalf of offenders at disposition hearings. The case management system coordinates the provision of services for both the client and his or her family. The focus is on "high risk" juveniles whose personal circumstances make them ripe for delinquency. Research on DDAP found that it was effective in providing services and in reducing recidivism (referral to juvenile court for a new offense) among its clients. The recidivism rate for the DDAP group was almost twice as low (34 percent) as that of the comparison group (60 percent) that was not treated. In addition, the members of the comparison group were more likely to engage in serious crime and have more than two referrals. The lower recidivism rate for DDAP clients was also true among juveniles classified as "high risk." On the basis of this evidence, it seems that programs that divert juveniles and provide needed social services can impact delinquency rates.[17]

The Transfer of Juveniles to Adult Court

As we have seen, the juvenile court was designed to prevent juvenile offenders from being treated and tried in the same courts as adult offenders. It was established to "save children" from the adult system. Recent criticisms sponsored by the "get tough" movement have called for severe punishments for juvenile offenders who commit serious crimes. From this point of view, juvenile offenders escaping just punishment for their crimes and the aims of deterrence and incapacitation of serious delinquents were not being met in juvenile court. In the 1990s, most state legislatures introduced punitive measures in response to rising rates of youth crime. One particular measure was the transfer of an increasing number and range of adolescents to adult criminal courts for prosecution. This procedure, known as **remanding,** waives juvenile court jurisdiction over a youth and sends the case to the adult criminal court.

An option in some states since 1920, a juvenile case can be transferred to adult criminal court in one of three ways (see also Chapter 6):[18]

- Judicial waiver
- Prosecutorial discretion
- Statutory exclusion

In any state, one, two, or all three methods may be in place. Of the three, judicial waiver is the most common transfer provision. Most statutes are limited to juveniles who are no longer amenable to treatment. The factors leading to this determination typically include previous offense history and dispositional outcomes. Statutes typically instruct the juvenile court to consider the availability of dispositional outcomes for treating the juvenile, the time available for sanctions, public safety, and the best interests of the child. A reverse transfer is also possible with adult criminal courts returning a case to juvenile court. Until 1966, transfers of juveniles were made without full benefit of due process of law. In the *Kent* decision, the U.S. Supreme Court ruled that juveniles facing a waiver to adult court had a right to a hearing, representation by counsel, access to records, and a right to a written statement of the reasons for the decision made by the court.[19]

During a waiver hearing, a juvenile court judge is asked to waive jurisdiction over a matter and transfer the case to criminal court so the juvenile can be tried as though he or she were an adult. Waiver decisions are often based on a number of factors, including

- The seriousness of the offense
- The juvenile's prior record
- The youth's amenability to treatment.

The waiver procedure has grown in popularity in recent years. In 1998, juvenile court judges waived 8,100 delinquency cases. The number of cases waived in 1998 was 1 percent more than in 1989, 9 percent less than in 1997, and 33 percent less than in 1994, the peak year. Of the cases waived in 1998, 36 percent (2,900) were for personal offenses, 40 percent (3,200) were property offenses, 16 percent (1,300) involved a drug law violation, and 8 percent (700) involved a public order offense as the most serious charge.[20] For the period 1988 to 1997, it was estimated that only 8 out of 1,000 formally handled delinquency cases were waived to adult criminal court.[21]

The trend toward more punitive responses to delinquency is most evident in new laws that facilitate the transfer of young offenders to criminal court without the traditional waiver hearing. The most highly controversial of these streamlined transfer methods is prosecutorial waiver. It allows prosecutors to choose whether to initiate proceedings in juvenile or criminal court.

A number of criticisms have been raised about the transfer decision. Specifically, transfer policies have been called into question for sending many minor and nonthreatening juvenile offenders to the adult system, aggravating racial disparities, and moving special needs adolescents into adult correctional systems that are ill prepared to handle them. Also, the evidence that transfer results in more severe penalties for some juvenile offenders and achieves a deterrent effect is questionable.[22]

SUMMARY

The administration of the juvenile justice system is in some ways more difficult than its adult counterpart. In other ways, it is much easier. The problem of whether the police, courts, and corrections agencies should develop complete and separate apparatus for juveniles or absorb them into the existing adult criminal justice system is one of long standing. The separate subsystems have had varying degrees of success in seeking autonomy for juveniles. The most successful of these has been the juvenile courts, which have had almost absolute power over the juvenile offender under the doctrine of *parens patriae.*

The trend in administration seems to be heading toward a more selective jurisdiction over offenders, focusing on the seriousness of the offense instead of the status of the offender. As attitudes change toward making juveniles more accountable for their actions, the adult and juvenile justice systems will become less distinguishable. As a result, the administration of juvenile justice will become more and more formalized. The traditional *parens patriae* approach will give way to a more legalistic one. Administration officials, who want and need rules as guidelines, will favor this process, but its impact upon the youth is yet to be determined.

TERMS TO REMEMBER

Adjudicated
Adjudicatory hearing
Children in need of services
   (CHINS)
Decarceration
Deinstitutionalization
Delinquency petition
Diversion
Dual beneficiaries

Goal conflict
Prosecutorial discretion
Radical nonintervention
Remanding
Status offenses
Statutorily excluded
Transfer of juveniles to adult court
Waiver petition
Widening of the net

REVIEW QUESTIONS

1. Why has the concept of *parens patriae* become difficult to maintain in the present juvenile justice environment?
2. What alternatives are usually used by the police in juvenile incidents?
3. Where do juvenile probation officers get their referrals? Where do most come from?
4. What is the role of the prosecutor in the juvenile justice process?
5. What takes place at a dispositional hearing?
6. How should status offenses be dealt with?
7. Analyze the goals of diversion. What are the benefits and problems associated with this process?
8. What are the goals of the transfer of juveniles to adult court? Why or why not should this process be used?
9. How can a juvenile be transferred to adult court? How do these processes differ?
10. Can the juvenile justice system meet the goals of treatment and punishment?

NOTES

[1]Kevin N. Wright, "The Desirability of Goal Conflict in the Criminal Justice System," *Journal of Criminal Justice,* Vol. 9 (1981), pp. 209–218.

[2]Peter M. Blau and W. Richard Scott, *Formal Organizations: A Comparative Approach* (San Francisco: Chandler, 1962).

[3]"Juvenile Justice Facts & Figures." Office of Juvenile Justice and Delinquency Prevention web site: http://ojjdp.ncjrs.org/facts/caseflowexplan.html, p.1.

[4]John P. Kenney and Dan Pursuit, *Police Work with Juveniles and the Administration of Juvenile Justice* (Springfield, IL: Charles W. Thomas, 1989), pp. 104–107.

[5]"Juvenile Justice Facts & Figures," p. 3.

[6]Ibid, p. 2.

[7]Ibid.

[8]Ibid, p. 3.

[9]Ibid, p. 4.

[10]Edwin Schur, *Radical Non-intervention: Rethinking the Delinquency Problem* (Englewood Cliffs, NJ: Prentice Hall, 1973).

[11]Robert Meier and Gilbert Geis, *Victimless Crime?* (Los Angeles: Roxbury Publishing, 1997).

[12]Institute of Judicial Administration, American Bar Association, *Standards Relating to Interim Status: Release, Control and Detention of Accused Juvenile Offenders Between Arrest and Disposition* (Cambridge, MA: Ballinger, 1980).

[13]*McKeiver v. Pennsylvania,* 403 U.S. 541 (1971).

[14]*Breed v. Jones,* 421 U.S. 519 (1975).

[15]M. A. Bortner, M. L. Sunderland, and R. Winn, "Race and the Impact of Juvenile Deinstitutionalization," *Crime and Delinquency,* Vol. 31 (1985), pp. 35–46. See also J. E. Fagan, E. Slaughter, and E. Hartstone, "Blind Justice? The Impact of Race on the Juvenile Justice Process." *Crime and Delinquency,* Vol. 33 (1987), pp. 224–258.

[16]M. Ezell, "Juvenile Diversion: The Ongoing Search for Alternatives," in Ira M. Schwartz, ed, *Juvenile Justice and Public Policy: Toward a National Agenda* (New York: Macmillan, 1992), pp. 45–58.

[17]Randall G. Shelden, *Detention Diversion Advocacy: An Evaluation* (Washington, D.C.: U.S. Department of Justice, Office of Juvenile Justice and Delinquency Prevention, 1999).

[18]Howard N. Synder and Melissa Sickmund, *Juvenile Offenders and Victims: A National Report* (Washington, D.C.: Office of Juvenile Justice and Delinquency Prevention, 1995), p. 26.

[19]Barry C. Feld, "Delinquency Careers and Criminal Policy: Just Deserts and the Waiver Decision," *Criminology,* Vol. 21 (1983), pp. 195–212.

[20]Anne L. Stahl, *Delinquency Cases in Juvenile Court, 1998* (Washington, D.C.: Office of Juvenile Justice and Delinquency Prevention, 2001).

[21]Charles M. Puzzanchera, *Delinquency Cases Waived to Criminal Court, 1988–1997* (Washington, D.C.: Office of Juvenile Justice and Delinquency Prevention, 2000).

[22]Donna M. Bishop, "Juvenile Offenders in the Adult Criminal Justice System," in Michael Tonry, ed., *Crime and Justice: A Review of Research, Volume 27,* (Chicago: University of Chicago Press, 2000), pp. 81–167.

chapter 5

JUVENILES AND THE POLICE: WHERE THE SYSTEM STARTS

As the initial gatekeeper to the juvenile justice system, police are granted perhaps the most critical discretion of any decision maker in the response to juvenile crime: whether or not to arrest and pursue formal processing. The role of the police in determining the type and level of diversion has also long been recognized.

— Gordon Sizemore & Scott Senjo

CHAPTER OVERVIEW

The quote above reveals the central role of the police as an entry point for the entire justice system, whether for adults or juveniles. The police are typically the first social agency on the scene, responding often without knowing or caring if the juvenile is the offender or the victim. Their powers are varied, from arrest to diversion, but they usually fit into the *parens patriae* style of the juvenile justice system. The desire to help is paramount, yet the power to arrest and the ability to help often conflict. But, with the advent of community policing and problem solving, the police have become more proactive in their involvement with juveniles. In recent years, police officers have directly offered services to youth to prevent their involvement with both drugs (D.A.R.E.) and gangs (G.R.E.A.T).

In this country, people are hired, appointed or elected to wear uniforms, carry badges and guns, and be, as President Grover Cleveland put it, "servants of the *people* to execute the laws which *people* have made."

These public servants include town constables, city police, county sheriffs and deputies, state patrol officers, warehouse guards, institutional guards, and truant officers. Each and every one of these control and law enforcement agents could and often do have contact with America's children. In this chapter, we will review the use of these powers and responsibilities these myriad agencies and their involvement in the juvenile justice system. By virtue of their position on the "leading edge" of the system, the role of the police is significant.

EMERGENCE AND GROWTH OF POLICE DEPARTMENTS

Although people from many European countries originally settled the United States, English customs and the concept of common law have had the greatest influence on the American system—adult and juvenile.

The **night watch** was the prevalent form of policing in the villages, towns, and cities of the new colonies. An early version of the present-day sheriff kept the peace by policing agricultural areas, especially in the South. The night watch, consisting of volunteers who took turns, soon became a very distasteful duty. Many Americans shunned this obligation because they were too busy or unconcerned. Those who could afford it hired "shiftless folk" to stand watch in their stead. Under the night watch system, which was the only form of law enforcement in many American towns until the mid-1800s, crime was rampant.

Clearly, untrained and unqualified and poorly paid or trained night watch "police" could not do the job. Citizens complained loudly that these hit-or-miss police practices were bringing about social chaos and disorder. After nearly thirty years of discussing reform, Philadelphia, Pennsylvania, became the first city to engage a fully paid and trained, round-the-clock police force. Following its example, many other cities soon began to set up their own police forces.

Modern policing in the United States began in 1844, when the New York state legislature authorized funds for day-and-night police forces throughout the state and empowered communities to organize police departments. In 1845, the New York City police forces were consolidated, the old night watch system was abolished, and the day-and-night shifts were organized. Chicago followed suit in 1851. New Orleans and Cincinnati in 1852, Baltimore and Newark in 1857, and Providence in 1864. By the 1870s, most of the nation's major cities had full-time police departments. At the turn of the century, few American cities were without full-time police forces.[1]

In the nineteenth century, salaries for officers were extremely low, and long lines did not form at the police recruiting offices. Those few who did show up were needed so badly that the recruiting officer often looked the other way in judging an applicant's qualifications. "The aim of the police department was merely to keep a city superficially clean and to keep everything quiet that was likely to arose public ire."[2]

Police forces, although becoming formally recognized and organized, were still ineffectual in crime control. The **spoils system,** the brainchild of President Andrew Jackson, was one of the primary reasons. Rotation in office enjoyed so much popular favor that police positions, of both high and low standing, were constantly changing hands, with political fixers determining the price and conditions of each change. The whole question of police corruption simply churned around in the public mind and eventually became identified with the corruption and degradation of city politics and local governments in the period.[3] The **Pendleton Act,** which established the civil service system at the federal government level, was passed in 1883. This monumental concept, adopted eventually at all levels of government, marked the end of the spoils system, and the consequent stability in local government eased many of the problems of the burgeoning police departments.

Until the late 1800s and the early 1900s, juveniles were subject to the same laws and punishments and the same treatment by the police as adults. There were no separate juvenile courts or juvenile laws to regulate the treatment and protection of children. Early courts and correctional systems followed English common law in cases involving juveniles.

Until the problems of the big city slums began to affect the lives of the "refined" citizenry, not much thought was given as to what should done to, or for, youths in trouble. At the turn of the century, citizens started urging the police to protect them from delinquents and youthful beggars. The police approach at that time, however, was to act only as only guardians of the peace, not as social workers. The concept of special juvenile police units patrolling neighborhoods and helping to stop delinquency before it started had not been adopted, and the somewhat brutal police methods of the time were applied to youthful criminals, as well as adults.

Protests favoring differential treatment of juveniles eventually caught the public fancy, creating a general clamor for change throughout the nation. As a result of the efforts of the Society for the Prevention of Cruelty to Children (composed mostly of women), in 1877 the New York state legislature passed the first law in this country that dealt specifically with police treatment of juveniles.[4] It read, in part:

> Any child under restraint or conviction, actually or apparently under the age of 16 years, shall not be placed in any prison or place of confinement, or in any courtroom or in any vehicle for transportation in company with adults charged or convicted of crime except in the presence of proper officials.[5]

Additional laws to protect and separate juveniles from adult criminals were passed in the ensuing years. One of the most important, and the cornerstone of the present system, was an act designed "to regulate the treatment and control of dependent, neglected, and delinquent children," signed into law in Illinois in April 1899. This was the first act in the United States that included a definition of juvenile delinquency: "Any child under the age of 16 who violates any law of this state or any city or village ordinance" was held to be a juvenile delinquent. The law was designed to avoid treating the child as a *criminal,* placing emphasis on rehabilitation of juvenile offenders rather than on punishment.[6]

With the passage of the Illinois act, a policing authority was introduced with a specific duty to work with delinquents. This authority was to be known as the juvenile probation officer, an official position even to this day. Many modern metropolitan police departments have special units to deal with juveniles exclusively; other police forces cooperate with county probation workers. In smaller communities, the same police who sometimes shoot it out with major criminals also investigate vandalism by roving gangs of youths.

For example, the Midvale (Utah) Police Department has established the following policy for officers dealing with juveniles in enforcement and custody situations:

> This agency's interests concerning juvenile offenders reflect the interest of the community to prevent juvenile delinquency. This agency expects all members to handle juveniles consistent with state laws and common sense. The best interest of the community may dictate a limited application of arrest powers regarding juveniles and officers may handle errant juveniles informally in certain instances.[7]

Here, the broad powers and authority that the police bring to the situation are apparent. Flexibility and discretion are also highlighted. The officer must assess the situation and use the method that is most appropriate to the individual case.

POLICE: THE FIRST CONTACT WITH THE SYSTEM

A youth's first contact with the police is the most important contact they may ever have with the juvenile justice system. The way in which the police treat them initially will have a decided influence on their perception and impression of both the juvenile and adult justice systems.

The police determine whether or not youths become further involved with the juvenile justice system. In many cases, police make what is referred to as "on-the-spot" adjustments, also known as **street corner**

justice. These adjustments may take the form of a warning to the youth, a ride home in the police cruiser, or possibly a meeting with parents or guardians. Some readers of this text may have experienced on-the-spot adjustments first hand when growing up. Consider for a moment whether your life would have been different had the police decided to refer the case to court for an adjudicatory hearing. Such police discretion is a valuable tool when used properly, but it can be open to abuse if not carefully monitored and supervised.

Generally, the first role of the police in dealing with juveniles is the *control function* of detection, investigation, and arrest.[8] Yet, we shall also see that police departments have become increasingly concerned about their *prevention function:* involving the community in the solving problems and improving conditions that can lead to crime and delinquency.[9]

Detection

Detection of a crime or response to a complaint will normally lead to an investigation by the police and may result in an arrest. Detection is often left to persons or agencies outside the police department. Even today, only the larger or more sophisticated forces have juvenile officers out on the streets. When police are assigned to a specific neighborhood and know that neighborhood, its people, its problems, and its resources, they become effective forces in the detection and deterrence of delinquency or abuse.

Alleged gang members are led away by Los Angeles police officers after being arrested following a brawl during the Cinco de Mayo celebration. (Douglas C. Pizac/*AP/Wide World Photos*)

Once the police are aware that a delinquent act may have been committed, they find themselves in the role of investigators.

Investigation

During the investigation of a delinquent act the suspects, if any, may be held in detention, released to parents, or some other disposition. It is therefore extremely important that the police investigate the act as thoroughly as possible . . . so that the youth might not be falsely labeled as a delinquent.

In the course of interviewing the suspect, witnesses, and other parties who are involved, the police face a crucial test of their effectiveness in the community. Often they come into a hostile situation where all concerned distrust the police. This attitude is especially prevalent in traditionally high-crime and low-income areas.

The officer has to learn as much about the alleged offense or abuse as possible in the shortest time possible. Interviewing is more art than science and often must be learned only by experience. The officer must be flexible. For example, interviewing a 16-year-old girl picked up for countless crimes and prostitution and who is wanted on a drug charge will not be, and should not be, the same as interviewing a 10-year-old girl who got caught stealing candy bars.

In questioning suspects in criminal cases, several restrictions have been placed on the police. Whether these restrictions provide safeguards against overzealousness or whether they are well meaning but unrealistic erosion of necessary police authority is open to debate. Nonetheless, the practical result is that the effectiveness of interrogations as a police technique is seriously curtailed in many cases, especially with suspects who are, in fact, guilty. These few suspects have learned to rely upon these restrictions for protection from punishment, knowing full well that if they cannot be interviewed adequately, this manner of proving guilt is denied the police. On the other hand, the innocent are denied opportunity to prove their innocence without being formally charged. The people, not the police are the ultimate victims of these restrictions. The police do not seek the privilege of denying suspects their rights, but they do feel that some balance between rights and cooperative responsibilities must be achieved in the public interest.

If the interview is successful, the police will normally have sufficient proof of a suspect's guilt or innocence. If there was no clear suspect at the onset of the investigation, well-conducted interviews will often provide one. While interviewing may not be the most important cog in the investigatory wheel, it is not always feasible or successful. Many delinquent acts have no witnesses at all, or at least none that will cooperate. In such cases, investigatory techniques (piecing together clues, fingerprints, and physical evidence) must come into play.

Arrest

Assuming that the investigation does turn up a suspect, the next step is confrontation and/or arresting the suspected offender. Here, too, the conduct of the police weighs heavily on the attitudes of the youth, his or her peer group, and the community. Citizen cooperation is extremely important to the police in all their dealings with the young. Many times the police, with citizen cooperation and consent, are able to waive legal guidelines, such as search warrants. Citizen cooperation saves time and money and should be encouraged. As adults, these citizens have the right to waive legal proceedings because they are considered to be mature persons and to understand what they are doing.

Questioning and arresting juveniles presents special problems to the police. In *Haley v. Ohio,* the courts stated, in considering whether a juvenile's statements are voluntary, that the length of questioning, the child's age, the time of day or night of questioning, whether the child was fed and allowed to rest, whether the child was allowed child's rights are all extremely important factors.[10]

> One of the best tests of a child's rights is whether the child has been treated with "fundamental fairness." Factors to be considered by the police in making this decision . . . in addition to the age of the child . . . are; apparent intelligence and all-around maturity, experience or lack of experience in such situations involving the police, the seriousness of the violation suspected of having been committed, and the extent of continuing danger to society in the situation. Even when the police decide that the child is mature enough to make these decisions every effort should be made to notify parents at the earliest possible moment so that they can furnish their support and advice.[11]

The concept of **fundamental fairness** varies in significance and definition according to different jurisdictions. Police administrators should seek the counsel of legal advisors on what the law is and how it is interpreted in the local jurisdiction before a youth is questioned, searched, or arrested.[12]

In *Miranda v. Arizona* (384 U.S. 436), the court ruled that a suspect must be advised of his or her rights (for example, the right to remain silent) when in any way deprived of freedom of movement. California incorporated these requirements into its juvenile rules for arresting youths. Several other states have followed suit since then. (See Box 5.1.)

However, even the *Miranda* ruling does not guarantee that, once read his or her rights, a juvenile knows what they mean. Since many authori-

---

Box 5.1 *Miranda Warnings*

1. You have the right to remain silent.
2. Any statements you make may be used as evidence against you in a criminal trial.
3. You have the right to consult with counsel and to have counsel present with you during questioning. You may retain counsel at your own expense or counsel will be appointed for you at no expense to you.

Even if you decide to answer questions now without having counsel present, you may stop answering questions at any time. Also, you may request counsel at any time during the questioning.

---

ties consider a child's problem to be a family problem, one of the best safeguards of a child's rights is to have the parents present at all police proceedings.

Whether or not a child is arrested or taken into custody, another role of the police is brought into play. That is to act as judge, jury, and executioner. As pointed out earlier, many youthful offenders never enter the juvenile justice system. They are released, reprimanded, or punished before the court ever enters into their lives. The old story of a child picked up in a rich neighborhood, driven home to mom and dad, and given a stern weekend in detention, is not at all unrealistic. Different police practices in different neighborhoods are undeniable and often necessary. Large inner-city police forces often do not have the personnel to deal with youths in any other way than to arrest them and get them off the streets. In smaller or well-to-do communities where crime rates are lower, the police are often more understanding and lenient toward disruptive or delinquent youths. Thus, there is a developing and serious need for clear and realistic guidelines for police dispositions.

GUIDELINES FOR POLICE DISPOSITION: THE POWER OF DISCRETION

In any situation, the course of action the police may choose may vary considerably among departments and among individual officers. The course of action is governed to some extent by departmental practice, either explicitly enunciated or tacitly understood. Some well thought out and recommended guidelines follow:

- Police should exercise, whenever practical, every alternative at their disposal before applying for a petition to the court. To do this they must know agencies other than the court to which they can and should make referrals.
- If on-the-spot adjustments are used, they should be used equally, regardless of the juvenile's skin color or which part of town he or she comes from or who the parents are.
- While diversion from formal court procedures is desired, police should not withhold evidence or other relevant facts concerning a case from the courts.
- Police should be trained and educated so as to be better able to judge the juveniles they are confronting. They need to be able to evaluate the effect of their disposition decisions. A sad-eyed lad running a long con story may require something stronger than a warning, whereas a youth who ran away from home because his father beat him continuously may not benefit from being driven back to the source of his problem.
- Police should make periodic checks on those they have diverted. Continuous warnings do the youth no more good than do continuous harassment and arrest. The power of helpful discretion must be brought to bear.

These guidelines are presented to give the student an idea of the specific areas that have to be considered. For every police administrator, flexibility in applying guidelines and policies used by the police will be needed in dealing with juveniles in their specific environment.

Again, the Midvale, Utah, Police Department provides some specific examples of police procedures concerning juvenile matters. For example, they provide for taking a child into custody if

- There is a legal detention order.
- Custody is necessary for the safety of the child or if the child seriously endangers others.
- Custody is necessary to insure the child's appearance in court.
- The child has committed a felony.
- The child had committed a misdemeanor in the officer's presence.
- The child is a runaway.
- The child is a truant.[13]

Such policies are difficult to evolve; indeed, in many instances policies cannot be made specific enough to be helpful without being too rigid to accommodate the vast variety of street situations. Nevertheless, it is important that, wherever possible, guidelines be formulated for the police in their dealings with juveniles. Without specific, standardized, and universal guidelines, it is extremely difficult for both the police and the citizenry to know when an adequate job is being done. What may be more reasonable and practical, of course more helpful, is that practices be at least standard within each precinct or department.

Guidelines, when they are formulated, must meet the local needs and must be flexible enough to allow for individual treatment of each case. The fact is that, in most cases, all laws that local police departments become involved with are therefore bound to guidelines made by the state legislature or the federal courts. This does not necessarily mean that any nice, neat, clear, and understandable guidelines actually exist. For this very reason, police departments have or should develop their own practices and guidelines for dealing with juveniles.

The Decision to Arrest

As the gatekeepers of the juvenile justice system, the police control access of juveniles. They determine whether the juvenile will enter the system at all and at what point or if they will be diverted. Of course, these decisions are significant. If they are racially biased in any way, minority youth may be more at risk later during the correctional processing stages.[14] Studies of police arrests of juveniles reveal the following factors (either alone or in combination) that affect decision making:

- Demeanor: Police view demeanor as a predictor of future behavior. Hostile or fawningly respectful behavior arouses both action and suspicion.
- Seriousness of the offense: Incidents of minor legal significance are more likely to be diverted.
- Group offenses: They are treated as an obvious indicator of gang activity. This factor is known as "the group hazard hypothesis."[15]
- Victim priorities: If the victim calls for action, the police are more likely to oblige them.
- Race and socioeconomic status.
- Sex: In general, males are more likely to be arrested for violent and drug offenses, and females for status offenses.[16] As female involvement in more serious offenses changes, so will the arrest rate.[17]

Further, these variables are likely to be correlated. For example, juveniles in a group may be more likely to "act out" and talk back to the police. Here, the group action and demeanor may combine to make arrest more likely. Minority groups are overrepresented among the poor. The poor are more likely to be arrested. Poor, minority-group victims are more likely to complain and demand action from the police. Thus, evidence of racial discrimination is difficult to absolutely determine, but several studies of police arrest practices have documented its existence.[18] On the other hand, Bittner has asserted that "The decision to arrest someone may have more to do with the routines of police work than with the accountable merits of the case."[19]

Box 5.2 Juvenile Curfew Programs

Curfews for juveniles have been touted as a method of controlling juvenile crime and preventing juvenile victimization. It is not a new or novel idea. In America, curfews have been imposed for over a century. From the 1890s to during World War II, curfews were used in large cities to decrease crime among immigrant youth and to help parents busily engaged in the war effort. As a result of a perceived increase in juvenile crime, they have recently been proposed in a number of cities. For example, Charlottesville, Virginia, adopted a curfew ordinance in 1996 that had the following goals:

- To promote the general welfare and protect the general public through the reduction of juvenile violence and crime within the city;
- To promote the safety and well-being of the city's youngest citizens, persons under the age of 17, whose inexperience renders them particularly vulnerable to becoming participants in unlawful activities, especially unlawful drug activities, and to being victimized by older perpetrators of crime; and
- To foster and strengthen parental responsibility for children.

To generate support for this program, the Charlottesville Police Department used its school resource officers to inform students and school personnel about its operations.

Citing this program, Ward offers the following suggestions on how juvenile curfews should be implemented:

- Create a dedicated curfew center or using recreation centers and churches to house curfew violators;
- Staff these centers with social service professionals and community volunteers;
- Offer referrals to social service providers and counseling classes for juvenile violators and their families;

continued

Box 5.2 *Juvenile Curfew Programs* (continued)

- Establish procedures such as fines, counseling, or community service for repeat offenders;
- Develop recreation, employment, anti-drug, and anti-gang programs; and
- Providing hot lines for follow-up services and crisis intervention.

He also recommends that the police develop consistent curfew enforcement policies that are known to parents and juveniles. It should include an accurate record-keeping information system that will facilitate follow-up with affected citizens. Ward also noted that the program led to a dramatic decrease in the number of juveniles on the street and that all parties associated with the program felt that the curfew was implemented properly. However, the research evidence concerning the effectiveness of juvenile curfews in reducing crime is mixed.

- In Vernon, Connecticut, researchers noted that the pattern of curfew stops, arrests, and the timing of Part I (Index) crime changes could not be attributed to enforcement of the nighttime curfew.
- In New Orleans, Louisiana, victimizations of both adults and juveniles and juvenile arrests during curfew hours did not decrease significantly following program implementation. There was some evidence of displacement by time. During non-curfew hours, some victimizations increased significantly. Yet, interviews with juveniles revealed that, although they did not know the full extent of the curfew law, they disobeyed it. Although they complained about unfair police practices, juveniles supported the curfew because they felt it would promote safety—something they desire from both the police and their parents.
- An early study of the impact of a curfew on crime in Detroit, Michigan, (1976) also reported evidence of displacement. While the curfew suppressed juvenile crime, juvenile criminal activity simply moved to earlier hours of the day.
- On a more positive note, a study of fifty-seven major American cities considered the impact of curfew laws on homicides (from 1976 to 1995) and on juvenile arrests for other crimes (from 1985 to 1995). Following the passage of curfew laws, county (or rural) areas registered decreases in burglary, larceny, and simple assault. Homicide and other crime rates and did not change.

continued

Box 5.2 Juvenile Curfew Programs (continued)

Overall, this experience with curfews again confirms the conclusion that juvenile crime is immune to a quick-fix approach.

Consistent with the community policing model, police may wish to assume a partnership role with other agencies. The long-term effect of a Chicago-based program that stressed pre-school involvement and dropout prevention was particularly promising. Pre-school participation was linked to lower rates of juvenile arrests (including violent crimes) and lower rates of school dropout. Acting in conjunction with other agencies, police in San Diego, California, helped reduce re-arrest rates for juveniles involved in a program that stressed graduated sanctions ranging from informal handling to probation and restitution.

Sources: J. Richard Ward, Jr., "Implementing Juvenile Curfew Programs," *FBI Law Enforcement Bulletin* www.fbi.gov.; Mike A. Males, "Vernon, Connecticut's Juvenile Curfew: The Circumstances of Youths Cited and Effects on Crime," *Criminal Justice Policy Review,* Vol. 11 (2000), pp. 254–267; K. Michael Reynolds, Ruth Seydlitz, and Pamela Jenkins, "Do Juvenile Curfew Laws Work? A Time-Series Analysis of the New Orleans Law," *Justice Quarterly,* Vol. 17, (2000), pp. 205–230; K. Michael Reynolds, William Ruefle, Pamela Jenkins, et. al., "Contradictions and Consensus: Youths Speak Out About Juvenile Curfews," *Journal of Crime and Justice,* Vol. 22 (1999), pp. 171–192; A. Lee Hunt and Ken Weiner, "The Impact of a Juvenile Curfew: Suppression and Displacement in Patterns of Juvenile Offenses," *Journal of Police Science and Administration,* Vol. 5, (1977), pp. 407–412; David McDowall, Colin Loftin, and Brian Wiersema, "The Impact of Youth Curfew Laws on Juvenile Crime Rates," *Crime and Delinquency,* Vol. 46 (2000), pp. 76–91; Arthur J. Reynolds, Judy A. Temple, Dylan L. Robertson, et. al., "Long-Term Effects of an Early Childhood Intervention on Educational Achievement and Juvenile Arrest: A 15-Year Follow-Up of Low-Income Children in Public Schools." *Journal of the American Medical Association,* Vol. 285, (2001), pp. 2339–2346; Susan Pennell, Christine Curtis, and Dennis C. Scheck, "Controlling Juvenile Delinquency: An Evaluation of an Interagency Strategy," *Crime and Delinquency,* Vol. 36, (1990), pp. 257–275.

POLICE AND THE NEGLECTED OR ABUSED CHILD

Thus far, this discussion has focused mainly between police and *delinquent* youths. However, there are several types of children/juveniles who come under the purview of the police.

Childhood is a reasonably happy and secure time for most children; they have parents or relatives who love them, provide for them, protect them, and give them a sense of security. But there are many children whose childhood has been lost or scarred by parents who fail them altogether or who inadequately meet their basic needs. These children are called *neglected*. They come from all kinds of homes and income strata. Rich children can be as easily considered **neglected** as those who are poor.

Typically, police become involved in neglect or abuse cases when a report is filed. Then, an immediate investigation is in order, for the protection and safety of the youth(s) in question.

- The investigating officer shall make all attempts to locate and conduct an interview with the abused child or juvenile as soon as possible.
- In cases involving severe injuries to a child, medical attention should be sought for the child immediately.
- Attempts shall be made by the investigating officer to identify and locate all additional victims, witnesses, and suspects in abuse cases.
- The investigating officer shall attempt to identify and secure any physical evidence.[20]

Police must make sure that the alleged neglect or abuse actually does exist when handling a case of this nature. Their methods of investigation and interview should be much the same as when responding to delinquency cases. An additional tool useful to police is the photograph or videotape; it will help to substantiate the condition of the child or his or her home at the time contact is made.

In dependent neglect cases it is usually persons other than the parents who make the complaint. As a result, it can often be difficult for the police to gain the cooperation of the parents in their investigation. The investigating officer must be certain to find out if the reported neglect or abuse is an isolated incident or only one event in a history of such occurrences.

The officer should make an immediate assessment of the situation and determine if action to protect the child must be taken. Many answers to complaints from interested parties, schoolteachers, social workers, and so forth, can be handled with a warning or reprimand to the parents. The officer may choose to simply inform the parents that any further complaints regarding the treatment of their children may result in a court appearance.

For example, the Cicero (Illinois) Police Department defines an *abused minor* as "any minor under 18 years of age whose parent or immediate family member, person responsible for the minor's welfare, or any person residing in the same home or a paramour of the minor's parent

- Inflicts, causes or allows to be inflicted upon such minor physical injury which causes death, disfigurement, impairment or physical or emotional health, or loss or impairment of any bodily function;
- Creates a substantial risk of physical injury to such minor;
- Commits or allows to be committed an act or acts of torture;
- Inflicts excessive corporal punishment, or;
- Whose environment is injurious to his or her welfare."[21]

Based on the officer's judgment, recommending professional counseling for the family may be advisable. Here, the officer's knowledge of community resources is vital. With the parent's cooperation and a referral to the appropriate source, the child may be saved the agony of further moral, mental, emotional, or physical punishment at his or her parent's hands.

Factors in Police Action

The following are factors that either alone or in combination require immediate police intervention:

- Evidence of the **battered child syndrome** and fear of recurring abuse by parents.
- Lack of appropriate adult supervision, discipline, and/or guidance.
- Lack of adequate physical care and/or protection from potentially harmful things or events.
- A parent's sexual exploitation of children, whether incestuous or for money (i.e., child pornography).
- Failure to provide for the child's basic needs of food, clothing, and shelter appropriate to the climate in which the child lives.

Rumors and actual accounts of abuse of children at the hands of their parents or others are numerous. Police departments, courts, and social agencies have records and photographs on file that would turn anyone's stomach. The ways in which children are abused stand as an indictment of the inventiveness of humankind . . . ranging from boiling an infant alive on the stove to locking a 6-year-old in a box or closet for several years.

Alternatives in Police Action

Assuming that the situation warrants punishment of the parents or removal of the child from the home, what are the alternatives available to the police?

Just as laws dealing with delinquency vary from state to state, so, too, do laws and police procedures. For example, in Illinois, **minors requiring authoritative intervention (MRAI)** are defined as

- Any minor under 18 years of age who is taken into limited custody;
- Is absent from home without the consent of the minor's parent, guardian, or;
- Is beyond the control of his or her parent, guardian, or custodian and in circumstances which constitute a substantial or immediate danger, and;
- Refuses to return home and whose parents cannot agree to placement *after* crisis intervention services have been tried.

Such juveniles may be taken into custody for up to six hours until they can be served by mandated crisis intervention agencies (including family preservation and family reunification). Officers must inform the juvenile of the reason for such custody and must make a good faith attempt to notify the parents or guardian(s) before the crisis intervention agency is contacted.[22]

Police are normally the ones who will take the child from his or her home. For example, procedures for the Cicero (Illinois) Police Department state that officers may (without a warrant) take into temporary custody a minor who (with **reasonable cause**) is believed to be

- Neglected, abused, or dependent (adjudicated as a ward of the court);
- Suffering from any sickness or injury that requires care, medical treatment or hospitalization when found on any street or public place.

Police officers have the legal responsibility and authority to place an abused or neglected child in protective custody and remove the child from parents (or a harmful situation) only when the child's safety is endangered.[23]

Whenever possible, the police should consult with community social agencies when custody is required. Many communities have "shelters for kids," foster homes, and group homes. All too often, however, a neglected child will spend days or even months in a county jail cell. Such a situation stems from inadequate planning and coordination of community resources on the part of the community leaders.

Unknown to many parents is the fact that they may be financially liable for all or part of the costs incurred for housing, feeding, and clothing their children while they are in protective custody. In some cases, parents are liable in cases involving both delinquent and dependent neglected children, but the amount assessed is usually based on the parent's ability to pay.

The question of the police role in the handling of neglected or abused children is an old and complex one. The police and the child are usually part of the same community (except in the case of runaways) and the problems of kids in need of help are the problems of the community. Consequently, only when everyone becomes aware of this community problem and understands its nature will the thousands of abused and battered kids have a hope of being found, heard, and eventually helped. The police are the important and crucial first step in this process. Given the money, the resources, and the training, they can become, as an extension of those they serve in the communities, a more effective force.

POLICE AND DELINQUENTS

As documented in Chapter 3, data from the Uniform Crime Reports indicate that the juvenile crime rate is slowing down. In 1999, law enforcement agencies in the United States made 2.5 million arrests of persons under 18.

- The most serious charge in more than half of these juvenile arrests were for larceny-theft, simple assault, drug abuse violation, disorderly conduct, or a curfew violation.[24]
- Compared to adult arrests, one in six arrests made by the police involved juveniles. Together, they accounted for 33 percent of all burglary arrests, 25 percent of all robbery arrests, 24 percent of weapons arrests, 13 percent of drug arrests, and nine percent of all homicide arrests in 1999.
- Based upon their proportion in the population, juveniles were disproportionately involved in arrests for arson, vandalism, motor vehicle theft, burglary, larceny-theft, disorderly conduct, robbery, and weapons law violations.
- They were underrepresented in arrests for murder, aggravated assault, forcible rape, and drug abuse violations in 1999.[25]
- Between 1980 and 1999, the violent crime arrest rate for juveniles fell. The greatest decline was registered among black juveniles. However, female arrest rates over the period remained relatively high.[26]

Although the peaks of the 1990s appear to have slowed down, these figures document the massive juvenile involvement with the police.

One of the best ways to keep juveniles from becoming statistics in the FBI Crime Index is to reach them before they become adults. During the past few decades, police departments have begun to place special emphasis on working with young people. More and more police services for juveniles, including special police units, are being established. See Boxes 5.2, 5.3, and 5.4 for descriptions of the Curfew, D.A.R.E. and G.R.E.A.T. programs sponsored by police.

It has been alleged that the nuclear family unit in the United States is breaking down and that this breakdown is a source of delinquency. Police often assume a more central role in containing juvenile acting-out behavior (i.e., rebelliousness, deviancy, and other actions or attitudes that make juveniles difficult to handle) and delinquent behavior. Whether they

---

Box 5.3 D.A.R.E.—*Drug Abuse Resistance and Education*

One of the most famous police prevention programs in history—D.A.R.E.—is grounded in the belief that something can be done about delinquency without directing sustained attention to the social forces that push adolescents in delinquent directions. In the specific case of D.A.R.E., the belief is that uniformed police officers teaching children about drugs and the problems drugs can cause will overcome the effects of macro-level factors such as poverty and micro-level factors such as parental supervision. Begun by the Los Angeles Police Department in 1983, the D.A.R.E. curriculum emphasizes the following goals:

- Give students the knowledge and skills to recognize and resist peer pressure to experiment with tobacco, alcohol and other drugs.
- Enhance self-esteem.
- Learn assertiveness techniques.
- Learn about positive alternatives to substance abuse.
- Learn anger management techniques and conflict resolution skills.
- Develop risk assessment and decision-making skills.
- Reduce violence.
- Build interpersonal and communications skills.
- Resist gang involvement.

The key component of the program is the presence of a uniformed officer in the classroom, serving as an instructor and a role model for the students. From its California roots, the program became a national sensation. More than 75 percent of America's school districts have adopted the program.

continued

Box 5.3 *D.A.R.E.—Drug Abuse Resistance and Education* (continued)

Despite its widespread adoption, formal, scientific assessments of the effectiveness of the D.A.R.E. program have produced mostly negative results. While considering a number of different outcomes (positive attitudes toward police, increasing attitudes toward drug abuse) as well as drug and alcohol use, D.A.R.E. programs in different states have failed to register long-term impact upon youths. In fact, one juvenile expert, Richard J. Lundman, recommends that D.A.R.E. be abandoned because it produces only short-term effects that disappear with the passage of time and fails to address the known causes of delinquency.

Despite these findings, the D.A.R.E. program is immensely popular and its reputation is intact. In fact, other studies indicate that D.A.R.E. is more effective when combined with other prevention activities (Just Say No Clubs, Red Ribbon Week) and with community policing in general.

Sources: Richard J. Lundman, *Prevention and Control of Juvenile Delinquency* (New York: Oxford University Press, 2001), p. 67; Bureau of Justice Assistance, *Fact Sheet: Drug Abuse Resistance Education (D.A.R.E.)* (Washington, D.C.: U.S. Department of Justice, 1995), p. 1; D.A.R.E. America web site, D.A.R.E. Scientific Advisory Board—FAQs, "Background," www.dare.com; Harold K. Becker, Michael W. Agopian, and Sandy Yeh, "Impact Evaluation of Drug Abuse Resistance Education (DARE)," *Journal of Drug Education,* Vol. 24 (1992), pp. 293–291; M. A. Harmon, "Reducing the Risk of Drug Involvement Among Early Adolescents: An Evaluation of Drug Abuse Resistance Education (D.A.R.E.)," *Evaluation Review,* Vol. 17 (1993), pp. 221–239; E. Wysong, R. Aniskiewicz, and D. Wright, "Truth and D.A.R.E.: Tracking Drug Education to Graduation and as Symbolic Politics," *Social Problems,* Vol. 41 (1994), pp. 448–472; R. L. Dukes, J. B. Ullman, and J. A. Stein, "An Evaluation of D.A.R.E. (Drug Abuse Resistance Education) Using a Solomon Four-Group Design with Latent Variables," *Evaluation Review,* Vol. 19 (1995), pp. 409–435; Richard T. Sigler and G. B. Talley, "Drug Abuse Resistance Education Program Effectiveness," *American Journal of Police,* Vol. 14 (1995), pp. 111–121; D. S. Kochis, "The Effectiveness of Project D.A.R.E.: Does It Work?" *Journal of Alcohol and Drug Education,* Vol. 40 (1995), pp. 40–47; Dennis P. Rosenbaum and Gail S. Hanson, "Assessing the Effects of School-Based Drug Education: A Six-Year Multilevel Analysis of Project D.A.R.E.," *Journal of Research in Crime and Delinquency,* Vol. 35 (1998), pp. 381–412; Donald R. Lynam, Richard Milich, Rick Zimmerman, et. al., "Project DARE: No Effects at a 10-year Follow Up," *Journal of Consulting and Clinical Psychology,* Vol. 67 (1999), pp. 590–593; Joseph F. Donnemeyer and Russell R. Davis, "Cumulative Effects of Prevention Education on Substance Use Among 11th Grade Students in Ohio," *Journal of School Health,* Vol. 68 (1998), pp. 151–158; David L. Carter, *Community Policing and DARE: A Practitioner's Perspective* (Washington, DC: Bureau of Justice Assistance, 1995).

Box 5.4 *G.R.E.A.T.—Gang Resistance Education and Training*

Similar to D.A.R.E., the G.R.E.A.T. program features a police officer offering a defined curriculum to students in school. Typically, the curriculum features:

- An introduction to acquaint students with the G.R.E.A.T. program and presenting officer.
- Crime/Victims and Your Rights—Students learn about crimes, their victims, and their impact on school and neighborhood.
- Cultural Sensitivity/Prejudice—Students learn how cultural differences impact their school and neighborhood.
- Conflict Resolution (two sessions)—Students learn how to create an atmosphere of understanding that would enable all parties to better address problems and work on solutions together.
- Meeting Basic Needs—Students learn how to meet their basic needs without joining a gang.
- Drugs/Neighborhoods—Students learn how drugs affect their school and neighborhood.
- Responsibility—Students learn about the diverse responsibilities of people in their school and neighborhood.
- Goal Setting—Students learn the need for all goal setting and how to establish short- and long-term goals.

In short, it is a classic, broad-based prevention strategy that is found in medical immunization programs.

As with D.A.R.E., the early evaluations of this program were less than impressive. Their implementation was questionable and the ability of exposed students to resist gang involvement was minimal. A recent evaluation found a significant program effect for five of the outcome measures (victimization, negative views about gangs, attitudes toward the police, prosocial peers, and risk seeking) were positive although gang involvement was not impacted. Once again, given the immensity of the problem and its potential for damage, the G.R.E.A.T. programs are likely to continue. The estimated cumulative number of students who have received the G.R.E.A.T. program is more than 2 million.

Sources: Finn-Aage Esbensen, D. Wayne Osgood, Terrance J. Taylor, Dana Peterson, and Adrienne Freng, "How Great is G.R.E.A.T.? Results from a Longitudinal Quasi-Experimental Design," *Criminology and Public Policy,* Vol. 1 (2001),

continued

Box 5.4   G.R.E.A.T.—Gang Resistance Education and Training (continued)

pp. 88–89; D. J. Palumbo, R. Eskay, M. Hallett, et. al., "Do Gang Prevention Strategies Actually Reduce Crime?" *Gang Journal,* Vol. 1 (1993), pp. 1–10; D. J. Palumbo and J. L. Ferguson, "Evaluating Gang Resistance Education and Training (G.R.E.A.T.): Is the Impact the Same as that of Drug Abuse Resistance Education (D.A.R.E.)?" *Evaluation Review,* Vol. 19 (1995), pp. 597–619; Thomas L. Winfree, Finn-Aage Esbensen, and D. Wayne Osgood, "Evaluating a School-Based Gang Prevention Program," *Evaluation Review,* Vol. 20 (1996), pp. 181–203; Thomas L. Winfree, Dana P. Lynskey, and James R. Maupin, "Developing Local Police and Federal Law Enforcement Partnerships: G.R.E.A.T. as a Case Study of Policy Implementation," *Criminal Justice Review,* Vol. 24 (1999), pp. 145–168. See the G.R.E.A.T. web site at www.atf.treas.gov/great.

---

like it or not, the police are becoming painfully aware that juvenile delinquency is a social condition that they—and this country—can no longer afford. Simple use of investigation and arrest with a lack of concern for the *why* of delinquent acts is plainly not enough. The police are also finding themselves used as a primary *treatment* tool.

THE PROMISE OF COMMUNITY POLICING

Community policing has become the dominant reform movement within policing. More of a theory rather than a specific plan of action, the idea of community policing is difficult to define. As a result, community policing has become mistakenly synonymous with certain tactics and methods. It is more than beat, foot, or bicycle patrols. It is and should be viewed as a philosophy and organizational strategy. It has specific applications to juveniles.[27]

Defining Community Policing

By its very title, **community policing** infers a partnership between the police, the neighborhoods and the people they serve. This partnership is designed to improve the quality of life in the community through the introduction of strategies designed to enhance neighborhood solidarity and safety.[28] Under this model, the police and the community work together to offer solutions to serious social problems they face. This bond between the police and the community is encouraged and officers are usually given time and authorization by their department to get to know the community's habits, wishes and customs. The assumption and belief is that when the police are able to truly relate to a community, they can be in the position to offer creative responses to local problems.

Community policing is different from the traditional/professional model of policing essentially because it demands that officers and their departments adopt proactive strategies and tactics to repress crime, fear, and disorder within local neighborhoods. In turn, community members are also expected take a proactive stance in helping the police and other government entities set policy. It is through this exchange process the citizens receive real input into setting organizational goals, objectives, and departmental values.

Community policing has a set of priorities, which assume that crime problems are different in each community and each area should be policed in accordance with neighborhood needs and values. It is understood that the traditional bureaucratic model, in which one policy should be enforced throughout a jurisdiction no longer applies. Police and strategies must be set in accordance with local norms and values. This decentralized approach to policy development allows citizens to be better protected, and officers to adjust their responses to best serve the community they serve.[29]

Therefore, officers and agencies must do more than simply respond to crime. They must be proactive and anticipate the social and law enforcement concerns before they become problems. Officers within departments that embrace the community policing philosophy are viewed as intelligent agents of the community and the criminal justice system who are able to intellectually and emotionally react to citizen concerns. These characteristics are summarized in Box 5.5.

Community policing is an operational and organizational philosophy designed to address problems and correct them. Under community policing, law enforcement agencies acknowledge that they are responsible for the crime problem and must work on prevention. By partnering with the community, the police seek effective long-term solutions to persistent crime problems.[30]

Problem Oriented Policing (POP)

Many departments use community policing within a framework of **problem-oriented policing (POP)** as a means of enacting it. Under POP, an analysis of the problems handled by the police will indicate how they can be handled in a long-term fashion. POP requires that the police develop a systematic process for examining and addressing the problems that the public expects them to handle. It requires identifying these problems in more precise terms, researching each problem, documenting the nature of the current police response, assessing its adequacy and the adequacy of existing authority and resources, engaging in a broad exploration of alternatives to present responses, weighing the merits of these alternatives, and choosing from among them.

Box 5.5   Characteristics of Community Policing

1. An admission that the police alone cannot solve the problem and that direct participation by citizens is also required.

2. A shift in the focus of problem definition to a customer orientation and a corresponding concentration on those problems identified by the citizens themselves as being of the greatest concern.

3. An emphasis on proactive, rather than reactive, policing, replacing a total preoccupation with 911 calls with efforts targeted at particular problems.

4. The identification and implementation of a range of nontraditional approaches.

5. The redirection of officers from their cruisers into more direct contacts with the community, along with the delegation of decision-making authority to the patrol officer's level.

Source: E. Sweeney, "Community-Oriented Traffic Policing," *The Police Chief,* Vol. LIX (1992), p. 13.

POP emphasizes identifying and analyzing problems (criminal, civil, or public nuisance) and implementing solutions to resolve the underlying causes of the problem. It emphasizes proactive intervention rather than reactive responses to calls for service, resolution of root causes rather than symptoms, and use of multiparty, community-based problem solving rather than a unilateral police response.[31]

POP focuses on a problem in a long-term, comprehensive manner, rather than handling the problem as a series of separate incidents to be resolved via arrest or other police action.

How can community policing and POP help solve the problem of delinquency? Past research on juvenile arrest practices indicates the nature of the problem between police and juveniles:

1. Relations between police and juveniles are almost necessarily characterized by tension and antagonism.

2. Since the majority of encounters between police and juveniles involve relatively minor and nuisance offenses, the bulk of police work with juveniles centers around order maintenance and social services.

3. These studies confirm that youths have a low arrest rate and that between one-third and 40 percent of all juvenile cases are handled in-

formally within police departments or referred to local community services.

4. The decision to arrest is often based upon the response to such individual characteristics as race, gender, and demeanor.[32]

Community policing has the following implications for police work with juveniles:

1. The frequency of contact and level of intimacy should increase as a result of efforts to prevent and reduce opportunities for crime by greater presence in the neighborhood.

2. The already wide discretion exercised by police is expected to increase under POP as police are encouraged to place increased emphasis on solving underlying problems believed to cause crime, to increase the proportion of officer activity directed at order maintenance and to work with neighborhoods in "community building" efforts.

3. Both problem solving and order maintenance activities are expected to result in more proactive efforts to engage citizens and more opportunities for police to participate in community life than has been the case under the professional model of policing.[33]

Thus, under community policing, the relationship between juveniles and the police should change considerably.

POLICE OPERATIONS

A national standard bearer, The Commission on Accreditation for Law Enforcement Agencies sets the following standard for juvenile police operations:

> When dealing with juveniles, law enforcement officers should always make use of the least coercive among reasonable alternatives, consistent with preserving public safety, order, and individual liberty. Generally speaking, law enforcement agencies have four sets of alternatives from which to choose when dealing with juveniles: they may release the offender and take no further action; they may divert the offender to any of a number of social service agencies; they may dispose of the case themselves; or they may (in the case of serious offenders) refer the youth to juvenile court (intake). Because a range of alternatives exists, agencies should establish guidelines and criteria for the use of each.[34]

Accordingly, Kenney and his colleagues have offered this list of the standard ways that a juvenile police unit can handle a case:

1. **Application for petition:** A petition is filed when the circumstances of the case are such that only the juvenile court can reasonably be expected to safeguard the interests and welfare of society and the juvenile concerned. A petition means that the youth is subject to its jurisdiction and may be brought before the juvenile court.

2. **Transfer of case:** Juvenile cases are transferred when another agency has jurisdiction, such as a probation department, state training school, or other law enforcement agency.

3. **Referral to other agencies:** A referral is made when it is believed that the case in question should be investigated further and some rehabilitative program set in motion for the guidance and adjustment of the juvenile.

4. **Action suspended:** In cases where it appears that the parents and juvenile, alone and unaided, can affect a satisfactory adjustment, no further action need be taken.

5. **Insufficient evidence:** When there is conflict in evidence or when there is reasonable doubt as to the responsibility of the juvenile and the evidence is of such a nature as to preclude a determination of involvement, the juvenile should be released and no further action taken.

6. **Exoneration:** When the investigation clearly indicates that a juvenile is not responsible for the delinquency charged, he should be released and exonerated, or cleared of all involvement.

7. **Voluntary police supervision:** This form of disposition is employed when it is felt that the parents unaided are incapable of affecting the child's rehabilitation, but that the officer and the parent working cooperatively can assist the child to self-adjustment without the help of the juvenile court or probation department or other agency. This disposition consists of furnishing guidance and counsel to the juvenile with the consent and full cooperation of the parents. Without such acquiescence it is valueless.

8. **Proves to be adult:** When investigation discloses that the true age of the person arrested as a juvenile to be over the juvenile court age limit, the charges shall be suspended and prosecution of the charge or charges handled as with an adult.

9. **Declared unfit:** The juvenile officer may recommend in the application for petition to the juvenile court that the juvenile be declared unfit for further consideration by the juvenile court and be remanded for trial under the general laws in the criminal court.

10. **Detention:** Although at times detention may form a part of the treatment process, it is presumed to be protective in nature, never punitive. All detention not under the order of the courts is temporary in nature. A child must be held no longer than is reasonably necessary for effective placement or for being brought to the attention of the court.[35]

One of these standard methods, diversion, is particularly significant. Nationwide, police diversion programs vary regarding goals, screening, and services provided. One innovative example of diversion involving the police is the community conferencing program in Woodbury, Minnesota. Here, the police refer cases to the program. Again stressing the potential of community policing, this program emphasizes community involvement to hold offenders accountable and to provide benefits directly to victims of juvenile crime.

The program follows the **family group conferencing** model from far-away Australia. A trained officer (either specially trained police officers or community volunteers) coordinates the program. They contact offenders, their parents, victims, and affected community members to explain the process and seek their voluntary participation. The conference is aimed at resolving the conflict between all concerned parties. They must decided who is the victim and how the harm caused can be set right, and attempt to prevent future victimization. Agreements are reached by a consensus of the participants and the community.

Offenders must complete agreements to successfully complete the program. Until then, prosecution is always an option. If they are successful, further involvement in the system and the creation of a juvenile record are avoided. The program is based on the beliefs that people most affected by a crime should resolve cases. It benefits the community by setting, maintaining, and enforcing norms of behavior and conduct via a partnership with the police. Of course, the offender avoids stigma and is able to make amends constructively.

Through the year 2000, this program had conducted approximately fifty conferences per year. Approximately 82 percent of the cases assigned to conferencing are successfully completed. In the remaining cases, about half were settled in preconference stages, and half were sent to juvenile court. Only two cases resulted in a failed agreement. This program runs a restitution payment success rate of over 95 percent compared to the court system rate of just over 50 percent. The overwhelming majority of persons involved in the process (over 90 percent) were satisfied with the outcome of their case.[36] Overall, this program represents the potential of police-community partnerships to solve the problems of juvenile delinquency.

SUMMARY

Juveniles are neither exempt from the law nor are they immune from the enforcement of the law. They must answer for their deeds just like anyone else. Immaturity and youth are not excuses for theft, rape, murder, or vandalism. Just as police are not always permitted to use force when arresting someone just because he or she is an adult does not mean that police may not use force when arresting someone simply because he or she is a child.

Basically, then, there are no real differences in police philosophy toward adults or juveniles. There are, however, various differences in the adaptations and application of that philosophy. These differences do not change basic police objectives, but they do affect the procedural methods used in handling a juvenile.

The similarity of police philosophy toward an adult criminal and juvenile criminal should not be misunderstood or misinterpreted. Police departments are genuinely concerned about rehabilitating juveniles who get into trouble with the law. Because of their acceptance of this growing public policy, police departments are more than ready and anxious to cooperate with other community agencies.

In the following chapter, we will go on to the juvenile court to examine how youths are processed through the system.

TERMS TO REMEMBER

Action suspended
Application for petition
Battered child syndrome
Community policing
Declared unfit
Detention
Exoneration
Family-group conferencing
Fundamental fairness
Insufficient evidence
Minors requiring authoritative
    intervention (MRAI)

Neglected
Night watch
Pendleton Act
Problem-oriented policing (POP)
Proves to be adult
Reasonable cause
Referral to other agencies
Spoils system
Street corner justice
Transfer of case
Voluntary police supervision

REVIEW QUESTIONS

1. What should a police officer do with a juvenile that he or she has taken into custody for committing a delinquent act?
2. How should an officer handle a child abuse or neglect case?

3. What role should the police officer play in a community program to prevent and control juvenile delinquency?

4. What do the D.A.R.E. and G.R.E.A.T. programs attempt to do? What are the questions surrounding their implementation and effectiveness?

5. What are the problems for the police in coping with juvenile crime? What suggestions can you make to help the police cope with this task more effectively?

NOTES

[1] Richard W. Kobetz, *The Police Role and Juvenile Delinquency* (Gaithersburg, MD: International Association of Chiefs of Police, 1971), pp. 139–141.

[2] Arthur M. Schlesinger and Dixon Ryan Fox, eds., "The Rise of the City, 1878–1897," in *History of American Life*, Vol. 10 (New York: Macmillan, 1934), p. 115.

[3] Bruce Smith, *Police Systems in the United States*, 2nd rev. ed. (New York: Harper & Row, 1960), pp. 105–106.

[4] Kobetz, *The Police Role and Juvenile Delinquency*, p. 147.

[5] Timothy Hurley, *The Origins of the Illinois Juvenile Court Law* (Chicago: Visitation and Aid Society, 1907), p. 14.

[6] Kobetz, *The Police Role and Juvenile Delinquency*, p. 148.

[7] International Association of Chiefs of Police net, Document Display, Document #559103, "Juvenile Offenders," Midvale Police Department (2/11/2002) www.iacpnet.com.

[8] John P. Kenney, Donald E. Fuller, and Robert J. Barry, *Police Work with Juveniles and the Administration of Juvenile Justice* (Springfield, IL: C. C. Thomas, 1995), p. 57.

[9] Ibid., pp. 57–58.

[10] *Haley v. Ohio*, 332 U.S. 596 (1948).

[11] Kenney, Fuller, and Barry, *Police Work with Juveniles*, p. 24.

[12] Ibid.

[13] International Association of Chiefs of Police, Midvale Police Department.

[14] Carl E. Pope and William Feyerherm, *Minorities and the Juvenile Justice System: Research Summary* (Washington, DC: U.S. Department of Justice, Office of Juvenile Justice and Delinquency Prevention, 1993), p. 10.

[15] Maynard Erickson, "Group Violations and Official Delinquency: The Group Hazard Hypothesis," *Criminology*, Vol. 11 (1973), pp. 127–160; Michael J. Hindelang, "With a Little Help From Their Friends: Group Participation in Reported Delinquent Behavior," *British Journal of Criminology*, Vol. 16 (1976), pp. 109–125; William Feyerherm, "The Group Hazard Hypothesis: A Re-examination," *Journal of Research in Crime and Delinquency*, Vol. 17 (1980), pp. 56–58; Mary Morash, "Establishment of a Juvenile Record: The Influence of Individual and Peer Group Characteristics," *Criminology*, Vol. 22 (1984), pp. 97–112.

[16] Christy A. Visher, "Gender, Police Arrest Decisions, and Notions of Chivalry," *Criminology*, Vol. 21 (1983), pp. 5–28; Ruth Horowitz and Anne E. Pottieger, "Gender Bias in Juvenile Justice Handling of Seriously Crime-Involved Youths," Journal of Research in Crime and Delinquency, Vol. 28 (1991), pp. 75–100; Jean E. Rhodes and Karla Fischer, "Spanning the Gender Gap: Gender Differences in Delinquency among Inner-City Adolescents," *Adolescence*, Vol. 28 (1993), pp. 879–889.

[17] Meda Chesney-Lind and Vickie V. Paramore, "Are Girls Getting More Violent? Exploring Juvenile Robbery Trends," *Journal of Contemporary Criminal Justice*, Vol. 17 (2001), pp. 142–166.

[18] Irving Piliavin and Scott Briar, "Police Encounters With Juveniles," *American Journal of Sociology*, Vol. 70 (1964), pp. 206–214; William F. Hohenstein, "Factors Influencing the Police Disposition of Juvenile Offenders," in Thorsten Sellin and Marvin E. Wolfgang, eds., *Delinquency: Selected Readings*, (New York: John Wiley, 1969), pp. 138–149; Neal L. Weiner and Charles V. Willie, "Decisions by Juvenile Officers," *American Journal of Sociology*, Vol. 77 (1971), pp. 199–210; David Black and Albert J. Reiss, Jr., "Police Control of Juveniles," *American Sociological Review*, Vol. 35 (1970), pp. 63–77; Richard J. Lundman, Richard E. Sykes, and John P. Clark, "Police Control of

Juveniles: A Replication," in Richard J. Lundman, ed., *Police Behavior: A Sociological Perspective* (New York: Oxford University Press, 1980), pp. 130–151; M. Wordes and T. S. Bynum, "Policing Juveniles: Is There a Bias Against Youths of Color," in K. K. Leonard, C. E. Pope, and W. F. Feyerherm, eds., *Minorities in Juvenile Justice* (Thousand Oaks, CA: Sage, 1995), pp. 47–65.

[19]Egon Bittner, *Aspects of PoliceWork* (Boston: Northeastern University Press, 1990), p. 341.

[20]International Association of Chiefs of Police net, Document Display, Document #557880, "Child Abuse—Physical/Sexual/Neglect," Craig (CO) Police Department (12/06/2001) www.iacpnet.com.

[21]International Association of Chiefs of Police net, Document Display, Document #546802, "Juvenile Processing Handbook," Cicero (IL) Police Department (08/12/1999) www.iacpnet.com.

[22]Ibid.

[23]Ibid.

[24]Howard N. Snyder, *Juvenile Offenders and Victims: National Report Series—Law Enforcement and Juvenile Crime* (Washington, DC: Office of Juvenile Justice and Delinquency Prevention, 2001), p. 9.

[25]Ibid., p. 10.

[26]Ibid., p. 13.

[27]Jeffrey T. Walker and Louie C. Caudell, "Community Policing and Patrol Cars: Oil and Water or Well Oiled Machine," *Police Forum,* Vol. 3 (July 1993), pp.1–9.

[28]Robert Trojanowicz and Bonnie Bucqueroux, *Community Policing: A Contemporary Perspective.* (Cincinnati: Anderson, 1990), p. xii.

[29]Albert J. Reiss, Jr., "Police Organizations in the Twentieth Century," in Michael Tonry and Norval Morris, eds., *Modern Policing* (Chicago: University of Chicago Press, 1992), pp. 91–94.

[30]Jerald R. Vaughn, "Community-Oriented Policing . . . You Can Make It Happen," *Law and Order* (June 1991), pp. 35–39.

[31]George E. Capowich and Janice A. Roehl, "Problem-Oriented Policing: Actions and Effectiveness in San Diego," in Dennis P. Rosenbaum, ed., *The Challenge of Community Policing: Testing the Promises* (Thousand Oaks, CA: Sage Publications, 1994), pp. 127–128.

[32]Gordon Bazemore and Scott Sanjo, "Police Encounters with Juveniles Revisited: An Exploratory Study of Themes and Styles in Community Policing," *Policing: An International Journal of Police Strategies & Management,* Vol. 20 (1997), p. 62.

[33]Ibid., p. 64.

[34]Commission on Accreditation for Law Enforcement Agencies, Inc. *Standards for Law Enforcement Agencies: The Standards Manual of the Law Enforcement Agency Accreditation Program* (Fairfax, VA: Fourth Edition, 1999), Standard 44.

[35]Kenney, Fuller, and Barry, *Police Work with Juveniles,* pp. 107–108.

[36]Innovations in American Government, "Restorative Community Conferencing," www.innovations.harvard.edu.

chapter 6

THE JUVENILE COURT

The mission of the juvenile or family court in addressing delinquency should be defined by carefully balancing competing, yet complementary goals—the welfare of children and the protection of the community. Since youths are developmentally different from each other, the correction of juvenile delinquents through services that are expressly designed to treat their behaviors and problems in an individualized fashion is best capable of preventing future offenses. Because they are developmentally and socially different from adults, they are more likely to be rehabilitated by carefully designed and tested treatment programs than by a purely punishment-based sanction system. The child protection focus of the court must receive even more attention than it has now. The court should work to integrate child welfare and delinquency services in the community and in the juvenile justice system.

— Robert E. Shepard, Jr.

CHAPTER OVERVIEW

A juvenile court is a judicial tribunal established to deal in a special way with children's cases. Juvenile courts exist in most jurisdictions throughout the country; they are also known as *family courts*. Regardless of the name, the functions and duties of these courts are the same. They handle only cases involving children up to statutorily defined ages, usually from 10 to 18. The juvenile court hears cases involving neglect, dependency, child abuse, and delinquency.

Referrals to the juvenile court generally come from parents, school agencies, or law enforcement officers. The majority comes from the police.

The juvenile court may be a completely separate court with a given jurisdiction or it may be a functional component of another court. Juvenile courts established by state constitutions require special legislation to define the powers that these courts may exercise. The authority of the juvenile court depends on the legislative body and its current attitudes. A state legislature can also decide to place the duties and functions of the juvenile court with other courts, granting these courts authority by statute. In Washington, for example, the superior court in each county functions as a juvenile court; in New York, there is a family court in each county; and, in Ohio, a few counties have an independent juvenile court, whereas other counties hear juvenile matters in the court of common pleas.

Juvenile courts have been described in a number of ways. "Throughout the brief history of the juvenile court, the debate on the nature of the court has often been ambiguous, leading to the conclusion that the juvenile court is a polymorphous agency which changes its identity like a chameleon, sometimes assuming the role of a criminal court, at other times serving as a social welfare agency, and in the interim being the kindly, benevolent father figure for those children who behave in an anti-social manner."[1]

It is this bipolar structure of the juvenile court system as both a court of law and a social service agency that has come under so much criticism of late. Many leading criminologists have attacked the juvenile court's tendency to over legislate morality and to disguise punishment as treatment.

Rulings and pronouncements on the purpose, role, and definition of the juvenile court have been issued over the years. Here is a sample:[2]

- The purpose of the statutes creating juvenile courts was not to provide additional courts for the punishment of crime; rather, the purpose is to establish special tribunals having jurisdiction within prescribed limits, of cases relating to the moral, physical, and mental well-being of children to the end that they may be directed away from paths of crime.[3]
- A district court's jurisdiction encompasses all criminal offenses and exclusive original jurisdiction over all felonies and of all persons brought therein charged with the commission of crime. The juvenile court is not a separate and distinct court, but the district court with enlarged powers.[4]
- The juvenile court is not a criminal court, but rather a statutory court having special jurisdiction of a parental nature over delinquent and neglected children, and its purpose and procedure are governed by rules applicable in civil cases.[5]

- Juvenile courts are generally defined as courts having special jurisdiction of a parental nature over delinquent and dependent children and are frequently referred to as specialized courts.[6]
- The juvenile court is not designed as a trial court in the ordinary sense. Its purpose is more informative than punitive, and its operating methods differ decidedly from those of a criminal court. Technicalities and formalities are largely done away with, and its simple procedure is designed to gain the confidence of those coming before it, and to enable the judge to best control and guide his or her wards, with more consideration for the future development than their past shortcomings.[7]
- The objectives of a statute creating a juvenile court are to provide measures of guidance and rehabilitation for the child and protection of society, not to fix criminal responsibility, guilt, and punishment.[8]
- In *Gault*, the Supreme Court stated that the extension to children of fundamental constitutional procedural rights . . . does not mean a total substitution of the adult criminal system for the present children's system.[9] The court further stated that "the problems of preadjudicative treatment of juveniles . . . are unique to the juvenile process; hence what we hold in this opinion with regard to the procedural requirements at the adjudicative stage has no necessary applicability to other steps of the juvenile process.[10]
- The [District of Columbia] Court of Appeals held that "there is sufficient dissimilarity between juvenile proceedings to deny application of the doctrine (pretrial discovery) to this issue. Criminal trials are comparatively formalistic. But flexible and informal procedures are essential to the *parens patriae* function of the juvenile court, and we have not been made aware that the juvenile court in this jurisdiction departs in practice from that philosophy."[11]

One theme that threads itself throughout the juvenile court as just described is that the juvenile court is not to be the same as an adult court. Just how much longer this distinction will continue to survive is, however, debatable. The *Gault* decision, for example, for all practical purposes destroyed the concept of *parens patriae* in the juvenile court. And with *Gault, Kent, Winship,* and others there has been a definite trend away from the informal, paternalistic models of the past in favor of greater formality. This trend has also created serious stresses in the administration of the juvenile justice and juvenile court systems.

There are those, however, who feel that granting the juvenile court the full adversary functions and duties of the adult court would greatly hamper and detract from its informal approach. In *McKeiver v. Pennsylvania,* for example, where the major question being raised was a juvenile's right to trial by jury (a right fully granted to adults), Justice Blackmun stated that

> Imposition of trial by jury as a matter of constitutional precept [in juvenile proceedings] would (1) possibly remake the juvenile proceeding into a fully adversary process, (2) put an effective end to the idealistic prospect of an intimate, informal, protective proceeding, (3) not strengthen greatly, if at all, the fact-finding function, (4) provide an attrition of the juvenile court's assumed ability to function in a unique manner, (5) not remedy the defects of the juvenile court system, (6) impede further state experimentation in dealing with the problems of the young, and (7) inject into the juvenile court system with traditional delay, the formality, and the clamor of the adversary system and, possibly, the public trial.[12]

The reality of the situation, in spite of any one group's likes or dislikes, has been vastly altered by the Institute of Judicial Administration/ American Bar Association (IJA/ABA) Juvenile Justice Standards Project and the Juvenile Justice and Delinquency Prevention Act. Further discussion of the Standards Project and the Juvenile Justice Act, and of the role and future of the juvenile court, will be taken up later in this chapter. For now, let us briefly examine the history and background of the juvenile court and court system.

History of the Juvenile Court

The juvenile court system in America was part of a movement aimed at removing youngsters from the criminal law process and creating special programs for delinquent, dependent, and neglected children.

The English common law concept of *parens patriae* was a major influence on the development of American juvenile law and eventually the juvenile court. The development of the juvenile court stemmed from the court of Chancery jurisdiction of England, which provided special consideration for children. Under this jurisdiction the crown asserted the power of *parens patriae* over children on the assumption that they were wards of the state. Until a special judicial tribunal for children was set up in Massachusetts in 1874 and the first official juvenile court was created in Cook County, Illinois, in 1899, criminal jurisdiction over juveniles lay with the regular criminal courts.

Increased urbanization, industrialization, immigration, and a growing concern for crime prevention in the nineteenth century led to various reform and welfare movements regarding children. One of these movements—the wave of humanitarian efforts by feminist groups (such as the Chicago Women's Club and Hull House), penologists, and philanthropists—led to the founding of the juvenile court in Illinois. Based on a medical model of scientific investigation, the juvenile court's original goals were to investigate, diagnose, and prescribe treatment, not to adjudicate guilt or to fix blame. Lawyers were not seen as necessary as the juvenile courts would not be of an adversary nature. In fact, the traditional juvenile court became part of a juvenile justice system that expressed considerable leniency and tolerance toward youths who engaged in antisocial conduct. Instead of processing children through a formal criminal justice system where they would be stigmatized as criminals and subject to punishment, the state would deal with delinquents in an *ex parte* civil process, which was to be both benign and paternalistic.

For some, the reforms that preceded the development of the juvenile court and those that followed were not sufficient. Judge Julian Mack, a well-known judge in the early juvenile court, commented on the juvenile court's development as an outgrowth of the general reform movement in the treatment of children: "What we did not have was the conception that a child that broke the law was to be dealt with by the State as a wise parent would deal with a wayward youth."[13]

Once conceived, the idea of juvenile courts spread with amazing speed. In April 1899, the Illinois legislature passed the Juvenile Court Act, which created the first statewide court for children. The Juvenile Court Act brought dependency, neglect, and delinquency cases under one jurisdiction and created features that have since characterized the juvenile court in the United States.

Within twelve years, thirty-two states had followed Illinois's example, and by 1925 all but two states had juvenile courts. By 1975, juvenile courts had jurisdiction over youth under 18. They could only be transferred to adult court, if the juvenile court waived its jurisdiction.[14]

Much has been written regarding the humanitarian philosophy behind the development of the juvenile court. The more traditional explanations of the "child-saving movement" have emphasized the noble sentiments and tireless energy of middle-class philanthropists. But well-intentioned people who desired to save children were not solely responsible for the acceptance of the juvenile court concept. The development of the court, and of similar reforms in corrections, was born out of the needs of the times. It was looked upon as a solution to the increasing numbers of homeless, wayward, and delinquent youths. If the conditions that helped to produce so many delinquent youths had not occurred, the juvenile court might never have been necessary.

The original goals of the juvenile court were based on the concept that children needed the state to act as a kindly parent and protect them from the severity of adult courts and penal institutions. The emphasis was on the child's need and not the deed. Courts were concerned primarily with rehabilitation and treatment, not with guilt or punishment or even innocence. The desire was to provide a range of treatment options to serve "the best interests of the child." The treatment would be administered until the child was "cured" or became an adult (age 21).

By the 1960s, this rehabilitation ideal had been called into question. Landmark Supreme Court decisions (as discussed in Chapter 7) led to the protection of the due process rights of juveniles. The Juvenile Justice and Delinquency Prevention Acts of 1968 and 1974 (and amendments passed in 1980) made several changes in juvenile justice operations. By the 1980s, the juvenile court system was viewed as too lenient, especially in dealing with violent crimes, and waiver procedures to adult court were established.[15]

JUVENILE COURT JURISDICTION

A good definition of jurisdiction as it applies to the juvenile court is as follows:

> Jurisdiction of a court is that power conferred upon it by law, by which it is authorized to hear, determine, and render final judgment in an action, and to enforce its judgments by legal process.[16]

Before the juvenile court can make its valid, enforceable order, the case must be brought properly before the court and the court must then make a finding. Certain requirements must exist before the case can be brought before the court. The court must have geographical jurisdiction over the accused. The court must also have jurisdiction over the conduct of the juvenile. Almost every juvenile court has jurisdiction over delinquency, dependency (incorrigibility), and abuse cases. Some extend this jurisdiction to adoptions, court-ordered support, paternity actions, divorce, permanent termination of parental rights, custody over mentally ill or retarded children, and, less often, family offenses and foster care placement and review. Therefore, the subject youth upon which the order is made must by law fall into one of the categories granted by statute to the juvenile court.

The age of the child is also a jurisdictional element. State statutes define both minimum and maximum age limits. For example, sixteen states set the youngest age for juvenile court delinquency jurisdiction. The youngest is 6 years of age in North Carolina. However, in cases involving status offenses, abuse, neglect, or dependency matters, many states have jurisdiction through age 20. It is recognized that there is really no established chronological age at which a child becomes sufficiently mature so that delinquency jurisdiction should thereafter begin. Under ideal circumstances, the selection of a minimum age should be based upon the juvenile's maturation level. There seems little sense in authorizing juvenile court delinquency jurisdiction over juveniles too immature or too young to realize that they have committed a criminal act.

While typically set at 18, the maximum age in delinquency cases is set as low as 15 in Connecticut, New York, and North Carolina and as high as 24 in California, Montana, Oregon, and Wisconsin.[17] The U.S. Children's Bureau recommends age 18 as the upper jurisdictional age limit. Approximately two-thirds of the states adhere to this recommendation. However, it is statutorily possible for the juvenile court judge to seek a transfer *(bind over)* of a juvenile to an adult criminal court. This usually occurs when the juvenile is older and has committed certain serious acts, such as murder or rape. Some geographic jurisdictions, in fact, automatically exempt from the juvenile courts juveniles 16 or older "charged by the United States attorney with murder, forcible rape, burglary in the first degree, armed robbery, or assault with intent to commit any such offense."[18] The Supreme Court has passed on such exemptions and has found them to be constitutional.[19]

Jurisdictional Problems

The juvenile courts are faced with certain problems when they lose jurisdictional rights over a juvenile who has reached the upper age limit. As frequently occurs, the juvenile will pass the upper age limit of the juvenile court's jurisdiction before the charges against him or her are adjudicated. The juvenile court must then decide from what point to measure the juvenile's age for jurisdictional purposes. Some courts measure the youth's age from the date of the offense. Others use the time of the judicial proceedings as the deciding factor, and still others measure from the date the actual trial begins. Most state codes provide that juvenile court jurisdiction attaches at the time of the offense, as opposed to the juvenile's age at the time of arrest or adjudication. Under these laws a juvenile who commits an offense prior to his eighteenth birthday remains subject to juvenile court jurisdiction even if age 18 is reached before the time of apprehension or adjudication. The model acts uniformly support this position. There are, however, a fair number of state codes that take a contrary position. According to the Task Force on Juvenile Justice and Delinquency Prevention, such a position can be problematic.[20] If the age of the juvenile at the time of arrest and/or adjudication is used to govern the juvenile court's jurisdiction, the possibility exists that police might delay making an arrest and/or prosecutors might delay initiating proceedings against a juvenile who is close to his or her eighteenth birthday until that juvenile has passed that maximum age. This would allow police and/or prosecutorial discretion unintended by the statutes by setting the stage for the juvenile's prosecution in an adult court.

State statutes giving the juvenile court jurisdiction over delinquents within a certain age range apply to dependents as well. The element of need of treatment and rehabilitation becomes a factor here. It is generally conceded that the status offender, who has committed no criminal offense, has different needs from a delinquent counterpart. It is also agreed that these needs, which are not being met by the juvenile court, can best be served elsewhere. In Ohio, a juvenile who attempts to marry without parental consent comes under the jurisdiction of the juvenile court. Georgia makes it illegal for a juvenile to patronize a bar. Adding cases of this nature to the juvenile court docket is questionable, at best. And, as previous discussion in this chapter has suggested, the juvenile court's delinquency jurisdiction over noncriminal offenders should be seriously questioned, debated, and challenged.

The jurisdiction of juvenile courts varies from state to state. The state legislature or other rule-making body decides what the court's jurisdiction will be. Since there are no federal juvenile courts, juvenile court jurisdiction is a matter for state policy. Juveniles under the age of 18 who violate a federal law not punishable by death or life imprisonment may have their case transferred to the juvenile court of the state in which they reside. The juvenile court can enforce its orders by legal action and should not therefore make an order that cannot be enforced by such action. According to Hahn, there are three prerequisites that the court must meet before it can make an enforceable, binding order. They are the following:

- The subject (person) upon whom the order is made must fall within one of the categories granted by statute to the juvenile court.
- Service of summons in accord with the particular statutory requirements, and the case law interpreting same, must have been had (subject to emergency orders).
- After service, a hearing, in accord with the procedures set forth in the *Gault* case, must have been had, and the court must have found, not by the civil standard or degree of proof of a mere preponderance of the evidence, but by the criminal court standard of "beyond a reasonable doubt," that the juvenile has been found to be delinquent or is otherwise within the jurisdiction of the court.[21]

Transfer of Juveniles to Adult Criminal Court

Although most transfers of jurisdiction, whether sought by the law enforcement official, a probation officer, the prosecutor, and the juvenile defendant himself or herself, or the court, involve older youths, the transfer of young defendants is not out of the question.

Before the American juvenile court was invented in 1899, juvenile offenders were treated no differently than adults. Under the infancy defense, children under age 7 were immune from prosecution because they lacked moral responsibility. Prosecutors had to prove that children between ages 7 and 14 were criminally responsible and that the individual juvenile was culpable. Beyond the age of 14, juveniles were deemed as responsible for their criminal acts as adults.[22] Under *parens patriae,* the aim of the juvenile court was to treat young offenders separately and rehabilitate them. Yet, by the 1940s, several states had procedures in place to try juveniles as adults if they met certain age and offense criteria.

Transfer is another example of the get-tough movement against juvenile crime. There are several ways that waiver fits into this punitive philosophy. First, it directly addresses public disgust with the "lenient" juvenile justice system by making a stand against delinquency. Second, it can allow the juvenile court to focus upon those juveniles who need services and attention beyond the problem of delinquency. Third, transfer aims to reduce juvenile crime through incapacitation—dealing with the most serious crimes and criminals. The hope is that the deterrent effect of sentencing will reduce juvenile crime.[23]

The boundaries of juvenile court jurisdiction changed as state legislatures became concerned about the seriousness of juvenile offenses. The rehabilitative focus on the individual case was lost. From 1992 through 1997, forty-four states and the District of Columbia passed laws to try juveniles as adults.

The mechanisms in place to transfer juveniles to criminal court vary according to the decision maker responsible for the waiver. They fall into three general categories:

- **Judicial waiver:** The juvenile court judge has the authority to waive juvenile court jurisdiction and transfer the case to criminal court. States may use terms other than judicial waiver. Some call the process *certification, remand,* or *bind over* for criminal prosecution. Others *transfer* or *decline* rather than waive jurisdiction. In most states, judicial waiver provisions are limited by age and offense criteria or to juveniles who are "no longer amenable to treatment" as a result of their offense and disposition history.

- **Concurrent jurisdiction:** Both criminal and juvenile courts share original jurisdiction for certain cases, and the prosecutor has discretion to file such cases in either court. Transfer under concurrent jurisdiction provisions is also known as *prosecutorial waiver, prosecutor discretion,* or *direct file.*

- **Statutory exclusion:** As of 1997, twenty-eight states had these provisions in the law, excluding certain juvenile offenders from juvenile court jurisdiction. Under statutory exclusion provisions, cases originate in criminal rather than juvenile court. Typically, they target certain serious, violent, or repeat juvenile offenders. Statutory exclusion is also known as *legislative exclusion* and *mandatory waiver.* In 1996, an estimated 218,000 juvenile cases were tried in adult criminal court under such provisions.[24]

Twenty-five states have no minimum age specified in their statutes. The youngest minimum age (10) is registered by Vermont and Kansas. Colorado, Missouri, and Montana list 12, whereas Illinois, Mississippi, New Hampshire, New York, North Carolina, and Wyoming use 13 as the minimum age for waiver. Sixteen state statutes specify 14 as the minimum age for transferring juveniles to adult court. The oldest minimum belongs to New Mexico at 15.[25] Between 1989 and 1994, the number of delinquency cases waived to criminal court rose by 51 percent. From this peak, it declined 33 percent through 1998.[26]

The U.S. Supreme Court in the *Kent* decision established the rights of juveniles under the transfer process. Here, the Court highlighted the due process rights of juveniles that must be provided for in the waiver decision. Juveniles have the right to the following:

- A hearing on the motion to waive jurisdiction of the juvenile court.
- Legal representation in waiver proceedings.
- For that counsel to have access to records and reports used to reach the waiver decision.
- A written statement of reasons for the decision made by the court.

These procedures were incorporated into transfer proceedings.[27]

Another option between juvenile and adult court jurisdiction is **blended sentencing.** By the end of 1997, twenty states had blended sentencing statutes. They allow courts to impose juvenile and/or adult correctional sanctions on certain young offenders. The juvenile court can impose an adult sentence or extend their sentencing jurisdiction into early adulthood. Typically, they cover the same class of serious or violent juvenile offenders as the various transfer provisions listed above. Here is a listing of the types of blended sentencing available:

- Juvenile-exclusive blend: The juvenile court may impose a sanction involving either the juvenile or adult correctional systems (example: New Mexico).
- Juvenile-inclusive blend: The juvenile court may impose both juvenile and adult correctional sanctions. The adult sanction is suspended pending a violation and revocation (examples: Connecticut, Kansas, Minnesota, Montana).
- Juvenile-contiguous blend: The juvenile court may impose a juvenile correctional sanction that may remain in force after the offender is beyond the age of the court's extended jurisdiction. At that point, the offender may be transferred to the adult correctional system (examples: Colorado, Massachusetts, Rhode Island, South Carolina, Texas).

- Criminal-exclusive blend: The criminal court may impose a sanction involving either the juvenile or adult correctional systems (examples: California, Colorado, Florida, Idaho, Michigan, Oklahoma, Virginia, West Virginia).
- Criminal-inclusive blend: The criminal court may impose both juvenile and adult correctional sanctions. The adult sanction is suspended, but is reinstated if the terms of the juvenile sanction are violated and revoked (examples: Arkansas, Iowa, Missouri, Virginia).[28]

Blended sentencing schemas have the potential to insulate eligible juveniles from the negative consequences of transfer but also raise the possibility that widening of the net will occur.

In their review of blended sentencing in Colorado and Michigan, Redding and Howell make several recommendations regarding its use. They maintain that blended sentencing should operate out of the juvenile court. The adult or extended juvenile sentence should be conditionally suspended if the juvenile is successfully rehabilitated and does not commit a new offense. The juvenile court judge should have authority over the transfer decision. Since they make up the bulk of juveniles targeted for transfer, blended sentencing should be targeted for use with habitual offenders.[29]

Several studies have examined the factors that influence the waiver decision. These factors are related to the discretionary powers of the actors involved, either judges or prosecutors, depending upon the type and nature of the waiver involved.

- Offense: Juveniles convicted of violent crimes were more likely to be waived.[30]
- Race: African-Americans were consistently treated more harshly than whites.[31]
- Age: Older juveniles were more likely to be transferred than younger juveniles.[32]
- Prior record: Juveniles with more prior referrals were more likely to be waived.[33]
- Family structure: Juveniles from single parent households were more likely to be transferred.[34]
- Gang membership and drug use: Transfer to adult court was more likely for juvenile gang members.[35]

Of course, the most important issue here is race. The other variables could be viewed as evidence that the transfer process is working—targeting the most serious offenders and their offenses. But discrimination is unacceptable. Minority communities lack the resources to fully prevent delinquency, including specialized juvenile programs. Many of the other listed variables (prior record, gang involvement) are strongly correlated with race. The system must be careful to avoid racial profiling, allowing bias to influence transfer procedures. Treatment and punishment must not be selectively based on race.[36]

Figure 6.1 presents statistics on delinquency cases waived to adult criminal court between 1988, 1993, and 1997. The percentage of waived delinquency cases involving personal crimes rose dramatically between 1988 and 1993 but declined slightly in 1997. Property crime cases waived fell to 38 percent in 1993 and remained at that level in 1997. Drug cases waived to adult court rose to 15 percent of the total number of cases in 1997, indicating an increased problem with substance abuse. The number of public order cases fell to 7 percent of the total in 1997. It is also notable that the number of waived cases rose substantially in 1993 but fell just as dramatically in 1997. This finding indicates that the type of cases transferred to adult court is in decline.

OPERATIONS UNDER THE JUVENILE COURT

The operation of the juvenile court system is not autonomous. It is, instead, dependent upon society at large, the juvenile justice system as a whole, and the dictates of individual communities. Without adequate integration of the court within these parameters, it would be like a horse without a rider—possibly going somewhere, but lacking direction on the best way to get there. Juvenile Justice Box 6.1 lists the important factors that separate juvenile court proceedings and adult criminal proceedings.

Most Serious Offense	1988	1993	1997
Person	28%	43%	40%
Property	53%	38%	38%
Drugs	11%	11%	15%
Public Order	8%	9%	7%
Number of Waived Cases	6,700	11,000	8,400

FIGURE 6.1 Offense Profile of Delinquency Cases Waived to Criminal Court in 1988, 1993, and 1997. *Source:* Charles Puzzanchera, Anne L. Stahl, Terrance A. Finnegan, Howard N. Synder, Rowen S. Poole, and Nancy Tierney, *Juvenile Court Statistics 1997* (Washington, DC: Office of Juvenile Justice and Delinquency Prevention, 2000), p. 14.

Box 6.1 Terms of Juvenile Proceedings

The principal features that distinguish current juvenile delinquency proceedings from adult criminal proceedings can be summarized as follows:

1. **Absence of legal guilt.** Legally, juveniles are not found guilty of crimes but are "found to be delinquent." Juveniles are not held legally responsible for their acts. Juvenile status, like insanity, is a defense against criminal responsibility. It is not, however, an absolute defense because of the possibility of waiver to criminal court.

2. **Treatment rather than punishment.** Whatever action the court takes following a finding of delinquency is done in the name of treatment or community protection, not punishment, as is the case for adult felony offenders.

3. **Absence of public scrutiny.** Juvenile proceedings and records are generally closed to the public. What goes on in court is presumed to be the business only of juveniles and their families. This position clearly has its roots in the early child-saving mission of the court. Hearings for serious juvenile offenders are now being opened to the public.

4. **Importance of a juvenile's background.** Juveniles' needs and amenability to treatment can, it is widely presumed, be deduced from their social history, prior behavior, and clinical diagnosis. This presumption is used to justify the wide discretionary powers granted to probation officers in screening petitions, to the court in deciding fitness and making dispositions, and to youth correction agencies in deciding when a ward should be released.

5. **No long-term incarceration.** Terms of confinement for juveniles are considerably shorter than those for adults.

6. **Separateness.** The juvenile system is kept separate from the adult criminal justice system at every point, from detention at arrest to the identities of the officials who handle the case in court, and in subsequent placements as well.

7. **Speed and flexibility.** Delinquency cases are disposed of more quickly than comparable adult criminal cases, and the juvenile court judge has a broader range of disposition alternatives.

The juvenile justice system is comprised of people who make decisions. It is not institutions, buildings, or agencies. Similarly, the juvenile court, which has been referred to as an institution, should portray itself in a more personal and humanistic way as a group of flesh-and-blood people, both those helping and those being helped.

Juvenile court statistics reveal the amount and nature of cases dealt with. For example, juvenile courts handled almost 1.8 million delinquency cases in 1997—an increase of 48 percent over the number processed in 1988.[37] In fact, juvenile courts handled four times more cases in 1996 than they did in 1960.[38]

Figure 6.2 presents the manner in which delinquency cases were processed by juvenile courts in 1997. Among petitioned cases, probation was the most common sanction—55 percent of the adjudicated and 21 percent of the nonadjudicated cases. A high percentage of both the nonpetitioned (44 percent) and the nonadjudicated (59 percent) cases were likely to be dismissed.

Across age groups, the percentage of delinquency case rates increased for all groups except age 10 (down 5 percent). The greatest increase was among persons age 16 (39 percent).[39] Males were involved in 77 percent of the delinquency cases handled by juvenile courts in 1997 and were responsible for the majority of person (74 percent), property (76 percent), drug (85 percent), and public order (76 percent) offense cases.[40] While female cases have risen sharply, their pattern did not match the

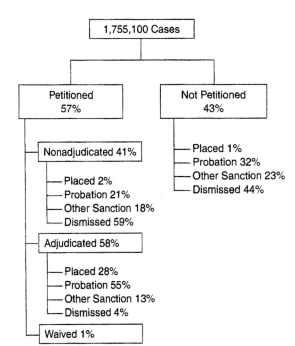

FIGURE **6.2** Juvenile Court Processing of Delinquency Cases, 1997. *Source:* Charles Puzzanchera, Anne L. Stahl, Terrance A. Finnegan, Howard N. Synder, Rowen S. Poole, and Nancy Tierney, *Juvenile Court Statistics 1997* (Washington, DC: Office of Juvenile Justice and Delinquency Prevention, 2000), p. 9.

severity of male cases. In 1997, female cases were less likely to involve drug law violations (7 versus 12 percent) but were more likely to involve personal offenses (25 versus 21 percent).[41]

By race, the number of delinquency cases involving white youths increased 43 percent between 1988 and 1997. Cases involving black and youth of other races increased 57 percent. Among all three groups, the smallest increase was registered among property offenses. For black juveniles, public order cases showed the greatest increase (112 percent). Among white juveniles and youths of other races, drug cases increased the most (144 percent and 137 percent each).[42] In terms of detention, the greatest variation between races was for drug law violations. 38 percent of the drug violation cases involving blacks were detained, compared to 16 percent of those involving youths of other races and 14 percent of white youth cases.[43]

The Court Intake Function

As Figure 6.2 revealed, over half of all cases referred to juvenile intake do not proceed to the point of formal adjudication. Because of this and the fact that the intake process often presents the initial contact between the juvenile and/or his or her family and the juvenile justice system, the **court intake function** must be considered one of the most important components of the entire juvenile justice system. How, when, and for what purpose it is utilized affects not only the youth whose future it may hold in the balance but the community as well.

Most juvenile courts have established a system whereby inappropriate cases are diverted from their attention. Called the *intake, screening, and adjustment process,* its dominant goal is to divert the juvenile from the court in order to prevent unnecessary court proceedings.

The police actually initiates intake screening outside the court in many cases. The police make extensive and informal adjustments in the field and at the police station. Factors that influence this decision include the following:

- The prior record of the youth. Prosecutors especially note this factor.
- The type of offense and the role of the juvenile in it.
- The attitude of the victim or complainant.
- The family situation of the offender.
- The potential community resources that might be utilized for correction.
- The general appearance and attitude of the offender toward the police.
- The possible overcrowding at the Youth Study Center.
- The police officer's anticipation of the juvenile court action should an arrest be made.[44]

The final point creates confusion and frustration for both the police and the courts. How often have you heard this statement on one of the police shows on television: "What good does it do for us to arrest them, when the courts just turn around and set them free?" Cooperation is up to the police and the courts on this matter. Police departments must make sure that their staffs are educated in the legal and technical aspects of juvenile court policy. Juvenile courts must share and update their policies with the police and other agencies that might encounter the delinquent, dependent, or abused child.

If the police determine that court action is appropriate or if someone else has filed a petition, it is normally the juvenile court's probation staff that continues the intake screening process. The dispositional screening by the probation staff is the crux of the court's intake and screening process. In its initial stages it will involve short investigations, social studies, and informal hearings that frequently involve both parents and child. After considering and weighing the information gathered at this point of the intake screening process, the probation staff determines a course of action. The case may be dismissed, disposed of in an informal manner such as informal probation, or the probation officer may feel that a formal petition requesting appropriate adjudication should be filed. The probation staff also determines where the juvenile should be detained pending court action. While some state statutes extend to juveniles the right to bail, most youths are released to their parents, unless, of course, circumstances of the case actually require detention.

It has already been stated in this chapter that the juvenile courts suffer from a definite lack of clearly written guidelines. Coupled with the movement to add further legalized procedures to all stages of juvenile court proceedings, this criticism has caused legislators and professionals in the field to seek formal guidelines to govern prejudicial proceedings of which intake and screening are major components. However, the American Bar Association has established standards for juvenile court proceedings that will serve as the basis of our examination of juvenile court operations.

Attorneys in the Juvenile Court

As the juvenile courts move closer to becoming adversarial, the presence of attorneys in the courtroom will become commonplace. In the *Gault* decision, the Supreme Court held that a juvenile accused of committing a crime had the right to counsel. Legal advocacy can begin at the prejudicial stage of the court process or during the trial itself. While attorneys representing juveniles are now generally accepted as a fact of life, the role of the prosecuting attorney has been less readily accepted. Traditional juvenile court process did not include a prosecutor in the sense of a legally trained person to represent the state in court proceedings. Prior to *Gault*, it was the accepted notion that adversaries (and therefore lawyer-advocates, whether for the child or the state) were best kept out of the juvenile court. Since *Gault,* many such notions have been abandoned. The rationale is as follows:

- The prosecutor is an advocate of the State's interest in juvenile court. The "State's interest" is complex and may vary with the type of proceeding and the nature of the particular case. Foremost, it includes (a) protection of the community from the danger of harmful conduct by the restraint and rehabilitation of juvenile offenders, and (b) concern, shared by all juvenile justice system personnel, as *parens patriae,* with promotion of the best interests of juveniles.
- To the extent that the State's interest in community protection may conflict with its interest as *parens patriae* in promoting the well being of a particular child, the prosecutor will be required to balance the interests based upon the nature and facts of the particular case. For example, to the extent that interests have to be balanced in given cases, the balance should be struck in favor of community protection when the juvenile presents a substantial threat to public safety, but of promoting the well-being of a child for most other types of offenses.
- In his role as advocate, the prosecutor has responsibility to ensure adequate preparation and presentation of the State's case, from the stage of police investigation through postdisposition proceedings.[45]

For these reasons, the American Bar Association has recommended that juveniles in court be provided with quality legal representation. The juvenile defense attorney must perform a number of crucial tasks, including (1) gathering information regarding clients' individual histories, families, schooling, and community ties, in order to assist courts in diverting appropriate cases; (2) preventing unnecessary pretrial detention, avoiding unnecessary transfers to adult court, and ordering individualized dispositions. They must protect their clients' interests at every stage of the proceedings, from arrest and detention to pretrial proceedings, from adjudication to disposition to postdispositional matters.[46]

Process and Authority of the Juvenile Court Proceeding

Once a case approaches or reaches the point of an adjudicatory hearing, the judge has the most extensive discretionary power in disposing of the case. It is interesting to note that juvenile court legislation does not specify the type of formal response that the juvenile is to make to the charges brought against him or her. The judge will generally, however, accept the common plea of guilty or not guilty.

The Supreme Court held, in *In re Winship,* that the proof against a juvenile must be beyond a reasonable doubt.[47] In juvenile cases the defense has a great advantage over the prosecution in regard to the standard of proof. The defense need only raise a reasonable doubt. The prosecution must establish each and every element of the crime or ungovernable act, and, in so doing, establish the court's jurisdiction beyond a reasonable doubt.

Again, the ABA stresses the need for quality defense counsel in these proceedings. Many public defenders and private counsel are not appointed until the detention hearing. In several locations, a single attorney handles most detention hearings and accepts the appointment of counsel for a panel of attorneys. Cases are then sent "downtown" for proper assignment of counsel later on, delaying the beginning of actual representation for many days.[48]

Adjudication

In the juvenile court, the adjudication hearing is relatively formal and is attended by the judicial officer, county attorney, defense attorney and the juvenile. Normally, the parents and/or guardians and a juvenile probation officer also attend, along with any victims or witnesses required. Typically, juvenile proceedings begin with a petition. The petition alleges that the juvenile is delinquent, neglected or abused, dependent, or in need of supervision. This petition can be filed by any interested party (police, prosecution, probation officers, victims, parents, etc.). It lists the charges and defines why the court has jurisdiction over the case and lists the options available to the court. It also informs the juvenile and his/her family of the charges made so that adequate representation may be acquired and a defense prepared.

The juvenile delinquency adjudication proceeding is like a bench trial in adult criminal court. Since detention is a possible outcome, juveniles have certain recognized constitutional rights to due process clause, such as the assistance of counsel, the privilege against self-incrimination, and the right to confront and cross-examine adverse witnesses and proof beyond reasonable doubt.[49]

Motions in Juvenile Court Proceedings

The proceedings in most juvenile courts remain informal, with most motions being presented orally. However, it is advisable to put some motions in writing.

That the motion is in writing, and hence ripe for purposes of appeal, is not lost on the judge. Written papers also prevent a judge unfamiliar with the particular question of law from being caught unawares and ignorant of the issues involved. Putting the judge in such a situation is impolitic and can be disastrous to an advocate's case. There is perhaps nothing more difficult than convincing a judge to reverse himself because he was "wrong."[50]

Both the defense and the prosecution should be aware of and prepared to respond to the various motions that can be made at the pretrial stage of the juvenile court process. There are four such major categories of motions, each with several subcategories. They are:

- Motions addressed to face the petition
- Motions addressed to the preparation of the case
- Motions addressed to the conduct of hearings or the trial
- Motions seeking the termination of court proceedings

These motions are listed merely to acquaint the reader with their form. A thorough discussion of each separate motion is beyond the scope and intent of this text.[51]

Again, the ABA notes particular problems in the motions process. Here, high caseloads again create problems for adequate representation. Attorneys who barely have time to cover all of their cases on a particular day do not have the time or energy to research and write effective pretrial motions. The inadequacy (or absence) of training is another serious problem, as is lack of professional supports such as specialized texts, computerized legal research, access to paralegals, availability of bilingual staff or translators, and adequate space for interviewing and meeting with clients.[52]

The Trial

The entering of the plea, the motions and countermotions, and the plea bargaining are all preludes to the main event (if the case is not diverted first): the actual trial. The juvenile court trial is also referred to as a *fact-finding* or *adjudicatory hearing.*

Trial Motions

During the trial, the prosecution and defense present witnesses, seek or deny evidence, and generally argue the points of the case. There are a number of **trial motions** that can be made by either advocate. They are commonly (1) motions to strike evidence or lines of questioning, (2) motions to declare a mistrial, (3) motions to dismiss due to the failure to develop *prima facie* evidence, and (4) motions to dismiss because of failure to prove the case beyond a reasonable doubt.[53]

Dispositional Stage of Trial

After the opening statements, presentation of evidence, trial motions, and closing statements comes the dispositional stage of the trial. The dispositional power of the juvenile court is far broader and more discretionary than the criminal courts. The criminal courts prescribe sentences and lengths of sentences to meet the particular offense (e.g., five to twenty years for robbery). The juvenile courts do not. The length of juvenile court commitment is indefinite in most states, but cannot exceed the twenty-first birthday.

There are restrictions on the broad dispositional powers of the judges, however. Their decisions must be based realistically on the availability of diagnostic, rehabilitative, alternative, and treatment facilities. In fact, the dispositional process is a direct result of the alternatives available to each particular judge in each and every court.

Juvenile court judges are empowered to do the following:

- Dismiss the case
- Suspend judgment pending further study
- Order protection (e.g., order the parents to desist from behavior linked with causing the child's delinquency)
- Order probation
- Order commitment or placement in an institution

Whatever the pending disposition, it is wise for the court to be reminded that the more involved an offender becomes with the juvenile justice system, and the more often he or she is moved through it, the greater is the potential for continued delinquent behavior.

While institutionalization is the most controversial and criticized of all juvenile court dispositions, it is also generally the least often used. Massachusetts, for example, which institutionalized its large training schools statewide, commits only about 10 percent of its youths to secure (traditionally institutional) care.

Recently, the criminal and juvenile justice systems have moved away from the traditional court disposition based on judicial discretion. This trend has gained impetus with the juvenile court's coming of age as more of an adversary court. The movement concerns possible mandatory or maximum sentences for juveniles convicted of delinquent acts. A severity index list of crimes is developed and requires a specific, not indefinite sentence based upon the crime committed and the youth's attitude, background, and potential for rehabilitation. The imposition of mandatory or maximum sentences for juveniles is not yet a widely accepted or even acknowledged alternative to the present open-ended discretional powers of the court. But it may become so, in which case the serious student of juvenile justice will wish to keep abreast of its development.

Juvenile court judges often offer the youth an alternative to institutionalization, such as the payment of a fine, or restitution to the victim or public for damages, or both. One relatively new option is **restorative justice.** (See Box 6.2.)

Box 6.2 Balanced and Restorative Justice

Sponsored by the Office of Juvenile Justice and Delinquency Prevention (OJJDP), the Balanced and Restorative Justice (BARJ) Project promotes increased use of restitution, community service, victim-offender mediation, and other innovative programs designed to hold juvenile offenders accountable, protect the community, and develop the competency of juveniles. Through its grantee, Florida Atlantic University in Fort Lauderdale, Florida, OJJDP provides training, technical assistance, and information/resources to states and local jurisdictions interested in implementing BARJ programs.

One project in Indianapolis, Indiana, has produced the following results. Conferences were implemented in a fashion consistent with the philosophy and principles of restorative justice. They were more effective than many other court programs in addressing victim needs. Both parents and offending youth felt very much involved in the process.

In terms of future offending, research compared program completion data and recidivism rates of restorative justice conference participants with those of youth in a control group. *Recidivism* was defined as a re-arrest after the initial arrest that brought the youth to the juvenile justice system, and recidivism analysis was conducted for both groups at six- and twelve-month intervals.

- **Program completion.** Youth participating in restorative justice conferences demonstrated a significantly higher completion rate (82.6 percent) than youth in the control group, who were assigned to other diversion programs (57.7 percent).

- **Six-month re-arrest rates.** The restorative conference group included fewer recidivists than the control group by a margin of 13.5 percent. This statistically significant difference represents a 40 percent reduction in rates of re-arrest.

continued

Box 6.2 Balanced and Restorative Justice (continued)

- **Twelve-month re-arrest rates.** Of the full sample of youth participating in the restorative conference program, 30.1 percent had been re-arrested within 12 months, compared with 42.3 percent of youth in the control group. This statistically significant difference represents a 29 percent reduction in recidivism.

- **Rearrest rates by offense, sex, and race.** Researchers conducted limited analyses of six-month re-arrest rates for selected subgroups of offenders. Youth who committed offenses against property had lower re-arrest rates than youth who committed offenses against persons. This difference was comparable for conference and control group youth. Both males and females in the conference group experienced lower re-arrest rates than their counterparts in the control groups. This difference was greater for females than for males. There were no racial differences in re-arrest rates for conference and control group youth. The overall reduction in re-arrest rates found for conference group youth was the same for whites and nonwhites. Thus, the effects of conferences appear consistent for youth across groups based on offense, sex, and race.

These preliminary research findings indicate that alternatives to traditional juvenile court processing should continue to be considered and developed in the future.

Source: Edmund F. McGarrell, "Restorative Justice Conferences as an Early Response to Young Offenders," *OJJDP Juvenile Justice Bulletin,* (August 2001). Washington, DC: Office of Juvenile Justice and Delinquency Prevention.

THE JUVENILE COURT TODAY

What is it that hampers the effectiveness of the function and operation of the juvenile court today as in the past? The problem is one basic to most large social institutions. It is that juvenile courts are continually given more duties and responsibilities than resources with which to perform those duties and responsibilities. Today's juvenile court continues to carry a dual role (bipolar structure) that contributes to the results in its dysfunction as a social institution. Not only is the court expected to carry out its original purpose as a welfare agency for the rehabilitation of wayward youths, it is also expected to protect society from the foul deeds of the juvenile delinquent. It becomes readily apparent that, while providing a child with the elements of a good and useful life (education, economic security, and emotional maturity), the court's role may be entirely incompatible with its other function of protecting the public from his or her antisocial behavior.

Burdened with these two conflicting obligations, the court finds it difficult to perform either one to anyone's satisfaction. Regrettably, it is often used as a scapegoat for the problems of delinquency and the juvenile justice system as a whole. The divergent range of responsibilities given to the juvenile courts has therefore made them somewhat ineffectual. When one realizes that the juvenile court operates foster homes, detention facilities, aftercare facilities, treatment facilities, and offers welfare services for young people, the seriousness of the problem becomes clearer.

The court is also expected to handle teenage traffic offenses and child abuse and neglect cases and, in some instances, to provide the legal sanction for the adoption of children. On top of these duties it serves as the disciplinary arm of the schools and community and of parents who cannot control their unruly children.

Status Cases versus Delinquent Cases

Compounding the problems of the juvenile courts are the numbers of nondelinquent cases that, in spite of the provisions of and amendments to the 1974 Juvenile Justice Act, continue to overload court dockets. The juvenile court is generally reluctant to refuse to hear a case for which it has a legal responsibility. For example, juvenile courts are mandated to deal with incorrigible, neglected, abused, and/or dependent children. School truancy is a status offense. If the schools decide that they do not want to handle matters of truancy, they can shift the burden for those matters to the juvenile courts.

It is generally conceded among those in both the juvenile court systems and the field of juvenile corrections that status offenders should not be locked up, either prior to or following their dispositions. It is also generally agreed that their needs are better met by nonlegal social service agencies, family courts, or youth service bureaus. The juvenile courts, under this scheme, are then freed to focus on the problems of the delinquent juvenile.

In 1997, the total number of delinquency cases was estimated at 1,755,100—an increase of 48 percent over the 1988 total. Crimes against persons totaled 390,800 (led by simple assaults—248,800). Property offenses were listed at 841,800 (the highest was larceny-theft at 401,300). Public order and drug law violations registered 340,100 and 182,400 respectively.[54] Status offenses about doubled between 1988 and 1997, rising to an estimate of 158,500 cases. They were led by liquor (40,700) and truancy (40,500) violations.[55]

Status Offenders: Deed versus Need

Supreme Court rulings in the area of juvenile justice have led to a gradual switch from the court's original concern with the child's needs to a mandate to cope with the child's deeds. The courts have taken on a definite adversary atmosphere—an atmosphere of the criminal court.

Court rulings such as *In re Gault* and others have granted constitutional due process rights to juvenile offenders who have committed criminal acts. To our knowledge, status offenders have committed no criminal offenses. But if these rulings are interpreted literally, the courts could be mandated to provide the same constitutional rights to status offenders. They, too, are in jeopardy of being deprived of their freedom for an indefinite period of time. Status offenders are theoretically entitled to all of the due process rights granted to adults (with the exception of trial by jury, *McKeiver v. Pennsylvania*) when they are adjudicated in the juvenile courts. Demands by status offenders that these due process rights be enforced could drastically disrupt and tie up court dockets and create a major crisis for the juvenile courts.

Figure 6.3 presents statistics on the juvenile court processing of status offense cases in 1997. A slight majority (52 percent) of all status offense cases were adjudicated. Of these cases, probation (62 percent) was the leading sanction. Among the nonadjudicated cases, the majority (67 percent) was dismissed. These figures indicate that large portions of the status offense cases are removed from the juvenile justice system.

Much debate continues regarding the care, treatment, and even jurisdiction of the juvenile court over juveniles who commit status offenses. As mentioned earlier in this text, the **Juvenile Justice and Delinquency Prevention Act** of 1974 calls for the deinstitutionalization of status offenders, while the IJA/ABA **Juvenile Justice Standards Project** initiated in 1971 recommends the elimination of delinquency jurisdiction of the juvenile courts over the status offender. Most states, however, continue to include status offenders in the delinquency category. The remaining 40 percent or so have created special categories for the status offender using a variety of acronyms, which include PINS (Persons in Need of Supervision), MINS (Minors in Need of Supervision), CHINS (Children in Need of Supervision), JINS (Juveniles in Need of Supervision), and FWSN (Families with Service Needs). Regardless of what clever name they are given,

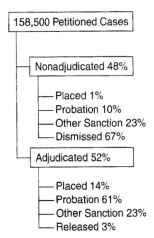

FIGURE 6.3 Juvenile Court Processing of Status Offense Cases, 1997. *Source:* Charles Puzzanchera, Anne L. Stahl, Terrance A. Finnegan, Howard N. Synder, Rowen S. Poole, and Nancy Tierney, *Juvenile Court Statistics 1997* (Washington, DC: Office of Juvenile Justice and Delinquency Prevention, 2000), p. 39.

the jurisdictional arrow is aimed at the same target—the judicial intervention into noncriminal cases.

The IJA/ABA Juvenile Justice Standards Project in February 1979 had seventeen of its original twenty-three volumes ratified. At that time, however, six of the most controversial standards were withdrawn. These included the volume on *NonCriminal Misbehavior,* which recommended the elimination of any juvenile court jurisdiction over the status offender. In February 1980 the ABA House of Delegates again refused to support the volume on *NonCriminal Misbehavior,* even though Judge Irving Kaufman, Chairman of the Juvenile Justice Standards Commission, stated that adoption of this volume would be the most important result of the commission's work. And, according to many in the field, the volume on *NonCriminal Misbehavior* is the philosophic cornerstone of the entire standards project.

The American Psychiatric Association (APA), via its Ad Hoc Task Force, has recently challenged the standards project on several issues.[56] The APA Task Force, for example, recommended the qualified retention of delinquency jurisdiction by the court, as opposed to total jurisdiction over certain acts by status offenders. These acts include severe and unresolved truancies, prolonged runaway behavior, and overt aggression. The APA Task Force also recommended encouraging sensitivity on the part of the juvenile courts to the developmental differences between children and adolescents and children and adults. The Task Force agreed that a juvenile who has not committed a crime by adult standards should not be subject to delinquency jurisdiction of the juvenile court. And, finally, the APA Task Force urged the juvenile court to establish specific services for serious noncriminal misbehavior.

When all is said and done, one issue paramount to the future of the juvenile court will be its handling of the status offender. And although it would appear to many in the field that the simplest solution would be the total removal of these offenders from any and all juvenile court jurisdiction, this might not only be ineffective but unrealistic as well. An analysis of status offenders nationwide will show a population beset by growing pains and problems. Jenkins reports that psychological testing of runaways (status offenders) using the Minnesota Multiphasic Inventory instrument revealed that they were more pathological than were their delinquent counterparts. This study also revealed that, compared with felony delinquents, runaways had higher recidivism and adult conviction rates. Males in the runaway group were characterized as typically much more rejected and unwanted with apparent failure in the parent-child relationship than were members of the delinquent group.[57]

If, in fact, the removal and/or diversion of status offenders from the juvenile court's jurisdiction are ever to become a reality, there must be workable alternatives. This action must be planned and coordinated carefully within the entire juvenile justice system, the community, and the appropriate government agencies, including the legislature. There is a need for traditional youth-serving agencies, such as the Scouts, YMCAs, Boys'

Clubs, to extend their capabilities to enable them to work toward meeting the needs of these nondelinquent youth; such services could include family-child conflict resolution, drug and alcohol abuse counseling, and counseling programs for boy and girl prostitutes. In any case, someone—if not the court, then social service agencies such as those mentioned must meet the needs of the status offender. To abandon this category of youths is not the answer.

Other Problems

Although the question of jurisdiction over status offenders and the failure of the court to define its role and set guidelines for its actions appear to be the major problems to be overcome by the juvenile justice system, the court's problems do not cease here.

Most state statutes invest the juvenile court judge with the powers to make rules, procedures, and appointments. However, if the judge fails to meet with other court personnel over a period of months or years to review the rules and procedures, the staff's ability to conduct the court's business properly can be hindered greatly. For example, if rules, procedures, and staff needs are not reviewed periodically, they will become outdated and difficult to administer. This could lead to case backlogs, delays, poor morale, and a decreased ability to function.

The operation of the juvenile court involves much more than the judicial treatment of cases. A number of juvenile courts have responsibilities for a variety of treatment and prevention-oriented options. For example, **juvenile drug courts** (see Box 6.3) have been established to focus substance abuse as a contributor to delinquency.

Defenders of the juvenile court blame the court's shortcomings on the lack of public support. They assert that the insufficient number of skilled personnel to staff the court's diagnostic treatment facilities and public disagreement over the court's role in the rehabilitative process are primary causes of court failure. They contend that the juvenile court plan is workable, if only someone would make a serious attempt to try it.

Juvenile courts are troubled by the lack of other resources also. In most court jurisdictions there is a growing need for adequate placement facilities for young people, such as foster homes, or halfway houses. There is also a lack-of-needed-service provision that could allow the placement of a youngster in his or her own home. Psychiatric services, for example, which are mentioned in most juvenile court standards, are in fact rarely provided in practice.

To overcome the shortage of placement possibilities and services, many court judges opt for the easy solution and simply commit the child to a juvenile institution. Others, who hesitate to do this, grasp at the barest of straws to keep the youth in the community. The result is a revolving-door policy. Children are released to the community no better prepared to survive than before they were brought before the bench. Within no time, the

Box 6.3 Juvenile Drug Courts

Juvenile drug courts are intensive treatment programs established within and supervised by juvenile courts to provide specialized services for eligible drug-involved youth and their families. Cases are assigned to a juvenile drug court docket based on criteria set by local officials to carry out the goals of the drug court program. Juvenile drug courts provide (1) intensive and continuous judicial supervision over delinquency and status offense cases that involve substance-abusing juveniles and (2) coordinated and supervised delivery of an array of support services necessary to address the problems that contribute to juvenile involvement in the justice system. Service areas include substance abuse treatment, mental health, primary care, family, and education.

Although tailored to the needs and resources of individual jurisdictions, juvenile drug court programs are characterized by the following common and essential elements:

- Establishment of a drug court team to include, at a minimum, a judge, prosecutor, defense attorney, treatment provider, evaluator, and school representative working collaboratively to meet the needs of the juvenile and his or her family.

- Intervention by the court as soon as possible following the juvenile's initial contact his/her family face (e.g., the juvenile's substance use, family and educational needs, and behavioral problems as they affect his or her ability to lead a drug-free life).

- Coordination of treatment and other services provided.

- Ongoing monitoring of the juvenile's progress in the program through frequent random urinalysis, continuous supervision, and proactive case management.

- Immediate judicial response to the progress of each participating juvenile or his or her noncompliance with the court's program conditions.

- A judge who is concerned about juveniles and their families, sensitive to cultural and other factors unique to each participant, and interested and trained in adolescent development and behavior, substance abuse, and pharmacology.

- A program philosophy that focuses on capitalizing on the strengths of each juvenile and his or her family.

continued

Box 6.3 *Juvenile Drug Courts* (continued)

Although most juvenile drug courts are still relatively new and remain in the process of documenting the full range of their impact, most have demonstrated the following results:

- Substantial reductions in recidivism.
- Substantial reductions in drug use, as measured by the frequency of positive urinalyses (compared with urinalyses of a comparison group).
- School progress of program participants, as measured by percentages of participants who remain in school, return to school, or obtain a general equivalency diploma (GED).
- Improved family functioning.
- Development of participants' life skills to promote their capacity to live crime- and drug-free.

Sources: Carolyn S. Cooper, "Juvenile Drug Court Programs," *Juvenile Accountability Incentives Block Grant Program Bulletin* (May 2001), http://www.ncjrs.org/html/ojjdp/jaibg 2001 5 1/contents.html; Marilyn Roberts, Jennifer Brophy, and Caroline Cooper, "The Juvenile Drug Court Movement," *Office of Juvenile Justice and Delinquency Prevention Bulletin* (March 1997).

---

same child appears before the court dozens of times. Institutionalization, even to the most sympathetic judge, becomes the inevitable solution. The revolving-door policy extends to youths on parole who find themselves no better equipped to return to the community after being institutionalized than those who are on probation.

In light of the problems discussed in this section, it is no wonder that students of the juvenile court have become extremely critical of the way in which it is run. The lack of adequate placement facilities, undertrained and inadequate personnel, lack of proper training for judges and probation officers (both of whom have broad discretionary powers over the lives of juveniles), and the apparent lack of role definition have led individuals and groups interested in civil liberties, especially the American Civil Liberties Union, to press for reforms. In the past, the outcome of the reforms has been Supreme Court decisions such as *Kent, Gault,* and others. The nature of future court decisions could depend on how quickly and how far the juvenile justice system moves toward court reform.

Professionals in the field are far from the only critics of the present juvenile court system. To the youth being adjudicated, all the court talk of rehabilitation and personalized justice can become meaningless and a cruel joke. Some merely feel contempt for the court system. Various features of their court processing may cause juveniles to develop a definite sense of injustice.

It appears that present-day courts cause juveniles to feel that their right of access to fairness or justice is being violated. Mixing youths who commit criminal acts with those who are merely status offenders adds to disillusionment. The 10-year-old who is habitually running away from home may not be quite sophisticated enough in knowledge of court proceedings to understand receiving the same or harsher punishment as another teenager who steals automobiles.

Taking into consideration the criticisms of professionals in and out of the juvenile justice system, and of the youth themselves, the juvenile court must campaign actively for the continued diversion and/or removal of status offenders from, if not all juvenile court jurisdictions, at least delinquency jurisdiction. They should also advocate policies that provide for the utilization of their official duties by the community only as a last resort. Although there are many in the field that would agree with these suggestions, there are still those who fear the wrath of the National Council of Juvenile Court Judges, child welfare agencies, and other related groups who have unfortunately come to regard coercion as an essential tool for dealing with juveniles. And, according to others, "The 1974 Juvenile Justice and Delinquency Prevention Act is only serving as a grant program to take status offenders out of security confinement but leaves them within the jurisdiction of the court."[58]

Changes in operations, such as **teen courts,** have also been suggested to maintain the fundamental premise of juvenile court—to help the youth. (See Box 6.4)

SUMMARY

After more than 100 years, the Juvenile court must review its present and future goals and objectives and its functions within the overall juvenile justice system. This is especially true in light of ongoing changes in the legal and political climate, the current philosophy of the juvenile justice system, and the continuing criticism of the court's very existence.

The days when the juvenile courts were largely a domain for social workers disappeared in 1967 with the *Gault* decision. Since then, the courts have increasingly become a battleground for lawyers. Even with *Gault,* however, some courts continued to treat delinquency proceedings as entirely civil and applied the same procedural safeguards and standards of proof as required in ordinary parental custody suits. That practice, too, came to an end with a court decision *(Winship)* in 1970.

The trend of today's court seems to be to send violent offenders up to the adult court, not only to deinstitutionalize but also to move gingerly in the direction of eliminating the status offender jurisdiction, and then to

Box 6.4 Teen Courts

Teen courts are an alternative to typical juvenile court process for young (age 10 to 15), first-time (no prior arrest), less serious (e.g., shoplifting, vandalism, disorderly conduct) offenders. It is designed as a voluntary, positive alternative process that can expand possible interventions for such youths. They are based on the premise that positive peer pressure might help steer juveniles away from trouble.

Although there are variations in structure, youths typically direct teen court operations and sanctions. In fact, the key to all teen court programs is that youth play a significant role in the deliberation of charges and the imposition of sanctions on juvenile offenders. A national survey of teen courts revealed that sanctions were aimed toward repairing the damage caused by the initial offense to either the community or toward specific victims. Over 75 percent of the teen courts surveyed listed community service, victim apology, a written essay, and teen court jury duty as sanctions that were "often" or "very often" imposed.

In terms of recidivism, a study conducted by researchers at the Urban Institute in a four state (Alaska, Arizona, Maryland, Missouri) evaluation found very similar (and sometime lower) re-arrest rates.

In Alaska, Arizona, and Missouri, the recidivism rates of teen courts participants were compared with that of other young, first-time offenders. Youth handled by teen court were less likely to commit another crime and be re-referred to the juvenile justice system within six months. In Alaska, recidivism among teen court youth was 6 percent, compared with 23 percent of those handled by the traditional process. In Missouri, the recidivism rate was 9 percent for teen court youth and 27 percent for the traditional process. In Arizona, the rate was 9 percent, compared with 15 percent in the traditional system (though this difference is not statistically significant). In Maryland, the results of the teen court process were compared with a more proactive police diversion program that provided similar services. Recidivism rates of both groups were extremely low—8 percent among teen court youth and 4 percent among youth in the police diversion program. This difference was not statistically significant.

Along with positive attitudes displayed by teen court participants, these results indicate that teen courts have the potential to offer a positive, low-cost alternative to traditional juvenile court processing. Teen court offers a way to prevent low-risk cases from becoming serious problems and thus saving youth.

Sources: Jeffrey A. Butts and Janeen Buck, "Teen Courts: A Focus on Research," *OJJDP Juvenile Justice Bulletin* (Washington, DC: Office of Juvenile Justice and Delinquency Prevention, 2000); Jeffrey A. Butts, Janeen Buck, and Mark B. Coggeshall, *The Impact of Teen Court on Young Offenders* (Washington, DC: The Urban Institute, 2002), www.urban.org.

subject the residual group of delinquents to uniform sentencing relatively devoid of individualized treatment—waived to adult court. This trend may not be unrealistic considering that the court has failed to accomplish its goals of diagnosis, rehabilitation, and treatment, presumably owing to lack of sufficient resources. The court's dual role as dispenser of punishment and source of rehabilitation has proven an unmanageable burden. There has been and continues to be inadequate staff, money, resources, and societal pressure to accomplish either, let alone both at once.

The court's roles need to be defined clearly or redefined. It needs autonomy to establish its own priorities. It has been overburdened and underassisted by outside agencies and the public. To abandon the juvenile court system altogether is, however, not the answer. We must be wary of marching toward such simplistic solutions as "procedural safeguards" and "responsibility and accountability." Scotland has abandoned its courts for children. England has restricted the appearance of juveniles until age 14. The European Welfare Panel uses nonjudicial techniques for its dealings with juvenile delinquents. And, the United States and Canada have become more procedural than ever before. All these systems are, however, evolutionary at best. They grow and die in cycles that become evident when one examines closely the history of the juvenile justice system. In the United States we are neither in a state of perfection nor imperfection regarding our juvenile courts. Rather, we are in a state of constant change based upon the ebbs and flows of the rest of our American society.

Still, the revamping and restructuring of the juvenile court system is a necessity, not a luxury. Contrary to its intended purpose, the court can produce and perpetuate delinquency. In its procedures and its decisions, the court must be sensitive to possible negative and damaging ramifications in what it does. It must require realistic, humane, and practical methods of processing and treating juveniles if it is to be considered an effective component of the juvenile justice system.

We have already discussed the present status of the IJA/ABA Juvenile Justice Standards Project in this chapter. While that project may go a long way toward reforming the juvenile court and juvenile justice systems, it does offer some shortcomings of which the reader should be aware. The standards, for example, do not continue the court's practice of postjudicial follow-up of the delinquent once guilt has been determined. This omission borders on contempt for the court's apparent failure at rehabilitation. The standards also imply massive diversions from both the courts and institutions, a diversion that can be expected to increase rapidly if the volume on *NonCriminal Misbehavior* is ever adopted. Unfortunately, there will still be juveniles locked away for considerable periods. The absence of clear statements of purpose in the standards as to the court's sanctions relating to the postjudicial process does impart the feeling that its principal purpose is to punish. This lack of interest after the fact also severely limits a sentenced youth's desire to effect behavioral changes and to become a contributing member of society; in essence, the youth feels set adrift in an uncaring atmosphere of rules, regulations, and limits on his or her freedom of choice without a meaningful explanation of what it is all about. We mention these shortcomings only as a caution to the reader that no single panacea exists for the solution of the problems evidenced by the juvenile courts and the overall juvenile justice system of which they are a crucial component.

As a final note, there are programs and projects either already developed or being developed to help monitor and, thus, suggest positive steps for change within the juvenile court system. Drug courts, restorative justice programs, and other alternatives should be pursued.

TERMS TO REMEMBER

Blended sentencing
Concurrent jurisdiction
Court intake function
Ex parte
Judicial waiver
Juvenile drug courts

Juvenile Justice and Delinquency
   Prevention Act
Juvenile Justice Standards Project
Restorative justice
Statutory exclusion
Teen courts
Trial motions

REVIEW QUESTIONS

1. Define the following terms:

   - Juvenile court
   - Juvenile court jurisdiction
   - Venue
   - *Parens patriae*
   - Status offender
   - Court administrator
   - Adversary function

2. What are the goals of the juvenile court?
3. What are the major problems facing the juvenile court today? What solutions are available?
4. How does the juvenile court relate to the rest of the juvenile justice system? The juvenile court may become more adversarial in nature (i.e., adultlike); would such a change affect the juvenile system as a whole? Why or why not?
5. What Supreme Court decision has had the most impact on the juvenile court system? Explain.

6. Based upon your personal experiences, how effective would you say the juvenile courts have been in fulfilling their roles? Explain. How do you think the performance of the court's role can be improved?

7. Keeping the original three goals of the juvenile court in mind, discuss how and why the court has failed to meet these goals. If you feel that the courts have met their goals, please explain.

8. What are the functions of waiver? What types are available and what are the strengths and weaknesses of each approach?

9. What are the goals of blended sentencing?

10. What do alternatives like drug courts and restorative justice attempt to do? Are they valuable?

NOTES

[1]Richard W. Kobetz and Betty B. Bosarge, *Juvenile Justice Administration* (Gaithersburg, MD: International Association of Chiefs of Police, 1973), p. 210.

[2]Ibid., pp. 210–213.

[3]*Lindsay v. Lindsay,* 257 111. 328, 100 N.E. 892 (1913), and *In re Turner,* 94 Kan. 115, 145, p. 871 (1915).

[4]*State v. Overby,* 209 N.W. 552, 554, 54 N.E. 295 (1926).

[5]*Bryant v. Brown,* 118 So. 184, 188, 151 Miss. 398, 60 A.L.R. 1325 (1928).

[6]*In re Santillanes,* 138 P.2d. 503, 508, 47. N.M. 140 (1943).

[7]*In re Dargo,* 81 Cal. App. 2d 205, 183 P.2d. 282 (1947).

[8]*Kent v. U.S.,* 383 U.S. 541, at 555, 556 (1966).

[9]*In re Gault,* 387 U.S. I at 30 (1967).

[10]Ibid., at 31.

[11]*District of Columbia v. Jackson,* 261 A. 2d 511 (D.C. Ct. of App., 1970).

[12]*McKeiver v. Pennsylvania,* 403 U.S. 528 S.Ct. 1976, 29 L. Ed. 2d 647 (1971).

[13]*Jane Addams, My Friend, Julia Lathrop* (New York: Macmillan, 1935) p. 137.

[14]Office of Juvenile Justice and Delinquency Prevention, *Juvenile Justice: A Century of Change* (Washington, DC: U.S. Department of Justice, 1999), p. 2.

[15]Ibid., pp. 3–4.

[16]14 O. Jur (2d); Courts; Section 93.

[17]*A Century of Change,* p. 9.

[18]D.C. Code Ann. § 16-2301 (3)(A)(1973).

[19]*United States v. Bland,* 472 F.2d 1329 (D.C. Cir. 1972).

[20]*Report of the Task Force, Juvenile Justice and Delinquency Prevention.* Standard 9.4, p. 301.

[21]Paul H. Hahn, *The Juvenile Offender and the Law* (Cincinnati: Anderson, 1971), p. 272.

[22]Robert E. Shepard, Jr., "The Juvenile Court at 100 Years: A Look Back," *Juvenile Justice,* Vol. VI (1999). http://www.ncjrs.org/html/ojjdp/jjjournal1299.

[23]Richard Redding, "Examining Legal Issues: Juvenile Offenders in Criminal Court and Adult Prison," *Corrections Today,* Vol. 61, (1999), pp. 92–98; David S. Tanenhaus, "The Evolution of Transfer Out of the Juvenile Court," in Jeffrey Fagan and Franklin E. Zimring, eds., *The Changing Borders of Juvenile Justice: Transfer of Adolescents to the Criminal Court* (Chicago: University of Chicago Press, 2000), pp. 13–44.

[24]Howard N. Synder and Melissa Sickmund, *Juvenile Offenders and Victims: 1999 National Report* (Washington, DC: Office of Juvenile Justice and Delinquency Prevention, 1999), p. 102. OJJDP Statistical Briefing Book, http://ojjdp.ncjrs.org/ojstatbb/html/qa087-98.html.

[25]*OJJDP Statistical Briefing Book,* http://ojjdp.ncjrs.org/ojstatbb/html/da089.html; Patrick Griffin, Patricia Torbet, and Linda Szymanski, *Trying Juveniles as Adults in Criminal Court: An Analysis of State Transfer Provisions* (Washington, DC: Office of Juvenile Justice and Delinquency Prevention, 1998).

[26]Ibid., http://ojjdp.ncjrs.org/ojstatbb/html/da191.html.

[27]*Kent v. United States,* 383 U.S. 541 (1966).

[28]Synder and Sickmund, *Juvenile Offenders and Victims,* p. 108.

[29]Richard E. Redding and James C. Howell, "Blended Sentencing in American Juvenile Courts," in Jeffrey Fagan and Franklin E. Zimring, eds., *The Changing Borders of Juvenile Justice: Transfer of Adolescents to the Criminal Court* (Chicago: University of Chicago Press, 2000), pp. 145–180.

[30]Charles W. Barnes and Robert S. Franz, "Questionably Adult: Determinants and Effects of the Juvenile Waiver Decision," *Justice Quarterly,* Vol. 6 (1989), pp. 117–135; M. A. Bortner, "Traditional Rhetoric, Organizational Realities: Remand of Juveniles to Adult Court," *Crime and Delinquency,* Vol. 32 (1986), pp. 53–73; C. Rudman, E. Hartstone, J. Fagan, and M. Moore, "Violent Youth in Adult Court," *Crime and Delinquency,* Vol. 32 (1986), pp. 75–96.

[31]J. Fagan, M. Forst, and T. S. Vivona, "Racial Determinants of the Judicial Transfer Decisions for Violent Juvenile Offenders," *Crime and Delinquency,* Vol. 33 (1987), pp. 259–286; M. J. Leiber and K. M. Jamieson, "Race and Decision Making within Juvenile Justice: The Importance of Context," *Journal of Quantitative Criminology,* Vol. 11 (1995), pp. 363–388; M. R. Podkopacz and B. C. Feld, "Judicial Waiver Policy and Practice: Persistence, Seriousness, and Race," *Law and Inequality,* Vol. 14 (1995), pp. 73–178; H. N. Synder, M. Sickmund, and E. Poe-Yamagata, *Juvenile Offenders and Victims: 1996 Update on Violence—Statistics Summary* (Washington, DC: Office of Juvenile Justice and Delinquency Prevention, 1996); C. R. Tittle and D. A. Curran, "Contingencies for Dispositional Disparities in Juvenile Justice," *Social Forces,* Vol. 67 (1988), pp. 23–58.

[32]Synder, Sickmund, and Poe-Yamagata, *1996 Update on Violence.*

[33]Mary J. Clement, "A Five-Year Study of Juvenile Waiver and Adult Sentences: Implications for Policy," *Criminal Justice Policy Review,* Vol. 8 (1997), pp. 201–219; Patricia Kirkish, Shoba Sreenivasan, Robert Welsh, et. al., "The Future of Criminal Violence: Juveniles Tried as Adults," *Journal of the American Academy of Psychiatry and the Law,* Vol. 28 (2000), pp. 38–46; Tammy M. Poulos and Stan Orchowsky, "Serious Juvenile Offenders: Predicting the Probability of Transfer to Criminal Court," *Crime and Delinquency,* Vol. 40 (1994), pp. 449–492.

[34]Simon I. Singer, "The Automatic Waiver of Juveniles and Substantive Justice," *Crime and Delinquency,* Vol. 39 (1993), pp. 253–261.

[35]Kirkish, Sreenivasan, Welsh, et al., "Juveniles Tried as Adults"; Howard N. Synder, Melissa Sickmund, and Eileen Poe-Yamagata, *Juvenile Transfers to Criminal Court in the 1990s: Lessons Learned from Four Studies* (Washington, DC: Office of Juvenile Justice and Delinquency Prevention, 2000).

[36]M. A. Bortner, Marjorie S. Zatz, and Darnell F. Hawkins, "Race and Transfer: Empirical Research and Social Context," in Jeffrey Fagan and Franklin E. Zimring, eds., *The Changing Borders of Juvenile Justice: Transfer of Adolescents to the Criminal Court,* (Chicago: University of Chicago Press, 2000), pp. 277–320.

[37]*Juvenile Offenders and Victims: 1999,* p. 5.

[38]Ibid., p. 145.

[39]Ibid., p. 17.

[40]Ibid., p. 21.

[41]Ibid.

[42]Ibid., p. 27.

[43]Ibid., pp. 27–28.

[44]Ibid., p. 143; Don C. Gibbons, Delinquency Behavior (Englewood Cliffs, NJ: Prentice Hall, 1976), p. 44.

[45]U.S. Department of Justice, Law Enforcement Assistance Administration, *Prosecution in the Juvenile Courts: Guidelines for the Future* (Washington, DC: U.S. Government Printing Office, December 1973), pp. 28–29.

[46]American Bar Association, "Executive Summary: A Call for Justice," http://www.abanet.org.

[47]*In re Winship,* 397 U.S. 358, 365–66 (1970).

[48]"A Call for Justice."

[49]*Gault; Winship.*

[50]Douglas J. Besharov, *Juvenile Justice Advocacy: Practice in a Unique Court* (New York: Practicing Law Institute, 1974), p. 265.

[51]The reader interested in learning the particulars of these motions is directed to Besharov's work or one of a number of law texts on the subject of juvenile court proceedings.

[52]"A Call for Justice."

[53]Besharov, *Juvenile Justice Advocacy,* p. 362.

[54]Charles Puzzanchera, Anne L. Stahl, Terrence A. Finnegan, Howard N. Synder, Rowen S. Poole, and Nancy Tierney, *Juvenile Court Statistics 1997* (Washington, DC: Office of Juvenile Justice and Delinquency Prevention, 2000), p. 5.

[55]Ibid., p. 37.

[56]Of all the agencies in this country dealing with the care of children invited to critique the IJA/ABA Standards Project, only the American Psychiatric Association responded.

[57]Richard L. Jenkins, "Status Offenders," *Journal of the Academy of Child Psychiatry* (Spring 1980), pp. 62–70.

[58]Milton G. Rector, president of the National Council on Crime and Delinquency, letter to authors, May 17, 1977, p. 2.

chapter 7

JUVENILES' LEGAL RIGHTS

Juvenile Court history has again demonstrated that unbridled discretion, however benevolently motivated, is frequently a poor substitute for principle and procedure. . . . The absence of substantive standards has not necessarily meant that children receive careful, compassionate, individualized treatment. The absence of procedural rules based upon constitutional principles has not always produced fair, efficient, and effective procedures. Departures from established principles of due process have frequently resulted not in enlightened procedures, but in arbitrariness.

— *In re Gault* 387 U.S. 1 (1967)

CHAPTER OVERVIEW

Since the late 1960s, decisions laid down by the U.S. Supreme Court have led to changes in juvenile court operations that have turned the system away from its original rehabilitative posture. The "criminalization" of the juvenile court has changed it to what Feld refers to as a second-rate criminal court that provides neither therapy nor justice.[1] Despite these rulings, the rights of juveniles have not been extended past the situation cited by the Court in the *Kent* decision, with juveniles getting "neither the protection accorded to adults nor the solicitous care and regenerative treatment postulated for children."[2]

Justice for the child in trouble is touted as an official goal for a modern society. However, in practice, children are often dealt with in ways that would be totally unacceptable if used for adults. The constitutional rights of juveniles are often violated, and there is little regard for their integrity, human dignity, and privacy.

Television, which attempts to reflect the realities of our society, has many popular series involving the police. But seldom does one see a juvenile being informed of his or her constitutional rights (*Miranda* warnings) before being taken into custody by the police. In reality, children are not constitutionally guaranteed the privilege of being informed of their rights.

Police must have probable cause for stopping, detaining, or even questioning an adult suspect. If the police handle an arrest incorrectly, it is quite possible that the adult offender cannot be found guilty at trial because of a technicality. However, it is not uncommon practice for police to stop, detain, and question a juvenile for little or no cause. Seldom does the police release a juvenile offender from custody because of a legal technicality resulting from improper arrest procedures.

In this chapter, juvenile rights will be explored. Emphasis will be placed on what has been done, and on what seems to remain to be done to reach equity. If juveniles are expected to abide by the law, does it not logically follow that they, too, should have equal protection under the law?

A Brief History

The earliest precedent related to the development of a modern-day juvenile code is the case of the ***Duke of Beaufort v. Berty*** (England, 1721). The basic principle of that case was that children should be treated differently from adults, primarily for the purpose of prevention rather than punishment. The principle flowing from this case did not receive immediate acceptance, but it is considered to be fundamental to juvenile law.

The principle of individualized justice for youth came with the decision *Rex v. Delaval* (England, 1763). The concept of *parens patriae,* which allows the state, through the courts, to assume parental responsibility for any child under its purview, evolved from *Ellesley v. Ellesley* (England, 1828).

Early American practices did not reflect a strong feeling for children, as evidenced by their treatment in the New England colonies. In fact, children who committed crimes in colonial times were often punished more severely than were adults.

By the nineteenth century, however, several champions had surfaced to lead the crusade for children's rights. More and more Americans were becoming aware that children might not be as responsible for their criminal acts as adults. By 1858, in California, a youth industrial school was established as an institution for children under the age of 18 who were leading "idle or immoral" lives. And, in 1887, California held that it was unlawful to confine persons under the age of 16 years in jails.

The nation's first juvenile court was established in Cook County, Chicago, in 1899. *Mill v. Brown* (Utah, 1907) states the importance of the laws establishing early juvenile courts: "The juvenile court law is of such vast importance to the state and society that, it seems to us, it should be administered by those who are learned in the law and versed in the roles of procedure, effective and individual rights respected. Care must be exercised in both the selection of a judge and in the administration of the law."

In 1923, the National Probation Association's Annual Conference proposed a Standard Juvenile Court Act. The last state to adopt this act was Wyoming, in 1945. Between 1925 and 1945, various states defined their own juvenile code.

The "new" court system, which was over 100 years in coming, defined all procedures of the juvenile courts as *civil*, rather than criminal. (**Civil suits** relate to and affect only individual wrongs, whereas **criminal prosecutions** involve public wrongs.) It is evident, therefore, that the greatest effort in the juvenile justice system has been aimed at creating a separate court system for youths and delinquents. This separate system and the perpetuation of the doctrine of *parens patriae* have resulted in a system that has largely chosen to ignore the legal rights of juveniles. Those rights accorded adults, such as the right to a speedy trial, the right to trial by jury, the right to bail, the right to confront one's accusers, and the right to protection from self-incrimination, were deemed to be unnecessary for juveniles.

However, as the rights of adults were being pursued, as in *Miranda v. Arizona,* some court decisions did have a bearing on juvenile rights. The decision in **Gideon v. Wainwright,** 372 U.S. 335 (1963), set the stage for legislation regarding due process. Although concerned with the right to legal counsel in adult, noncapital felony cases, several states have required that indigent children who request counsel be so provided and at public expense. *Gault* established this as a right for juveniles.

Some Landmark Cases

Kent v. United States, 383 U.S. 541 (1966). In the landmark opinion of **Kent v. United States,** the Supreme Court at long last evaluated juvenile court proceedings and juveniles' constitutionally guaranteed rights. As previously mentioned, due to its rehabilitative origins, juvenile court proceedings were regarded as civil rather than criminal in nature. In *Kent,* the Court noted that the child involved in certain juvenile court proceedings was deprived of constitutional rights and at the same time not given the rehabilitation promised under earlier juvenile court philosophy and statutes. It pointed out "there may be grounds for concern that the child receives the worst of both worlds."[3]

The Court attempted to institute due process requirements in juvenile court with this decision. Waiver to adult court was recognized as a serious proposition for juveniles. Accordingly, the Court ruled that juveniles had rights in such proceedings in accordance with the due process clause of the Fourteenth Amendment. Since waiver to adult court is a "critically important" stage in the juvenile court, juveniles are entitled to the following:

1. A hearing
2. To be represented by counsel at such a hearing
3. To be given access to records considered by the juvenile court
4. A statement of the reasons in support of the waiver order.

The bottom line of this decision is that "a juvenile must be given due process before being transferred from a juvenile court to an adult court."[4]

The *Kent* decision upheld a juvenile's **right to a judicial hearing.** The Supreme Court ruled that the lower court decision on the waiver of this right was unconstitutional. In making this ruling, the Court emphasized that although juvenile court procedures were still civil in nature and that consequently juveniles were not entitled to all the protections given to adult criminals, waiver hearings must still provide all of the protections implied in the Fourteenth Amendment's due process clause.

Kent was 21 when the Court issued its opinion, so he could not be remanded to juvenile court. The Supreme Court sent his case to the U.S. District Court of the District of Columbia with instructions to hold a waiver hearing. This court held that, "the waiver of Morris A. Kent was, on the merits, appropriate and entirely consistent with the purpose of the Juvenile Court Act." This act called for the waiver of juveniles charged with certain crimes to be sent to adult criminal court. Kent was then found guilty of six counts of housebreaking and robbery but "not guilty by reason of insanity," on two counts of rape.[5]

In the *Kent* decision, the court also addressed the factors the judge should consider in the transfer decision process: the seriousness of the offense, violence demonstrated, maturity and sophistication of the child, and rehabilitative resources available to the court.[6] In a later, related decision *(Breed v. Jones)*, the Court held that a juvenile who had been adjudicated delinquent in juvenile court could not be convicted of the same crime in adult court due to the constitutional provision against double jeopardy.[7]

In re Gault, *387 U.S. 1 (1967).* On May 15, 1967, the Supreme Court rendered its first decision in the area of juvenile delinquency procedure **(in re Gault)**. Gerald Gault allegedly made a telephone call to a woman living in his neighborhood, during which he used some obscene words and phrases. The use of a telephone for such purpose violated an Arizona statute, and hence Gerald, age 16, was subject to adjudication as a juvenile delinquent. The adjudication was in fact made after a proceeding in which he was not offered the basic procedural protections to which he would have been entitled had he been charged in a criminal court. In this decision, Justice Abe Fortas ruled that a child alleged to be a juvenile delinquent had at least the following rights:

1. Notice must be given in advance of proceedings against a juvenile so that he or she has reasonable time to prepare a defense.
2. If the proceedings may result in the institutionalization of the juvenile, then both the juvenile and the parents must be informed of their right to have counsel and be provided with one if they cannot afford to obtain one on their own.
3. Juveniles have the protection against self-incrimination. The juvenile, parents or guardians must be advised of the right to remain silent.
4. Juveniles have the right to hear sworn testimony and to confront the witnesses against them for cross-examination.[8]

The *Gault* decision ended the presumption that the juvenile courts were beyond the scope or purview of due process protection. The primary lesson learned here was that juvenile courts would have to become courts of law and follow standard procedures concerning the constitutional rights of those on whom they passed judgment. Juveniles have basic constitutional rights when they face an adjudication hearing that could result in incarceration in a juvenile facility.[9]

Here is a review of the basic procedural due process rights that were granted to juveniles via the *Gault* decision.

Right of Notice of Charges.   The *Gault* case established that a juvenile has a constitutional right to be given a timely notice of the charges against him or her. The **right to a notice of charges** is required in order to give the juvenile's defense counsel adequate time to prepare for the trial.[10] To provide this timely notice, most states use a summons. A summons is the legal instrument to give notice to the accused of the proceedings against him or her. *Gault* held that the due process requirements of notice in juvenile court proceedings were to be the same as in other criminal or civil proceedings.

Right To Counsel.   In *Gault,* it was held that the accused juvenile has the **right to counsel.** Counsel may be of the person's own choosing or may be appointed by the court for financial or other reasons. By the time the *Gault* decision was made, several states had already taken steps to provide legal counsel for juveniles. Since *Gault,* however, the regular participation of defense counsel in juvenile court has become commonplace. However, whether the juvenile uses private or assigned counsel, such defense counsels are likely to be unfamiliar with the proceedings of a juvenile court, for many will have had only civil court experience. Notice of the juvenile's right to counsel must be clearly understood by both the child and the family and should be given both in writing and orally. This notice contains two important elements: (1) the child and/or parents may be represented by counsel; (2) if they cannot afford and therefore cannot employ counsel, the child and parents are, in the absence of a competent waiver, entitled to be represented by counsel at public expense.

Procedures direct that notice of the right to counsel shall be given to the child and parents at the first intake interview, or when the child is admitted to a detention center or shelter-care facility. Counsel should be given to children whenever possible. No simple action holds more potential for achieving procedural justice for the juvenile in court than does legal representation.

Rights of Confrontation and Cross-Examination.

The juvenile's **rights of confrontation and cross-examination** of hostile witnesses was upheld in *In re Gault*. Most states apply this ruling to only the first phase of the criminal court proceedings—that is, to that part dealing with the determination of one's guilt or innocence. However, many statutes and cases allow the juvenile the right of confrontation and cross-examination at dispositional hearings at which the second phase of criminal court proceedings is carried out, designed to determine appropriate sentencing. For example, in *Strode v. Brorby*,[11] a commitment order that would have sent a boy to an industrial school rather than place him on probation was reserved. The court ruled that the juvenile had been refused the opportunity to present witnesses in his favor that would have testified that he deserved probation rather than institutionalization.

Right of Privilege Against Self-Incrimination.

The Fifth Amendment right to remain silent (that is, the **right of privilege against self-incrimination**) is the last entitlement conferred upon juveniles by the *Gault* decision. The Court concluded that the constitutional privilege against self-incrimination is as applicable in juvenile cases as it is in adult cases.

If the juvenile court judge in the *Gault* case had reached a decision on Gerald Gault's guilt, based on Gault's own admissions, it would have been based on admissions obtained without regard to his privilege against self-incrimination. In ruling on the *Gault* decision, Justice Abraham Fortas obviously felt that juvenile court judges should not be influenced by confessions, admissions, and like acts that may have been obtained under dubious circumstances and without regard to the provisions of the Fifth Amendment. Court decisions since *Gault* have extended the privilege against self-incrimination during judicially required examinations (i.e., psychological evaluation) as part of a transfer proceeding.[12]

However, *In re Gault* failed to answer one question: whether a juvenile must be advised of his or her rights at some point in the prejudicial stage. When serious offenses are involved and the juvenile might be transferred to an adult criminal court, some police forces are giving such warnings.

In re Winship, *397 U.S. 358 (1970).* Some states, such as California, apply *Miranda* restrictions as a rule to juvenile interrogation. In the landmark case ***In re Winship,*** the Supreme Court held that, to justify a court finding of delinquency against a juvenile, there must be **proof beyond a reasonable doubt** that the juvenile committed the alleged delinquent act.[13]

Twelve-year-old Samuel Winship was adjudicated delinquent as the result of a theft of $112 from a woman's purse. Consequently, he was committed to a training school for one and one-half years, subject to annual extensions of commitment, until his eighteenth birthday. The case was appealed to the New York Court of Appeals and was upheld by that court. The Supreme Court, however, later reversed that decision. The Supreme Court contended that the loss of liberty is no less significant for a juvenile than for an adult. Therefore, no juvenile may be deprived of his or her individual liberty on evidence less precise than that required depriving an adult of his or her individual liberty. With this ruling the Court mandated that the criminal law burden—rather than the traditionally less stringent civil law burden of the mere preponderance of all evidence—is applicable in juvenile cases.

Before this case, the requirement seemed to be that the judge be influenced only by a preponderance of evidence against the accused delinquent. As in *Gault,* the implications of this decision were limited to cases where juveniles were charged with crimes, not status offenses or cases of neglect or dependency. They are faced with the possibility of incarceration and curtailment of freedom.[14]

McKeiver v. Pennsylvania, *403 U.S. 528 (1971).* Finally, the Supreme Court agreed to hear arguments about whether juveniles had a constitutional **right to a jury trial.** In the ***McKeiver v. Pennsylvania*** decision, the Court implied that the due process standard of "fundamental fairness" applied to juveniles, but the Court rejected the concept of trial by jury for juvenile cases. The Court contended that the "juvenile proceeding has not yet been held to be a 'criminal prosecution' within the meaning and reach of the Sixth Amendment . . ."[15] The Supreme Court stated that it was as yet unwilling to "remake the juvenile proceeding into a full adversary process" and put "an effective end to what has been the idealistic prospect of an intimate, informal protective proceeding."[16] The Court concluded by encouraging the states to "seek in new and different ways the elusive answers to the young."[17] However, the Supreme Court was careful to note that there "is nothing to prevent a juvenile court judge in a particular case where he feels the need, or when the need is demonstrated, from using an advisory jury."[18]

Jury trials for juveniles in most cases, however, are the exception rather than the rule, unless a motion specifically requesting the statutory provision of a trial by jury is made in the court jurisdiction in which the case is to be heard.[19] Sanborn asserts that several structural changes would be required to grant the right to trial by jury in juvenile court. They would include making delinquency records and probation officer treatment plans unavailable to judges. Such changes would completely alter the *parens patriae* nature of the proceedings and duplicate procedures of adult criminal court.[20]

Thus, the right to trial by jury is one of the few constitutional rights that are not provided to juveniles. The other constitutional rights *not* extended to juveniles are: the right to a public trial, the right to bail, and the right to a grand jury indictment.[21]

Legislative Changes

The Supreme Court has not been the only source of change in the area of juvenile rights. Federal acts and legislation have also played an important role. For example, until the Uniform Juvenile Court Act of 1968, police or others could still take a child into custody in a situation in which the Fourth Amendment would have exempted an adult. The Uniform Juvenile Court Act therefore set some limits on nondiscriminatory home removals of children. It provides for the removal of a child from his or her home only if there are reasonable grounds to believe that the child is suffering from illness or injury or is in immediate danger from the environment and that removal from that environment, therefore, is necessary.

In 1974, the U.S. Congress passed the Juvenile Justice and Delinquency Prevention Act (Public Law 93-415). The legal impact of this legislation and its amendments are presented in Box 7.1.

It appears, then, that the courts and the legislative bodies (state and federal) are still reluctant to allow children to be treated as if the legal equals of adults. As a doctrine, *parens patriae* is as firmly entrenched as was the earlier doctrine to treat delinquent children by having them whipped and put to bed without supper.

As noted, these decisions extended due process rights to juveniles when they are faced with significant sanctions—waiver to adult court and incarceration. Compared to adults, juveniles do not have full protection under the law. When facing the bars or being sentenced as an adult, juveniles charged with delinquency have equal protection under the law.[22] Blending the philosophy of *parens patriae* with criminal responsibility again presents significant difficulties for the juvenile court and its charges. The original goal was to give the juvenile court unlimited ability to extend benefits to juveniles in trouble. When their behavior is serious,

Box 7.1   The Core Requirements of Juvenile Justice and Delinquency Prevention Act

The Juvenile Justice and Delinquency Prevention Act of 1974, as amended, establishes four custody-related requirements for juveniles:

1. The "deinstitutionalization of status offenders and non-offenders" requirement (1974) specifies that juveniles not charged with acts that would be crimes for adults "shall not be placed in secure detention facilities."

2. The "sight and sound separation" requirement (1974) specifies that, "juveniles alleged to be or found to be delinquent and [status offenders and non-offenders] shall not be detained or confined in any institution in which they have contact with adult persons incarcerated because they have been convicted of a crime or are awaiting trial on criminal charges." This requires that juvenile and adult inmates cannot see each other and no conversation between them is possible.

3. The "jail and lockup removal" requirement (1980) states that juveniles shall not be detained or confined in adult jails or lockups. There are, however, several exceptions to this requirement. Regulations implementing the Act exempt juveniles held in secure detention facilities if the juvenile is being tried as a criminal for a felony or has been convicted as a criminal felon. In addition, there is a six-hour grace period that allows adult jails and lockups to hold delinquents temporarily until other arrangements can be made. Jails and lockups in rural areas may hold delinquents up to twenty-four hours under certain conditions. Some jurisdictions have obtained approval for separate juvenile detention centers that are collocated with an adult jail or lockup facility.

4. The "disproportionate confinement of minority youth" requirement (1992) specifies that states determine the existence and extent of the problem in their state and demonstrate efforts to reduce it where it exists.

Regulations effective December 10, 1996, modify the act's requirements in several ways:

- Clarify the sight and sound separation requirement—in nonresidential areas brief, accidental contact is not a reportable violation.
- Permit time-phased use of nonresidential areas for both juveniles and adults in collocated facilities.

continued

Box 5.2 The Core Requirements of Juvenile Justice and Delinquency Prevention Acts (continued)

- Expand the six-hour grace period to include six hours both before and after court appearances.
- Allow adjudicated delinquents to be transferred to adult institutions once they have reached the state's age of criminal responsibility, where state law expressly authorizes such transfer.

The revised regulations offer flexibility to states in carrying out the act's requirements. States must agree to comply with each requirement to receive Formula Grants funds under the act's provisions. States must submit plans outlining their strategy for meeting the requirements and other statutory plan requirements. Noncompliance with core requirements results in the loss of 25 percent of the state's annual Formula Grants program allocation.

As of 1998, fifty-five of fifty-seven eligible States and territories are participating in the Formula Grants program. Annual state monitoring reports show that the vast majority are in compliance with the requirements, either reporting no violations or meeting the *de minimis* or other compliance criteria.

Source: Office of Juvenile Justice and Delinquency Prevention, *1999 National Report Series, Juvenile Justice Bulletin—Juvenile Justice: A Century of Change* (Washington, DC: U.S. Department of Justice, 1999), p. 4.

---

the nature of the proceedings and the protections afforded juveniles change accordingly.

Other Procedural Rights

As a result of the Supreme Court cases mentioned earlier, procedural guarantees are extended to juveniles via the due process provisions of the Fourteenth Amendment of the Constitution. **Procedural rights** are rights pertaining to statutory laws and are accorded to juveniles during the fact-finding process of a juvenile case.[23]

Thus far, the procedural rights guaranteed to juveniles in court proceedings are (1) the right to adequate notice of charges against him or her; (2) the right to counsel and to have counsel provided if the child is indigent; (3) the right to confrontation and cross-examination of witnesses; (4) the right to refuse to do anything that would be self-incriminatory; (5) the right to a judicial hearing, with counsel, prior to the transfer of a juvenile to an adult court;[24] and (6) the right to be considered innocent until proven guilty beyond a reasonable doubt. In addition to procedural rights in court, juveniles do have certain other procedural rights within the various stages of the juvenile justice system.

Arrest. Many states, though they do not consider the taking of a child into custody by police an arrest, do require that this act be legal under the state and federal constitutions. Since the *Gault* decision, many courts have required that the police have **probable cause** before taking a child into custody as a suspect in a criminal act. "In the near future, courts will have to decide whether the taking of a juvenile into custody for non-criminal misbehavior, or ungovernability is subject to these or other standards. Certainly, there are some constitutional limitations on how the police handle problem children."[25]

Though laws applicable to the arrest of adults may be applicable to the arrest (or taking into custody) of juveniles, provisions found in juvenile acts relating to detention, custody, and interrogation may differ decidedly from those accorded adults. Juveniles can only be arrested (or be the target of a warrant) if probable cause is demonstrated.[26]

The requirements of the Fourth Amendment apply to the search and seizure process with juvenile arrests. Evidence obtained via juvenile arrests is subject to the **exclusionary rule** (the prohibition against the use of illegally obtained evidence in court).[27] This standard also applies to "warrantless searches" that are conducted during the arrest process. As with adults, the police must have a reasonable suspicion that a juvenile suspect has committed a crime before a search takes place.[28] Regarding juveniles, specific court decisions have been made that limit searches. Juveniles cannot be searched simply because they are in an area where a crime has been committed.[29]

However, the Supreme Court has lifted some of these restrictions, ruling that exclusionary rule may be limited when the police have acted in "good faith" to seize evidence while protecting the rights of citizens.[30] These restrictions apparently do not apply to searches conducted by school officials. They only need "reasonable grounds" to search juveniles—not a warrant nor probable cause.[31]

Interrogation. The issue of whether warnings (*Miranda* decision) must be given at the interrogation of a juvenile suspect has yet to be decided by the Supreme Court. As noted earlier, the *Gault* decision gives the accused juvenile the right to refuse to give self-incriminating evidence; however, this privilege has generally been applied to court proceedings only. In fact, the Supreme Court in the *Gault* decision declined to discuss the questioning of juveniles by the police.

The Supreme Court concluded that the very fact of custodial interrogation exacts a heavy toll on individual liberty and trades on the weakness of individuals. If the Court felt this way about confessions abstracted from adults, they logically would be even more sensitive to those obtained from juveniles. If, according to *Miranda,* an individual does not knowingly waive his or her constitutional privilege against self-incrimination, then the police cannot submit that person to custodial interrogation. Court rulings have thoroughly examined the waiver issue for juveniles:

1. Coerced confessions by juveniles are not admissible in court.[32]
2. If a juvenile is held in isolation, any obtained confession may be regarded as involuntary.[33]
3. When juveniles invoke the right to remain silent, it must be respected. The courts have recognized asking for a grandmother to be present during questioning as evidence of this right.[34]
4. Waivers must be knowingly, voluntarily, and intelligently given.[35]

To summarize, efforts have been made in juvenile cases to bind police officers to procedures similar to those used in adult arrests.

Detention.   Since the decision to detain a juvenile before court proceedings affects the way the court will later see that child, it is important that this decision be arrived at fairly. Placing a juvenile in a **detention** facility simply because he or she has no place else to go, for example, appears to be a questionable practice, especially in light of the potential harm it may cause the juvenile. Court decisions have established the following principles regarding juvenile detention:

1. Preventive detention of juveniles awaiting adjudication is constitutional. The *Schall v. Martin* decision was based upon the desire to protect society from repeated acts of delinquency.[36]
2. A probable cause hearing must be conducted before detention is continued.[37]
3. Holding accused status offenders in adult jails prior to adjudication is unconstitutional.[38]

State statutes often justify detention of juveniles on the basis of the probability that they will flee, if they are dangerous to themselves or others and have poor home conditions. Protection of youths remains paramount.[39] See Chapter 9 for a further discussion of the definition and appropriate uses of detention for juveniles.

Bail.   State statutes typically specify a time limit in which a detention hearing for juveniles must be held. Usually, this limit falls between forty-eight and seventy-two working hours after the youth is detained. The U.S. Supreme Court has not determined if juveniles have a constitutional right to **bail.**[40] However, with the increasing attention to waiver to adult court, the right to bail may become a significant issue.

There are many factors to be considered in regard to bail for juveniles. For example, where does a 14-year-old teenager get the money for bail, especially when his or her parents cannot pay it? Would the right to bail simply widen the gap between justice for the rich and justice for the poor? Bail is a constitutional guarantee in most adult cases, and the disparity between rich and poor exists there. The adult who posts bail usually suffers if he or she skips bail, especially if the bail money was his or her own or a friend's or a relative's. Would a juvenile feel any responsibility to the person who put up the money to ensure the child's temporary freedom? Would bail bondsmen be willing to provide bail money for indigent juveniles, especially those who receive no financial support from their parents?

These and other questions will have to be considered in devising a system of bail for juveniles accused of criminal acts, especially if the courts rule in favor of this provision as a constitutional right for juveniles.

Rights of Incarcerated Juveniles

The last of the procedural rights of juveniles at other stages of the juvenile justice system involves the rights of incarcerated juveniles. Concern for incarcerated or institutionalized juveniles comes from a similar concern in adult cases. The primary issues are prisoner rights and the right to treatment.

In its examination of the causes of the Attica prison riot of 1971, a tragedy in which over forty people died, the McKay Commission cited a long record of disregard of legitimate grievances arising from inadequate medical care, bad food, and the absence of recreational facilities; obstacles to any form of communication with the outside world; rules that were "poorly communicated, often petty, senseless, or repressive and . . . selectively enforced," and a "relationship between most correctional officers and inmates that was characterized by fear, hostility, mistrust, nurtured by racism."[41]

If the proper grievance practices had existed at the time, the riots at Attica and the New Mexico prison might never have happened. The need for just grievance procedures is as real in juvenile institutions as in adult prisons. As yet there have been no juvenile equivalents of either the New York or New Mexico riots. However, this should not be taken to mean that injustices do not take place within juvenile institutions. The basic aim is to establish fairness in institutional proceedings. Grievance procedures can be set up to guide operations.

Grievance procedures enable a child to grieve daily life issues that do not involve discipline (e.g., food quantity or quality). The basic elements of adequate grievance procedures are (1) notice to the children of the availability of grievances, (2) a clear and simple procedure for children to present their grievances to staff, (3) prompt investigation of grievances (usually 3 days), (4) opportunity for children to present grievances to an impartial person, (5) notice to children of the decision of the impartial person, and (6) the taking a final action.[42]

Although this section is limited to a brief overview, there are other issues related to the rights of incarcerated juveniles. They are mail and censorship; dress codes; personal appearance; visitations; religious freedom; notice of rules; searches; work assignments; right to care and treatment (expanded upon below); the use of corporal punishment; the use of physical, mechanical, and/or medical restraints; room confinement; loss of privileges; disciplinary procedures; and transfers.

The Right to Treatment

The issue of the individual's **right to treatment** has been the subject of several court rulings over the past two decades. The majority of these rulings involved the involuntary confinement of adults in mental institutions or similar treatment facilities, and it has been just recently that their application was considered for persons confined to prisons or correctional facilities, adult or juvenile. Birnbaum (1960) was perhaps the first to articulate the right to treatment:

> The courts, under their traditional powers to protect the constitutional rights of our clients should begin to consider the problem of whether or not a person who has been institutionalized solely because he is sufficiently mentally ill to require institutionalization for care and treatment actually does receive adequate medical treatment so that he may regain his health, and therefore, his liberty, as soon as possible; that the courts do this by means of recognizing and enforcing the right to treatment; and that the courts do this, independent of any action by the legislature, as a necessary and overdue development of our present concept of due process.[43]

Since this beginning, the right to treatment has been established in two key cases that apply to the rights of adult mentally ill persons: *Wyatt v. Stickney* (1971) and *Donaldson v. O'Connor* (1975). In *Wyatt,* the Court ruled that the due process clause of the Fourteenth Amendment guarantees mental patients a right to receive treatment, given a reasonable opportunity to be improved or cured.[44]

Because the inmates of training schools and juvenile institutions are confined against their wills, the right-to-treatment issue regarding juveniles was inevitable. As such, many courts have held that an institutionalized child must receive appropriate treatment or be released. Some states, therefore, require periodic progress reports on the juvenile, and cases have been brought before the courts to require juvenile correctional systems to improve institutional services and to release children when these services are inadequate or in violation of the juvenile's right to an "acceptable home substitute" as his or her place of detention.[45]

In *Creek v. Stone,* the Court of Appeals for the District of Columbia interpreted the local juvenile court act to mean that a juvenile has a statutory right to treatment.

> The purpose stated in the 16 D.C. Code § 2316(3)—to give the juvenile the care "as nearly as possible" equivalent to that which should have been given by his parents—establishes not only an important policy objective, but an appropriate case, a legal right to a custody that is not in conflict with the parens patriae premise of the law.[46]

Certainly, the recognition of a juvenile's legal right to treatment would be consistent with the ideal of *parens patriae.*

In the courts, this right became entwined with conditions of confinement in juvenile institutions. In *Nelson v. Heyne,* a federal court coupled a right to treatment under the due process clause of the Fourteenth Amendment with the right to be free from cruel and unusual punishment (Eighth Amendment). Held at the Indiana Boys School, the plaintiffs asked for a restraining order to protect them against the use of corporal punishment and psychotropic drugs. The court stated:

> In our view, the "right to treatment" includes the right to minimum acceptable standards of care and treatment for juveniles and the right to individualized care and treatment. Because children differ in their need for rehabilitation, the individual need for treatment will differ. When a state assumes the place of a juvenile's parents, it assumes as well the parental duties, and its treatment of its juveniles should, so far as can be reasonably required, be what proper parental care would provide. Without a program of individualized treatment, the result may be that the juvenile will not be rehabilitated, but warehoused, and that at termination of detention they will likely be incapable of taking their proper places in free society, their interests and those of the state and the school thereby being defeated.[47]

Although the U.S. Supreme Court has never established a juvenile's right to treatment, this concept was also strengthened in another lower court ruling. In ***Morales v. Turman,*** the court ruled that juveniles housed in the facilities of the Texas Youth Council had a constitutional right to treatment. As in *Nelson,* the conditions of confinement at these institutions were held as violations of the Eighth Amendment prohibition against cruel and unusual punishment.[48]

There is a myth that there is a common model in the juvenile justice system. The reality is that there is a "model muddle." The term *model muddle,* although coined originally for application to the mental health system, applies equally as well to the juvenile justice system. Each element of the system seems to have a different viewpoint as to just what the system is, or what it is supposed to do. Juvenile court judges, parole and probation officers, law enforcement personnel, correctional staff, and others are far from agreeing on what model is best to use in processing juvenile offenders through the system. One of the most prevailing and presently controversial of these models is the treatment model.

The **treatment model** assumes basically that delinquent behavior has its root cause in a physical, mental, emotional, educational, sociological, or occupational handicap of the offender. It likens the delinquent to someone who is "sick" and advocates that, if the underlying problem can be identified and a liberal dose of medicine applied, the "patient" will be "cured" of any further delinquent or deviant behavior. The treatment model is, however, under heavy attack—first, because it often deals only with behavior and has yet to prove its efficacy to "cure" a case of shoplifting or armed robbery, for example; and second, because it has seldom been given a chance; that is, it has seldom been given the financial and professional resources required to administer the treatments for which the delinquent has been confined. In this event, treatment merely becomes custody. Without treatment, the confinement for treatment has no validity and the treatment model fails. If one accepts this premise, however, then the recent failure of the courts to guarantee treatment rights to incarcerated delinquents could be viewed as one more nail in the treatment model's coffin lid.

Two rights are related tangentially to the right-to-treatment issue that are not widely discussed or generally examined in a text on juvenile delinquency: (1) the right to refuse treatment and (2) the right to punishment. Normally the right to refuse treatment is claimed in cases involving mental patients, but an inmate of a correctional facility can use it. The acceptance or rejection of treatment seems at first to be the individual's prerogative. However, if a patient or inmate is allowed to refuse treatment, he or she would more than likely remain a burden on society.

One could hypothesize that the increasingly high rate of recidivism among juveniles released from institutions may be a result of their refusal to accept treatment; this is, however, doubtful. One would have to prove that treatment had been offered in the first place before one could conjecture that it had been refused.

The right to refuse treatment is closely related to, but not the same as, the right to choose punishment rather than treatment. Both these proposed rights are alternative and theoretical companions to the right to treatment. The courts have both supported and refuted the right to refuse treatment, but they have yet to decide a case involving the issue of "right to punishment."

The right to choose punishment may seem absurd at first, but it is plausible when looked at in the following manner. Just as the right to treatment is based on statutory law, the right to punishment under the law is supportable under the same concept. This concept is applicable to the offender who is criminally responsible for his or her crime. The delinquent could object to conventional treatment by citing the First Amendment right to privacy and then demand a statutory right to punishment based on a state criminal code designating a specific length of imprisonment as punishment for the crime for which he or she was convicted or committed.

The theoretical approach to a right to punishment is clarified further by the following argument. Treatment often takes place in confinement. Confinement itself has been defined as punishment.[49] Therefore, treatment, when it takes place in confinement, can be punishment. If the inmate has the right to accept or refuse treatment and possibly even choose what kind of treatment, then it would seem that the inmate may, therefore, have the right to choose punishment (confinement) as his or her treatment. This may seem somewhat oblique, but such an interpretation is theoretically correct and could be put into practice. Courts have not decided such a case, but individuals sentenced in criminal or juvenile court that are classified as psychopaths and receive indeterminate sentences may be expected to raise this issue in the near future.

PROCEDURAL RIGHTS OUTSIDE THE JUSTICE SYSTEM

Do juveniles, both delinquent and nondelinquent, have rights other than those associated specifically with the juvenile justice system? If so, what are they? To a limited extent, juveniles do have the same rights as other citizens. The term **limited extent** is used because these rights are not always acknowledged or honored. One of the major reasons for this lack of acknowledgement is that a juvenile's age of majority (adulthood) is adult-defined, and, until this age is attained, a juvenile is considered a child, or a second-class citizen. These limited-extent rights include rights under laws governing employment and employment practices; driving; contracts and legal agreements; voting; drinking; taking drugs; marriage, sex, and abortion; operating a business; rights in educational institutions; rights with regard to parents and home; and the right to the means to maintain an adequate standard of living.

The two most important institutions that hold almost totalitarian control over the life of the juvenile are the school and the family. These institutions have the greatest amount of contact with and both formal and informal control over juveniles.

The number of children receiving public assistance in the form of Aid for Dependent Children (ADC) reflects the right to an adequate standard of living. Aside from ADC, the Social Security system and the Veterans Administration provide assistance to qualified families, regardless of income level. There is also Child Development Head Start, Child Development–Child Welfare Research and Demonstration Grants, Public Assistance–Social Services, Work Incentive Programs, and Community Service Training Grants.

While some people may decry "welfare cheaters" and claim that most persons on welfare are not willing to work, it is generally accepted that children, at least, should receive public assistance.

Another right of juveniles is the right to employment and protection against employer abuses.[50] The labor market experience of juveniles has been discussed in national juvenile justice administration policy sessions for many years. Initially, there was concern because of the high rate of unemployment, but later the emphasis shifted to poor job preparation and insufficient occupational training for youths who enter the labor market with less than a college degree.

SUBSTANTIVE RIGHTS OF MINORS

Substantive rights are the basic rights of a human being, such as life, liberty, and the pursuit of happiness that are not dependent on laws made by humankind. Although there has been some resolution in the area of procedural rights for juveniles, the issue of the **substantive rights of minors** has remained virtually unexamined.

Substantive rights are especially important when discussing children who present no real threat either to themselves or to society. Laws, regulations, and rules that would make an adult's lifestyle unbearable often control these children.

Substantive rights used to be expressed in terms of protection and welfare. The new substantive rights are a decidedly different breed; they include the right to refuse an unwanted service, the right to make or participate in choices that affect one's life, and the right to be free from unnecessary restrictions in individual development. "Underlying all efforts to define these new rights is the question of whether children, as well as adults, have a fundamental interest in privacy that might be expressed as the **'right to be left alone.'**"[51]

For example, the courts have ruled on the juvenile's right to confidentiality. Juvenile court was designed to be a confidential process. Protecting the privacy of the juvenile would also prevent harm to youths. Of course, this right conflicts with the desire to protect the public from further delinquent or criminal acts at the hands of juveniles. To address such issues, the courts have established the following principles:

1. The legal status of a juvenile witness can be brought out on crossexamination in court.[52]

2. Under prescribed circumstances and their rights under the First Amendment, the press may report the results of juvenile court proceedings.[53]

3. The Federal Juvenile Delinquency Act does not violate the First Amendment by mandating the closure of juvenile court proceedings.[54]

4. Juveniles can be legally required to register as sex offenders.[55] However, the Kentucky appellate court has ruled that a juvenile cannot be required to give a blood sample to be compiled in the state's centralized DNA database. While adjudicated delinquent for sex offense, the juvenile in question was not convicted of a felony, as required by state law.[56]

As these decisions demonstrate, it is difficult to balance the rights of society and those of juvenile offenders.

SUMMARY

In this chapter, we have discussed the procedural rights of juveniles within the court system and how this relates to their substantive rights. What will be the eventual impact of the recent "revolution" in juvenile rights on the juvenile justice system has yet to be determined. However, as juveniles gain equal rights and protections under the law, they are losing the sometimes useful and heretofore "protective" cover of *parens patriae.*

If juveniles are eventually treated as equals with adults, will they then be also exposed to the potential dangers that might befall adults? If an adult attempts an escape from prison, he or she may be shot, even killed, in the process. Thousands upon thousands of youths "run" (abscond) or escape from training schools and juvenile institutions each year. What would be the public reaction if several of them were wounded or killed in their attempts? Adult correctional facilities, staffed with armed guards, are places where security and control are guiding considerations. Should we turn our relatively insecure youth camps into likenesses of these facilities?

Currently, juveniles are protected from being identified in newspapers and from being fingerprinted until age 16. Should we change these practices and ensure exacting equality between juveniles and adults?

One thing is relatively clear: the juvenile offender of today is often the adult offender of tomorrow. How we treat and react to these juveniles now may have great bearing on whether or not we will have to deal with them later, as adults, when they are at least guaranteed their full constitutional rights.

TERMS TO REMEMBER

Bail
Civil suit
Criminal prosecution
Detention
Duke of Beaufort v. Berty
Exclusionary rule
Gideon v. Wainwright
In re Gault
In re Winship
Kent v. United States
Limited extent
McKeiver v. Pennsylvania
Morales v. Turman
Probable cause

Procedural rights
Proof beyond a reasonable doubt
Right of privilege against self-
  incrimination
Rights of confrontation and cross-
  examination
Right to a judicial hearing
Right to a jury trial
Right to a notice of charges
Right to be left alone
Right to counsel
Right to treatment
Substantive rights of minors
Treatment model

REVIEW QUESTIONS

1. Define the following terms:
   a. Procedural rights
   b. Substantive rights
   c. Due process
2. Discuss the major court cases upon which the procedural rights of juveniles within the court are based.
3. What ramifications would the right to trial by jury have on the juvenile justice system? Explain.
4. What are the advantages and disadvantages of juveniles receiving the same protection and constitutional rights as adults?
5. What is meant by the terms *right to treatment* and *right to punishment?* How do these rights apply to the juvenile justice system? Explain.
6. Discuss the potential psychological impact that due process rights might exert on children.

NOTES

[1]Barry C. Feld, *Bad Kids: Race and the Transformation of the Juvenile Court* (New York: Oxford University Press, 1999).
[2]*Kent v. United States* 383 U.S. 541 (1966); F. A. Orlando and G. L. Crippen, "Rights of Children and the Juvenile Court," in Ira M. Schwartz, ed., *Juvenile Justice and Public Policy: Toward a National Agenda* (New York: Macmillan, 1992).
[3]*Kent v. U.S.*
[4]Rolando V. del Carmen, Mary Parker, and Frances P. Reddington, *Briefs of Leading Cases in Juvenile Justice* (Cincinnati: Anderson, 1998), p.137.

[5]O. W. Ketcham, *"Kent* Revisited," *Juvenile Justice Update,* Vol. 2 (1996), pp. 1–2, 11–12.

[6]*In re Marven C.,* 39 Cal. Rptr. 2d 354 (Cal. App. 1995); del Carmen, et al., *Briefs of Leading Cases in Juvenile Justice,* p.134.

[7]*Breed v. Jones* 421 U.S. 517 (1975).

[8]*In re Gault,* 387 U.S. 1 (1967); A. Neigher, *"Gault* Decision: Due Process and the Juvenile Courts," in Barry W. Hancock and Paul M. Sharp, eds., *Criminal Justice in America: Theory, Practice, and Policy* (Upper Saddle River, NJ: Prentice Hall, 1996), pp. 305–320.

[9]del Carmen, et al., *Briefs of Leading Cases in Juvenile Justice,* p. 173.

[10]For example, see *M. v. Superior Court,* 4 Cal. App. 3d 370, 482 P.2d 664, 93 Ca. Rptr. 752 (1971).

[11]In Tennessee a juvenile is entitled to a jury trial on an appeal *de novo* from a juvenile court decision. (A trial *de novo* is a trial that is held for the second time, as if there had been no former decision.)

[12]*United States v. J.D.* 517 F.Supp. 69 (S.D.N.Y. 1981); *R.H. v. State* 777 P.2d 204 (Alaska App. 1989); del Carmen, et al., *Briefs of Leading Cases in Juvenile Justice,* pp. 153–155; 160–162.

[13]*In re Winship,* 397 U.S. 358, 365-66 (1970). See also *Debacher v. Bainard,* 396 U.S. 28, 6 Crl 3001 (1970).

[14]del Carmen, et al., *Briefs of Leading Cases in Juvenile Justice,* p. 179.

[15]See, for example, *In re Richard S.,* 27 N.Y. 2d 802, 264 N.E. 2d 353, 315 N.Y.S. 2d 861 (1970).

[16]The doubt expressed must be one that a reasonable man or woman would express when presented with all of the evidence.

[17]Joseph Senna and Larry Siegel, *Juvenile Law: Cases and Comments* (St. Paul, MN: West Publishing Co., 1976), p. 344.

[18]Douglas J. Basharov, *Juvenile Justice Advocacy: Practice in a Unique Court* (New York: Practicing Law Institute, 1974), p. 287.

[19]Children's Bureau, U.S. Department of Health, Education, and Welfare, *Legislative Guide for Drafting Family and Juvenile Court Acts* (Washington, DC: U.S. Government Printing Office, 1973), p. 20.

[20]Joseph B. Sanborn, "Remnants of *Parens Patriae* in the Adjudicatory Hearing: Is A Fair Trial Possible in Juvenile Court," *Crime and Delinquency,* Vol. 40 (1994), pp. 599–615.

[21]del Carmen, et al., *Briefs of Leading Cases in Juvenile Justice,* p. 181.

[22]*Boyd v. State* 853 S.W.2d 263 (Ark. 1993).

[23]The requirements of due process were also extended to cover short term, school suspension cases in *Goss v. Lopez* 419 U.S. 565 (1975). del Carmen, et al., *Briefs of Leading Cases in Juvenile Justice,* p. 183.

[24]*Ex parte State ex rel.* Simpson, 288 Ala., 535, 263, So. 2d. 137 (1972).

[25]U.S. Department of Justice, Law Enforcement Assistance Administration, *Standards for the Administration of Juvenile Justice* (Washington, DC: U.S. Government Printing Office, July 1980), p. 190.

[26]Rush defines probable cause as "A set of facts and circumstances that would induce a reasonably intelligent and prudent person to believe that a particular person had committed a specific crime; reasonable grounds to make or believe an accusation." George E. Rush, *The Dictionary of Criminal Justice* (Guilford, CT: Dushkin/McGraw-Hill, 2000) p. 268.

[27]Ibid., p. 129. See *Mapp v. Ohio* 367 U.S. 643, 6 L.Ed. 2d 1081, 81 S.Ct. 1684 (1961).

[28]*Terry v. Ohio* 392 U.S. 1, 20 L.Ed. 2d 889, 88 S.Ct. 1868 (1968).

[29]del Carmen, et al., *Briefs of Leading Cases in Juvenile Justice,* pp. 40–41.

[30]*United States v. Leon* 468 U.S. 897, 82 L.Ed. 2d 677, 104 S.Ct. 3380 (1984); *Massachusetts v. Shepard* 468 U.S. 981, 82 L.Ed. 2d. 737, 104 S.Ct. 3405 (1984).

[31]*New Jersey v. T.L.O.* 469 U.S. 325 (1985); *Cason v. Cook* 810 F.2d. 188 (8th Cir. 1987); del Carmen, et al., *Briefs of Leading Cases in Juvenile Justice,* pp. 24–26; 36–38.

[32]*Haley v. State of Ohio* 68 S.Ct. 302 (1984); del Carmen, et al., *Briefs of Leading Cases in Juvenile Justice,* pp.19–20.

[33]*Gallegos v. Colorado* 370 U.S. 49 (1962); del Carmen, et al., *Briefs of Leading Cases in Juvenile Justice,* pp.21–22.

[34]*Fare v. Michael C.* 442 U.S. 707 (1979); *Smith v. State* 623 So. 2d 369 (Ala. Cr. App. 1992); *In re Gilbert E.* 38 Cal. Rptr. 2d. 866 (Cal. App. 1994); del Carmen, et al., *Briefs of Leading Cases in Juvenile Justice,* pp. 22–24, 38–40, 44–45.

[35]*State v. Sugg* 456 S.E. 2d 469 (W. Va. 1995); del Carmen, et al., *Briefs of Leading Cases in Juvenile Justice,* pp. 47–48.

[36]*Schall v. Martin* 104 S. Ct. 2403 (1984); del Carmen, et al., *Briefs of Leading Cases in Juvenile Justice,* pp. 88–89.

[37]*Baldwin v. Lewis* 300 F. Supp. 1220 (E.D. Wis. 1969); del Carmen, et al., *Briefs of Leading Cases in Juvenile Justice,* pp.90–92.

[38]*D. B. v. Tewksbury* 545 F. Supp. 896 (D. Or. 1982); del Carmen, et al., *Briefs of Leading Cases in Juvenile Justice,* pp. 98–100.

[39]Gennaro F. Vito, Deborah G. Wilson, Richard Tewksbury, *The Juvenile Justice System: Concepts & Issues* (Prospect Heights, IL: Waveland Press, 1998) p. 93.

[40]del Carmen, et al., *Briefs of Leading Cases in Juvenile Justice,* pp. 85–86.

[41]J. Michael Keating et al., *Grievance Mechanisms in Correctional Institutions* (Washington, DC: U.S. Government Printing Office, September 1975).

[42]David W. Roush, *Desktop Guide to Good Juvenile Detention Practice* (Washington, DC: Office of Juvenile Justice and Delinquency Prevention, 1996), p. 141.

[43]M. Birnbaum, "The Right to Treatment," *American Bar Association Journal,* Vol. 46 (1960), pp. 449–503.

[44]*Wyatt v. Stickney* 325 F. Supp. 781 (M.D. Ala. 1971); *Donaldson v. O'Connor* 422 U.S. 563 (1975).

[45]Juvenile Court of the District of Columbia, *In the Matter of Joseph Franklin Savoy and Tony Hazel,* p. 16.

[46]*Creek v. Stone* 379 F.2d 106, 111 (D.C. Cir. 1967).

[47]*Nelson v. Heyne* 491 F.2d 352 (7th Cir. 1974); see Senna and Siegel, *Juvenile Law,* p. 478.

[48]*Morales v. Turman* 383 F.Supp. 53 (E.D. Tex. 1974): del Carmen, et al., *Briefs of Leading Cases in Juvenile Justice,* pp. 234–236.

[49]*Cross v. Harris* 418 F.2d 1095.

[50]See Frances Fox Piven and Richard A. Cloward, *Regulating the Poor* (New York: Pantheon, 1971).

[51]Ibid., p. 77.

[52]*Davis v. Alaska* 415 U.S. 308 (1974); del Carmen, et al., *Briefs of Leading Cases in Juvenile Justice,* pp. 274–275.

[53]*Smith v. Daily Mail Publishing Co.* 443 U.S. 97 (1979); del Carmen, et al., *Briefs of Leading Cases in Juvenile Justice,* pp. 276–277; *Oklahoma Publishing Company v. District Court in and for Oklahoma City* 480 U.S. 308, 97 S.Ct. 1045 (1977).

[54]*United States v. Three Juveniles* 862 F. Supp. 651 (D. Mass. 1994); del Carmen, et al., *Briefs of Leading Cases in Juvenile Justice,* pp. 281–283.

[55]*State v. Acheson* 877 P.2d 217 (Wash. App. 1994); del Carmen, et al., *Briefs of Leading Cases in Juvenile Justice,* pp. 283–284.

[56]*J.D.K., a Juvenile, Appellant, v. COMMONWEALTH of Kentucky, Appellee* 2001 WL 92996 (Ky. App).

JUVENILE PROBATION— CHEAPER OR BETTER?

I bailed nineteen boys, from 7 to 15 years of age, and in bailing them it was understood, and agreed by the court that their cases should be continued from term to term for several months, as a season of probation; thus each month at the calling of the court docket, I would appear in court, make my report, and thus the cases would pass on for 5 or 6 months. At the expiration of this term, twelve of the boys were brought into court at one time, and the scene formed a striking and highly pleasing contrast with their appearance when first arraigned. The judge expressed much pleasure as well as surprise at their appearance, and remarked, that the object of the law had been accomplished and expressed his cordial approval of my plan to save and reform.

— John Augustus[1]

CHAPTER OVERVIEW

Today, with continuing emphasis on community-based services for juveniles, it is recognized that not all juveniles who are adjudicated delinquent belong in institutions. **Probation** (Box 8.1) is one method of court disposition that the juvenile justice system may impose, once the youth is determined to be delinquent. In fact, probation is the most frequently used juvenile court disposition at the present time. Nationwide, in 1999, 39.9 percent of cases in juvenile court proceedings resulted in probation.[2] This

---

Box 8.1 Probation

Probation is a sentence not involving confinement that imposes conditions. The sentencing court retains authority to supervise, modify the conditions, and resentence the offender if conditions are violated. Probation is increasingly being linked with a short sentence to jail, followed by a period of probation.

---

figure represents a 43 percent increase in the number of juvenile probationers since 1990.[3]

Current statistics from 1999 reveal more patterns in juvenile probation. There were 670,901 juveniles under probation supervision in 1999. Of that number, 76 percent (509,933) were male and 24 percent (160,968) were female. By racial category, 70 percent (466,765) of the probationers were white, 27 percent (184,151) were black, and 3 percent (19,985) from other groups. The age group figures for juvenile probationers in 1999 were 5 percent (32,272) under 12, 6 percent (38,109) age 12, 11 percent (73,739) age 13, 17 percent (112,922) age 14, 22 percent (155,623) age 15, 23 percent (155,623) age 16, 15 percent (102,518) age 17, and 1 percent (10,144) over 17. By referral offense, most probationers committed a property offense (43.2 percent, or 290,093), followed by offenses against persons (23.1 percent, or 155,178), public order offenses (21.6 percent, or 145,148), and drug crimes (12 percent, or 80, 482).[4]

As it relates to juvenile offenders, probation is the "workhorse" of the Juvenile Justice System:

> Juvenile probation is the oldest and most widely used vehicle through which a wide range of court-ordered services are rendered. Probation may be used at the "front end" of the juvenile justice system for first-time, low-risk offenders or at the "back end" as an alternative confinement for serious offenders.[5]

Ordinarily, juveniles on probation submit to a set of conditions established by the court that are related to the offense committed. The "basic set" of juvenile probation functions includes intake screening of cases referred to juvenile and family courts, predisposition or presentence investigation of juveniles, and court-ordered supervision of juvenile offenders.[6]

HISTORICAL BACKGROUND OF PROBATION

Basically, the history and development of modern probation for juveniles follows the same lines as that for adults. The antecedents of our present concept of probation started when those who dispensed the law tried to be both fair and compassionate to the convicted or accused offender by giving him or her an opportunity to avoid punishment under certain conditions. Typically, probation is a suspended sentence. The right to sanctuary, a predecessor of probation or the suspended sentence, permitted a convicted criminal freedom from arrest so long as the person remained in the sanctuary. There are several examples of the right to sanctuary cited in the Bible; in fact, holy places were often set aside for this purpose.[7] This early practice, abandoned in England in the seventh century, was a far cry from probation practices. But it did provide a criminal with a form of reprieve or stay of punishment.

In the Middle Ages, secular punishment could be avoided through a practice called **benefit of clergy.** Persons could use this device to escape the sanguine, often capital, punishments of English common law. While benefit of clergy first applied only to members of the clergy, it eventually was extended to any person who could quote Psalm 51 from the Bible and thus beg personally for mercy. Benefit of clergy may be seen as an early form of suspended sentence. As it became available to more and more classes of accused persons, it lost its original intent and clerical meaning and became "a clumsy set of rules which operated in favor of all criminals to mitigate in certain cases the severity of the criminal law."[8] Gradually, the state acquired total jurisdiction from the church and benefit of clergy was eventually abolished. By 1827, it could no longer be claimed by commoners, and in 1841 it was no longer available to English peers. Benefit of clergy survived in the American colonies until only shortly after the Revolution.

Another early form of suspended sentence was **judicial reprieve,** the temporary suspension of the imposition or sentence by the court. The granting of such reprieve usually allowed the defendant to go free pending final disposition of the case. Its purpose was to allow the defendant to have time to appeal a case to the Crown or to apply for a pardon. It was also granted when the judge was not satisfied with the evidence presented against the accused. Although judicial reprieve did offer a form of suspended sentence, sometimes indefinite suspension, it did not set forth any conditions by which the accused was to be governed during this reprieve. This form of suspended sentence was not probation, which by earlier definition must carry with it some degree of supervision.

Recognizance (the obligation to appear in court), with or without bail, is deeply embedded in English law. Originally, it was used as a method for assuring that a defendant would appear at trial. It was also used as a form of provisional suspension until the final disposition of a case. Today, it is used for only the first purpose. Recognizance originated as a form of preventive justice. It "consists of obliging those persons, whom there is a probable ground to suspect of future misbehavior, to stipulate with and to give full assurance to the public, that such offense as is apprehended shall not happen. . . . This 'assurance to the public' is given by entering into a recognizance or bond (with or without sureties) creating a debt to the state that becomes enforceable, however, only when the specified conditions are not observed. The recognizance is entered into for a specified period of time."[9] Recognizance and provisional release on bail in a very real sense were the first rudimentary stage in the development of probation.

EARLY PROBATION IN THE UNITED STATES

The Warwickshire Quarter Sessions, an English criminal court, practiced the conditional release of youthful offenders to the supervision of their masters or parents in England as early as 1820. But a Boston cobbler by the name of **John Augustus** (Box 8.2) deserves the title of the "father of probation," for he was the world's first probation officer.

Augustus spent a great deal of time observing the proceedings of the Boston police court. He became interested in the common drunks in jail. Because they could not pay their fines, he often paid them himself. In fact, by 1858 he had bailed out over 1,152 men and 794 women and girls. In addition to this, he would offer to help young girls and women who had either no place to go or no one to care for them.

Augustus undertook the task of supervising and guiding the behavior of those he bailed out during the period prior to the court's final disposition. The courts encouraged Augustus in his endeavors by not sentencing the convicted criminals to the usual stay in the House of Corrections. In-

---

Box 8.2 John Augustus (1785–1859)

Augustus, the "father of probation," was a Boston shoemaker interested particularly in the temperance crusade in the 1840s. As a member of the Washington Total Abstinence Society, he worked at getting men to give up alcohol. Part of his voluntary service in Boston was to visit courts and request temporary suspensions or postponements of sentence for those whom he judged were ready to quit liquor. During the next brief few weeks, Augustus would work with the bailed person, and return to court to encourage a fine (usually one penny and court costs) for the men he felt would remain sober and law abiding. He bailed almost 2,000 men, women, and children and, of the first 1,100, only one forfeited a bond. He died almost penniless, after having established a new way of dealing with offenders: probation.

stead, if they had shown signs of good behavior and reform during the period between their release on bail and their final court date, the judge would impose only a nominal fine and order the defendant to pay court costs.

Augustus' work resulted in the establishment of a visiting probation agent system in Massachusetts, in 1869. This system was devised primarily to assist delinquent children; the method of supervision employed was described as follows:

> If the offense of the convicted one appears exceptional to his general good conduct, and his appearance and surroundings are such as to give promise of future correct behavior, and if it be the first offense, the child is put on probation, with the injunction, "Go and sin no more," and becomes one of the wards of the state by adoption, over whom we exercise such guardianship as we may. If there is hope without strong promise that the offender may do well if released on probation, he is formally and legally committed to the agent of the Board of State Charities, and comes under his control independent of the parents, except as the agent permits; but he is allowed to return to the parents, and remain with them so long as he does well; although he may remain with his parents or friends, he becomes a ward of the State by due process of law, and a subject of visitation.[10]

Because of the humanitarianism of this one man, the nation's first probation law was passed in Massachusetts in 1878. In 1891, a second Massachusetts law required the criminal courts to appoint probation officers and to extend the provisions of the first law generally. By 1900, there were only four other states that recognized and used this new approach for the disposition of criminal cases. They were Missouri, beginning in 1897; Rhode Island, in 1899; New Jersey, in 1900; and Vermont, in 1900. Not until the creation of the first juvenile court in Chicago in 1899 was the idea of probation or suspended sentence with proper supervision considered in regard to juveniles.

By 1927, all but two states had passed laws similar to that of Illinois to establish juvenile courts, and all but one of those had established juvenile probation systems. The link between juvenile courts and the provision of probation services for juveniles so prevalent in the system today may be said to have originated at the very beginnings of the juvenile court movement.

Although probation sources have expanded greatly, there remains a valid challenge to practitioners in the juvenile justice system, particularly to the juvenile courts and probation officers, to see that the system does indeed work as intended.

PROBATION TODAY

Probation has become a major part of the juvenile justice system as well as a complex social institution that touches the lives of literally hundreds of thousands of young people each year. Underlying the practice of probation is the basic belief that there are juvenile delinquents who pose neither a threat nor a risk to society. Placing such juveniles in institutions would be in neither the youths' nor society's best interests. This is especially true if one accepts the Glueck's premise that most juvenile delinquency is self-correcting—the youth usually outgrows it whether or not there is official intervention by the juvenile justice system.[11] Indeed, placing juveniles in more than the "least restrictive environment" required for society's protection can lead to further law violations and more dangerous forms of delinquency. Putting a probation-eligible youth in an institution is also not cost effective to the state. It costs significantly more to maintain a juvenile in an institution, camp, or ranch than it does to supervise that same youth on probation in the community. For example, a Texas study determined that the cost of juvenile incarceration was $110.11 per day compared to $8.44 per day for community supervision in 1998. In addition, a Rand Corporation study estimated that community supervision could prevent seventy serious crimes per every $1 million expenditure.[12] A very important task for probation personnel therefore, is to identify those youths who pose no threat to the community. If the adjudicated delinquent poses no jeopardy to the community and demonstrates law-abiding behavior to the court, it is in the best interests of all concerned to consider placing the youth on probation.

Why Probation?

The primary goal of probation is to provide services designed to help youthful offenders in dealing with their problems and their environments. If the probation is successful, the factors that brought the youths into contact with the law should be resolved, and at the same time, a reintegration process for the youths into the community should be carried out. Probation is to be preferred over institutionalization for several reasons:

1. Probation allows the juvenile to function at a fairly normal level in the community, while at the same time affording protection for the community against further law violations.
2. Probation helps the juvenile to avoid the negative effects of institutionalization, which often hinder the progress of rehabilitation and the return to law-abiding behavior.

3. The verbal description of the offense in a probation case is often worded in a less severe manner than is that for other dispositions. For example, instead of a case description of "grand larceny," the words "bicycle theft" may be used. This decreases the impact of the labeling process on the juvenile.

4. The youth's rehabilitation program is greatly facilitated by keeping the youth in the community, living at home, and, if feasible, attending school, participating in extracurricular activities, working, and so forth.

5. Probation is much less expensive than is incarceration. In fact, figures indicate that probation costs only one-sixth as much as incarceration.[13]

Of course, probation is not a suitable or desirable disposition in all cases. In some states statutes define certain offenses as ineligible for probation. All offenders convicted of these offenses must be incarcerated, regardless of circumstances. In these cases, the court must accept the questionable assumption that dispositional decisions for such offenders can be based on the offense alone and that other conditions such as personality, attitude, and life circumstances are inconsequential factors in the dispositional decision for the offender.

Even if an offense is probation eligible, the community may be so outraged by the crime committed by the youth that pressure is applied on the court to place the youth in an institution. It may also be clear from the youth's past behavior or attitude that there is a predictable risk to the community and that probation would be inappropriate. In most cases, however, probation is feasible if given a chance. A great deal depends upon the training and attitude of the probation staff and the level of their commitment to making it work.

GRANTING PROBATION

How, then, is the judge to decide between placing a juvenile offender on probation and sending him or her to an institution? In 1973, the International Association of Chiefs of Police Delinquency Prevention/Juvenile Justice Conference devised criteria to guide the juvenile court judge in such a decision. The factors to be considered are still valid today:

1. Does the court have a probation department? If so, is it adequately staffed to insure maximum supervision of and counseling assistance to clients?

2. The nature and circumstances of the offense. How serious is the offense, both to the victim and to the public? What amount of criminal

sophistication was evidenced in the planning and commission of the offense?

3. The history and character of the offender. Is he currently on probation for another offense? Was he previously incarcerated? Did he admit his guilt or involvement? What are his attitudes toward the offense, society, and juvenile justice officials?

4. The offender's family situation. Would placing him back in an unstable family jeopardize chances for rehabilitation? Are the parents willing to assist their child or do they want to "get him off their hands"?

5. Availability of community resources. The juvenile court judge must establish excellent liaison procedures with community juvenile justice service agencies in order to be able to refer the probationer to these agencies for assistance with his problem. The child's school must be willing to readmit him and assist him in making a satisfactory readjustment.[14]

We supplement these original guidelines with new provisos developed by the Office of Juvenile Justice and Delinquency Prevention. In their revised *Desktop Guide to Good Juvenile Probation Practice,* they envision the role of probation as a catalyst to develop safe communities and healthy youth and families. This role will be fulfilled by the following:

1. **Holding offenders accountable.** By exercising their proper function, probation officers protect the community via aggressive enforcement of conditions (i.e., curfews, drug testing), effective communications with families of offenders or providing timely help in a time of crisis.

2. **Building and maintaining community-based partnerships**. Ties should be developed and maintained between probation officers and the police, community members, schools, churches, and other community agencies.

3. **Implementing results-based and outcome-driven services and practices.** As the juvenile offender is accountable to victims, juvenile probation offices must have clear and firm expectations of performance. Goals like fairness and consistency are paramount.

4. **Advocating for and addressing the needs of victims, offenders, families, and communities.**

5. **Obtaining and sustaining sufficient resources.**

6. **Promoting growth and development of all juvenile probation professionals.**[15]

This statement of principles stresses that juvenile probation is a catalyst. In order to accomplish its mission, entities and individuals other than the probation officer must be involved in the prevention of delinquency.

Formal and Informal Probation

Put simply, formal probation occurs when the child's petition for probation is brought before the court and the court in turn decides that a formal hearing is necessary. A youth must normally be an adjudicated delinquent, dependent, or incorrigible before being placed on formal probation.

If a juvenile is given formal probation, he or she is placed under direct supervision of an assigned probation officer and must abide by the conditions tailored to fit that situation.

A majority of cases never reach the formal court hearing stage. Informal, or "vest pocket," probation may occur for one of a number of reasons. One of the most common is an overcrowded juvenile court calendar. To place a juvenile on informal probation, a petition must be filed with the court. This petition may be filed by just about anybody, but it is usually handled by the police, the probation office, a social service agency, or in some cases by the juvenile court's intake service.

The juvenile court, in conference with those involved with the case (e.g., the probation officer, court intake officer, and so forth), reviews the juvenile's case and determines if the offense, behavior, or life circumstances warrant a formal court hearing. If not, the juvenile can be placed on informal probation and is, therefore, technically under the supervision of the probation office.

> Informal dispositions are not always in the youth's best interests, however: The rationale for pre-judicial handlings rests on the greater flexibility, efficiency, and humanity it brings to a formal system operating within legislative and other definitive policies. But pre-judicial methods that seek to place the juvenile under substantial control in his pattern of living without anyone's consent are not permissible. The difficult task is to discriminate between the undesirable use of informality, benevolent as well as punitive, and tolerable, desirable modes of guidance.[16]

"Pre-judicial" means that the case does not reach the formal hearing stage, not that the court has not been involved. Most juvenile courts have juvenile probation departments that are defined and legitimized under statute and are part of the court.

Filing a Petition

Generally, a **petition** is filed when the legal authority of the juvenile court is needed to ensure either the welfare of the child or the safety of the community. Anyone who has firsthand knowledge of the case can file a petition with the court. The petition must, however, be reviewed and found to be justifiable by a juvenile probation officer or by a juvenile court intake officer. If there is no charge in the petition, they will not be required to offer a defense. Although a petition may be amended to include all charges, such an amendment should not be necessary if special attention is paid to completeness and accuracy in the first place.

A completed petition should contain the following sections, if possible:

1. A positive identification of the child, including both true name and alias (if any), date of birth, place of birth, sex, and current address and telephone number. If the petitioner does not know any of this information, he or she should so state.
2. A positive identification of the parent or guardian, including true names and aliases (if any), marital status, current address and phone, specific relationship to the youth (this should state whether this relationship is natural, legal, putative, adoptive, or deceased), and the name and address of the persons with whom the youth is presently living.
3. A specific statement of the facts of the case. This statement should enable the court to determine its jurisdiction over the juvenile and over the subject matter of the proceedings and should be phrased in plain language and with a reasonable definiteness and particularity.
4. A request for an inquiry into the case by the court, that is, that the court look into the welfare of the child and make such order as the court shall find to be in the best interests of the juvenile and the community.
5. A copy of or statement regarding previous court orders concerning the youth in question; this should include dates of the orders and the current legal status of the juvenile.

Figure 8.1 is a generalized example of a petition that might be used by a juvenile probation department.

The initial investigation required to enable a person to file a petition is not enough. Once the petition is accepted, the juvenile court intake worker, the probation officer, or any other party who filed the petition must conduct a further investigation. Witnesses (if applicable) must be found and interviewed, evidence must be compiled, and a case must be composed that will convince the judge that the court must intercede either to protect the child or to safeguard the community.

FUNCTIONS OF JUVENILE PROBATION

The contemporary juvenile probation department serves three major functions: (1) intake and screening, (2) investigation, and (3) supervision.

IN RE THE WELFARE OF B.D.   LEGAL NO

                                                                  PETITION

_____

I represent to the Court as follows

Name of child

Place of residence

Name of person child resides with and relationship

Name of father   Residence

Name of mother   Residence

Marital status of parents

     That the child is

     That the child is within or residing within County and is in need of care and planning by the court.

     Wherefore your petitioner prays that the Court inquire into conditions and enter s such an order as shall be for the child's welfare, pursuant to Chapter 13.04 of the Revised Code of _____.

                                          _____

                                          Petitioner

STATE OF _____

COUNTY OF _____

                                          _____

                                          Petitioner

                                          _____

                                        Agency or Relationship
                                          or Residence

_____ being first duly sworn on oath, deposes and says:
     That with (s)he is the petitioner herein, that (she has read the foregoing petition, knows the contents thereof.

                                            _____

                                          _____

SUBSCRIBED AND SWORN TO before me this _____day _____of 20____.

                               SUPERIOR COURT CLERK by Deputy

                                          _____

             or

                                    Notary Public in and for the
                                         State of _____, residing at

                                         _____

continued

NOTICE TO CHILD AND PARENTS OR CUSTODIAN
READ CAREFULLY

The Court after appropriate hearings in open court may:

1. Commit a delinquent or incorrigible child to the Department of Social and Health Services, Division of Institutions or

2. Decline or waive jurisdiction in delinquency cases, to treat a child as an adult by referral to an appropriate adult court or prosecuting authority, or

3. Place a delinquent, incorrigible or dependent child in the parents custody subject to a probation plan or

4. Place a delinquent incorrigible or dependent child in the temporary custody of a group home or foster home or

5. Make any social plan for the best welfare of a delinquent incorrigible or dependent child

Hearing set for:
N & S to
Officer:

FIGURE **8.1** A sample petition

Intake and Screening

The primary function of intake and screening is to determine whether those juveniles for whom petitions have been made fall under the jurisdiction of the court. Most states have statutes that define what kinds of cases may be handled by the probation department. Thus, each case sent to the department must be screened thoroughly to make sure it is an appropriate referral.

Many referral sources do not have the time, money, or staff to properly explore each case they refer. Often, the probation officer has to confer with the child, the family, and the referral source to find out whether the probation office should handle the case directly or by referral to other community resources.

In addition to statutory deferment, other circumstances may prevent the involvement of the probation department. For example, most probation offices cannot offer services for the psychotic, the retarded, or the severely handicapped child. The preliminary investigation at intake should include an interview with the juvenile at which time the juvenile should be advised of his or her legal rights. The probation department should also contact the youth's parents or guardians to inform them of the status of the case and of their right to contact an attorney.

It is possible that the case may be resolved at this early screening stage by what has been called previously an informal disposition. This occurs if it is decided that the juvenile need not go to court but may instead be supervised by the probation department with the consent of the parents or guardian.

A crucial part of the intake and screening process is to decide whether the child should be admitted to, continued in, or removed from detention prior to the final disposition of the case. Removal from the home may constitute a major threat to the child and/or family and may deal a severe psychological blow to the youth. While removal may be necessary and even helpful for some, it may be damaging and inappropriate for others. The problem is rendered even more complex by the fact that, in the 1960s and 1970s many juvenile detention facilities degraded and brutalized their inmates rather than rehabilitated them.

The importance of doing a good job during the intake and screening process must be emphasized. Inappropriate referrals and wrong decisions can do a great deal of harm to the youths involved.

Investigation

In addition to the preliminary investigation in regard to filing a petition, the probation department must develop a comprehensive social history on each youth who is scheduled for a hearing in juvenile court.

The juvenile court can be a dominant power in the life of a juvenile in trouble. Since the juvenile delinquent may be returned home, placed in an alternative living situation, or removed from society entirely for several years, depending on the action of the court, the social study or diagnostic study is extremely important to the future of the child.

> Such a study involves the awesome task of predicting human behavior. The focal concern is the probable nature of the child's response to the necessary demands of society. Will he or will he not be able to refrain from offending again if permitted to continue to reside in the free community? An even more complicated question is: What will be his adjustment under the various possible conditions of treatment, i.e., if he is returned home without further intervention, or if he is provided differing sorts of community supervision and service, or if he is confined in an institution? Only by illuminating such questions can the social study be of value to the court's dispositional decision.[17]

The probation department staff is charged with a major responsibility. The crucial and difficult task of pretrial investigation requires hard work, dedication, intelligence, and the ability to describe human behavior. Effective interview techniques and the ability to coordinate resources and knowledge represented by other disciplines such as law, medicine, and psychiatry must be used as backup to the investigator's own personal skills.

It is not always possible to immediately delineate a child's problems and formulate a precise treatment for those problems after the social diagnosis. The treatment process is often a gradual process in which a continuing relationship between the child and the probation staff is involved. Starting with the problem as defined by the juvenile, and determining what that juvenile wishes to do about it, many other areas of difficulty are uncovered. It is not possible or even desirable for the probation officer to contend with everything that surfaces diagnostically. For example, many fatherless boys are in need of a strong father figure. Casework training (Box 8.3) may give the probation officer the flexibility to provide such a figure. But time, caseload size, or the danger of the youth's becoming overly dependent upon the probation officer may make this option unrealistic.

Supervision

The overall picture of juvenile probation is muddied by the total lack of standardization. This problem exists in state jurisdictions and in the courts within a single state. This is true in regard to the provisions of probation in general and the provision of supervision in particular.

There appear to be no standardized procedures regarding the conditions of probation, the training of probation officers, the organization of the probation staff, or the provision of services. Probation procedures, in

---

Box 8.3 Casework

Casework generally refers to the social-work model of offering services to the client based on an analysis of the case, diagnosis of client needs and problems, and designing a treatment plan to rehabilitate the offender. This approach reflects a "medical model" of corrections that raises the two questions: "Who are offenders, and what shall we do with them?" The answers are: "They are sick, and corrections should heal them and make them well."

Faced with the realities that most federal probation officers are not well prepared to provide casework and that most clients do not require this approach, the Federal Probation Service has shifted emphases to a Community Resource Management Team model. Basically, this approach argues that the offender should be reintegrated in the community, using existing community resources. Team members, usually specializing in one aspect of client needs (such as employment, drug abuse problems, emotional counseling), serve as "brokers," referring clients to local facilities and services. This team approach is believed to be a more effective reintegration approach than an officer would provide through conducting classical casework therapy.

fact, seem to be determined by individual courts and by individual cases. This multiplicity of procedures requires that probation supervision be discussed in generalities rather than in specifics. Probation supervision involves three major factors: (1) surveillance, (2) casework service, and (3) counseling or guidance.

1. **Surveillance.** The officer must keep in touch with the juvenile, the parents, the school, and other persons or agencies involved with the case. The degree of this **surveillance** depends on the amount of time the officer must spend on routine paperwork, the size of the caseload, and the individual philosophy of the court. Surveillance is intended to keep the probation officer informed about the child's progress, attitude, reactions to the treatment plan, the parents' relationship with the child, and other aspects that would indicate the child's progress or lack of progress toward reintegration into the community. Surveillance should not be used as a threat to the child. If conducted properly, it can point out the responsibilities and the demands that life and society can make on each member of a community. By acting only as a monitor and reminder of failures, it can be a strong *negative* force.

2. **Casework.** The probation officer is expected to utilize social **casework** methods to diagnose, treat, and generally deal with a juvenile. The officer makes home visits, conducts interviews, has discussions with the juvenile and parents, arranges for referrals to service agencies, works with the school, and engages in other tasks that are required in effective casework. The officer must determine to what extent the problems confronting the youth may be alleviated by involvement in community services or by his or her own personal intervention. The officer must then coordinate such services and present them in an organized program aimed at helping the child and the parents to make effective use of them.

3. **Counseling or guidance. Counseling** and/or guidance in supervision works hand in hand with the other two aspects and makes them both possible to perform.

Auxiliary Functions

Depending on the jurisdiction, the probation department provides several other services aside from surveillance, casework service, and counseling. Large probation departments often administer their own treatment or diagnostic services. These programs may include such things as foster care, group homes, drug treatment centers, and forestry camps. They may also be involved in organizing and planning community resources, and some may even operate delinquency prevention programs.

In summary, the supervision of juveniles by the probation department depends on several factors. Some of the more significant are the size and staffing of the department and available financial resources.

The amount of success that the probation department experiences in carrying out its supervisory tasks depends in large measure on the ratio of probation officers to juveniles. To emphasize this point, Douglas Besharov offers the following observation regarding juvenile probation supervision:

> The realities of probation supervision do not live up to those hopes of the theory. Few communities are blessed with sufficiently staffed probation services. Many probation departments are so completely overwhelmed that they provide almost no supervision or follow-up. Individuals on probation may be seen as infrequently as once every two months during a perfunctory office interview. This affliction of probation systems is so common that it even has a name: "token probation." Although the available evidence indicates that the size of a probation officer's caseload does not affect his success, it is reasonable to assume that the effect of "token probation" on a troubled youth is worse than no supervision at all. He sees that the end of court process was a sham and he loses further confidence, or fear in the system.[18]

Supervision Styles of Probation Officers

Supervision styles are framed by the manner in which officers view the job. This worldview defines the primary role that they follow. These roles revolve around the classic treatment (help the offender) and surveillance (protect the public) dichotomy.

1. **The punitive officer** perceives his or her role as the guardian of middle class morality. He/she attempts to coerce the offender into conforming by a means of threats and punishment, and emphasizes control, the protection of the community against the offender, and the systematic suspicion of those under supervision. Typically, they view themselves as law enforcers.

2. **The protective officer** vacillates literally between protecting the offender and protecting the community. The tools are direct assistance, lecturing, and, alternatively, praise and blame. He/she is perceived as ambivalent in his/her emotional involvement with the offender and others in the community as he/she shifts back and forth in taking sides with one against the other. They view themselves as therapists who try to blend treatment and surveillance.

3. **The welfare officer** has as the ultimate goal the improved welfare of the clients, achieved by aiding them in their individual adjustment within limits imposed by the client's capacity. Such an officer believes

that the only genuine guarantee of community protection lies in the client's personal adjustment, since external conformity will only be temporary, and, in the long run, may make a successful adjustment more difficult. Emotional neutrality permeates relationships. The diagnostic categories and treatment skills are employed from an objective and theoretically based assessment of the client's needs and capacities.

4. **The passive officer** sees the job as a sinecure requiring only minimum effort. He or she "fakes it" and "never has enough time" to manage his or her "trouble-free caseload." He or she is marking time until retirement.[19]

Research on probation officer attitudes reveals that juvenile probation officers are likely to express strong support for the rehabilitation and case worker type (treatment) of supervision strategy.[20] However, they also express a high degree of cynicism about the ability of the system to achieve the goal of offender rehabilitation.[21]

Probation officers thus have a broad range of supervision styles. They must blend the need for control with the need for treatment. Their choice of style is also dependent upon the nature of the client and the demands of the situation.[22] Treatment and enforcement are two sides of the same correctional coin.

CONDITIONS OF PROBATION

At the present time the conditions under which probation is granted are not standardized. Some courts dictate these conditions on an individual basis, while other courts follow state statutes.

The conditions of probation that do exist range from vague, general directives—for example, "Stay out of trouble" to specific stipulations, which may include attending school regularly; being home by a certain hour (curfew); getting a job; undergoing specific treatment or counseling; avoiding delinquent peers; refraining from the possession of firearms, dangerous weapons, or an automobile; refraining from drinking or use of drugs; living at home and obeying parents; living in a foster or group home; restoring damage to victims (**restitution;** see Box 8.4); doing volunteer public service work or chores; enrolling in special classes for vocational training; and regularly reporting to the probation officer.

The purpose of these conditions is to alter the juvenile's environment of past delinquent behaviors in the hope that, by removing those factors that were a negative influence, the youth will be less likely to misbehave. It can also be argued that conditions of probation may cause more misbehavior than they prevent. By imposing conditions on a youth that do not constrain his or her nonprobationer peers, the juvenile may feel picked on,

Box 8.4 Restitution

A court-ordered condition of probation that requires the offender to repair the financial, emotional, or physical damage done (a reparative sentence) by making financial payment of money to the victim or, alternatively, to a fund to provide services to victims. In addition, restitution programs are frequently ordered in the absence of a sentence to probation. It is an example of a community service alternative that is designed to make the offender directly accountable for crime while simultaneously protecting the public. It is based on the concept of restorative justice—that the offender will make amends to both the victim and the community.

Almost every state has restitution programs in operation, although Florida, Minnesota, and Michigan appear to be leaders in the development of American restitution programs. (Restitution programs have been extensively implemented and evaluated in Great Britain.) In Minnesota, parolees may also be required to reside in a residential center and pay part of their wages to victims. Other jurisdictions require victim-offender conferences to establish the amount of financial compensation to be given the victim.

A new model in this area is the "Balanced Approach and Restorative Justice" (BARJ) philosophy. It emphasizes the establishment of closer ties between community agencies and granting equal status to needs of the offender, the victim, and the community. Victim-offender mediation is a strong component of these models. The BARJ model is a part of juvenile legislation in Pennsylvania and Indiana.

Research findings on juvenile restitution programs report a small but significant impact upon recidivism. They also demonstrate that restitution program participants, both offenders and victims, express strong support concerning their participation and involvement in them.

Sources: David M. Altschuler, "Community Service Initiatives: Issues and Challenges," *Federal Probation,* Vol. 65 (2001), pp. 28–32; Gordon Bazemore and Mark S. Umbright, *Balanced and Restorative Justice for Juveniles: A Framework for Justice in the 21ˢᵗ Century* (Washington, DC: Office of Juvenile Justice and Delinquency Prevention, 1997); Ronald J. Seyko, "Balanced and Restorative Justice Efforts in Allegheny County, Pennsylvania," *The Prison Journal,* Vol. 81 (2001), pp. 187–205; Bruce A. Arrigo and Robert C. Schehr, "Restoring Justice for Juveniles: A Critical Analysis of Victim-Offender Mediation," *Justice Quarterly,* Vol. 15 (1998), pp. 629–666; Office of Juvenile Justice and Delinquency Prevention, *Guide for Implementing the Balanced and Restorative Justice Model* (Washington, DC: U.S. Department of Justice, 1998).

alienated, or left out. Examples of such arbitrary conditions could include curfews, not driving, obeying all laws (including crossing a street against the light, etc.), or going directly home after school. For some youths on probation, the conditions of their probation are so arbitrarily restrictive that to live normal lives they have no choice but to violate these conditions.

Probation should have conditions, but these conditions should be studied carefully before being mandated. They should be realistic and should be tailored as much as possible to fit a workable plan for both the youth and the community. They should also be flexible enough to allow for special circumstances such as letting a youth with a curfew go to a special school function, maintain employment that may keep him or her out after curfew, and so forth. Conditions should be stated in a fair and comprehensive manner. The youth involved should know exactly what is or is not expected of him or her and what he or she can expect from the court, including how to, and under what circumstances the youth can, approach his or her probation officer regarding negotiation of conditions. Probation conditions can also apply to the parents, guardians, or custodians of the youth on probation. For example, the court may order that the parents maintain closer control over the juvenile, undergo family therapy at a community mental health center, or participate in other suggested treatment programs. Similar considerations regarding the imposition of conditions on parents as discussed concerning youths should be followed.

If the child (or parents) violates the conditions of probation, he or she may be returned to the court for a new disposition based upon the latest misbehavior. Because probation is a means of retaining the youth in the community (and thus a means of eliminating the problems of reintegration after being in an institution), every effort is normally made to refrain from removing the child from the family and community. It is not uncommon for a youth to be returned to probation status time and time again. The courts tend to look for things such as current violations, their impact on the community, the child's past record, his or her attitude toward probation and society, and other factors. These factors were of course considered when the original disposition of probation was granted. The informal probationer who violates the condition of probation may expect to go before the court for a formal hearing and be adjudicated as either a delinquent or an incorrigible. For the youth on formal probation, the conditions of that probation may be made tighter. Often, the youth has to report more often to his or her probation officer and the hours under curfew are increased significantly.

If it appears that the youth may have to be brought before the court again, the probation officer can assume disciplinary control over the client. If the officer has a large and unmanageable caseload, disciplinary control has little or no impact. In such a situation, the threat of return to the court becomes an arbitrary action, based on infrequent or totally negative contact with the juvenile.

If one accepts that youths should remain in their communities, if at all possible, it is not surprising to see that some courts bend over backwards to avoid sending youths to institutions, even if they repeatedly violate the conditions of their probation. There is a limit, however, to the tolerance of even the most concerned courts. The violation of probation can and often does result in an order remanding the youth to a correctional facility.

There are those who interpret a violation of probation as a failure of the individual officer. This tends to force many officers to make sure that, if a violation does occur, the blame falls on the juvenile and not the officer. To deflect the blame, however, the probation officer must resist committing him or herself to the youth. Thus, if the probationer does fail, the officer can exonerate him- or herself of any responsibility and say that it is the juvenile's entire fault. Pressure of this sort certainly does not strengthen the effectiveness of the correctional concept of reintegration.

DURATION OF PROBATION

As in the case of conditions of probation, the length of time a youth must spend on probation varies from state to state where statutes exist or from court to court within each state. Some statutes limit the maximum time of the probation. And in some states, the maximum term of probation may be extended one or more times after required notice and a court hearing.

If a statute is either nonspecific about the limit or does not establish one at all, the maximum extended length is usually considered to be until the juvenile reaches majority, normally age 18.

If the juvenile has proven that he or she can responsibly meet the conditions of probation including no further law violations, the courts can shorten the term of probation and release the youth to the community on an unsupervised, normal citizen, status.

ORGANIZATION AND ADMINISTRATION OF PROBATION

Administratively and organizationally, juvenile probation has traditionally been a local function. Generally, there are three major types of organizational structures used by the states in their provision of juvenile probation services:

1. A centralized, statewide system
2. A centralized county or city system supported by state supervision, consultation, standard-setting, staff development assistance, and partial state subsidies

3. A combined state-local structure, with the largest jurisdictions operating their own probation departments and the state providing services in other areas.

Local courts or the state administrative office of the courts in twenty-three states and the District of Columbia administer probation services. Fourteen other states administer probation via a juvenile court in urban counties and through a state executive system in smaller counties. Ten states administer probation through a statewide, executive branch department. In the remaining three states, the county executive is in charge of probation services.[23] These organizational structures create complex intergovernmental problems, chiefly because, as mentioned earlier, most states place the administrative responsibility for juvenile probation services on the shoulders of the juvenile courts.

Juvenile probation has suffered and continues to suffer because there is no uniformity of standardization of administrative procedures. Administration by more than one level of government is a major cause of trouble. If juvenile probation administration continues to be divided among several units of government, then a strong, centralized state-level agency should be responsible for setting goals and standards in probation services for those departments that are unable to set their own.

Where the question of state versus local administration of juvenile probation services is raised, the best solution, from an organizational standpoint, is to have supervision from the state and administration through the counties. Such a plan

1. Has greater potential for assuring uniformity of standards and practice, including provision of services to rural areas.
2. Makes more feasible certain kinds of research, statistical and fiscal control, and similar operations.
3. Best enables recruitment of qualified staff and provision of centralized or regional in-service training and staff development programs.
4. Permits staff assignment to regional areas in response to changing conditions.
5. Facilitates relationships to other aspects of the state correctional program.[24]

However, even if everyone agreed that the administration of probation services belongs at the local level, this consensus would not completely solve the problem of intergovernmental relations. County or city probation services are administered either by the court or by an administrative agency that is a separate function of the local government. Some system professionals feel that the probation function should be part of the local corrections component; conversely, others maintain that the responsibility for probation services should remain with the juvenile court because of the court's legal jurisdiction (the sentence is suspended while the offender is on probation, yet the court maintains legal control and can revoke the suspension, if warranted, and commit the offender to an institution).[25]

Major police organizations contend that the administration of juvenile probation should be the function of the county or district courts and not at the community level. This is part of the movement toward consolidating such services at more cost-effective levels.

THE PROBATION OFFICER

With proper administration, sound organizational structure, and the commitment of state and local governments to providing competent probation services, probation still requires one more ingredient—the dedicated, well-trained, and concerned juvenile or probation officer.

"All juvenile courts have an auxiliary staff to provide the court's social service function. The same staff usually operates the intake and adjustment service, the predispositional investigation and report service, and the probation supervision service."[26] These staff members are sometimes called *juvenile counselors,* but more frequently they are known as *juvenile probation officers.* This name originated because of their traditional role of supervising juveniles on probation. Generally, state statutes spell out the specific powers and duties of the juvenile probation officer.

Duties

The duty and responsibility of the juvenile probation officer is to carry out the functions of juvenile probation: (1) intake and screening, (2) investigation, and (3) supervision. How much success the officer has in fulfilling these functions will be determined by several factors, some of which are beyond the officer's control. For example, the number of probation officers a court can hire will be limited by the court's budget, and the number of officers has a direct bearing on the size of each caseload. The training (when there is training) an officer receives is the prerogative of the court under its mandate to provide staff to oversee probation.

Although considered low in professional standing within the juvenile justice system, the probation officer generally receives the necessary court backing to enable him or her to do the job effectively. In many respects, the probation officer may be viewed as being second only to the juvenile court judge in the degree of power he or she holds within the juvenile justice system. The probation officer has the power to direct cases to and from the court system, to decide whether a juvenile is to be kept in detention or not, to influence the court's disposition through his or her ability to color the court's picture of the child and the child's family, and to exert a general influence over the outcome of a case.

Qualifications

Community supervision staff (this includes juvenile probation officers) should possess the necessary educational background to enable them to implement effectively the dispositional orders of the court. The staff should possess a minimum of a bachelor's degree in one of the helping sciences (e.g., social work, psychology, counseling, or criminal justice).[27] The juvenile probation officer should also have emotional maturity and integrity; a belief in the ability of youths to change; an interest in working with and helping children; a basic respect for the law; an ability to work well with other professionals and community members; a desire to grow professionally; and a firm belief in the dignity and worth of young people.

These qualities are an essential part of a prospective juvenile probation officer. Persons who meet these requirements or standards should receive extensive on-the-job training regarding the diagnosis and treatment of the juvenile probationer. They should be encouraged to avoid the trap of the routine administration of social services at the expense of support and treatment.

Survey results indicate that there are an estimated 18,000 juvenile probation officers at work in the United States. The majority of them (85 percent) are involved in the delivery of basic services (intake, investigation, supervision) at the line officer level. The remaining 15 percent administer probation offices or manage probation staff.[28]

Training

There should be forty hours of initial and eighty hours of ongoing training each year in the subject areas in which community supervision staff, including juvenile probation officers, are required to work. This training should begin with an orientation program for new workers to enable them to become familiar with court or agency policies, attitudes, and demands. In-service training, casework supervision, and procedures for educational leave should be included in on-the-job training.

In-Service Training. In-service training should be designed to meet the needs of the staff at various levels, including supervisory and administrative. Larger agencies should assign a full-time person to conduct in-service training; appropriate state departments in organizing training regionally should assist smaller agencies.

Casework Supervision. Casework supervision involves instruction for the probation officer in the proper use and application of diagnosis and treatment. Without specific instruction of this kind, it is difficult for the untrained worker to apply what has been learned in the training program to practical situations involving juveniles, their families, and the community.

Educational Leave.   The probation department should not only offer but should actively encourage educational leave and stipends so that both part- and full-time staff members have the opportunity to broaden their education, meet desired qualifications, and improve their professional abilities and competence.

It is unrealistic to assume that all the educational and training needs of the probation officer can be met during an in-service training period. For this to happen, there must be well-prepared personnel to carry out the necessary supervision and training of those who need it; unfortunately, this is seldom the case. Maximum contributions to the field of probation will not be realized unless staff members are encouraged to advance, learn, and grow. Graduate professional training is an excellent way to accomplish this goal. Advanced professional training can be pursued by taking a master's degree in social work, which normally requires two full years' work beyond a bachelor's degree, or a graduate degree in sociology, psychology, criminology, or public administration. These degrees require one or two years' study beyond the undergraduate degree.

A survey of juvenile probation officers in all fifty states and the District of Columbia reflected their views concerning training. Nearly half of the states responded that their jurisdiction was considering the certification of juvenile probation officers, making it a professionally credited position with certain stated requirements. The survey also revealed that organizations tended to emphasize pre-service training but more in-service training was now required.[29]

Method of Appointment

Probation staff should be selected in accordance with civil service laws where there is an organized civil service system. Where these laws do not apply, the staff should be selected on the basis of the merit of the applicants. The selection process should include a thorough review of the applicant's education, experience, and training. A merit examination should be used in making appointments. It should be open to all persons who meet the qualifications.

The evaluation and/or examination should test basic skills and knowledge required for good performance. It should not be concerned with matters that are meant to be learned on the job. Once appointed, the new probation officer should be given a reasonable period of time in which to become acquainted with his or her new duties and responsibilities.

Salaries

Salaries for newly appointed probation officers are as nonstandardized as the function and terms of probation itself. In a survey of juvenile probation officers, more than half (53 percent) of the line officers reported earnings of less than $40,000 per year. Thirteen percent earned $40,000 per year or more. About 30 percent of the administrators reported annual earnings of more than $49,999. Regarding job concerns, 42 percent of the probation officers surveyed expressed fear that their job was becoming more dangerous. About one-third of the officers reported that they had been assaulted on the job in their career.[30] It is apparent that the job of a probation officer is not lucrative. The desire to serve the public and juvenile clients is the driving force in this profession.

Probation standards call for salaries commensurate with employment in similar positions of trust and responsibility. Because of low salary rates, most of the nation's probation departments cannot compete with other government agencies in recruiting the caliber of staff member that they need and want. It is little wonder that the majority of probation departments identify lack of staff as their biggest problem in administering and conducting juvenile probation services.

Caseload Size

As mentioned earlier, a decisive factor in the quality of probation services is the size of the officer's caseload. All facets of the probation officer's work, from preliminary investigation to supervision, are affected by the caseload. An overcrowded caseload will usually result in a cursory investigation in which many pertinent and potentially crucial facts may be totally overlooked.

Recent survey results of juvenile probation officers found that the size of caseloads in departments ranged from 2 to 200. The median (midpoint) of active caseload size was 41, but the officers suggested that the optimal caseload size should be 30 clients.[31]

Supervision, other than formal reporting and infrequent checks at school, work, and home, is literally impossible with a large caseload. Large caseloads not only limit supervision to a cursory police-type function, but they also tend to move probation services further away from professional social casework standards for diagnosis and treatment to a more authoritarian role.

INNOVATIONS IN JUVENILE PROBATION

A number of programs and supervision supplements have been devised to supplement juvenile probation. A sample of these different strategies is presented in this section.

Probation Subsidy

No discussion of juvenile probation would be complete without a look at what has come to be known as the probation subsidy program. (See Box 8.5.) It has been pointed out that the lack of staff and the overload of case assignments can greatly lessen the impact that probation might otherwise have on diverting juveniles from the formalized system. The probation subsidy program was started to alleviate this situation; it is used in several states today.

Simply stated, **probation subsidy** provides funding and guidance necessary to enable participating courts to develop and implement community based treatment programs as alternatives to institutionalization. Normally, funding is provided by the state to the local courts. It is based on the number of youths that each court is able to divert from the state system.

The aim of the subsidy program, therefore, is to reduce the necessity for commitment of juveniles to state correctional facilities by strengthening and improving the supervision of juveniles placed on probation by the juvenile courts. The program encourages the courts to develop a wide range of special programs that may include counseling and placement services; contracts for psychiatric, psychological, and medical services; special day care centers; vocational and educational programs; family and group counseling; tutoring services; extensive use of volunteers; use of case aides, work and recreational programs, educational counseling, and myriad other services integral to effective probation supervision programs.

Box 8.5 Probation Subsidy

A *probation subsidy* is a program run by a state. The subsidy provides money to counties and local jurisdictions for not committing offenders to prisons. The intents of subsidies are to bolster local probation services, encourage expansion of probation services, develop innovative probation strategies, and lessen the prison overcrowding problem.

Probation subsidies originated in California and, for a period before the resurgence of neoclassical ideology forced sharp changes in an otherwise enlightened environment, reduced the proportion of felon offenders sentenced to California penal institutions. Increasing probation service strength also saved the California prison system millions of dollars in the interim. Coupled with intermediate punishments, particularly intensive supervised probation, such subsidies could form the backbone of a correctional reform in many states suffering from prison overcrowding.

The functions of probation (i.e., intake, investigation, and supervision) are also functions of probation subsidy workers. Essentially, except for funding base and allocations, regular probation and probation subsidy officers operate in a similar manner. Staff assignments and caseload sizes may vary, however, for probation subsidy officers. For example, some states have regular, local probation officers who handle the nonsubsidy probation caseloads and probation subsidy officers who handle nothing but subsidy caseloads.

Since probation subsidy is meant to go beyond regular probation in diverting children from the correctional program, subsidy officers generally have caseloads comprised of youths who are on informal probation or who have not yet reached the formal hearing stage. This type of caseload, which generally requires less routine paperwork, allows the subsidy workers to spend more of their workday providing or coordinating direct services for youths on their caseloads.

The probation subsidy program, where it has been tried, has had a far greater success rate than ever anticipated. It has reduced the social and individual cost of juvenile delinquency by reducing treatment costs, reducing the pattern of institutional commitments, and meeting the treatment needs of delinquent youths within the community.

Some states have also tried what is called a **negative subsidy** (Box 8.6), in which a state charges each county a sum of money for every offender the county commits whose crime was a lesser offense.

Volunteers in Probation

The use of volunteers to supplement the efforts of paid correctional and juvenile justice system personnel are an increasingly common practice. Most probation department administrators endorse it enthusiastically.

Box 8.6 Negative Subsidy

In addition to the policy option of subsidizing probation services in counties that commit fewer than expected offenders to prison every year, or for meeting state requirements and standards, some states have decided that certain types of offenders ought to be kept in their local community under probation control. To encourage such retention, Oregon charges each county $3,000 for every committed offender whose crime falls in the "least severe" category. This means that a check for $3,000 must accompany the commitment papers when the least risky case offender is transported to prison. This is a *negative subsidy,* designed to encourage local communities to accept responsibility for providing correctional care and control for their own residents.

Probation itself, the reader will recall, actually began as a volunteer service in the nineteenth century. In recent years, rising probation caseloads, lack of staff, and increased costs have brought about a renewed dependence on the assistance of community volunteers in probation. With the emphasis today on community-based programs for both adult and juvenile offenders, community volunteers are especially useful, and in the courts, the number of volunteers has increased significantly in the past fifteen years.

Voluntary work in probation is a documented subject, and several works have been written that explain all facets of volunteer programs in probation.

In a volunteer program, the probationer remains under the supervision of the probation department after having been placed on probation. However, the youth's primary contact is with a volunteer, usually on an individual basis within the community setting.

Case assignments are made on a common sense basis. Volunteers and children should be matched for the most rewarding relationship. The matching should be based on the needs of the probationer and the skills and interests of the volunteer. Both the youth and the volunteer must feel comfortable with each other or nothing will be accomplished. Many of the larger probation departments have a volunteer coordinator who oversees and supervises the pairing of youths and volunteers and the supervisory responsibilities during the probation period.

There are risks involved in matching probationers and volunteers. One of the risks concerns matching that ends in failure. This is a major problem because the professional staff member must pick up the pieces and attempt to keep the youth interested in the program and out of trouble. The youth may already be badly alienated from the system and may cause the regular probation officer more concern and problems than if the child had been assigned to his or her caseload in the first place. Under these circumstances, regular professional probation officers become resentful or extremely skeptical of volunteers who may undermine the system through their inexperience, lack of professional training, or inability to perform probationary tasks.

Intensive Supervision

Intensive supervision is designed to address a number of different systemwide, supervision problems and issues. First, it aims to generate increased contact between the officer and the client by decreasing caseload size. This increased contact will benefit society through the close monitoring of high-risk offenders. It will also provide improved service delivery and more effective treatment for clients. Lundman defines intensive supervision programs (ISPs) as follows:

ISPs are an example of the United States' current "get tough" policy with respect to adolescent crime. Intensive probation and intensive parole programs are *tough* ways of doing time in the community. Small caseloads allow for the strict enforcement of the routine conditions of probation and parole. Officers have time to make sure clients are in school or at work each weekday and home each night and weekend.[32]

Intensive supervision typically features small caseloads of ten to fifteen clients with officers working in teams of two. It is combined with such program features as education, community service, restitution, employment, and electronic monitoring.[33] Intensive supervision also targets high-risk offenders who would be incarcerated if the program were not available.[34] The hope is that intensive supervision will lead to a reduction in the institutional population and lower recidivism rates.[35] However, research findings on several ISPs fail to demonstrate any appreciable difference in recidivism rates between ISP clients and other juvenile offenders in the community.[36] Yet, the ability of intensive supervision to achieve a "break even" result with reduced costs of incarceration is a positive finding.[37]

Electronic Monitoring

Another "get tough" approach to the community supervision of juvenile offenders is **electronic monitoring.** Using a tracking device worn by the client, electronic monitoring tracks movement. It can be used to monitor curfews imposed by the court or take the place of institutional confinement, using the home as the site of punishment.[38]

Evaluations of electronic monitoring programs cite several beneficial aspects of this program. First, it is less costly than incarceration. Second, it can easily be combined with other forms of treatment because the juvenile is in the community. Third, the offender is not removed from social supports—school, family, churches, and so on. Participants did not complain that electronic monitoring was overly intrusive and a violation of their privacy.[39]

School Probation

Historically, schools have been recognized as a delinquency prevention institution. The hope was that education would open up opportunities for juveniles and give them a stake in conformity. Thus, schools have been a focal point of recent violence prevention and restitution efforts.[40]

As a result, like their police counterparts, juvenile probation officers have often moved their offices directly into middle and high school buildings to have closer contact with their clients. This move provides more effective monitoring and also increases communication between the officer, the client, other community agencies and, of course, teachers and school authorities. Pennsylvania has widely adopted **school probation** with programs in fifty of its sixty-seven counties. Some 150 officers working in 300 schools have served more than 16,000 juveniles. Preliminary research evidence demonstrates that school probation has a desirable impact upon both school attendance and behavior.[41]

SUMMARY

There is one major problem facing the success of probation—careless overuse.

> Probation supervision tends to be a dumping ground for all those difficult juveniles whom the judge is afraid to send back into the community without some protection from future misgiving or criticism. He does not wish to place them and yet he "must do something" with them. Mentally retarded children, who are in need of very specialized types of services, also are often placed on probation because there is no other place for them. The effect is the dilution and misapplication of limited resources. For many juveniles, then, the circumstances of probation invite failure.[42]

The trend in corrections is more and more toward community-based programs, programs that are being asked to offer diagnosis, diversion, and treatment, and to reduce stigma. As this trend continues, greater use will be made of probation as an alternative to institutionalization. With this increased use comes the threat of overuse of the program as an effective means of dealing with youth in trouble.

The nationwide use of probation is the preferred disposition, preferably without the subsequent adjudication of guilt within the particular case. It is also recommended that volunteers serve in all capacities in the probation process. We agree with Richard Lundman: "It is recommended that routine probation remain as the first and most frequent sentencing option for moderately delinquent juveniles convicted of index crimes against property."[43]

There are persuasive arguments in favor of probation over institutionalization. They are (1) a reduced stigma for the youth involved; (2) the advantage of remaining in the community; (3) the availability of a wealth of resources offered in the community that are generally absent in the institution; (4) the number of youth served and diverted from the formal system; and, most important, (5) the reduced costs of probation as compared with those of institutionalization. We must ensure, however, that reduced cost does not just make probation cheaper without also making it better.

TERMS TO REMEMBER

Benefit of clergy	Petition
Casework	Probation
Counseling	Probation subsidy
Electronic monitoring	Recognizance
Intensive supervision	Restitution
John Augustus	School probation
Judicial reprieve	Supervision styles
Negative subsidy	Surveillance

REVIEW QUESTIONS

1. Outline the historical beginning of the modern probation system.
2. Define the term probation. Explain what is meant by formal and informal probation.
3. What are the functions of probation today? How are they administered best?
4. What is a petition and how is it filed? Why is it filed?
5. What qualities are important in an applicant for the job of probation officer? Are these qualities or qualifications being met?
6. Explain probation subsidy. How does this program and the use of volunteers in probation fit into the goals of probation? Cite any experience or knowledge you have regarding subsidy or volunteer programs.
7. Do you think probation works? Why or why not?
8. Go to the web site for *Easy Access to Juvenile Court Statistics,* http://ojjdp.ncjrs.org/ojstatbb/ezajcs, and update the figures on the number of probationers contained in this chapter.
9. Which of the new forms of supervision discussed in this chapter do you think is the most promising? Why?
10. What should be the dominant philosophy of juvenile probation officers? Why?

NOTES

[1]U.S. Department of Justice, *Juvenile Justice: A Century of Change* (Washington, DC: Office of Juvenile Justice and Delinquency Prevention, 1999), p. 2.

[2]A. Stahl, T. Finnegan, and W. Kang, *Easy Access to Juvenile Court Statistics: 1990–1999,* http://ojjdp.ncjrs.org/ojstatbb/ezajcs.

[3]Ibid.

[4]Ibid.

[5]Patricia McFall Torbet, *Juvenile Probation: The Workhorse of the Juvenile Justice System* (Washington, DC: Office of Juvenile Justice and Delinquency Prevention, 1996), p. 1.

[6]Ibid, p. 2.

[7]W. S. Holdsworth, *A History of English Law,* vol. 3, p. 294, quoted in *Probation and Related Matters* (New York: United Nations, Department of Social Affairs, 1951), footnote, p. 17.

[8]Ibid.

[9]Robert M. Carter and Leslie T. Wilkins, eds. *Probation, Parole, and Community Corrections* (New York: John Wiley, 1976), p. 83.

[10]Board of State Charities of Massachusetts, *Sixth Annual Report* (Boston: State of Massachusetts, 1869), p. 269.

[11]Sheldon Glueck and Eleanor Glueck, *Delinquents and Nondelinquents in Perspective* (Cambridge, MA: Harvard University Press, 1968), pp. 151–152.

[12]U.S. Department of Justice, Law Enforcement Assistance Administration, *Annual Report of National Institute for Juvenile Justice and Delinquency Prevention* (Washington, DC: Government Printing Office, March 1980), p. 21.

[13]Tom Reed, *Oranges to Oranges: Comparing the Operational Costs of Juvenile and Adult Correctional Programs in Texas* (Austin, TX: Texas Criminal Justice Policy Council, 1999) pp. 39–46. Peter W. Greenwood, Karyn E. Model, C. Peter Rydell, and James Chiesa, *Diverting Children from a Life of Crime: Measuring Costs and Benefits* (Santa Monica, CA: Rand Corporation, 1996) pp. 57–66.

[14]R. W. Kobetz and B. B. Bosarge, *Juvenile Justice Administration* (Gaithersburg, MD: International Association of Chiefs of Police, 1973), p. 325.

[15]Patrick Griffin, "Rethinking Juvenile Probation: *The Desktop Guide to Good Juvenile Probation Practice* Revisited," *NCJJ In Focus,* Vol. 2 (November 2000), p. 2; Joseph B. Sanborn, "The Juvenile, the Court, or the Community: Whose Best Interests Are Currently Being Promoted in Juvenile Court," *Justice System Journal,* Vol. 17 (1994), pp. 249–266; Gordon Bazemore and Lynette Feder, "Rehabilitation in the New Juvenile Court: Do Judges Support the Treatment Ethic," *American Journal of Criminal Justice,* Vol. 21 (1997), pp. 181–212; W. D. Burrell, "Juvenile Probation and Prevention: Partners for the Future?" *Community Corrections Report on Law and Corrections,* Vol. 6 (1998), pp. 3–4, 16.

[16]President's Commission on Law Enforcement and Administration of Justice, *Task Force Report—Juvenile Delinquency and Youth Crime* (Washington, DC: U.S. Government Printing Office, 1967), p. 16.

[17]President's Commission on Law Enforcement and Administration of Justice, *Task Force Report—Corrections,* (Washington, DC: U.S. Government Printing Office, 1967), p. 132.

[18]Douglas J. Besharov, *Juvenile Justice Advocacy, Practice in a Unique Court* (New York: Practicing Law Institute, 1974), p. 383.

[19]Adopted from Lloyd E. Ohlin, Herman Piven, and D. M. Pappenfort, "Major Dilemmas of the Social Worker in Probation and Parole," *National Probation and Parole Association Journal,* Vol. 2 (1956), pp. 21–25; Daniel Glaser, *The Effectiveness of a Prison and Parole System* (Indianapolis, IN: Bobbs-Merrill, 1969); Carl Klockars, "A Theory of Probation Supervision," *Journal of Criminal Law, Criminology, and Police Science,* Vol. 63 (1972), pp. 550–557.

[20]Richard D. Sluder and Frances P. Reddington, "An Empirical Examination of the Work Ideologies of Juvenile and Adult Probation Officers," *Journal of Offender Rehabilitation,* Vol. 20 (1993), pp. 115–137.

[21]Jeffrey P. Rush, "Juvenile Probation Officer Cynicism," *American Journal of Criminal Justice,* Vol. 16 (1992), pp. 1–16; Russell L. Curtis, William A. Reese, and Michael P. Cone, "Cynicism Among Juvenile Probation Officers: A Case of Subverted Ideals," *Journal of Criminal Justice,* Vol. 18 (1990), pp. 501–517.

[22]Harry E. Allen, Chris W. Eskridge, Edward J. Latessa, and Gennaro F. Vito, *Probation and Parole in America* (New York: The Free Press, 1985), pp. 132–133.

[23]Torbet, *Juvenile Probation,* p. 2.

[24]Kobetz and Bosarge, *Juvenile Justice Administration,* p. 333–334.

[25]Ibid., p. 335.

[26]Besharov, *Juvenile Justice Advocacy,* p. 159.

[27]See Lori Colley, Robert G. Culbertson, and Edward J. Latessa, "Juvenile Probation Officers: A Job Analysis," *Juvenile and Family Court Journal,* Vol. 38 (1987), pp. 1–12.

[28]Torbet, *Juvenile Probation.*

[29]Frances P. Reddington and Betsy W. Kreisel, "Training Juvenile Probation Officers: National Trends and Practice," *Federal Probation,* Vol. 64 (2000), pp. 28–32.

[30]Torbet, *Juvenile Probation,* pp. 2–3.

[31]Ibid., p. 3.

[32]Richard J. Lundman, *Prevention and Control of Juvenile Delinquency* (New York: Oxford University Press, 2001), p. 166.

[33]B. Stanton, *Juvenile Intensive Probation Surveillance Techniques* (Washington, DC: Office of Juvenile Justice and Delinquency Prevention, 1992).

[34]Todd R. Clear, "Juvenile Intensive Probation Supervision: Theory and Rationale," in Troy L. Armstrong, ed., *Intensive Interventions with High-Risk Youths,* (Monsey, NY: Criminal Justice Press/Willow Tree Press, 1991), pp. 29–44; R. G. Wiebush and Donna M. Hamparian, "Variations in 'Doing' Juvenile Intensive Supervision: Programmatic Issues in Four Ohio Jurisdictions," in Troy L. Armstrong, ed., *Intensive Interventions with High-Risk Youths* (Monsey, NY: Criminal Justice Press/Willow Tree Press, 1991), pp. 153–188.

[35]Allen, Eskridge, Latessa, and Vito, *Probation and Parole in America,* pp. 194–196.

[36]William H. Barton and Jeffrey A. Butts, "Intensive Supervision Alternatives for Adjudicated Juveniles," in Troy L. Armstrong, ed., *Intensive Interventions with High-Risk Youths* (Monsey, NY: Criminal Justice Press/Willow Tree Press, 1991), pp. 317–340; Henry Sontheimer and Lynne Goodstein, "An Evaluation of Juvenile Intensive Aftercare Probation: Aftercare versus System Response Effects," *Justice Quarterly,* Vol. 10 (1993), pp. 197–227.

[37]Lundman, *Prevention and Control,* p. 180.

[38]I. Montgomery, "Electronic Monitoring: Overview of an Alternative to Incarceration for Juvenile Offenders," *Journal for Juvenile Justice and Detention Services,* Vol. 10 (1995), pp. 26–28.

[39]Michael T. Charles, "Electronic Monitoring for Juveniles," *Journal of Crime and Justice,* Vol. 12 (1989), pp. 147–169; John S. Clarkson and James J. Weakland, "A Transitional Aftercare Model for Juveniles: Adapting Electronic Monitoring and Home Confinement," *Journal of Offender Monitoring,* Vol. 4 (1991), pp. 1–15; Melvyn C. Raider, "Juvenile Electronic Monitoring: A Community Based Program to Augment Residential Treatment," *Residential Treatment for Children and Youth,* Vol. 12 (1994), pp. 37–48.

[40]Scott H. Decker, *Increasing School Safety Through Juvenile Accountability Programs* (Washington, DC: Office of Juvenile Justice and Delinquency Prevention, 2000).

[41]Patrick Griffin, "Juvenile Probation in the Schools," *NCJJ In Focus,* Vol. 1 (Winter 1999), pp. 1–11.

[42]Besharov, *Juvenile Justice Advocacy,* p. 384.

[43]Lundman, *Prevention and Control,* p. 303.

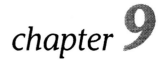

chapter 9

JUVENILE INSTITUTIONS: THE SUCCESS OF FAILURE

In theory, detention of youth fulfills three primary objectives. First, youth are detained if there is reason to believe that in the absence of such external controls the juvenile would be free to commit additional serious crimes, thereby posing a threat to the safety and security of the community. In this situation the child is incarcerated primarily for the benefit of the community. Second, juveniles also are detained in cases where the bad influences of a home environment necessitate placing the child in a more protective setting. In this case, children are viewed as being endangered and detention is construed a temporary measure until a more permanent home placement can be arranged. Finally, detention parallels the function of the bail system in adult criminal court, and ensures the appearance of the youthful offender at subsequent court dates.

— Barry Krisberg and James F. Austin[1]

CHAPTER OVERVIEW

No matter what it is called—juvenile institution, training school, correctional facility, detention center, shelter, youth camp, ranch, halfway house, jail, reformatory, or prison—each of these places is an institution in which a delinquent and dependent youth can be held.

Commenting on the rising number of commitments to juvenile correctional institutions, Marler and Scoble state:

While high-profile incidents of youth violence have gained national headlines during the past few years and politicians have vowed to "get tough" on juvenile offenders, the majority of adolescents in juvenile justice systems throughout the country are not violent offenders. In fact, more than half—about 70 percent—of juvenile offenders have been incarcerated for property offenses, multiple misdemeanors or controlled substance violations, and have substance abuse problems. Clearly, with this much variation, a one-size-fits-all approach to juvenile justice cannot work.[2]

Juvenile administrators must be prepared to counter the emotional reactions of the public to high-profile, juvenile crimes. They fuel the search for "quick-fix" solutions to delinquency that do not produce long-term results.[3]

The per capita operating expenditure by juvenile detention and correctional facilities has changed over the past twenty years. There has been a definite trend toward **privatization** (See box 9.1). Smith reports that total operational expenditures for juvenile facilities increased from $2.4 billion in 1974 to $3.8 billion in 1994.[4] This rate of increase was greater for private facilities (136 percent) than public facilities (25 percent) during this time period.[5] Methods, features, and benefits of privatization are listed in Box 9.1.

However, there are substantial differences between public and private institutions. A juvenile institution is intended to provide specialized programs for children who must be under some form of restraint to be treated. Accordingly, it normally houses the more hardened, unstable, or nontreatable youths who do not even meet the liberal standards for juvenile probation. The institution program attempts to prepare the youth for return to the community. Whether this reintegration with society will work depends on several interrelated factors, one of which is the quality of aftercare services, which are necessary to strengthen and reinforce

---

Box 9.1 Privatization

With lease-purchase, government officials have created a nonprofit entity that acts on behalf of their agency. With *privatization,* a profit-making company actually owns the institution because private investors have put up money to build it.

Financing provided by a private company is almost always more costly because a unit of government can obtain a lower interest rate than a private company. A major reason for the higher cost is that lease payments on a privately owned institution must be treated as taxable income. In the recent past, the higher cost of private financing

continued

Box 9.1 Privatization (continued)

has been somewhat reduced because special tax benefits may be available to a company raising capital for construction. When tax benefits are available, private owners of a facility may pass their savings through to the governmental entity in the form of reduced lease payments.

Private owners of correctional facilities have been eligible to claim such tax benefits as depreciation and investment tax credits. However, federal legislation passed in 1986 disallows most of the tax advantages of private ownership. Accordingly, the cost of private financing will probably be even higher than in the past.

Privatization may also involve private sector management and operation of a correctional facility. While private firms may offer contracts for both operations and financing, these issues should be examined separately. Although costs of operation may be discretionary, costs of private financing are necessarily higher when raising capital for construction.

Other features of private sector participation may be of interest to state and local officials. Many firms now offer a comprehensive package of services called *turnkey* or *design-build* contracts in which a single company provides a variety of services ordinarily divided among several different firms. Depending upon the laws of each jurisdiction, consolidation into one contract may be an efficient approach that results in faster completion of the correctional facility.

Industrial development bonds represent a public-private partnership. This approach offers tax-exempt income to investors because securities are issued with the authorization of a governmental entity. However, total financing must be limited to $10 million, and the unit of government must pay full, fair market value for the facility upon termination of the lease. Use of industrial development bonds is tightly restricted by federal law, and it is expected that Congress will impose further limitations on this approach in the future.

The number of juveniles held in private facilities is on the rise. In 1999, the number of juvenile offenders in residential placement in private facilities numbered 31,599—an increase of 7 percent over the number in 1997. The number of juveniles in residential placement in public facilities numbered 76,355 but they only increased by 1 percent over 1997.

Sources: National Institute of Justice, *Ohio's New Approach to Prison and Jail Financing* (Washington, DC: U.S. Department of Justice, November, 1986), p. 9; Melissa Sickmund, "Juvenile Offenders in Residential Placement: 1997–1999," *Juvenile Offenders and Victims—National Report Series* (Washington, DC: Office of Juvenile Justice and Delinquency Prevention, March, 2002), p. 1.

changes begun in the institution that can be tested and proved only during the course of normal community living. These types of programs are more likely to be run by public agencies. Private juvenile facilities are more likely to be ranches, forestry camps, farms, halfway houses, and group homes that feature rehabilitation services and greater contact with the community.[6] Despite the fact that more juveniles were held in private facilities during this period, the number of private juvenile facilities increased more than their public counterparts.[7]

Despite the vast expansion and growth of community-based facilities there has still been no major decline in the use of juvenile institutions. In the *Gault* decision, the Supreme Court emphasized the reality of institutionalization for a juvenile:

> Ultimately, however, we confront the reality. . . . A boy is charged with misconduct. The boy is committed to an institution where he may be restrained of liberty for years. It is of no constitutional consequence . . . and of limited practical meaning . . . that the institution to which he is committed is called an Industrial School. The fact of the matter is that, however euphemistic the title, a "receiving home" or an "industrial school" for juveniles is an institution of confinement in which the child is incarcerated for a greater or lesser time. His world becomes "a building with whitewashed walls, regimented routine and institutional hours. . . ." Instead of mother and father and sisters and brothers and friends and classmates, his world is peopled by guards, custodians, state employees, and delinquents confined with him for anything from waywardness to rape and homicide.[8]

HISTORICAL ORIGINS OF JUVENILE INSTITUTIONS

America's early juvenile institutions were patterned after nineteenth-century European models. In 1817, the London Philanthropic Society was founded and included in its purpose and practice the reformation of juvenile offenders. This organization opened the first English house of refuge for children, which became the prototype of similar houses of refuge in the United States.

Houses of Refuge

One of the first prisons in history was specifically designed for juvenile offenders. In 1704, Pope Clement XI built the Hospice of San Michele in Rome. It was designed to accomplish the aim of **expiation**—the atonement of sins through suffering. Its strict regimen could be summarized as follows:

The young offenders worked in association in a central hall at tasks in spinning and weaving. Chained by one foot and under a strict rule of silence, they listened to the brothers of a religious order while they droned through the Scripture of religious tracts. The incorrigible boys were separated, day and night, in little cubicles or cells. Large signs, hung throughout the institution, admonished "Silence." Floggings were resorted to as penalties for "past mistakes."[9]

Houses of refuge were the next organized attempt to control and treat juvenile delinquency. These institutions marked a major shift away from family-oriented discipline and toward treatment administered by society in specialized facilities. As houses of refuge spread throughout Europe and America, they retained a reformatory atmosphere, associated with education and with mechanical labor, as in the trades. Rauhe Haus, founded in Hamburg, Germany, in 1833 by Dr. John Henry Wichern, served as a model for the institution combining reform and refuge.[10]

New York, Boston, and Philadelphia were the centers of urban population in the early 1800s. The woeful plight of wayward youths confined with adults in jails in these cities prompted groups to study the ways in which juveniles were being handled in Europe. The philosophy upon which early American juvenile institutions were founded was, therefore, an indigenous one. It can be traced to several European leaders and educators such as Johann Heinrich Pestalozzi (1746–1827), who established a school for orphans at Neuhoff, Switzerland, in 1775.[11] Unfortunately, Pestalozzi's legacy to American school children—the reduction of physical abuse and punishment in common schools—made little impression on those who ran the houses of refuge or the reform schools.

The New York Society for the Reformation of Juvenile Delinquents, founded in 1823, organized the first of the institutional movements. Originating from a movement within the Society of Friends, the New York Society opened the first reformatory in the United States, the New York House of Refuge, in 1825. The New York house and those opened in Boston and Philadelphia generally accepted destitute and orphaned children as well as youths convicted of crimes in state and/or local courts. Life was hard for the children who grew up in these special houses. Their parents were looked down upon as too poor or too degenerate to provide them with the basic necessities of life. The refuge house managers considered immigrant youths, white female delinquents, and blacks of both sexes (generally, blacks were totally excluded from the refuges) inferior to white, American-born males.

The New York City House of Refuge experienced a rapid growth rate and similar growth occurred in other houses of refuge. Before long, they became overcrowded and filled with a mixture of hard-core juvenile delinquents and orphans. New York's answer was Randall's Island institution in the East River. Randall's Island allowed the Society for the Reformation of Juvenile Delinquents to apply a more systematic reformatory regime; one that they felt was the answer for dealing with delinquent and wayward youth.

The first public juvenile institution was a municipal reformatory for boys, established in New Orleans in 1845. Prior to that, the operation and maintenance of the institutions was a joint effort responsibility of state and private agencies. The first state reform school for boys was opened in 1845 in Westboro, Massachusetts. Known as the **Lyman School for Boys,** it was closed only in 1972.

The prevailing philosophy and educational practice of the times had a great deal of influence on the operation of juvenile institutions. During this time, it was believed that behavior was entirely a matter of self-control; thus, related influences were given little consideration. The early methods used in institutions were concerned with strict discipline, the inculcation of regular work and school habits, and the extensive use of punishment.

In 1835, Pennsylvania enacted legislation to add incorrigibility as a reason for commitment. The new law was challenged as unconstitutional after an incorrigible child had been committed to the House of Refuge without a jury trial. In *Ex Parte* **Crouse,** the Pennsylvania Supreme Court upheld the commitment, ruling that "The House of Refuge is not a prison, but a school, where reformation, not punishment, is the end." This case upheld the authority of the state to act in *parens patriae* for the benefit of juveniles.[12]

New York established a state agricultural and industrial school in 1849, and Maine, a training center in 1853. By 1870, Connecticut, Indiana, Maryland, Nevada, New Hampshire, New Jersey, Ohio, and Vermont could boast separate institutions or training schools for delinquents. By 1900, thirty-six states had followed suit, and today they are located in every state.

The original functions of the houses of refuge, reformatories, and juvenile institutions were threefold: (1) to get the poor, the wayward, and delinquent youths off the streets; (2) to separate youths from adult criminals; and (3) to save juveniles from crime through a regimented lifestyle, education, and training. Although juvenile institutions attempted to protect the children from the negative influence of adult institutions, the courts were still permitted to commit juvenile offenders to adult prisons if they desired.

Although the efforts to rescue juveniles in the early 1800s were crude and haphazard, they did offer a beginning. The religious environment and training of the early houses of refuge was largely Protestant, in keeping with the religious affiliation of early settlers in the eastern United States. To counter this Protestant influence, several private sectarian institutions were established. The Roman Catholic order of the House of Good Shepherd established institutions for girls, and the Christian Brotherhood assumed responsibility for parochial schools and for institutional care of delinquent Catholic boys. Protestant denominations also established institutions for delinquent youth of both sexes. After the major Jewish migrations near the end of the nineteenth century, American Jews began to build orphanages and training schools as well.

Reform Schools

During the period 1859–1890, the movement to set up houses of refuge was replaced by the reform school and preventive agency movement. The Boston House of Reformation was one of the more notable reform schools. Juvenile asylums were established, and the practice of "placing children out" became popular. By 1890 nearly every state outside of the South had some type of reform school for delinquent youths that was also responsible for the care of numerous destitute children. One of the major problems facing the reform schools then still exists today: the problem of agreeing to a legal definition of juvenile delinquency. Because of this, youths who had committed a crime, youths who had neither committed nor been convicted of a crime, and youths who were convicted of a crime for which the law had no penalty were all held together in the same school. Also housed there were children who had been abused or abandoned by their parents, or youths who had been committed by their parents for being unruly or unmanageable.

Although the reform schools devoted more time to schooling (usually half a day or more), many of them were otherwise indistinguishable from the early refuges. Most were large congregate institutions with regimented workshop routines. Many reformers sought to change the routines of these reform schools by introducing a more varied and aesthetic institutional life for the children, with guidance aimed at bettering the total child and not simply at making the child conform to the rigors of strict discipline, work, and training.

Cottage Reform School

The **cottage reform school** plan, founded by Wichern at Rauhe Haus, offered an opportunity to break away from the congregate placement of children in the institutions. Wichern's cottage plan was described as follows:

> Each house is to be a family, under the sole direction and control of the matron, who is the mother of the family. . . . The government and discipline are strictly parental. It is the design to give a home interest, a home feeling and attachment, to the whole family."[13]

Cottage reform schools spread widely throughout the United States. New Jersey (1864) and Indiana (1866) opened cottage schools, and some older institutions converted from the congregate to the cottage plan. The cottage system for housing institutionalized juveniles continues to be the most popular form in use today.

State Reformatories

The 1870s were marked by the beginning of yet another type of institution: state reformatories for young men 16 to 30 years old who were first offenders. This development aided in resolving the category of children referred to as juvenile delinquents. American penal reformers, influenced by European innovations, established the New York State Reformatory at Elmira in 1877, the Massachusetts Reformatory for Men in 1884, and a reformatory for women and girls convicted of misdemeanors, chiefly those involving sex offenses, in New York in 1893. With the growth of the reformatory movement, some juvenile delinquent institutions were relieved of their older and often more troublesome inmates, a relief that was welcomed.[14]

Multi-ethnic group of teen male wards in gray sweats marches at L.A. City Youth Authority. (A. Ramey/*PhotoEdit*)

Deficiencies of the Reform Movement

Early juvenile institutions had many failings. In the Eastern states, they were located in the large metropolitan cities, and these locations afforded the juveniles little change from the conditions that had so much to do with their being delinquent. With a vast amount of open land, Western states overcame this shortcoming by locating their schools in the countryside and organizing their institutional programs around agricultural work. By the 1890s, most western reform schools had introduced vocational education, along with military drill and organization, into their routines. But they were otherwise very similar to the older Eastern institutions and were bound toward a common destiny.

In the South, no provision was made for juvenile lawbreakers until long after the Civil War. The Populist political movement ushered in badly needed reforms. Prior to that time children were put in jail, in convict camps, in the country road gangs, or in prison farms along with adults.

As quoted by H. W. Charles in the last half of the nineteenth century, A. O. Wright of the Wisconsin Board of State Charities summarized the feeling of child-saving philanthropies of the time:

> If I were to classify the order of places, best or worst, in which people may be placed, especially children or young people, I say first of all, a good home; second best, a small institution rightly managed under proper persons, meaning by a small institution, one or two hundred inmates or less; thirdly, a large institution; fourth, a bad home.

Punishment in reform schools was often brutal, and reformatory institutions became known, in the words of one superintendent, as "not the first aid to the injured . . . the forlorn hope." At the Illinois Reformatory a boy was hung by chains on the wall for nearly three days. He was alternately beaten and given the "water cure" until he died with his back broken in three places.[15]

Noncriminal youth who did not attend school regularly or were unruly in school were spared the unhappy fate of reform school when parental or truant schools were started in 1900 just for those children. Thus youths who did not belong among the populations of juvenile institutions were kept out of them.

Strongly influenced by popular scientific notions about juvenile delinquency and its probable causes, reform school managers and institutional superintendents emphasized everything from physical conditioning, strict military discipline, and the learning of a trade to the attainment of "decent" moral standards.[16] Little progress has been made beyond the attempts of early correctional administrators. Today, basically the same problems are being faced. They are overcrowding, lack of public support and proper legislation, and a continuous debate on the link between cause and treatment of delinquency. The systems and practices started in the early houses of refuge, reform schools, reformatories, and juvenile institutions have remained with us. Throughout the country, many of our institutions are relics of the nineteenth century. In many cases, their programs have changed little since the founding date was put on their cornerstones.

FACILITIES FOR JUVENILES

Schools built to house the homeless and dependent children who roamed the streets of Europe in the nineteenth century became the model for many later established in the United States. In England, the Reformatory School Acts of 1854, 1857, and 1866 offered methods whereby courts could send offenders under the age of 16 to reformatories and, later, industrial schools. In 1825, the New York City House of Refuge became the first real American response to the juvenile problem. These early facilities were prison-like structures, and the courts were still allowed to send juvenile offenders to adult prisons instead if they so desired. Juvenile institutions attempted to protect the children from the bad influence of the adult institutions, even though the system was crude and decentralized. Most of these schools were established by private organizations that recognized the need for special attention to both juvenile offenders and neglected or dependent children. The first cottage housing systems for juveniles, now the most popular systems were founded in Massachusetts (1854) and Ohio (1858). Not until 1899, however, in Chicago, was the juvenile court system coordinated within a political jurisdiction as an integral part of the criminal justice system in the United States. Since that time, the juvenile court system has extended to cover every jurisdiction in the country, and a fairly standard pattern of juvenile confinement has ensued.

Adair youth detention facility. (Kentucky Department of Juvenile Justice)

JUVENILE INSTITUTIONS TODAY

The primary kinds of institutions for juveniles in the present-day United States are detention homes and training schools (See box 9.2).

Detention Centers

The main type of facility for juveniles today is the **detention center,** where juvenile victims of crime and juvenile offenders are often kept in the same facilities, with the same treatment afforded to both, under *parens patriae.* The Census of Juvenile Placement (CJRP) reported in 1997 that one in five (20 percent) juveniles were held in facilities with fewer than 31 residents and a similar proportion were held in facilities with more than 350 residents. In terms of security status, the majority of juveniles in residential placement (71 percent) were confined after school hours by at least one locked door or gate.[17] Many states have statutory provisions for the detention of juveniles in jails so long as they are segregated from adult offenders. Some states have statutes or policies prohibiting such detention, but practical problems frequently require the violation of these statutes.

Facilities designated exclusively for juvenile detention are usually not the best examples of how an ideal juvenile correctional facility should be designed and operated. Most of these structures were originally built for some other purpose and converted to their present use with as little expense as possible. Most are overcrowded before they reach their rated capacities. In the adult institutions the emphasis is on custody, and the same preoccupation with security shapes the programs and general environment in the juvenile facilities. Most are located in urban areas and are virtually sealed off from the community by their physical structure and other security measures. The youths are placed in dormitory-style housing, or single cells in some cases, often with the fixed furniture and dreary interiors that are typical of adult institutions. Most juvenile detention centers lack services and programs that might improve the residents' chances of staying away from crime. These juveniles are denied most of the good aspects of adult programs and are subject to the worst aspects of institutional programs (See box 9.3). Over twenty years ago, the National Advisory Commission on Criminal Justice Standards and Goals made specific recommendations for juvenile detention facilities. These recommendations remain sound and deserve review:

- The detention facility should be in a residential area and near court and community resources.

Box 9.2 Types of Juvenile Facilities

Juvenile facilities are classified by the term of stay and type of environment.

TERM OF STAY

Short-term Facilities that hold juveniles awaiting adjudication or other disposition.

Long-term Facilities that hold juveniles already adjudicated and committed to custody.

TYPE OF ENVIRONMENT

Institutional Environments impose greater restraints on residents' movements and limit access to the community. Most detention or diagnostic centers, training schools, and ranches are classified as having institutional environments.

Open Environments allow greater movement of residents within the facilities and more access to the community. Facilities with open environments mainly include shelters, halfway houses, group homes, and ranches, forestry camps, or farms.

- The population of detention centers should not exceed thirty residents. When the population significantly exceeds this number, separate components should be developed under the network system.
- Living areas should not house more than ten or twelve youngsters each, with single rooms and programming regarded as essential. Individual rooms should be pleasant, adequately furnished, and home-like rather than punitive and hostile.
- Security should not be viewed as in indispensable part of the physical environment but should be based on a combination of staffing patterns, technological devices, and physical design.
- Existing residential facilities within the community should be used in preference to building new facilities.
- Facility programming should be based on investigation of community resources and the possible use of them before determining the facility's in-house program requirements.
- Any new construction and renovation of existing facilities should be based on consideration of the functional interrelationships between program activities and program participants.

- Detention facilities should be coeducational and should have access to a full range of supportive programs, including education, library, recreation, arts and crafts, music, drama, writing, and entertainment. Outdoor recreational areas are essential.
- Citizen advisory boards should be established to pursue development of in-house and community-based programs and alternatives to detention.
- Planning should comply with pertinent state and federal regulations and the Environmental Policy Act of 1969.[18]

It would be well for administrators and legislators to dust off these documents and see where they stand two decades later in their implementation.

Box 9.3 Suicide Prevention in Juvenile Facilities

Suicide in juvenile detention and correctional facilities was more than four times greater than youth suicide overall. According to the Centers for Disease Control and Prevention (CDC), the suicide rate of adolescents ages 15 to 19 has quadrupled from 2.7 suicides per 100,000 to 11 suicides per 100,000 in 1994. CDC has also reported that more teenagers died of suicide during 1994 than of cancer, heart disease, acquired immune deficiency syndrome, birth defects, stroke, pneumonia and influenza, and chronic lung disease combined.

The U.S. Bureau of the Census has been collecting data on the number of deaths of juveniles in custody since 1989. In the first year of the survey, juvenile officials self-reported seventeen suicides in public detention centers, reception and diagnostic centers, and training schools during 1988. Fourteen such suicides were reported during 1993. Given the epidemiological data regarding adolescent suicide, coupled with the increased risk factors associated with detained and confined youth, the reported number of suicides in custody appears low. The National Center for Health Statistics, however, reported that 30,903 persons committed suicide in the U.S. in 1996. Of these, approximately 7 percent (2,119) were youth age 19 or younger. For youth younger than age 15, suicides increased 113 percent between 1980 and 1996. Because of statistics like these, many juvenile justice experts and practitioners believe that suicides are underreported. To date, no comprehensive study of deaths in custody has been undertaken.

Source: Office of Juvenile Justice and Delinquency Prevention, *Juvenile Justice—Youth With Mental Health Disorders: Issues and Emerging Responses* (April 2000), http://www.ncjrs.org/html/ojjdp/jjjnl_2000_4/sui_1.html

The issue of whether it is productive to place juveniles in institutions is being hotly debated in correctional circles. Jerome Miller mounted the most extensive attempt at decarceration when he served as Youth Commissioner for Massachusetts in 1969. Faced with official criticism of the operations of training schools in the state, Miller took the radical step of closing all reform schools and placing juvenile offenders on community supervision.[19] Although initial research found that juveniles under community supervision had slightly higher recidivism rates, the Massachusetts reform has proven to be effective. The small size of these community programs, coupled with secure confinement, have influenced the development of similar reforms in Utah, Missouri, Maryland, and other states.[20]

Institutions are the most expensive and least successful method of handling juvenile offenders.[21] But until the services needed for supervision and treatment in the community are forthcoming, judges often have no other choice but to commit offenders. The junior prisons are not all bad, but the custody philosophy is the prevailing model, and it creates the same problem at this level as at the adult level. The dangers that these institutions present to the civil rights of the juvenile offender were forcefully brought to public attention in a series of landmark court decisions, outlined in Chapter 7.

TODAY'S APPROACH TO INSTITUTIONS

Directors of early juvenile institutions were concerned chiefly with the protection of society. Youths confined within institutional walls were judged enemies of society, and their custody was looked upon as a disciplinary measure. How far have things advanced since then? Has there been measurable progress in the search for an answer to the problem of juvenile delinquency? For the past several decades, juvenile institutions have been subscribing, at least superficially, to a philosophy of social responsibility for the rehabilitation of deviant youth. As a consequence, today's institutions call for greater emphasis on education, vocational and personality training, and the inculcation of socially accepted living habits. Although recent Supreme Court decisions, such as *In re Gault,* have moved away from the *parens patriae* concept, it is still a widely held belief that society is responsible for juvenile delinquency. The collective social conscience of America has reacted with an incredible variety of programs meant to alleviate the problem.

Society has a way of placing its concerns in an order of priority, concerns that are social and technological. One often hears the inquiry, "If we can put a man on the moon, why can't something be done about crime?" Social problems that lead to, cause, or are associated with crime and delin-

Pod in a juvenile facility. (Kentucky Department of Juvenile Justice)

quency might be solved if top priority were given to solving these problems using the finest minds in the world and an unlimited budget. Such efforts are not likely in the near future, however, so debate, half-measures, and temporary solutions will have to do for the foreseeable future.

In the meantime, juvenile crime increases, public schools cease to function, and organized and armed youth gangs re-emerge as a menace in the community. A return to the extensive use of imprisonment, which stigmatizes youthful criminals as the enemies of society, may well be the future for juvenile corrections. Although not all youths belong in juvenile correctional institutions (e.g., status offenders, mentally or emotionally disturbed youth, or first-time offenders), economic pressures may force a line to be drawn.

The data in Table 9.1 reveal that there were 108,931 juvenile offenders in residential facilities on October 27, 1999. More than one-third of these offenders had committed an offense against the person. Although the percentage of juveniles held for some personal offenses had actually declined between 1997 and 1999, the number of these juvenile offenders had increased seven percent overall. Also note that the trend in residential placement of status offenses is decreasing. The percentage of juveniles in residential placement for status offenses declined between 1997 and 1999 (32 percent decrease).

The proponents of community-based programs and treatment for troubled youth may argue against it, but a return to old-fashioned discipline, large congregate institutions, and the reform school-style institutions, although not the most desirable response, may be unavoidable. However, if the increased use of institutions and the "get tough" policy is to be effective, the public will be faced with staggering costs for new and bigger institutions with more staff, and an increasing drain on limited resources.

TABLE **9.1**   Juvenile Offenders in Residential Placement, 1997–1999

MOST SERIOUS OFFENSE	NUMBER OF OFFENDERS	PERCENT	% CHANGE, 97–99
Delinquency	109,931	96	5
Person	38,005	35	7
Homicide	1,514	1	−21
Sexual Assault	7,511	7	34
Robbery	8,212	8	−13
Aggravated Assault	9,984	9	5
Simple Assault	7,448	7	12
Other Person	3,336	3	50
Property	31,817	29	−1
Burglary	12,222	11	−3
Theft	6,994	6	−5
Auto Theft	6,225	6	−5
Arson	1,126	1	23
Other Property	5,300	5	13
Drug	9,882	9	6
Drug Trafficking	3,106	3	2
Other Drug	6,776	6	9
Public Order	10,487	10	8
Weapons	4,023	4	−4
Other Public Order	6,464	6	17
Status Offense	4,694	4	−32
Total Juvenile Offenders	**108,931**	**100**	**3**

Source: Melissa Sickmund, "Juvenile Offenders in Residential Placement: 1997–1999," *Juvenile Offenders and Victims–National Report Series* (Washington, DC: Office of Juvenile Justice and Delinquency Prevention, March 2002), p. 1.

Detention

The National Juvenile Detention Association (NJDA) defines *detention* as follows:

> Juvenile detention is the temporary and safe custody of juveniles who are accused of conduct subject to the jurisdiction of the court who require a restricted environment for their own or the community's protection while pending legal action. Further, juvenile detention provides a wide range of helpful services that support the

juvenile's physical, emotional, and social development. Helpful services minimally include: education; visitation; communication; counseling; continuous supervision; medical and health care services; nutrition; recreation; and reading. Juvenile detention includes or provides for a system of clinical observation and assessment that complements the helpful services and reports findings.[22]

In addition, the American Correctional Association Detention Committee defined the seven essential characteristics of juvenile detention:

- **Temporary custody.** Of all the methods of incarceration within the criminal justice system, only juvenile detention stresses its temporary nature. Detention should be as short as possible.

- **Safe custody.** This concept implies freedom from fear and freedom from harm for both the juvenile and the community. This definitional theme refers to a safe and humane environment with programming and staffing to ensure the physical and psychological safety of detained juveniles.

- **Restricted environment.** The nature or degree of restrictiveness of the environment is generally associated with the traditional classifications of maximum, medium, or minimum security or custody.

- **Community protection.** In addition to the factors listed above, the court has a legitimate right to detain juveniles for the purpose of preventing further serious and/or violent delinquent behavior.

- **Pending legal action.** This theme includes the time spent awaiting a hearing, disposition, a placement, or a return to a previous placement.

- **Helpful services.** Programs are available to detained juveniles to help resolve a host of problems commonly facing detained juveniles. Because detention has the potential of creating a tremendously negative impact on some juveniles, it is important that programming have the depth of services required to meet the needs of a wide range of juvenile problems.

- **Clinical observation and assessment.** Most juvenile codes specifically refer to this theme as a purpose for detention. The controlled environment of juvenile detention often provides the opportunity for intense observation and assessment to enhance decision-making capabilities. Properly credentialed individuals who coordinate and conduct the observation and assessment process provide competent clinical services.[23]

Authorities generally agree that only certain youths should be detained involuntarily. They include those who would probably disappear prior to their hearing, those with a high probability of committing a dangerous offense while awaiting court disposition, and those who must be held for another jurisdiction. Federal guidelines emphasize that no youth should be detained unnecessarily, and those who can remain safely in their homes should be allowed to do so. These guidelines also specify that juveniles needing diagnostic evaluations should be able to receive them without being subjected to detention. In all, open facilities should be used for all youth not explicitly requiring a secure custodial setting.

Guidelines and recommendations, no matter how well intended or thought out, are useless unless they are put into practice. They are, however, useful as a yardstick against which to measure the real-life findings encountered by students of the juvenile justice system. Detention facilities can include jails, centers located above the juvenile court, converted mental wards, or anyplace in which youth can be imprisoned, pending a hearing or transfer.

The emphasis on custody, which pervades the adult institutions, also shapes the general environment of juvenile detention facilities. Most of these facilities are located in urban areas and are virtually sealed off from the community by their physical structure and other security measures. The youths are placed in dreary single cells or barracks-type housing with fixed furniture.

The chance of leaving a detention facility to return to a nondelinquent lifestyle is remote when one considers the lack of services and programs for youths in detention. They are denied most of the good in the adult programs, and are subjected to the worst aspects of institutional living.

Placing a Youth in Detention

There are several critical factors that have been linked with the courts' decision to place a youth in a detention facility:

1. Location of the detention unit
2. The time of the youth's apprehension
3. The location of that apprehension
4. Availability of intake personnel to screen referrals
5. The credibility of the referring source
6. The degree to which the court sees its detention policies as an area of community interest.[24]

For example, it has been observed that:

1. The further the detention unit is from the referring police units, the lower the rate of placement.

2. If a juvenile is apprehended after court office hours, he is more likely to be held in detention.

3. Youth are more likely to be detained if apprehended on the street or in public buildings where parents or concerned adults are less likely to be available to intervene.

4. When intake personnel are available for thorough screening and for detention hearings, juveniles are less frequently held in detention.

5. The higher the credibility of the referring source with court personnel, the greater the likelihood that a juvenile will be detained.

6. Time of year . . . especially as related to the school calendar, public attitudes, and interorganization relations of the court with other community agencies also affect how detention policies are implemented.[25]

INSTITUTIONS: FUNCTIONS AND THEORIES

Although the stated purposes of the juvenile detention facility and the juvenile institution (or state training school) are ideologically different, what they produce is quite similar. Adult prisons and juvenile institutions have been criticized repeatedly for their inherently degrading and dehumanizing effects on inmate populations. However, the continued use and survival of institutions indicates that they are performing functions and purposes acceptable to society, which continues to tolerate them.

In an article entitled "Tear Down the Walls? Some Functions of Prisons," the authors, Charles Reasons and Russell Kaplan, suggest that the actual survival of prisons and institutions depends on their "fulfilling four important manifest functions in varying degrees: (1) reformation, (2) incapacitation, (3)retribution, and (4) deterrence." However, Reasons and Kaplan also suggest that there are eleven latent functions of institutions more significant than the four manifest functions that also serve various interests and needs: "(1) maintenance of a crime school, (2) politicization, (3) self-enhancement, (4) provision of jobs, (5) satisfaction of authoritarian needs, (6) slave labor, (7) reduction of unemployment rates, (8) scientific research, (9) do-gooderism, (10) safety valve for racial tensions, and (11) birth control. These latent functions, largely unintended and generally unrecognized, suggest that abolition of the prison may not be as assured as some reformers suppose."[26]

Because institutions are considered the most expensive and least successful method of handling juvenile offenders, one must question whether these functions of institutions (or ones similar to them) are preserving them despite the costly operations and lack of success attributed to juvenile institutions. Alternatives to institutionalization, such as the provision of supervision and treatment in the community, are under close scrutiny to prove themselves. It no longer suffices simply to state that these services exist. With less tolerance for crime and criminals, adult and juvenile, these community services will have to prove effective almost immediately in order to be continued. All juvenile programs are under such scrutiny today; however, programs that break with tradition and contemporary innovations are usually most suspect and subject to early curtailment.

It appears, then, that the manifest and latent functions of institutions do outweigh their high cost and their lack of success with offender populations. This contention assumes that their purpose is *custody* as opposed to *treatment*. Unfortunately, the emphasis on custody as the prevailing model creates the same problems of civil rights at the juvenile level as it does at the adult level. The dangers that juvenile institutions hold for the civil rights of the offender were forcefully brought to public attention in the *Gault* decision.

The theory (that incarceration is an effective device for changing people and at the same time deterring others) is debatable, despite the *Gault* decision. Unfortunately, national statistics on recidivism after incarceration are generally not available to substantively refute this theory. Better statistics on the rate of recidivism of juvenile institutional populations after release would certainly provide us with useful information on the supposed deterrent effect of institutions. The incarceration of youths, in fact, can reach a point of diminishing returns. Studies have indicated that communities spend enormous sums of money keeping juveniles locked up longer than is necessary—so long, in fact, that the chances of realizing rehabilitation are greatly decreased. Findings emphasize the absence of a positive correlation between time served in institutions and subsequent criminal or delinquent behavior.

The juvenile justice system suffers from basic mistaken notions regarding the functions of institutionalization: first, punishment is of little importance, and, second, punishment and rehabilitation can occur in the same setting. In an article "When to Punish, When to Rehabilitate," Ellsworth Fersch suggests a two-step process-first punishment, then rehabilitation. He contends that this would restore faith in the criminal justice system and respect for the individual and society. "We need to separate these critical functions and provide short, swift, and humane punishment, followed by voluntary rehabilitation."[27] Fersch may be right, although the effects of punishment on a frightened youthful offender may well neutralize his or her receptivity to rehabilitative programs. Even voluntary participation by the youth may be consent merely to gain release from the institution or rehabilitative setting. If a system such as Fersch's is adopted, those responsible should take care to maintain the fine difference between being viewed as "prison screws" or "rehabilitative agents."

In review, there are four manifest and eleven latent functions that are attributable to juvenile institutions. The continued existence of juvenile institutions may be the result of their successful fulfillment of the latent functions, while fulfillment of the functions of reformation, incapacitation, retribution, and deterrence are of secondary consequence. But it is apparent that today's juvenile institutions have fallen far short of providing conclusive proof that theory in their favor is, in fact, valid.

INSTITUTIONAL TREATMENT AND REHABILITATION

The National Advisory Commission on Criminal Justice Standards and Goals offered extensive guidelines and standards to assist the juvenile institutions in their re-examination of educational and vocational training programs. Unfortunately, in spite of these standards and guidelines, actual experience has shown that most youths committed to juvenile institutions are simply "doing time." Their release is more often based on such non-treatment-related factors as overcrowding, administrative decisions, and, incredibly, *nontreatability*. Instead of being a constructive and maturing experience, incarceration in a juvenile institution is often harmful for the juvenile. Nonconstructive time spent away from family and community leads to a lessening of the sense of belonging and responsibility.

Both the public and the juvenile justice professional view institutionalization as a last resort, an alternative to be used when nothing else is available. In fact, there has been a recent decrease in the rates of institutionalization of juveniles at a time when juvenile court delinquency cases—the primary source of commitments to institutions—appear to be increasing. The decrease in institutional care, therefore, may reflect the recent emphasis on finding alternatives for the treatment of youthful offenders, using incarceration only where it is absolutely necessary to the child's welfare and/or to the protection of the community.

Services in Institutions

Institutionalized juveniles, for whatever reason they are in institutions, must be provided access to services required for individual growth and development. These services include meaningful, quality education and adequate vocational training programs.

Irving Kaufman suggests that to accomplish this end all sentences should be fixed terms. The court upon show of good cause should impose any subsequent change. "Indeterminate sentences have been rejected by the commission as a game of chance based on arbitrary decisions. Frequently in the past the most violent juveniles were released from institutions because they were, ironically, difficult to control. Power to determine the actual length of stay of a juvenile is thus removed from the hands of correctional authorities. To encourage good behavior, correctional administrators are allowed to reduce a youth's sentence by no more than 5 percent. The maximum term of incarceration should not exceed two years for any offense.[28]

Currently, even when the treatment staffs do plan a potentially meaningful program, they can seldom be assured of how long they have with their "client." As long as release is possible at any time, training programs are practically worthless. To believe, therefore, that youths are released from juvenile institutions only when they are successfully rehabilitated or "cured" is to believe a fantasy.

The use of fixed-length sentences would allow the juvenile to complete useful training programs. One must keep in mind, however, that the length of time a youth spends in an institution and the degree to which he or she is rehabilitated are not always related. To assume, for example, that the longer a youth spends incarcerated the more he or she will be rehabilitated, and vice versa, is not always true. To justify the use of fixed-length sentences, therefore, on the basis of allowing enough time for the completion of adequate training programs, and then not to provide these programs would be in violation of the principle of "right to treatment." Under a system of fixed-length sentences, it would be necessary for the institutional staff to tailor treatment programs to fit the varying periods of time youths could spend in the institution. It would defeat the purpose of the treatment plan, for example, if a youth sentenced to from two to four months were placed in a treatment program that required at least ten months to complete.

Morales v. Turman

Many people have assumed that a juvenile has the right to treatment once he or she comes under the auspices of the juvenile justice system, or at least that treatment does exist. However, the *right* of a juvenile to rehabilitation and/or treatment (whether or not treatment actually exists) in a correctional institution has until very recently gone uncontested. Most court cases concerning rights to treatment have involved adults, but in 1974 the U.S. District Court for the Eastern District of Texas in *Morales v. Turman* determined that constitutional rights of incarcerated minors had been violated and ordered the parties involved to submit a comprehensive plan for righting these violations.[29] This case has raised a wide range of issues regarding the nature and adequacy of procedures and programs adopted by the Texas Youth Council (TYC). The TYC has the responsibility under Texas law for minors adjudicated delinquent and involuntarily committed to its custody. In this case, the court withheld issuing a permanent order of relief in favor of the plaintiffs to give TYC a chance to make amends and to present a treatment plan favorable to all parties involved. This was done because the granting of requested relief could quite possibly entail extensive changes in virtually every phase of the TYC operations.

What the plaintiffs in this case accomplished was nothing less than an exhaustive attack on a set of policies and programs that, when taken as a whole, represent no less than a state's entire juvenile correctional system. The assurances requested by the plaintiffs should serve as examples to be followed by similar court action throughout the United States. *Morales v. Turman* and its implications for correctional attitudes, settings, and treatment rights are crucial to the future of the juvenile justice system. Although this case applied specifically to Texas, the conditions described therein are similar to those in a large number of other states in this country. It is hoped that these systems that have been or are moving in the direction of providing requests and assurances similar to those contained in the *Morales* case will continue to do so and that states that find their programs sadly behind the times and lacking in humane treatment practices will soon follow suit. If not, court action similar to that brought against the TYC may leave them no choice.

The whole concept of treatment or lack of treatment within our juvenile institutions raises the basic question, "Is it our intention to punish youth who violate the law or to rehabilitate them?" Put another way, this question is, "Are we for justice, or are we for laws?" According to Rossi:

> In the juvenile area, the system for training criminals throughout the United States is complete. Hardly a course is overlooked in the education of youth when they enter this exceptional and unequalled academy of learning. Quickly and proficiently they develop into criminals. Yet, juveniles are not brought into this world as potential, hardcore criminals. A criminal, like a surgeon, requires training and enlightenment, growth and extension. The manner and means of training and development a juvenile receives will determine whether or not he or she will become a criminal. Crime is not a talent! It is a means of survival and self-preservation and a way of life for many young individuals. It's not an artistic, creative endeavor such as music, painting, or architecture.[30]

If law is to be upheld, then a juvenile who violates the law should be accorded every right currently granted to adult offenders, including the right not to be detained or incarcerated for status offenses or incorrigible acts. If justice is to be served, we should see to it that only those youths for whom no alternative exists other than incarceration are committed to juvenile institutions and at the same time accord them all rights granted adults. Furthermore, incarcerated youths should be guaranteed humane rehabilitative treatment, and nonincarcerated youths should be placed in community-based treatment programs that promote their remaining in society as useful citizens.

Escape and Unauthorized Leaves

Among the many serious problems confronting juvenile correctional administrators and staff is escape or unauthorized leave from juvenile institutions. Unauthorized leaves both disrupt and destroy a juvenile's participation in residential treatment programs designed to make possible a successful re-entry into the community. In the past few years, professional staffs at institutions have become increasingly aware of this problem.

Increasing rates of unauthorized leaves apply nationwide. It is the authors' belief that the frequency and length of unauthorized leaves should be controlled. Reduction in the frequency of unauthorized leaves should reduce the rate of criminal behavior committed by juveniles in the community and should make the juvenile more available for treatment. A long-range reduction in delinquency is also probable.

An interstate agreement for juveniles (called the Interstate Compact on juveniles) was formulated in the early 1950s to cope with the many problems involved in supervising and controlling juveniles and juvenile delinquents. A major purpose of this agreement is to provide for a way to return captured escapees to the state from which they had escaped.

Under the compact, when the runaway child is apprehended in another state, the arresting agency usually contacts the institution or agency from whose jurisdiction the child ran. If problems are encountered, the Interstate Office may assist whenever possible.

The constitutionality of the compact has been challenged on the grounds that it has not received the consent of Congress and that it violates the protection privileges and immunities and due process clauses of the Fourteenth Amendment.[31] Ruling in a case that challenged the compact *(Chin v. Wyman et al.)*, a New York court said that in respect to the possible violation of due process, a hearing should be held in the state to which the youth had fled, on the question of whether he or she should be returned to the home state. Such a hearing, the court said, was necessary to satisfy due process requirements.[32]

Before leaving the subject of escape and unauthorized leave, the reader should consider two things:

1. The granting of full constitutional protection to juveniles carries potential hazards unrealized by many. For example, adult convicts attempting to escape from an institution can be legally shot. How acceptable would it be to allow a 13-year-old joy rider to be subjected to the same sort of life-endangering threat?
2. Of the thousands of young people who escape or take unauthorized leave from juvenile institutions each year, many are never caught and are not heard from again. Could it be that perhaps they have found their own successful means for rehabilitation outside the world

of our institutional treatment programs? (At least one juvenile institution recognizes this possibility and calls it "self-placement.")[33]

INSTITUTIONAL PUNISHMENT

Horror stories of brutal punishment, sexual and homosexual abuse and assault, and convict child labor were once commonly reported in newspapers, magazines, and other media. For the most part, the juvenile justice system has overcome these abuses; however, children still may suffer many dehumanizing acts when they are locked away in jails, institutions, and "kid prisons."[34]

Often funds and resources that could be used for education, health care, and positive treatment of youth are used up on negative programs. Many institutions continue to emphasize punishment or the threat of punishment as their primary means of controlling their youthful populations. Bizarre corporal punishments are common in juvenile institutions and detention facilities. A Harvard student, for example, who posed as a 16-year-old inmate of the John J. Connally Youth Center in Roslindale, Massachusetts, reported that one commonly used punishment was to hold a boy's head under water, and for minor infractions of the rules youths were beaten by the fists of teenagers forced to participate under threat of a beating themselves.

The use of solitary confinement or isolation is as widespread in juvenile detention facilities and institutions as is corporal punishment and the administration of calming or tranquilizing drugs. Its use continues despite condemnation from the theoreticians and practitioners.

Within juvenile correctional institutions, organizational traditions exist that compound the problems caused by mixing treatment and punishment. In treatment philosophy as in punishment philosophy, the primary source of the delinquent or incorrigible behavior is sought within the offender. As a consequence, the treatment philosophy has never really challenged the social functions of institutional punishment, nor has it indicated the extent to which caste-like correctional organizations may seriously hamper efforts at rehabilitative treatment. There is a tendency for youths to view whatever is done to them as punishment rather than treatment.

Part of the reason for this perception lies in the fact that treatment personnel, even if highly trained (and they are in short supply in most juvenile training schools), have a symbiotic relationship with clients which is subtle and paradoxical. The status of the professional, his helping role, his very place in the whole scheme of things depends heavily upon the client remaining in a subordinate relationship to him. The paradox is, therefore, that although the professional role ostensibly exists to help the client, it is, in fact, one which relies upon a super ordinate-subordinate relationship. As a result, it is difficult for the client to change unless his relationship to those above him changes also. Organizational arrangements are not available by which to encourage him to stop conceiving of himself as delinquent, inmate, or patient, and to conceive of himself, instead, as nondelinquent, employee, or student.[35]

Although some institutions are taking steps to move inmates step by step into new roles, there are still too few organizational structures within correctional institutions that allow the youth to be anything but an inmate and a delinquent. There are, therefore, two types of punishment practiced within our juvenile institutions: (1) actual physical punishment such as beatings, isolation, restraints, and so forth, and (2) a psychological attitude that causes the youth to view everything happening to him or her, while at the hands of an adult power structure, as punishment—even if that action is intended to be treatment-oriented and in the youth's best interest.

THE FUTURE OF JUVENILE INSTITUTIONS: PROGRAMS AND ISSUES

In recent years, delinquency has increased, and this has stimulated the development of numerous kinds of programs for the juvenile institutional field. Four of the most significant of these new programs are described briefly as follows:

a. **Community-Based Treatment. Community-based treatment** includes various methods of handling juveniles in a community setting as alternatives to commitment or for reducing the number of commitments. They are of special interest because of their relative economy compared with institutional commitment and because of the advantages of treatment in a setting as normal or "close to home" as possible.

   The principal vehicles include intensified and selected probation and parole caseloads offering special counseling and community help plus "in and out" and trial furloughs; group homes and agency-operated residential treatment programs; "day care" in specialized institutional programs that return youngsters home at night and on weekends; regional detention centers with diagnostic service intended to reduce "dumping" into institutions; special "closed" local facilities with intensive counseling; and family involvement.

b. **Group Treatment. Group treatment** techniques offer essentially the advantage of economy over one-to-one counseling relationships, plus treatment advantages gained from insights on behavior through viewpoints expressed from several sources. In the institutional setting they have included families of the trainees. Their common goal is acceptance of responsibility rather than satisfaction with shallow conformity.

c. **Diversification.** Development toward **diversification** is represented by the growth of small camp programs, halfway houses, group-treatment centers, reception and screening centers, vocational training centers, and special short-term programs. The breadth of these programs attempts to address the different problems faced by juveniles.

d. **Decriminalization and Deinstitutionalization.** Detention of juveniles would be drastically reduced if PINS and dependency-neglect cases were removed altogether from juvenile court jurisdiction. Decriminalization of conduct that is prohibited "for children only," would remove thousands of children from court-controlled institutions. This shift would work only if alternatives were available to respond to neglected and troubled children. One such mechanism is the system of "Youth Service Bureaus" advocated by the President's Crime Commission in 1967.[36]

In the future, juvenile justice administrators must guarantee that alternatives to institutionalization are as readily available to the children of the poor as to middle- and upper-class children. One may argue that poor children commit more wrongs, but the unequal handling of criminal cases may be because upper- and middle-class families are more often allowed to deal with the problem *outside* of the system. Ironically, poor children are often placed in juvenile institutions for their own protection and good, regardless of the seriousness of their offense(s), whereas children from prosperous backgrounds are usually released—also for their own good— even though they may have committed more serious offenses.

Boot Camps for Juvenile Offenders

Boot camps developed in the 1990s as a means to punish offenders while limiting institutional crowding. They are defined as:

Boot camp programs are modeled after military basic training. Offenders often enter the programs in groups that are referred to as platoons or squads. They are required to wear military-style uniforms, march to and from activities, and respond rapidly to the commands of "drill instructors." The rigorous daily schedule requires youths to wake up early and stay active throughout the day. Although programs differ somewhat, the schedule usually includes drill and ceremony practice, strenuous physical fitness activities, and challenge programs (e.g., ropes courses) as well as required academic ed-

Kentucky boot camp program. (Kentucky Department of Juvenile Justice)

ucation. Frequently, youths in the camps receive summary punishments, such as having to do pushups for misbehaviors.[37]

Thus, boot camps satisfy the popular demand for punishment while recognizing the youth's need for treatment and education.

> Boot camps are perhaps the most visible means of showing the public that those responsible for trying to curtain juvenile crime are taking the initiative. One question might be: do we use boot camps simply because they appeal to the public's image of "getting tough" on juvenile crime rather than because we believe they will accomplish the goal of reducing juvenile crime and recidivism? Phrased differently, we must ask ourselves if juvenile boot camps are so popular because of their political appeal rather than because they work.[38]

By 1996, forty-eight residential boot camps for juveniles were operating in twenty-seven states.[39]

Evidence of the effectiveness of these programs is mixed and limited. Juveniles who take part in the camps report positive responses to their institutional environment and its programs.[40] In addition, juvenile boot campers recorded improvement in their reading and math skills.[41] Across the board, boot camp participants have similar, if not higher, rates of recidivism than other juvenile, nonparticipant counterparts.[42]

The problem in sustaining the program gains from boot camp programs is tied to the availability and quality of aftercare programs. Upon release, the juvenile needs community-based programs to address their individual concerns.

> Aftercare programs must be broad-based and flexible enough to meet the particular educational, employment, counseling, and support needs of each participant. The aftercare component should form dynamic linkages with other community services, especially youth service agencies, schools, and employers.[43]

Boot camps are not the ultimate answer to juvenile delinquency but they appear to have the potential to be a part of the "response matrix in corrections."[44]

Disproportionate Minority Confinement

Disproportionate minority confinement is the overrepresentation of minority youth in juvenile institutions. It has been recognized as a problem in almost every state. This problem is usually a cumulative one—the result of decisions made at every stage of the juvenile justice system, from arrest to confinement to release.[45] Official figures indicate that minority group juveniles, especially African Americans, make up a higher percentage of juvenile arrests and were disproportionately held in detention centers and training schools.[46] Figures also indicate the following:

- Although proportions are declining, black juveniles are overrepresented at all stages of the juvenile justice system compared with their proportion in the population.
- Minorities accounted for 67 percent of juveniles committed to public facilities nationwide—a proportion nearly twice their proportion of the juvenile population.
- Interview data reveals that white males were less likely to have been in a gang than black and Hispanic males but more likely to have carried a gun.
- Black youth accounted for 15 percent of the juvenile population in 1997 but 26 percent of all juvenile arrests and 44 percent of arrests for violent offenses.
- Black juveniles accounted for 38 percent of the crimes against persons in 1996.
- All racial groups had large increases in drug case rates between 1991 and 1996: 116 percent for whites, 132 percent for blacks, and 167 percent for youth of other races.
- Between 1987 and 1996, the increase in the number of black juvenile cases involving detention was nearly four times the increase for whites.

- Minorities accounted for seven in ten youth held in custody for a violent offense.
- In 1997, half of the females in residential placement were minorities.[47]

In 1988, the Juvenile Justice and Delinquency Prevention Act of 1974 was amended to require states to meet four mandates:

1. Remove juveniles from adult jails.
2. Keep juveniles separated from adult offenders.
3. No longer incarcerate status offenders.
4. Reduce disproportionate minority confinement.

Legislation in 1992 required states to reduce the proportion of minority juveniles confined in secure facilities or face reduction in Federal funds available for their juvenile programs.[48] Later Federal legislation required local law and justice council advisory committees to submit an annual report on the proportionality of rehabilitative services, their effectiveness in relation to community supervision and parole, and citizen complaints regarding disproportionality in the county juvenile justice system.[49] The Office of Juvenile Justice and Delinquency Prevention provides training and grant supporting training and technical assistance to develop and test approaches to reduce disproportionate minority confinement.[50]

Explanations for disproportionate minority confinement follow two trends. One falls short of calling the system racist and refers to the treatment of minorities as "differential treatment."[51] Another argues that the greater involvement of minorities in violent and serious crime is the cause of disproportionality. A related theory notes the extended exposure of minority groups to socioeconomic, family, and educational problems that contribute to their involvement in crime and delinquency.[52]

Those studies that found that race made a difference have examined several stages of the juvenile justice process. Conley found that African American youths were severely over-represented at every stage of the process.[53] McGarrell observed trends in juvenile court processing from 1985 to 1989 in 159 counties from seventeen states. Nonwhite referrals increased significantly in juvenile court processing. Some of the increase was fueled by the rise in drug cases.[54] A cohort study of 50,000 youths followed from intake to judicial disposition found that race was a significant factor in determining outcome. Bishop and Frazier concluded that black youths were placed at a considerable disadvantage by the cumulative effect of differential treatment.[55] Another study followed a random sample of jurisdictions through three points of the juvenile justice system and found that race had a significant and independent effect on detention.[56] A Washington state study reported that minority youths were much more likely to be confined than white youths even when the violent crime rate was high. Negative stereotypes of minorities drove perceptions of dangerousness and led to confinement.[57]

Several studies found that a long arrest record and the seriousness of the present offense had more influence on sentencing decisions than race. Bell and Lang found that the number of prior offenses influenced sentencing decisions and that whites were consistently treated more leniently than other offenders.[58] A Florida study reported that minority overrepresentation in the commitment process was due to the seriousness and number of prior adjudicated offenses.[59] Finally, extensive and comprehensive research by Michael J. Leiber and his colleagues has documented that minorities (African Americans, Native Americans, and Hispanics) are more likely to receive serious sanctions for their delinquent acts than Whites throughout the juvenile sentencing process.[60]

Several states have attempted to develop innovative solutions to deal with disproportionate minority confinement. In response to research findings that minority juveniles accounted for 48 percent of all youths formally charged in juvenile court, Pennsylvania developed prevention and intervention strategies. They included youth clubs, truancy and dropout prevention projects. These projects had mixed results, reporting low levels of truancy, suspension and recidivism in some areas.[61] In 1991, pilot programs were also developed in five states (Arizona, Florida, Iowa, North Carolina, Oregon). These programs addressed the issue that minority representation was the result of the scarcity of resources for minority youth programs. In order to resolve this problem, programs that address the problems that lead to delinquency must be developed and made available to all juveniles.

Juveniles in Adult Jails and Prisons

Juveniles are being held in adult facilities. This is largely the result of new sentencing policies holding juveniles accountable for their offenses and trying them as adult offenders. Table 9.2 documents the rate of increase in this occurrence. Between 1983 and 1998, the number of juveniles held in adult jails more than tripled.

In Table 9.3, we can see the attributes of juveniles admitted to state prisons in 1985 and 1997. While the number of admissions has increased, it appears that fewer of these juvenile inmates had been admitted for a violent offense while juveniles convicted of drug offenses increased dramatically. While the proportion of white juveniles had decreased, increases were noted for both black and Hispanic offenders. Males make up the majority of these inmates, and they appear to be getting younger. While the average maximum sentence has decreased, the average minimum sentence increased by nine months.

TABLE **9.2**   Juveniles in Adult Jails, 1983 – 1998

YEAR	JUVENILES
1983	1736
1984	1482
1985	1629
1986	1708
1987	1781
1988	1676
1989	2250
1990	2301
1991	2350
1992	2804
1993	4300
1994	6700
1995	7800
1996	8100
1997	9105
1998	8090
% Change, 83–98	**366%**

Source: James Austin, Kelly Dedel Johnson, and
Maria Gregoriou, *Juveniles in Adult Prisons and
Jails—A National Assessment* (Washington, DC:
Bureau of Justice Assistance, 2000), p. 5.

Based on this information, Austin and his colleagues made the following recommendations to the Bureau of Justice Assistance and correctional administrators who manage juveniles held in adult institutions:

- Insure that classification instruments are valid for this subset of the adult correctional population and that risk and needs instruments reflect maturation issues and special needs of the juvenile population.
- Develop specialized programs responsive to the developmental needs of youthful offenders, including: educational and vocational programs, sex offender and violent offender programs, and substance abuse programs that take into account the roles these issues play in adolescent development.[62]

TABLE 9.3 Attributes of Juveniles Admitted to State Prisons, 1985 and 1997

ATTRIBUTE	1985 PRISON ADMISSIONS	1997 PRISON ADMISSIONS
Total Admissions	3400	7400
Offense Type		
Violent	82%	61%
Property	42%	22%
Drug	2%	11%
Public Order	4%	5%
Race/Ethnicity		
White	32%	25%
Black	53%	58%
Hispanic	14%	15%
Other	1%	2%
Gender		
Male	97%	97%
Female	3%	3%
Age at Admission		
17	80%	74%
16	18%	21%
15	2%	4%
14 & Younger	0%	1%
Average Sentence		
Maximum	86 months	82 months
Minimum	35 months	44 months

Source: James Austin, Kelly Dedel Johnson, and Maria Gregoriou, *Juveniles in Adult Prisons and Jails—A National Assessment* (Washington, DC: Bureau of Justice Assistance, 2000), p. 6.

SUMMARY

Juvenile institutions are as good or as bad as those in the adult system. Most people dislike seeing youths detained in jails and lockups, but this practice still persists in jurisdictions where there are either no, or limited, alternatives. In one southeastern Ohio community, for example, it is not uncommon for parents with unruly children to call the local sheriff. He obliges by locking them up for a few days to "teach them a lesson." This is done without the knowledge of the court and is a clear violation of the juvenile's rights to due process.

From numerous research projects conducted over the years, it is clear that detention and incarceration in juvenile institutions harm many youths. Despite the failures of the adult corrections system, society seems to prefer using a similar type of system for the youths who come in contact with the juvenile justice system. To counter this attitude, standards of treatment and guidelines for handling the problems of delinquents must be applied carefully to these youths in trouble. Otherwise, the impact upon society can be more negative than positive.

Just as important as the institutions are the alternatives to institutionalization offered by juvenile corrections administrators. The rights and recourses available to adults in the adult corrections system will probably soon be accessible to juveniles as well. While the two systems are not yet equal, the movement toward equalization seems irreversible. It is the job of the juvenile justice professional to ensure that these similarities are more on the positive side than the negative.

TERMS TO REMEMBER

Boot camps	Diversification
Community-based treatment	*Ex parte* crouse
Cottage reform school	Expiation
Detention center	Group treatment
Disproportionate minority confinement	Lyman School for Boys
	Privatization

REVIEW QUESTIONS

1. Define *detention* and *institutionalization*. What is the basic difference between them?
2. What is the purpose of juvenile institutions? Is that purpose realistic, given the structure of today's society? Why or why not?
3. What is meant by "right to treatment"? Discuss the major aspects of *Morales v. Turman* and how that case may have an impact on the national juvenile justice system as a whole.
4. Define and discuss the following terms:
   a. Unauthorized leave
   b. Isolation
   c. Institutional alternatives
5. Discuss the future of juvenile corrections in terms of detention and institutions.
6. Discuss the issue of punishment versus treatment as the most realistic goal of the juvenile institutions of the past, today, and the future.
7. Why is the issue of disproportionate minority confinement so important?

8. What do boot camps have to offer? Should the practice be continued and expanded?

9. What should be done about juveniles in adult institutions?

10. Go to the web site for OJJDP's Census of Juveniles in Residential Placement at http://www.ojjdp.ncjrs.org/ojstatbb/cjrp and update the figures contained in this chapter. Also, look up the figures for your state and see how the trends there compare to those of the entire nation.

NOTES

[1]Barry Krisberg and James F. Austin, *Reinventing Juvenile Justice* (Newbury Park, CA: Sage Publications, 1993), p. 74.

[2]Betty Marler and Marc Scoble, "Building a Juvenile System to Serve the Majority of Young Offenders," *Corrections Today,* Vol. 63 (April 2001), p. 86.

[3]Charles J. Kehoe, "Juvenile Corrections in a Changing Landscape," *Corrections Today,* Vol. 63 (April 2001), p. 6.

[4]Bradford Smith, "Children in Custody: 20-Year Trends in Juvenile Detention, Correctional, and Shelter Facilities," *Crime and Delinquency,* Vol. 44 (1998), p. 537.

[5]Ibid., p. 538.

[6]Ibid., p. 539.

[7]Ibid., p. 530.

[8]*In re Gault,* 387 U.S. 1, 27 (1967).

[9]Harry E. Barnes and Negley K. Teeters, *New Horizons in Criminology* (Englewood Cliffs, NJ: Prentice Hall, 1959), p. 334.

[10]Robert W. Mennel, *Thorns and Thistles: Juvenile Delinquents in the United States, 1825–1940* (Hanover, NH: University Press of New England, 1973), pp. 52–54.

[11]Ibid., pp. 25–26; S. Schlossman, "Delinquent Children: The Juvenile Reform School," in Norval Morris and David J. Rothman, eds., *The Oxford History of the Prison: The Practice of Punishment in Western Society* (New York: Oxford University Press, 1995), pp. 363–389.

[12]David W. Roush, *Desktop Guide to Good Detention Practice* (Washington, DC: Office of Juvenile Justice and Delinquency Prevention, 1996), p. 27.

[13]Horace Mann, "Account of the Hamburgh Redemption Institute" (n.p. 1843).

[14]Mennel, *Thorns and Thistles.*

[15]H. W. Charles, "The Problem of the Reform School," *Proceedings of the Conference for Child Research and Welfare 1* (1910); Clarissa Olds Keller, *American Bastilles* (Washington, DC: Carnaham Press, 1910), pp. 8–9.

[16]David Rothman, *Conscience and Convenience* (Boston: Little Brown, 1980); Alexander W. Pisciotta, *Benevolent Repression: Social Control and the American Reformatory-Prison Movement* (New York: New York University Press, 1994).

[17]*OJJDP Statistical Briefing Book.* Online. Available: http://www.ojjdp.ncjrs.org/ojstatbb. 28 February 2001; Joseph Moore, "Innovative Information on Juvenile Residential Facilities," *OJJDP Fact Sheet* (Washington, DC: Office of Juvenile Justice and Delinquency Prevention, 2000).

[18]National Advisory Committee on Criminal Justice Standards and Goals, *Report of the Task Force on Juvenile Justice and Delinquency Prevention* (Washington, DC: U.S. Government Printing Office, 1976), p. 695.

[19]Jerome G. Miller, *Last One Over the Wall: The Massachusetts Experiment in Closing Reform Schools* (Columbus, OH: The Ohio State University Press, 1991).

[20]Robert B. Coates, Alden D. Miller, and Lloyd E. Ohlin, *Diversity in a Youth Correctional System: Handling Delinquents in Massachusetts* (Cambridge, MA: Ballinger, 1978); Barry Krisberg and James Austin, "What Works with Juvenile Offenders: The Massachusetts Experiment," in Dan Macallair and Vincent Schiraldi, eds., *Reforming Juvenile Justice: Reasons and Strategies for the 21st Century* (Dubuque, IA: Kendall/Hunt Publishing, 1998), pp. 173–196.

[21]See Travis C. Pratt and Melissa R. Winston, "The Search for the Frugal Grail: An Empirical Assessment of the Cost-Effectiveness of Public vs. Private Correctional Facilities," *Criminal Justice Policy Review,* Vol. 10 (1999), pp. 447–471; Jeffrey Butts and William Adams, *Anticipating Space Needs in Juvenile Detention and Correctional Facilities* (Washington, DC: Office of Juvenile Justice and Delinquency Prevention, 2001); M. J. McMillen, "Planning Juvenile Detention Facilities: The Real Costs," *Journal for Juvenile Justice and Detention Services,* Vol. 13 (Spring 1998), pp. 44–57.

[22]Roush, *Desktop Guide to Good Detention Practice,* p. 83.

[23]Ibid., pp. 83–84.

[24]Rosemary C. Sarri, *Under Lock and Key: Juveniles in Jail and Detention* (Ann Arbor: University of Michigan, 1974), p. 21.

[25]Ibid., pp. 21–22.

[26]Charles E. Reasons and Russell L. Kaplan, "Tear Down the Walls? Some Functions of Prisons," *Crime and Delinquency,* Vol. 21 (1975), pp. 360–372.

[27]Ellsworth Fersch, "When to Punish, When to Rehabilitate," *American Bar Association Journal,* Vol. 61 (1975), pp. 1235–1237.

[28]Irving R. Kaufman, "Of Juvenile Justice and Injustice," *American Bar Association Journal,* Vol. 62 (1976), pp. 730–734.

[29]*Morales v. Turman,* E.D. Tex., 1974, 383 F. Supp. 53.

[30]J. Rossi, *Hard Cores Don't Come from Apples* (Pasadena, CA: Ward Ritchie Press, 1976), pp. 51–52.

[31]For further discussion on the subject of escapees and/or runaways, the reader is referred to: *Smallwood v. Hindle* (District Court of Iowa, Black Hawk County, October 11, 1964); and the Runaway Youth Act, Title III of the Juvenile Justice and Delinquency Prevention Act of 1974 (P.L. 93–415).

[32]*Chin v. Wyman et al.* (N.Y. Supreme Court Westchester County, December 31, 1963), 246 N.Y.S. 2d. 306.

[33]The institution referenced is Training Institute of Columbus, Ohio.

[34]Clemens Bartollas, Stuart J. Miller, and Simon Dinitz, *Juvenile Victimization: The Institutional Paradox* (New York: Halstead Press, 1976): Clemens Bartollas and Christopher M. Sieverdes, "Juvenile Correctional Institutions: A Policy Statement," *Federal Probation,* Vol. 46 (1982), pp. 22–26; John M. MacDonald, "Violence and Drug Use in Juvenile Institutions," *Journal of Criminal Justice,* Vol. 27 (1999), pp. 33–44.

[35]President's Commission on Law Enforcement and Administration of Justice, *Task Force Report: Corrections* (Washington, D.C.: U.S. Government Printing Office, 1967), p. 149.

[36]Ronald Goldfarb, *Jails: The Ultimate Ghetto* (Garden City, NY: Anchor Press, 1976), p. 315.

[37]Doris Layton MacKenzie, Angela R. Gover, Gaylene Styve Armstrong, and Ojmarrh Mitchell, "A National Study Comparing the Environments of Boot Camps with Traditional Facilities for Juvenile Offenders," *National Institute of Justice: Research in Brief* (Washington, DC: U.S. Department of Justice, August, 2001), p. 1.

[38]Jerry Tyler, Ray Darville, and Kathi Stalnaker, "Juvenile Boot Camps: A Descriptive Analysis of Program Diversity and Effectiveness," *Social Science Journal,* Vol. 38 (2001), p. 458.

[39]Mac Kenzie, Gover, Armstrong, and Mitchell, "A National Study."

[40]Ibid.

[41]Michael Peters, David Thomas, and Christopher Zamberlan, *Boot Camps for Juvenile Offenders: Program Summary* (Washington, DC: Office of Juvenile Justice and Delinquency Prevention, 1997), pp. 19–20.

[42]Ibid., pp. 21–22.

[43]Eric Peterson, "Juvenile Boot Camps: Lessons Learned," *Office of Juvenile Justice and Delinquency Prevention Fact Sheet# 36* (Washington, DC: U.S. Department of Justice, June, 1996), p. 2.

[44]Joanne Ardovini-Brooker and Lewis Walker, "Juvenile Boot Camps and the Reclamation of Our Youth: Some Food for Thought," *Juvenile and Family Court Journal,* Vol. 51 (2000), pp. 21–29.

[45]Karen B. Shepard, "Understanding Disproportionate Minority Confinement," *Corrections Today,* Vol. 59 (1995), pp. 114–115.

[46]Heidi M. Hsia and Donna Hamparian, *Disproportionate Minority Confinement: 1997 Update—Juvenile Justice Bulletin* (Washington, DC: Office of Juvenile Justice and Delinquency Prevention, 1997); Wayne N. Welsh, Phillip W. Harris, and Patricia H. Jenkins, "Reducing

Overrepresentation of Minorities in Juvenile Justice: Development of Community-Based Programs in Philadelphia," *Crime and Delinquency,* Vol. 42 (1996), pp. 76–98.

[47]Office of Juvenile Justice and Delinquency Prevention, *Minorities in the Juvenile Justice System—1999 National Report Series, Juvenile Justice Bulletin* (Washington, DC: U.S. Department of Justice, 1999).

[48]Vicky T. Church, "Meeting Disproportionate Minority Confinement Mandates," *Corrections Today,* Vol. 58 (1994), pp. 70–72.

[49]Bernard C. Dean, *Juvenile Justice and Disproportionality: Patterns of Minority Over-representation in Washington's Juvenile Justice System* (December, 1997) http://www.sgc.wa.gov/JJD/ JJD%20Report.HTM.

[50]Hsia and Hamparian, *Disportionate Minority Confinement.*

[51]Darlene J. Conley, "Adding Color to a Black and White Picture: Using Qualitative Data to Explain Racial Disproportionality in the Juvenile Justice System," *Journal of Research in Crime and Delinquency,* Vol. 31 (1994), pp. 135–148.

[52]Patricia Devine, Kathleen Coolbaugh, and Susan Jenkins, "Disproportionate Minority Confinement: Lessons Learned from Five States," *OJJDP Juvenile Justice Bulletin* (Washington, DC: Office of Juvenile Justice and Delinquency Prevention, 1998), p. 8; Charles J. Kehoe, "Juvenile Corrections in a Changing American Landscape," *Corrections Today,* Vol. 63 (2001), p. 6; Darnell F. Hawkins, John H. Laub, Janet L. Lauritsen, and Lynn Cothern, "Race, Ethnicity, and Serious and Violent Offending," *OJJDP Juvenile Justice Bulletin* (Washington, DC: Office of Juvenile Justice and Delinquency Prevention, 1998).

[53]Conley, "Adding Color."

[54]Edmund F. McGarrell, "Trends in Racial Disproportionality in Juvenile Court Processing: 1985–1989," *Crime and Delinquency,* Vol. 39 (1993), pp. 29–48.

[55]Donna M. Bishop and Charles E. Frazier, "The Influence of Race in Juvenile Justice Processing," *Journal of Research in Crime and Delinquency,* Vol. 25 (1988), pp. 242–263.

[56]Madeline Wordes, Timothy S. Bynum, and Charles J. Corley, "Locking Up Youth: The Impact of Race on Detention Decisions," *Journal of Research in Crime and Delinquency,* Vol. 31 (1994), pp. 149–165.

[57]George S. Bridges, D. J. Conley, R. L. Engen, and T. Price-Spratlen, "Racial Disparities in the Confinement of Juveniles: Effects of Crime and Community Social Structure on Punishment," in Kimberly Kempf-Leonard, Carl E. Pope, and William H. Feyerherm, eds., *Minorities in Juvenile Justice* (Thousand Oaks, CA: Sage, 1993), pp. 128–152.

[58]Duran Bell and Kevin Lang, "The Intake Dispositions of Juvenile Offenders," *Journal of Research in Crime and Delinquency,* Vol. 22 (1985), pp. 309–328.

[59]Florida Department of Juvenile Justice, "Seriousness of Delinquency History Relative to Disproportionate Minority Confinement," *Bureau of Data and Research: Research Digest, Issue #18,* (April 1998). http://www.djj.state.fl.us/RnD/r digest/Issue18/issue18.htm.

[60]Michael J. Leiber and Jayne M. Stairs, "Race, Contexts, and the Use of Intake Diversion," *Journal of Research in Crime and Delinquency,* Vol. 36 (1999), pp. 56–86; Michael J. Leiber and Katherine M. Jamieson, "Race and Decision Making Within Juvenile Justice: The Importance of Context," *Journal of Quantitative Criminology,* Vol. 11 (1995), pp. 363–388; Michael J. Lieber, "Toward Clarification of the Concept of 'Minority' Status and Decision-Making in Juvenile Court," *Journal of Crime and Justice,* Vol. 18 (1995), pp. 79–108; Michael J. Leiber, "A Comparison of Juvenile Court Outcomes for Native Americans, African Americans, and Whites," *Justice Quarterly,* Vol. 11 (1994), pp. 257–279.

[61]Hsia and Hamparian, *Disportionate Minority Confinement;* Welsh, Harris, and Jenkins, "Reducing Overrepresentation." For more information on disproportionate minority confinement, see the Office of Juvenile Justice and Delinquency Prevention website on this subject at www.ojjdp.ncjrs.org/dmc/.

[62]James Austin, Kelly Dedel Johnson, and Maria Gregoriou, *Juvenile in Adult Prisons and Jails—A National Assessment* (Washington, DC: Bureau of Justice Assistance, 2000), p. xi.

chapter **10**

JUVENILE PAROLE: USEFUL OR HARMFUL?

The success of any institutional treatment program depends to a large extent upon supervision done after a youngster is released on "juvenile aftercare." The Commission found, however, that aftercare is perhaps the most neglected aspect of the juvenile justice system. Juvenile aftercare, where it exists, entails cursory contact by underpaid, overworked counselors with excessive caseloads who often do not meet minimum qualifications to be counselors.

— Robert W. Winslow

CHAPTER OVERVIEW

What is Parole?

Before discussing juvenile aftercare, it is useful to define *parole*. This will help to eliminate some of the misconceptions regarding it. The terms *probation* and *parole* are often confused. In many instances, the word parole is used imprecisely when referring to various methods of release from an institution that may or may not be included in its actual meaning.

Juvenile parole is defined as the conditional release of a juvenile from a correctional institution at a time when he or she can best benefit from release and continued life in the community under the supervision of a counselor or parole officer. Parole is a method whereby society can be protected and the juvenile can be provided with continuing treatment and supervision.

There is no direct tie between juvenile court probation and juvenile parole as part of one correctional process. *Probation* is administered, in most cases by the courts on a county level; *parole*, on the other hand, is generally administered on a statewide basis by the agency that is responsible for providing institutional services. Juvenile probation is a pre-institutional procedure. A juvenile is sentenced to probation as an alternative to institutionalization. Parole is part of the correctional process and is used only after the juvenile has spent time in a juvenile correctional institution.

The term **aftercare** has also been used in reference to juvenile parole. Although it is not widely accepted or used within the field of juvenile corrections, *aftercare* will be used here interchangeably with juvenile parole to encourage its usage. Those who are concerned about providing social services to youths prefer this term to its adult counterpart—parole. Generally speaking, the practice of juvenile aftercare has gained more acceptance than has the term itself. The word *parole* derives from the French, in which it means "to promise." The term was probably first used in a correctional context by Samuel Howe, a Boston penal reformer of the mid-1800s.

Unlike the probationer, the parolee (one who is on parole) has already completed part of the period of his or her commitment. Release is conditional and may be revoked if the terms of the parole are violated prior to the end of the youth's parole period.

Parole, unlike probation, is administrative and quasi-judicial. It is an attempt to bridge the gap between the institution and the community and to ease the transition period from one to the other. Parole is meant to help the youth remain in the community and to decrease the likelihood of becoming involved again in delinquent behavior. The parolee is usually more of a problem to the parole officer or counselor than the probationer is to probation staff. The paroled juvenile has been locked away and may be bitter, resentful, remorseful, and hostile and may exhibit more acting out or antisocial behavior than a probation counterpart. Behavior is not predictable, however, for sometimes the parolee will be more cooperative, docile, and content than will a probationer. The parolee can have parole revoked and can be returned for another taste of institutional life, which is something that many juveniles on probation can only conjecture about and have not experienced. Whatever the individual youth's reaction to parole, hostile or cooperative, juvenile corrections is responsible for providing aftercare services as long as institutionalization of juveniles continues and as long as the mechanism of parole is an alternative "way out."

BRIEF HISTORY OF PAROLE

Parole, unlike probation, is basically more English and European than American in its roots. In England in the early nineteenth century, transportation, indenture, and other practices of placing children and adults in involuntary labor in both private and public settings became common practice. These programs, motivated by economic pressures rather than by humanitarian concerns, offered a conditional release from prison. As in parole, the transported or indentured individual was not altogether free, but rather was forced to work for a certain period of time (often as long as seven years) to regain his or her freedom. In early American history, offenders were sentenced to prison for a fixed length of time—the **determinate sentence**—and they were not released until that time had been served.

Breaking with this tradition, New York, in 1817, was the first state to pass a so-called **good time law.** Good time laws allowed for a reduction in a prisoner's sentence based on his or her cooperative good conduct and behavior in accordance with institutional rules. Subsequent good time laws passed by other states had rules that were firm and straightforward but that varied from one state to another. New York's, for example, enabled the correctional administrator to "reduce by one-fourth the sentence of any prisoner sentenced to imprisonment for not less than five years, upon certificate of the principal keeper and other satisfactory evidence, that such prisoner behaved well, and acquired in the whole, the net sum of 15 dollars or more per annum."[1] By 1916, all states and the District of Columbia had passed some form of good time law.

Although good time laws were a step in the right direction, they were really not much better than the methods used to gain pardons for prisoners serving excessively long sentences. Early laws sometimes dictated such oppressively long sentences for a prisoner that the *jury* often petitioned the governor to grant a pardon. Not unlike current practices, pardons were often used to empty out prisons to make room for newly sentenced offenders. Obviously, overcrowding of penal institutions is an age-old problem.

Meanwhile, by 1832, a new concept in corrections—the **indeterminate sentence**—was being developed and experimented with (See box 10.1). The idea of the indeterminate sentence is attributed to the combined efforts of England's Alexander Maconochie and Ireland's Sir Walter Crofton. At the 1870 meeting of the National Prison Association, the effectiveness of Crofton's "Irish system" was discussed. The system devised by Crofton, and presented by him in a paper on indeterminate sentencing at that meeting, consisted of a series of stages, each bringing the prisoner closer to freedom. In the first stage, the new prisoner was placed in solitary confinement and assigned to dull, monotonous work. The second stage involved assignment to public works and a progression through various grades, periods of time in which conduct was to improve. In the last stage, the prisoner was assigned to an intermediate prison where there was no supervision and the prisoner moved in and out of the free community. If his conduct continued to be good and if he was able to find a job, he was returned to the community on a conditional pardon or "ticket of leave." This pardon could be revoked at any time within the span of his original fixed sentence if conduct was not up to standards established by those who supervised the conditional early release. Crofton's plan was the first effort to establish a system of conditional liberty in the community.

In 1867, the Michigan legislature passed an indeterminate sentence act under continued pressure from the superintendent of the Detroit House of Corrections, Zebulon Brockway. Brockway pressed for the use of parole and the indeterminate sentence mainly because of the large number of prostitutes who were being shuttled in and out of his institution.

Indeterminate sentencing and parole as advocated by Crofton and Brockway were introduced in 1876 at the Elmira Reformatory in New York. In the form of parole worked out at Elmira, the prisoner was kept under the supervision and control of the prison authorities for an additional six months following release. By 1891, eight states had authorized the indeterminate sentence but only for first-time offenders. New York excluded first-time women offenders altogether.

For adult prisoners, true indeterminate sentencing has won acceptance more slowly than has parole. However, a genuine indeterminate sentence (one having no minimum or maximum length) has been used in the juvenile justice system for some time. One might question, however, if the juveniles are not released because of their willingness to conform to the model used to determine their ability to return to a free society (as is the case in a genuine indeterminate sentence). Another question is whether they are not released periodically merely because of overcrowded conditions, lack of sufficient funds and resources, or for other shortcomings of the system.

The American Law Institute's Model Youth Correction Authority Act of 1939 introduced the practice of granting the court the right to commit

---

Box 10.1 Indeterminate Sentence

An *indeterminate sentence* is a sentence to incarceration pronounced by a judge that sets minimum and maximum periods of incarceration of the offender (such as from one to five years). The minimum term would establish the earliest release date (adjusted for certain time credits for, as an example, jail time during pretrial detention) or the first time before the inmate could possibly be released. At the maximum term, the inmate would have to be released.

Underlying the indeterminate sentence are assumptions of rehabilitation, and early release, if the offender is treated and is reformed. The minimum and maximum periods (such as a one-to-five year sentence) reflect the inability of the sentencing judge to know when the offender will be reformed.

delinquent or dependent youths to the local youth authority for diagnosis and placement. This act is significant because it focused much attention on the youth authority model in the 1940s and 1950s. The model promoted the concept of parole release and aftercare supervision for committed youths. Today, every state has statutory provisions for both juvenile and adult parole.

Parole for juveniles can be traced back to the early houses of refuge established for children in the latter half of the nineteenth century. "Juvenile parole developed for several years as part of the general child welfare field, but recently, while still retaining a close involvement with child welfare programs, has assumed a more distinct status."[2] The concepts of foster care and group homes have also led to the emergence of parole as a specific practice. However, juvenile parole still remains one of the least developed of all aspects of the juvenile justice system.

JUVENILE PAROLE TODAY

After release from correctional institutions, most juveniles eventually go back to the neighborhoods from which they came. Unless the youth dies in the institution or is transferred to an adult correctional facility, he or she will be released and will be the charge of the juvenile justice system for some period of time. The excessively long sentences of the nineteenth century usually meant that most offenders, adult or juvenile, left prison bitter and broken. Today, almost every offender has a chance for parole before completing a prison term. The adult offender is usually released on parole long before the expiration of the maximum sentence. In the case of juveniles, they are usually paroled long before institutional treatment programs have reached them, or long after they have become hardened by and immune to the whole system.

More widespread than the practice of minimum confinement periods is the practice of requiring the committing judge to become involved officially before a juvenile can be paroled. Nine states have such a procedure. The problem with this practice is that the judge, often already too busy with court matters, must be aware of the child's problems and behavior in the institution, as well as current provisions and conditions in the child's local community. Providing both kinds of information to the judge has been difficult at best, and therefore the judge is required to act on incomplete or outdated knowledge. Another problem is that control by the court may impede institutional programs for the child by treatment staff that has the duty of preparing the youth for release. The vast majority of states have done away with judicial control over the release of committed juveniles.

Experts in the field of juvenile aftercare agree that the aims of parole are based on two separate but not mutually exclusive objectives: (1) the protection of the community and (2) the proper adjustment of the offender. With a growing emphasis on the integration and coordination of institutional and parole services, it becomes increasingly evident that the most important objective of the total correctional process is the protection of society. It seems to us that the question should not be the protection of society versus the rehabilitation of the delinquent but, rather, the protection of society through the offender's rehabilitation.

The immediate purpose or objective of parole is to assist the parolee in understanding and coping with the problems faced upon release, to get used to the status of being a parolee. The long-range goal of parole is to assist in the development of the juvenile's ability to take independent action and to make correct choices regarding behavioral standards that will be acceptable to society. This latter goal is essential, for it is of permanent benefit to both the parolee and the community.

The basic functions of juvenile aftercare are three: (1) classifying the offender to determine readiness for release and the risk factor upon release, among other things; (2) the rehabilitation and reintegration of the juvenile into the community; and (3) the reduction in the likelihood of the juvenile's committing further delinquent acts, that is, reduction in recidivism.

Overall, the usefulness and effectiveness of parole in achieving its goals and purposes depend on whether it performs two social tasks. The first is sound case disposition. This encompasses the selection of those juveniles from among the institutionalized offender groups who, at a certain point, would benefit from return to the community instead of remaining in the institution. Since most juveniles are eventually paroled, the primary concern becomes more one of when to release, as opposed to whom. The second social task is social treatment, which includes providing the offender with access to adequate community resources to aid in reintegration.

Both these social tasks place immense responsibility on the correctional system within juvenile justice. Case disposition involves "people processing" to select the right course of action to meet the needs of each individual youth, and social treatment necessitates intervention (sometimes welcomed, often not) into the social situation in which the individual functions in an attempt to change attitudes and behaviors. The final outcome is often nothing less than the actual shaping of the present and future lives of human beings.

THE PAROLE DECISION PROCESS: WHO DECIDES AND HOW?

Parole services in the juvenile justice system should be administered by the same state agency that is responsible for the institutional and related services to delinquent and dependent children. This agency is called the juvenile paroling authority.

Juvenile parole services as administered vary widely among the states and Puerto Rico. Unlike other programs for youths, such as public education, which is nearly always administered by a state educational agency, juvenile parole has no clear-cut organizational pattern. A youth authority, a child welfare agency, an adult correctional agency, a lay board, or the correctional institution staff may administer it.

Differing patterns of local jurisdiction have emerged for various reasons. Some state officials have chosen to give jurisdiction to local agencies, on the assumption that youth would receive better care from them than from the centralized, state-operated programs. In other states, the jurisdiction for parole has fallen to local agencies by default; there were simply no state agencies that could provide the needed supervision at a local level.

To ameliorate such non-standardized organizational arrangements for the administration of aftercare services, the law under which the youth is committed to a juvenile correctional institution should provide that the agency granted legal custody also be given the right to determine when the youth shall leave the institution.

For purposes of this text, the administering agency of juvenile parole will be referred to as the "juvenile paroling authority."

When to Release

Unlike the adult parole boards, most juvenile paroling authorities do not determine the length of time (at the postsentencing stage) of an offender's prison term.

Some juvenile paroling authorities do, however, require that the juvenile remain incarcerated for a certain period before release on parole. The period varies among states and jurisdictions. In most instances, however, the youth's length of commitment is determined by what is called "the progress toward rehabilitation." Progress is sometimes measured by a token system that awards a specific number of points for various positive actions. In most states, the criterion for measuring successful rehabilitation (and therefore, time of release) is whether or not the juvenile conforms or causes problems. Unfortunately, there exists no valid measure of a genuine rehabilitation or change of attitude. The youth's behavior may be tempered by knowledge of the release date or may be motivated solely to please "the man." By appearing to have been reformed, the youth receives the quickest release possible.

Institutions with the most adequate treatment services are the best prepared to judge the youth's readiness for parole. In these institutions, staff members should have the opportunity to come to know the juvenile as an individual, for they can then judge more accurately the progress, risk, and potential for successful reintegration into the community. In institutions where the process model has replaced the treatment model, the decision as to when a particular youth is ready for parole can be based upon little more than the behavior shown by that youth while institutionalized. In this case, factors to consider are the number of times isolation had to be used, and the number of fights, or other behavioral problems, caused by the youth. If the process model is to become the model used within juvenile correctional institutions, guidelines based on criteria other than good behavior are needed in determining preparedness for release.

For purposes of parole, there is general agreement that the youths should be released as soon as operative criteria determine they are ready. The use of the fixed sentence, with a minimum and a maximum, could well interfere with this conceptual approach.

Gains made by the youth in the institution (if any) must be strengthened when they are returned to the community by the basic functions of the parole process. Good release planning is a key to the success of the youth's "return life" in the community. Institutional staff, working in conjunction with parole staff, should prepare the juvenile for any negative reactions or other stumbling blocks to reintegration that may be encountered in the community. This prerelease planning should include the utilization of community resources during incarceration, if possible, and discuss post release problems, thus helping to bridge the gap between the institution and the community.

The question of when to release a juvenile on parole depends on the youth's future behavior and how far one can predict that behavior. There are several policy considerations that should be evaluated prior to granting parole:

- Whether the juvenile has profited by his or her stay in the institution.
- Whether reform has taken place so that it is unlikely that another offense will be committed.
- Whether behavior in the institution has been acceptable.
- Whether suitable employment, training, or treatment is available on release.
- Whether the juvenile has a home or other place, such as a group home, to which to go.
- Whether the youth's perception of his or her ability to handle reintegration into the community is viewed as acceptable.
- Whether the seriousness of past offenses and the circumstances in which they were committed are not sufficiently severe as to preclude release.
- Whether the juvenile's appearance and attitude prior to release are acceptable.
- Whether behavior on probation and/or former parole, if applicable, are acceptable.
- Whether institutional staff workers' perception of the youth's successful return to the community is positive.

In making parole selection decisions, the paroling authority generally runs the risk of making one of two types of errors. The first is granting release to a juvenile who will commit new offenses or parole violations. The second is not granting release to a youth who would have completed parole without violation. Since over 98 percent of all juveniles committed to institutions are eventually released, the chances are that, sooner or later, both of these errors will occur, perhaps often. A thorough evaluation of the policy considerations previously mentioned, coupled with a good knowledge of the youth, the system, and the setting to which the juvenile will be returned, will certainly aid the paroling authorities in their decision of when to release.

PAROLE SERVICES

Parole services consist of all the various components of the juvenile justice system required to facilitate the goals and basic purposes of parole. These include institutional efforts at classification, the efforts of the parole staff and juvenile paroling authority to assist the youth in reentry to the community, and efforts of the community on the juvenile's behalf.

Juvenile parole services begin with pre-parole investigations to establish the groundwork for parole supervision and to obtain the necessary background information on the child and family. Parole services continue until the discharge of the parole case. The average length of time the juvenile will spend on parole status varies from state to state. Some states keep their juveniles in active aftercare supervision programs for an average of one year or less; others give aftercare supervision for an average of one year or more. Girls generally are maintained on parole longer than boys; the reason may lie in society's attitude that the young female offender requires protection through supervision for a longer period than does the young male.

The service of supervising a paroled youth is a form of social work; hence it is helpful if the parole officer has had some social work training. Unfortunately, as is the case with probation and institutional staff, many of them do not. Parole officers experience many of the same problems as their probation counterparts: too many children to supervise, too large a territory to cover, and too much time spent in travel.

It is unrealistic to assume that the parole officer can be all things to all youths. Community involvement in the youth's rehabilitation is paramount to the success of any aftercare services program. Even though the parole agent can identify the juvenile's problems, developing solutions to these problems ultimately lies within the community. The community must be willing to reaccept the child and, through its acceptance, facilitate the primary goal of individual rehabilitation. Juvenile aftercare services should therefore act as an agent of community change.

Caseload Size

Caseload size is an important factor in the ability to deliver effective parole services. The report of the President's Commission on Law Enforcement and Administration of Justice called for a maximum caseload of fifty juveniles for the aftercare counselor (active supervision cases). One prerelease investigation was held to be equal to three cases under active supervision.

Aftercare programs should be set up for proper counseling and direction for all categories of offenders. It is preferable for the juvenile to maintain personal contact with the parole officer to ensure adequate supervision. Caseload sizes should not be so large that routine contact between the parolee and the parole agent is conducted only through telephone calls.

Although it is claimed that a reduction of the size of a parole officer's caseload would result in greater success for parolees, there is no evidence to prove it. Proposals to reduce caseload size still gain wide acceptance on the basis of promised improvement in success rates, even though research suggests that reducing the caseload size alone is not the answer.

The institutionalization of the fifty-unit concept is now firmly entrenched. Budgets for operating agencies, testimony before legislative bodies, standards of practice, and projections for future operational needs all center about this number. There is no evidence of any empirical justification for fifty, nor for that matter, any other number.[3]

Parole Staff

Without adequate staff, aftercare programs are likely to remain the stepchild of the juvenile system. The President's Commission on Law Enforcement and the Administration of Justice stated that the juvenile justice system spends ten times more money and resources to incarcerate a juvenile than it does for probation or aftercare. Low salaries, large caseloads, and lax professional standards are not conducive to attracting highly trained and qualified professionals to enter into a career of juvenile aftercare.

Ideally, parole staff should possess a master's degree in social work or a related field because of the nature and complexity of their tasks. This standard has proven virtually impossible to attain, however. To compensate for the lack of formal professional training in the diagnosis and treatment of behavioral problems, extensive in-service training and other methods of staff development are highly recommended.

Adherence to this recommendation would help to solve many problems currently facing juvenile aftercare staff. Furthermore, the staff could get down to the business of supervising and helping youths in need. This would be a clear improvement over simply trying to survive in a system that often seems not to give a damn.

CONDITIONS OF PAROLE

Although the **conditions of parole,** under which a juvenile is released in the community, are not quite as stringent as those for adults, they are complex. Among the specifications generally included in the conditional release of the juvenile are (1) not committing further offenses; (2) staying off drugs and away from alcohol; (3) not hanging around with the old gang or other persons who are known offenders or who could have a potentially damaging effect on the youth on parole; (4) reporting on a regular basis to the parole officer or other designated person; (5) staying in a specified geographical area; and (6) getting a job or obtaining training that will lead to gainful employment. Several states have an actual parole contract that the youth is required to read, understand, and sign prior to release.

Conditions may be changed and renegotiated after consultation with the juvenile parole counselor. This provision, practiced by other states as well, is an attempt to make the terms of a juvenile parole as flexible as possible, adjusting realistically to changing needs, desires, and opportunities. Violation of the conditions of parole can result in revocation by the parole authority. However, the only valid reason for parole revocation is clear evidence that the youth just cannot function properly in the community.

Once the decision to grant parole is made, the specifications attached to that conditional release often become the measure of a youth's freedom and responsibility. Since failure to observe a condition of parole may result in revocation, its legal significance is clear. The value of such conditions is that both the youth and the community is made to understand that parole, although a mechanism for release from the institution is not absolute freedom. The right to decide parole conditions within individual jurisdictions, the way in which these conditions are actually imposed, and the discretionary right of an individual parole officer to enforce these conditions are crucial continuing legal safeguards in both adult and juvenile corrections.

The basic legal issues associated with parole conditions may be summarized as follows:

- Conditions often affect such basic constitutional freedoms as religion, privacy, and freedom of expression.
- Too often they are automatically and indiscriminately applied, without any thought given to the necessities of the individual case.

- In many instances, conditions lack precision and create needless uncertainty for the supervised individual and excessive revocation leverage for those in authority.

- Some conditions are extremely difficult, if not impossible, to comply with.[4]

Revocation of Parole

Ordinarily, **revocation of parole** is within the purview of the juvenile paroling authority (if one exists). In most jurisdictions, the paroling authority must issue a warrant, or order, if it intends to detain a juvenile suspected of violating parole. A few states permit detention for parole violation without such a warrant. The discretionary powers of the paroling authority are very broad regarding its decision to revoke the juvenile's parole. Irregularities and failure to provide legal representation at revocation hearings have received careful scrutiny by appellate courts and, most recently, by the U.S. Supreme Court.

In late June 1972, the U.S. Supreme Court decided a most important case regarding parole revocation and revocation hearings. The case of *Morrissey v. Brewer* contained facts that were fairly typical of the standard practices regarding parole revocation as it existed in approximately twenty states where no hearings were held to determine the appropriateness of revoking the offender's parole.

The petitioners in *Morrissey* were two parolees originally sentenced to prison in Iowa for forgery. Approximately six months after being released on parole, their parole was revoked for alleged violations. The two men appealed an appellate court's decision on the ground that the revocation of the paroles without a hearing had deprived them of due process of law guaranteed by the Fourteenth Amendment.

The appellate court, in affirming the district court's denial of relief, reasoned that parole is only "a correctional device authorizing service of sentence outside a penitentiary" and concluded that a parolee is still "in custody"[5] and not entitled to a full adversary hearing, as would be mandated in a criminal proceeding. The Supreme Court reversed the court of appeals decision and held that:

> the liberty of parole, although indeterminate, includes many of the core values of unqualified liberty and its termination inflicts a "grievous loss" on the parolee and often on others. It is hardly useful any longer to try to deal with this problem in terms of whether the parolee's liberty is a "right" or a "privilege." By whatever name, the liberty is valuable and must be seen as within the protection of the Fourteenth Amendment. Its termination calls for some orderly process, however informal.[6]

The Supreme Court has since guaranteed the "orderly process" when it laid down guidelines establishing minimum standards of due process regarding parole revocation. In referring to these guidelines, the Court stated that:

> They include (a) written notice of this claimed violations of parole; (b) disclosure to the parolee of evidence against him; (c) opportunity to be heard in person and to present witnesses and documentary evidence; (d) the right to confront and cross-examine adverse witnesses (unless the hearing officer specifically finds good cause for not allowing confrontation); (e) neutral and detached hearing body such as a traditional parole board, members of which need not be judicial officers or lawyers; and (f) a written statement by the fact finders as to the evidence relied on and reasons for revoking parole.[7]

Although these requirements refer to the actual revocation hearing, the court required substantially the same requirements at a preliminary hearing conducted at a time prior to the revocation hearing and shortly after arrest or detention. The court said that this preliminary hearing should be "conducted at or reasonably near the place of the alleged parole violation or arrest and as promptly as convenient after the arrest while information is fresh and sources are available . . . to determine whether there is probable cause or reasonable ground to believe that the arrested parolee has committed acts that would constitute a violation of parole conditions."[8]

There is no doubt that the Supreme Court's ruling in reviewing *Morrissey v. Brewer* has enhanced the rights of a parolee, but it has also left several questions unanswered.

Revocation Rates

The rate of parole revocation is often used to measure the effectiveness of various parole programs. Prus and Stratton suggest:

> . . . if one is to use revocation rates as a measure or program success, one should be highly conscious of the processes by which decisions to revoke parolees are made. While known infractions draw attention to the parolee and make his status as a parolee problematic, violations are subject to multiple interpretations and the seriousness of a given offense can be readily defined away. The decision to revoke a parole reflects the agent's personal orientations and his perception of self-accountability to the goals and personnel of the system in which he works. Revocation is not a structured response to parole violations; it is a socially influenced definition.[9]

It cannot be stressed too strongly that parole revocation rates are meaningful only when the reasons and procedures by which parole may be revoked are clearly understood.

DISCHARGE FROM PAROLE

In most jurisdictions, the parole officer may recommend the juvenile on parole status for **discharge from parole** at any time after the juvenile's release from the correctional institution. Release from parole is, however, conditional and is based on criteria similar to those used in determining release from the institution. Keeping in mind that the major goal of parole is the protection of society *through* the rehabilitation of the offender, it is paramount that there is a reasonable assurance that the parolee can continue to adjust satisfactorily in the community once the parole supervision is removed. In many states, the discharge of the juvenile from parole jurisdiction is reserved for the juvenile paroling authority or its agent. The juvenile's parole counselor is responsible for recommending discharge and for submitting this recommendation in writing to the paroling authority prior to the actual discharge of the parolee.

The decision to discharge a juvenile from parole can have as many potential pitfalls as the decision to place him or her on parole in the first place. For some youngsters on parole, survival in the community is possible because they can depend on their parole counselor. At least the officer is supposed to have some interest in their existence. Once this crutch is removed, the parolee may regress in both behavior and attitude and may well end up back on the road to crime. Most jurisdictions are reluctant to discharge a juvenile from parole for at least one year after release from the institution. It is hoped that this is enough time for the competent and observant agent to recognize and work on the youth's long-range needs and to help him or her achieve independence from the juvenile justice system.

It was stated that juvenile aftercare is the poor stepchild of the juvenile justice system. Similarly, post aftercare services are the abandoned child. Once discharged from parole, most juveniles are left to their own devices until they either become 18 (and are considered adults) or commit crimes and are returned to the courts for yet another trip on the juvenile justice merry-go-round. This is too often a ride they must take because somewhere someone failed to prevent the circumstances leading to their original delinquent acts.

Research on post parole success rates is generally scant, even though there is a definite need for it. In the absence of solid data, juvenile justice officials continue to play youth and society against one another.

JUVENILE RECIDIVISM

Attention on juvenile recidivism rates during aftercare have been sparked by such concerns as:

- Escalating juvenile crime rates.
- Dramatic increases in the number of youth entering secure care.
- Spiraling institutional costs.
- The juvenile correctional system's demonstrated ineffectiveness in controlling or reducing delinquent behavior among aftercare populations.[10]
- The increased use of juvenile incarceration has not demonstrated measurable reductions in juvenile arrests following the release of incarcerated offenders.[11]

Traditionally, juveniles have demonstrated high recidivism rates on parole (from 55 to 75 percent).[12] Similarly, a study of juveniles released from Wisconsin institutions between 1986 and 1990 found that 37 percent were reincarcerated within two years. On average, youths were in the community for only seven months between commitments.[13] Research on community supervision programs for juveniles have also yielded disappointing results. In her research review, MacKenzie was unable to reach definitive conclusions regarding the effectiveness of such programs.[14] In response to these problems, new models of supervision and treatment of juvenile aftercare have been developed.

The Intensive Aftercare Program (IAP Model)

Developed by David Altschuler and Troy L. Armstrong, the **IAP Model** addresses the documented failure of juvenile incarceration and aftercare by emphasizing the following:

1. Preparatory institutional services that can be reinforced in the community.
2. A highly structured transitional experience that bridges the institution and the community.
3. The use of intensive supervision and follow-up services in the community.[15]

The IAP Model stresses juvenile case management in five components:

1. Assessment, classification, and selection criteria. High-risk youth are identified through the use of a validated risk-screening instrument.

2. Individualized case planning that incorporates family and community perspectives. Specific attention is given to youth problems in conjunction with families, peers, schools, and other social networks.

3. A mix of intensive surveillance and services. Staff must have small caseloads and provide services not only during the daytime during the week but also during weekends and in the evenings.

4. A balance of incentives and graduated consequences. Violations are dealt with in proportion to their seriousness. In addition, good performance should be recognized within a graduated system of meaningful rewards.

5. The creation of links with community resources and social networks.[16]

The Office of Juvenile Justice and Delinquency Prevention has funded projects based on the IAP Model in four states (Colorado, New Jersey, Nevada, and Virginia) that will be subject to intensive research by the National Council on Crime and Delinquency.

SUMMARY

In this chapter it was shown that the concepts of juvenile parole and juvenile aftercare are used interchangeably. Probation, which takes place before the institutionalization of a juvenile as a diversionary procedure, is separate from parole. Juvenile parole (aftercare) is used to bridge the gap back to the community after incarceration. The juvenile under the guidance of the juvenile parole officer is more likely to be a problem than the juvenile reporting to the juvenile probation officer. Parole for juveniles has a dual purpose: protection for the community and proper adjustment of the parolee.

Many attempts have been made to classify youths in correctional institutions as potentially "good" risks on parole. In this instance, classification refers to the prediction of behavior after release. Classification, if applied properly, contributes significantly in the assignment of parolees to the appropriate type of parole officer.[17] More effort must be expended in this area if juvenile parole is to be maximally effective.

The juvenile parole decision-making process is fragmented and varied throughout the states. Fragmentation is a major problem and one that needs to be addressed squarely in determining the kind of organizational structure for a juvenile paroling authority. Organizational muddle, combined with excessive rhetoric and little action, have tended to push juvenile parole into the same model as the adult systems. Whether this movement will prove useful or harmful remains to be seen.

TERMS TO REMEMBER

Aftercare	IAP Model
Caseload size	Indeterminate sentence
Conditions of parole	Juvenile parole
Determinate sentence	*Morrissey v. Brewer*
Discharge from parole	Parole services
Good time laws	Revocation of parole

REVIEW QUESTIONS

1. Describe the difference between probation and parole.
2. How does the historical background of parole differ from that of probation?
3. List and discuss the major goals and three basic purposes of aftercare. How are these being realized?
4. Discuss the importance of the decision of the U.S. Supreme Court in *Morrissey v. Brewer.*
5. What factors should be considered for the successful release from an institution to parole status and for the discharge of a youth from parole? Are these considerations similar? Why or why not?
6. Explain how parole fits into the juvenile justice system and how it relates to the rest of the system.
7. Who decides when to parole and on what basis?
8. In your opinion is juvenile parole working? Why or why not?

NOTES

[1]Harry E. Barnes and Negley K. Teeters, *New Horizons in Criminology,* 3d ed. (Englewood Cliffs, NJ: Prentice Hall, 1959), p. 568.

[2]President's Commission on Law Enforcement and Administration of Justice, *Task Force Report: Corrections* (Washington, DC: U.S. Government Printing Office, 1967), p. 60.

[3]Robert M. Carter and Leslie T. Wilkins, eds., *Probation, Parole, and Community Corrections* (New York: John Wiley, 1976), p. 212.

[4]Ibid., p. 667.

[5]*Morrissey v. Brewer,* 408 U.S., 471 (1972).

[6]Ibid., p. 489.

[7]Ibid.

[8]Ibid., p. 486.

[9]Robert Prus and John Stratton, "Parole Revocation Decision Making: Private Typings and Official Designations," *Federal Probation* (March 1976) 48.

[10]Richard G. Wiebush, Betsie McNulty and Thao Le, "Implementation of the Intensive Community-Based Aftercare Program," *OJJDP Juvenile Justice Bulletin* (July 2000), p. 1.

[11]David M. Altschuler and Troy L. Armstrong, "Reintegrative Confinement and Intensive Aftercare," *Juvenile Justice Bulletin* (July 1999), http://www.ojjdp.ncjrs.org/bulletin/9907_3/reintegrate.html.

[12]Barry A. Krisberg, James Austin and Paul Steele, *Unlocking Juvenile Corrections* (San Francisco, CA: National Council on Crime and Delinquency, 1991).

[13]S. Troia, "Correctional Institutional Recidivism Among Youth Released from DYS Institutions, 1986 to 1990," *National Institute of Justice* (Wisconsin Department of Health and Social Services, 1993).

[14]Doris Layton MacKenzie, "Commentary: The Effectiveness of Aftercare Programs—Examining the Evidence," *Juvenile Justice Bulletin* (July 1999), http://www.ojjdp.ncjrs.org/bulletin/9907_3/comment.html.

[15]David M. Altschuler and Troy L. Armstrong, "Intensive Juvenile Aftercare as a Public Safety Approach," *Corrections Today*, Vol. 60 (1998), pp. 118–123.

[16]Wiebush, McNulty, and Le, "Implementation," p. 2.

[17]Ryan M. Quist and Dumiso G. M. Matshazi, "The Child and Adolescent Functional Assessment Scale (CAFAS): A Dynamic Predictor of Juvenile Recidivism," *Adolescence,* Vol. 35 (2000), pp. 181–192; Robin A. Lemmon and Sharon K. Calhoon, "Predicting Juvenile Recidivism Using the Indiana Department of Correction's Risk Assessment Instrument," *Juvenile and Family Court Journal,* Vol. 49 (1998), pp. 55–62.

Group Homes, Foster Care, and Adoption

Adoption of children is an ever-changing tradition. In ancient Rome, the purpose of adoption was to provide elder men with sons to carry on the family name. By the mid-1920s in the United States, the goal was to find children for childless couples. Today the emphasis is on what is best for the adopted child.

— Joan McNamara

Chapter Overview

The trend of making the community responsive to and responsible for the care and well-being of all of its citizens, including juveniles, which began to take hold in the early 1970s, continues today. As a result of the 1974 Juvenile Justice and Delinquency Prevention Act, communities are faced with the responsibility of dealing with their incorrigible and dependent juveniles (status offenders) whether or not they like it or are prepared to handle it. The Juvenile Justice Act requires the deinstitutionalization of status offenders. Congress amended the JJDP Act in 1977 to bring "non-offenders" (such as dependent and neglected youth) under the DSO provision and to provide states with broader alternative placement for all juvenile clientele. In 1980, Congress specified that such juveniles must be removed from "secure" juvenile detention and correctional facilities and prohibited states from detaining juveniles in jails and local lockups. Congress also approved an exception to this mandate for juveniles who have violated a valid court order (VCO). In 1992, Congress added a fourth mandate requiring that states receiving JJDP Act Formula Grants provide assurances that they will develop and implement plans to reduce overrepresentation of minorities in the juvenile justice system.[1]

What should the juvenile justice system do with the troubled youths with whom it comes in contact, youths who often have nowhere to go except an institution? Avenues other than institutionalization must be explored. All elements of the juvenile justice system—the police, the probation officer, the judge, the parole officer, the institutional staff, and other professionals—agree that youths should be kept out of institutions. But of course these children cannot simply be let loose in the community. There have to be other choices, alternatives that are both acceptable and promising, or an institution may be the only choice left.

Some administrators operate on the "conventional wisdom" that the child's own home, no matter how bad, is better than no home at all. However, too often a bad or abusive home environment has caused the child to exhibit the very behavior that has resulted in involvement with juvenile justice in the first place. To return the child to such a home is analogous to patching the bullet holes in a target and then returning it to the shooting range. Some parents are not physically, mentally, emotionally, or financially capable of providing their children with proper care and supervision. In such cases, the problem can often be resolved with professional treatment or casework intervention. However, it may still be necessary to remove children from the home during rehabilitation, and a temporary placement may be the proper environment in which to carry this out.

If the home is simply not suitable for the return of the child, permanent alternatives must be sought. This chapter will examine three of the most commonly used alternatives to institutionalized or home living, either temporarily or permanently. These alternatives are group homes, foster care, and adoption.

Approximately 70 percent of all monies spent for juvenile corrections programs per year go for institutional programs, even though almost one-half of all those institutionalized become recidivists. And, concerning various states' efforts at the deinstitutionalization of juveniles, it is noted that in none of the states did the deinstitutionalization effort cause an increase in either the amount or seriousness of juvenile crime.

GROUP HOMES

Group homes are a relatively recent development in the United States. There are those who contend that today's group homes, both private and public, are simply an extension of the halfway house concept. At their onset, in the early 1960s, group homes may indeed have been halfway houses. At the time, they were perceived as a way to ease the rehabilitated youth's reentry into the community. In fact, they could be viewed as a kind of halfway-out house. The group home was responsible primarily for providing additional direction and support to the child, support needed to make the final adjustment to community living.

At first, group homes placed emphasis on making a youth self-sufficient, self-responsible, and self-reliant. To ensure the likelihood of success, institutions were often discouraged from referring to group homes boys or girls who had serious behavioral problems. This practice tended to rule out such offenders as the repeat automobile thief, the sexually deviant offender, or those who might commit extreme acts of violence to themselves or others.

In short, early group homes looked after the "low-risk" youth who could be eased into the community from the institution with the minimum amount of treatment or trouble. It was rare for the group homes to accept a youth who had not gone through the institutional "softening up" process.

Today, those responsible for group home operations shy away from the term **halfway house.** It is felt that this label connotes impermanence, both to those who find themselves as residents and those on the outside. In fact, for many residents the state group home has become a more permanent home than they have ever known. In this situation, the name "halfway" becomes disturbing to those who may be experiencing their first feeling of belonging.

Group homes exist throughout the country in one form or another. Most states sign contracts with private group homes and do not run the homes directly. A few states run, own, and operate the homes themselves.

In the 1970s, group homes broke out of the image of "transition warehouses" of the 1960s. In the 1980s, many provided extensive treatment programs. These new group homes are willing to work with youths from institutions, rejected by institutions, and assigned directly from a centralized diagnostic center. Their main purpose is the same—to ease the youth's re-entry to society—but they also provide group care, counseling, and/or treatment for whatever period seems to be appropriate.

Purpose of the Group Home

The group home is generally a small residence for six to fifteen youths. It is meant to be a place where adequate peer relationships can be formed, but where affectional ties to and demands from adults are kept at a minimum. Group homes impose needed external controls, but youths are not required to accept "substitute parents," as is the case in the foster home setting. Acceptance of a dependent role can be particularly difficult for the youth who, in his or her normal course of maturing, is in the process of achieving emotional independence from parental figures. Because in most cases those considered for group home placement are children between ages 13 and 18, group homes can promote the socialization process through small-group interaction, interaction that does not involve a father or mother figure.

The group home, which was introduced in 1916, offers interaction in small groups in which confidence in and conflicts with a limited number of people provide the requisite emotional support and opportunities for growth.

The group home concept is the result of the findings of interrelated studies conducted in various settings in which socialization takes place (i.e., the family, the community-treatment centers, and institutions) and of theoretical insight into what makes a person develop into a mature member of society (i.e., the normal development process).[2]

There are seven characteristics generally accepted as common to group homes:

- They are residential.
- They provide group care.
- They contain between six and ten residents.
- They are community based.
- They provide social services.
- They have a full-time staff.
- They serve youths who are capable of living in the community but who need, for a variety of reasons, an alternative to other natural homes.

The following is a workable definition of a group home from 1973, still valid today:

A group home is a small, community-based residential facility for a group of youths for whom a community-living situation is desirable, but who need an alternative to their natural homes. A full-time staff supervises the youth's activities and is responsible for coordinating the provision of social services, whether these services come from staff members themselves or from the community.[3]

Group homes are not a family enterprise. Professional and custodial staffs are employed to run group homes (state or private) on a salaried basis. Unlike foster homes or adoptions, a "normal" or "normative" family atmosphere does not generally exist in a group home. Instead, members often receive community services in a fragmented or piecemeal way from a number of unrelated agencies. With this kind of setup, the youth is not overburdened with outside involvement, involvement that is not only unrelated but also sometimes not well coordinated and where victimization of the juvenile clients can be a problem.[4]

School Facilities and Education

School facilities in the larger, more institutionalized group homes may be on the grounds of the home. The teaching staff is drawn from the group home staff. However, children in group homes often attend public schools in the community in which the home is located. Successfully integrating youths from group homes into the public schools depends in part on the cooperation and coordination efforts of group home staff, children, the public schools, and the community. Through their efforts, children with problems can be assimilated smoothly into schools designed to serve the average child.

Group homes with sufficient funds can hire a community intervention specialist whose task it is to facilitate the transition of the group home children into local community activities such as schooling. Many states have Title I teachers who either conduct classes for group home children at the local public school or, in situations that warrant it, at the individual group home. Classrooms may be set aside for Title I teachers to use as they require them. Group home youth can be given credit for work completed at school or carried out at the group home level, with credit being granted by the local school officials in coordination with Title I teachers. Every school-age child in a group home should receive a fundamental and meaningful education, whatever his or her point of entry into the program, tested ability, behavioral difficulties, or motivation.

Youths who enter group homes often come from an institutional educational program, where positive reinforcement methods are likely to be used. Positive reinforcement provides rewards, such as privileges and good grades, for exhibiting desired behavior. When youths from this environment are placed into a public school in the community near the group home, they suffer from a form of educational shock. The more stringent demands of the public school system often cause these youths to become discouraged, and their motivation wanes. Past experience has shown that some of these youths create disciplinary problems in the classroom, problems that result in their being removed from school. Sometimes dismissal is what they wanted in the first place.

Title I teachers can also act as tutors, guidance counselors, and overall educational coordinators for group home residents. In these capacities they can ease the overall educational shock syndrome experienced by many youths and help them to solve motivational shortcomings and ease tensions leading to disruptive behavior in the classroom. Relieved of this responsibility, the public school classroom teacher has more time to teach, time that might otherwise be wasted in overcoming administration and/or behavioral problems.

Title I teachers, or their facsimiles, ensure that the educational needs of the group home youth are met in a meaningful and compatible way, not only for the individual child but for the community as well. If neither is available, it becomes crucial that the group home either have its own internal educational system or an excellent working relationship with the local public school.

Group Home Admissions

In recent years, group homes have become increasingly popular within the juvenile justice system. In most states, a youth must be under court order or jurisdiction upon entering a group home. It is not uncommon for youths entering group homes do so on a *parole status*. This means that if they do something wrong their parole could be revoked and they might be returned to the institution or incur other disciplinary action. To avoid red tape and waste of staff time normally involved in a parole revocation, some states have changed the status of state group home youth from parole status to continued "institutional" status. Instead of revoking a youth's parole, the juvenile can simply be transferred back to the institution.

Licensing

Most states have the authority to license group homes as a specific category of childcare services. Licensing requirements also provide a description of the children and young expectant mothers that the group home serves. They are those

- Who need foster care but who cannot ordinarily adjust to the close personal relationships normally required by a foster family home.
- Who leave an institutional setting for a transitional period of care prior to returning to their own home or prior to achieving independence [e.g., job, armed services, and college].
- Who need emergency placement pending more permanent planning or during temporary disruption of a current placement.
- Who are emotionally disturbed or physically or mentally handicapped, or whose behavior is so bizarre as to be unacceptable to most foster parents; provided that the supervising agency, through its own program or by the marshalling of appropriate community resources, can provide the necessary specialized services that may be required by the group which the facility serves.[5]

Many states stipulate that group home operators must become licensed by the state. Licensing of operators ensures that professional standards are applied to group homes to prevent abuse and the existence of group homes of poor quality. There are some precedents that offer guidance to those concerned with the licensing of group home operators. Each state, for example, has a Nursing Home Administrator's License Board. This board interviews prospective operators, gives them a written test regarding their abilities as nursing home operators, and generally evaluates their capabilities, training, and experience. The problem with developing a written test for group home operators, however, is that there is no agreement among those in the field on a common body of knowledge that all group home operators require. This may reflect the fact that there has been no sufficient definition of the group home's role and responsibilities.

Program Services

The adequate provision of program services to juveniles is perhaps the single most important issue facing group homes today. These program services include educational counseling, tutoring, job placement, individual counseling, and life skills counseling. They are essential to the group home's goal of successfully reintegrating juveniles into the community. Those in the group home field should have a common understanding of what services group homes should offer and how those services fit into existing community resources.

The provision of services needed to adequately treat juveniles instead of "warehousing" them has emerged as a genuine concern of group home professionals in recent years. Problems with the provision of needed services to group home youths may arise if such factors as (1) whether the youths with varying needs and problems can be accommodated successfully within the same group home setting, or (2) whether youths in different age groups are compatible and able to be treated together are not taken into consideration.

Program evaluation is essential to the provision of program services and any treatment that may result. Proper evaluation can answer such questions as (1) What is the best way of assuring that a group home is actually providing quality services as efficiently and as effectively as possible? and (2) Which client assignments, staffing patterns, and interfacing with outside service agencies are in the best interests of the juveniles being served? The proper evaluation of group home services will move group homes a major step forward in their realization of their full potential as a childcare resource.

Group Home Referrals

What a group home program evolves into may be a far cry from what that program was actually intended to do. One reason for this is that inappropriate referrals are frequently made, referrals that often redefine the role and purpose of the group home and thus endanger its survival.

Staffing of Group Homes

The program of rehabilitation at a group home is determined by the kinds of residents in that home and their particular needs. It is the staff's function to see to it that the program meets those needs and that there are sufficient personnel resources to support it. In general, there is no single staffing pattern that will fit the needs of all group homes.

Group home staff and supplementary volunteers should be suited for the job, and they should be fully aware of and trained for the demands of the particular home's program. Although not a prerequisite for group home house parents, a college degree is an asset because of the semiprofessional aspects of the job.

Personal characteristics and attitudes such as sincerity, maturity, concern, patience, and an empathy with youth are extremely important attributes for group home house parents. However, group homes find it difficult to recruit good house parents because of the low salary levels. Few people with the desired character traits of good group home house parents can afford to take the job.

In addition to the personal characteristics mentioned, the operators of group homes should have administrative skills and the ability to act as liaison between the home and the community. Group home operators may find that they are required to provide in-service training for new staff. Finally, if the group home claims to provide a therapeutic service for its youth, then at least one person on the staff should have the credentials to act as a counselor.

Future of Group Homes

The following recommendations for future action in the group home field were made in 1973 by the state of Washington. These suggestions are still valid goals for group home operations.

- As a prerequisite for licensing, each group home should provide a comprehensive description, in writing, of its proposed service delivery plan.
- Copies of all new or updated description packages should be made available to all potential child-placing agencies and/or individuals. Such descriptions can often provide useful knowledge for the determination of an appropriate placement and can save the referral agency and the child time and trouble.
- To involve the community and to limit responsibilities for group home operations to a few individuals, each group home should be required to appoint a board of directors.

- To facilitate the functions listed, no member of the board of directors should be in a position to benefit financially from the group home's operation.
- Each group home should be evaluated based upon the development of a sound methodology.
- The evaluation of the group home should take place at least every six months.
- State-sponsored training should be provided for all group home staff personnel. Diversification in programs offered by group homes is beneficial to both the juveniles being served and the community.
- As a means of evaluating success rates and of tracking the post placement progress of former group home residents, those former residents should be subjects of appropriate follow-up studies.
- Coordination of the development of all group home programs, including future programs, should be strongly considered. Such a centralized group home planning function is essential to the provision of quality services that appropriately meet the needs of juveniles placed in a group home setting.[6]

Because of their general nature, the group home operators of other states could adopt these recommendations readily.

As far as the role of the group home in the juvenile justice system of any particular state is concerned, the state must define that role. Of special importance is the relationship between institutions and group homes. When the purpose of the group home is defined clearly and programs are funded and begun, only then can the group home programs realize their full potential as community-based juvenile corrections alternatives.

FOSTER CARE

The concept of *parens patriae* contains the doctrine that society shall have the ultimate parental responsibility for all children in the community. Thus, when a youth cannot or will not remain at home, society must provide a substitute living arrangement. One such alternative is foster care. **Foster care** is a generic term applied to any kind of full-time substitute care for children outside their own homes by persons other than their parents. Although this generic term could also be used to describe institutional care, group home care, adoptive care, and so forth, here it will mean specifically foster home care.

A foster home, unlike the group home, offers services to the youth who still has fairly strong dependency needs, rather than to the young person who is struggling to be free of adult control.

A *foster home* is a family paid by the state or local government to board a neglected, abused, or delinquent child. If the court feels that the child does not need the controls of a correctional institution but is not yet ready for the move to independence offered in a group home, the child will most likely be placed in a foster home. In 1933, 47.2 percent of the dependent, neglected, and emotionally disturbed children needing substitute care were placed in foster family homes, while the remaining 52.8 percent were institutionalized.[7] The trend in the past six decades has been away from institutional care to foster care.

Background of Foster Care Homes

The feudal practice of *indenture,* in which parents contracted to place their child with a master craftsman to learn a trade, is the forerunner of foster home care. In return for teaching the child a trade, the craftsman had his or her services for a given length of time.

Although the feudal system vanished, the practice of indenturing youth remained in the form of private and public placements of dependent or destitute children. Delinquent children were also indentured. From 1853 to 1879, the Children's Aid Society of New York placed 48,000 children in homes in Southern and Western states. These placements were unpaid—that is, the family agreed to feed, house, clothe, and educate the child at its own expense. In 1866, Massachusetts started placing children who were charged with delinquent acts with families who were paid board.[8] The Massachusetts plan was the first systematic attempt at providing foster home care for delinquent youths.

With the rise of the juvenile court movement in 1899 and the consequent effort to remove the stigma of delinquency, the use of foster home care emerged as a preferred alternative to correctional placements.

In Boston and Buffalo in the 1930s, foster homes were used to provide care for youths who needed secure custody. Foster parents were guaranteed a flat sum with an additional per capita rate for each child in residence.

The use of foster care homes has shown a steady growth in the second half of the twentieth century. But in the 1960s, concern was voiced about the effectiveness of foster care programs. During that period professionals were becoming aware that the supply of foster homes was limited, that the needs of children coming into care were changing, and that the sheer number of youths in need of service was growing at an alarming rate.

Foster family care also came under attack in the 1970s as widespread reports of foster parent child abuse were publicized. Because of these reports, the National Council of Juvenile and Family Court judges recommended a federal law requiring agencies receiving federal foster care funds to make plans for each child's removal, if possible, from foster care.

In a similar stand, the staff of the National Commission for Children in Need of Parents has urged mandatory reviews, by a court or other outside authority, of every agency's plans for every child each sixty days. However, in spite of this, foster care continues today to be the most frequently used alternative home placement for children of all ages.

The Need for Foster Care

Specific reasons why foster care may be needed can be grouped into two main categories: (1) *parent*-related problems and (2) *child*-related problems.

The most frequent **parent-related problems** are

- Parental inadequacy
- Parental rejection
- Mental illness
- Child abuse
- Child neglect
- Abandonment
- Addiction to drugs
- Alcoholism
- Imprisonment
- Inability to cope.

The most frequently observed **child-related problems** are

- Parent-child conflict
- Delinquent behavior
- Incorrigibility
- Emotional disturbance
- Physical handicap
- Mental handicap
- Child-sibling conflict
- Sociopathic behavior.

If one or more of these problems does exist, the following questions then arise: What type of child can be expected to benefit from an experience in a foster care home? What type of child would not be suitable for foster care placement? Although these questions are difficult to answer, experience and common sense do offer some basic clues for the right course of action.[9]

Separation of a child from its parents can become necessary for a wide range of reasons according to family problem. Some of these are

- The physical condition of the mother
- Mental illness of the mother
- Emotional problems of the children
- Severe neglect or abuse
- Family problems.

Providing adequate income, medical care, housing, or child supervision could avert many separations. However, a residual group appears to be prone to separation because of severe psychological problems.

If there were a profile of the "average" child in foster care, it would indicate that most children entering foster home care come from broken homes with either one or both parents absent. The children are usually from lower class, chronically deprived families that are living a crisis-oriented existence. The principal source of referrals for the children coming into foster care is their parents, followed by social service agencies, the courts, and the police. The average length of stay for children in foster family care is less than one year. However, many children placed in foster family care remain for three years or more.

The Decision to Remove

The removal of a child or children from their home and their subsequent placement in foster family care should occur only as a last resort, when such intrusive means of intervention cannot be avoided. Although removal may be the only practical answer for some children, evidence from several states indicates that such removals result all too frequently in inadequate foster care placements. In essence, we end up substituting poor care and neglect by the parents for poor care and neglect by the state.

The removal of endangered children from the home is authorized in almost all states when the court determines that such action is in the best interests of the child. The burden of proof should be on the court and/or the intervening agency to demonstrate the actual need for the removal of a child. Cases involving nonaccidental physical harm to the child should be determined by a preponderance of evidence. All other cases should be determined by clear and convincing evidence. In any event, the court should determine that the available foster home placement would not endanger the child or children.

Selecting the Foster Home

Once the decision to separate the child (or children) from the parents is made and all the pertinent placement information is gathered, the process of choosing a home to meet the child's specific needs should begin.

The range of homes available to the child-placing agency home realistically determines the criteria for an appropriate, whether private or public. In the past the majority of foster homes were located in low-income urban areas. The need to supplement income with the money received for taking in a foster child has often been criticized in cases where it seems the sole reason why a family will take a foster child in the first place. In these cases, the benefit to the child being placed should be questioned. In recent years, social agencies have been focusing their home-finding efforts in higher income suburban areas.

Assuming that delinquents from various ethnic backgrounds have a better chance of adjusting in a familiar environment, efforts have also been made of late to place minority children in ethnically appropriate homes. A good foster home, regardless of location, generally has the following characteristics:

- The foster father has a high degree of participation in the minor's care.
- The foster parents accept the natural parents as significant persons in the minor's life.
- The foster family is well accepted in the neighborhood and the community.
- The foster parents' own children seem secure and well adjusted.
- Relationships within the family are characterized by mutual respect.
- The foster parents help the minor understand that he can be loved.
- The foster parents give affection without expecting immediate returns.
- The foster family has a clear set of "ground rules" for behavior but a teenager's need for privacy and group activities is recognized.[10]

Foster Family Care: A Changing Image

Foster family care has recently come under severe criticism by experts in the field of childcare. These professionals are now somewhat more reluctant to favor foster family care as an alternative placement service than they once were. Foster family care has been used so widely (nobody keeps an accurate count) that it has become looked upon as the panacea for the ills of delinquent, dependent, incorrigible, and neglected and/or abused youngsters. Under our current system that allows these placements, children spend their formative years (onset of most placements is age 5) in a state of "nonidentity," being shifted from one foster home to the next. They grow up without roots, uncertain of their futures, and with calloused outlooks on life. Authorities in the field say that they will reach adulthoods filled with more welfare, unemployment, and crime than will their non-foster care counterparts.

Assuming this to be true, one could make the further assumption that children being placed in foster family care come from families where parents will not or cannot respond to the array of services being offered, services such as day care, homemaker help, protective services, and appropriate financial and medical care, all of which may make it possible for the child or children to remain in their own homes as opposed to being added to the ranks of foster care cases. Many youths, therefore, are coming from homes that are beyond rehabilitation. Consequently, the "temporary" nature of foster care has been greatly changed. More and more youths are apt to spend all their minority years in foster families. The longer a child remains in foster care, the more likely he or she is to remain there. One solution to this problem is to ensure that maximum efforts at providing these needed services are made early in the case history.

This solution is aimed at the top of the foster care funnel—the own home to foster home route. If, however, foster care placement cannot be avoided, the next solution is aimed at the middle of the funnel. This is where the juveniles remain captive due to incredible amounts of bureaucratic bungling and red tape. The middle of the foster care funnel has to be unclogged to allow for free flow out the other end, so that juveniles can either go back to their own homes or go into permanent adoptive placements. Unfortunately, children are kept in foster care by outmoded laws and by the self-preservation instincts of the social service industry, an industry that would rapidly move away from status quo if foster children were put into permanent homes. Hopefully, this situation can be remedied by adopting the provisions of the Federal Adoption Assistance and Child Welfare Act of 1980. It was designed to provide families with preplacement services to prevent the need for children to enter the foster care system, to provide proper care for children who are in the system, and to move children through the system and back into home or adoption as quickly as possible.[11]

Focusing on the Problem

Traditional emphasis in foster care has been on the children. Focus must now be centered on the failures of our social and economic systems that lead to the family dysfunctions that can lead to the need for foster care.

A child research project carried out at the Columbia University School of Social Work clearly pinpointed where changes should take place.

Knowledge about the kinds of family situations that lead children to enter foster care has implications for both practice and policy. It would, of course, be an oversimplification to consider all the families of children in placement as constituting a homogeneous group. But with the exception of some families of emotionally disturbed children, there are many characteristics common to this parent population. These common areas include pervasive poverty, high incidence of minority group membership, frequent receipt of public assistance, one-parent families, and physical and mental illness.

It is apparent that the social service system as presently structured does not have the capability to provide basic preventive services to strengthen family life. A majority of the families in the study were known to social agencies before the placement crisis. Yet these agency resources did not prevent the movement of these children into foster care. The child welfare system is forced to operate like firemen arriving after the house was burned . . . fulfillment of its service task is hampered by the extent of damage done prior to agency intervention. Disadvantaged circumstances, extreme pathology, and inadequate parenting are common precursors of placement, thus handicapping the most sincere professional efforts to give such children a chance before they reach adulthood.[12]

The characteristics that are common to the parent population in this study are also those often linked with the causes of crime and delinquency. Obviously, programs that would be effective in curbing the movement of children into foster care could prove useful in preventing delinquency. Basic preventive services to strengthen family life would, therefore, serve the juvenile justice system as a whole, including the families of children who must enter foster care.[13]

There are no complete solutions to the child-rearing dilemma. "In any society there will always be come children in need of substitute parenting. But enlightened social policies designed to improve living conditions of the urban poor could effect significant reductions in the number of children entering care."[14]

Until such time as social and/or economic resources are made available to those who must now rely on foster care, foster home placement as an alternative to institutionalization will remain ever present within the juvenile justice system. As such, it is incumbent upon the power structure to make necessary improvements in the foster care system.

ADOPTION

The third and final alternative to institutionalization to be discussed in this chapter is adoption. "**Adoption** is the social and legal process of becoming a parent. After adoption, parents and children have essentially the same reciprocal rights and responsibilities as if they were biologically related."[15] The problems that face natural parents and children are much the same, therefore, as those facing adoptive parents and adopted children. This is true in all aspects of family life, including those that could bring the children and parents in contact with the juvenile justice system. Children from group homes or foster homes may end up being adopted, and adopted children may end up being placed in a group or foster home.

Historical Background

To acquire heirs to their thrones, the ancient Assyrians, Egyptians, Babylonians, Greeks, and Romans instituted the practice of adopting children. Actually, adoption can be traced to the beginning of recorded history. The adoption of Moses by Pharaoh's daughter and Esther by Mordecai are both recorded in the Bible. The ancient Chinese considered ancestor worship so significant that they established the custom of allowing a childless male to claim the first-born son of his younger brother. Over four thousand years ago the Babylonians, in the code of Hammurabi, emphasized the importance of perpetuation of the family in the following section of their code:

> If a man take a child in his name, adopt him as a son, this grownup son may not be demanded back.[16]

Primitive tribes were known to have used the practice of adoption to settle quarrels with one another. One tribe would adopt a child, usually a male, belonging to a member of high status in another tribe.

Modern adoption law has its beginnings in the Roman Empire, where adoption became very popular for both social and religious reasons. The Roman father had total authority over his children and descendants, including the power of life and death. This dominance had a crucial effect on the development of adoption; it meant that the adoptive father had complete control over his adopted children. All previous family ties—biological, legal, religious, and economic—were severed. Once an adoption was formalized, there was no possibility of being reversed.

The adoption of children was practiced in European countries during the Middle Ages. However, it was unknown to the common law of England, from which much of American law is derived. The emphasis on blood lineage was the major reason English common law lacked regulations regarding the adoptive process. Feudal tradition was such that only a biological male child born during wedlock could inherit his parents' rights and property. A child born out of wedlock or one who was adopted was not a legal heir.

That is not to say the English were not concerned with the plight of homeless, parentless children. They were, but until the Adoption of Children Act of 1926, they chose means other than adoption to meet those needs. Apprenticeship or indentured servitude were two methods in common use, and when the English founded colonies overseas, these practices went with them. In the seventeenth century, a vast number of destitute English children became apprenticed as child laborers in Virginia, Massachusetts Bay, and other colonies. "The apprenticing of poor children to the Virginia Company began as early as 1620. . . . A record of 1627 reads: 'There are many ships going to Virginia and with them 1400 to 1500 children which they have gathered up in diverse places.' "[17]

During the eighteenth and nineteenth centuries in America, the apprenticeship system was still the preferred method of taking care of homeless children. No governmental or legal sanction existed for adoption. Blood relatives began taking complete responsibility for their family's orphaned or dependent children. And, soon it became a common practice for them to specify in their wills the relative with whom the orphaned child should live. Mark Twain's Tom Sawyer illustrates this practice. An aunt raised Tom after his own parents died.

Apprenticing of children began to die out during the rapid industrialization of the United States in the mid-1800s. Machines replaced apprentice tradesmen and craftsmen. Child welfare agencies were formed, agencies that attempted to place needy children in institutions or in foster and adoptive homes.

Opponents of adoption often criticized the placement of homeless children in private homes. Responses to such criticism, however, were often overzealous and lent a decidedly paternalistic air to the subject. Unfortunately, the paternalistic attitude continues today. This attitude is well illustrated by the following quote from the founder of the New York Children's Aid Society:

> It is feared that these children would corrupt the morals of the families to which they are sent. . . . We must remind such persons [the critics of adoption] of the wonderful capacity for improvement in children's natures under new circumstances; and we assert boldly, that a poor child taken in thus by the hand of Christian charity, and placed in a new world of love and of religion, is *more likely to be tempted to good,* then to tempt others to evil.[18]

Early adoption laws were considered to be *private laws*—that is, laws made available only to those select individuals to whom knowledge of a specific child to be adopted was made available. Members of the general public as a rule were uninformed of the adoption laws or of how they themselves could adopt a child. It was thought that only a member of the elite society could be entrusted with the duty of converting a poor, ignorant little child into a God-fearing member of decent society. The very notion that others less fortunate than themselves could be good, loving parents to adopted children probably never even entered the minds of the lawmakers of the day or those for whom the laws were made.

Adoption Today: Why and Who

In our society, a childless family has generally been thought to be an incomplete family. Consequently, the inability to conceive or bear children has been one of the primary reasons that people adopt. A new sense of social responsibility and a growing concern and awareness about overpopulation is leading many who are already natural parents to adopt children in need of parents. They are inclined to feel that it is better to adopt a child who is already here than to have a new child and add to the population of the world.

Adoption is open today for children of any age, not only infants. Furthermore, more attention is being paid to children who traditionally were difficult to place, such as older children, siblings, mentally, emotionally, or physically handicapped children, and children of a minority or mixed racial background.

In the United States, adoption statutes vary from state to state. Generally, however, any unmarried adult, single parent, or married couple, where both are adults, may file for the adoption of a child. If either of the prospective parents is a minor, the parties may jointly adopt the other spouse's child. In many states, anyone who is a resident of that state is allowed to adopt. Other states require that the adopting parents be a specific number of years older than the person to be adopted.

Rights and Responsibilities in Adoption

Every child has the right to have his or her own parents, and no child should be unnecessarily deprived of this right. A child has a right to grow up in a reasonably wholesome family setting that should offer affection, security, and the desire to see that the child develops in the best manner possible by providing all the necessities of childhood, including adequate medical care. As for responsibility, the child is obligated to obey the adoptive parents and to perform any other duties that would be expected of a child by his or her natural parents.

> Natural parents of children who may be adoptable have rights, too. In our culture and under our law, the natural parents or, if they are not married to each other, the mother, have the right to custody and control of children born to them. They also have the responsibility for their support, care, and upbringing. This right of the parents must be exercised for the child's benefit, and if not, must yield to the child's interest and welfare. A parent may not be deprived of his rights nor divest himself of his responsibility for the care of a child except through process of law with full protection of the child.[19]

Natural parents also have the right to have counseling in arriving at a decision of whether to give up their child for adoption, and they must have a full understanding of their rights and of the consequences of their decision, especially of the irreversibility of such a decision once the adoption is made final in court.

Problems in Adoption

In an adoption placement, several problems can slow or hinder its success. Some of these are outlined below.

- Adoptions arranged primarily for the convenience of the natural parents, to meet the need of the adoptive parents, or for the profit of the intermediary parties. In all such arrangements the welfare of the child is a secondary objective, if it is an objective at all.
- Delay in placement. . . . Loss of time in making permanent, adequate placement for an infant endangers his opportunity for healthy development and deprives his adoptive parents of their share of an interesting and significant period of his life.
- Multiple home placements. . . . When a child is subjected to multiple placements, whether by plan or default, his emotional development is jeopardized.
- Placement in a home that ultimately proves incapable of providing the wholesome atmosphere considered to be the child's right. A poor emotional environment is destructive to the child's development. Competent casework with the child's prospective parents prior to placement reduces the incidence of the abuse represented by gross misplacement.
- Failure to resolve problems of the natural parents. . . . The lack of able counsel at the proper time contributes to the persistence of unresolved conflicts in the parents that may affect their lives for a long time. Such trauma most often occurs when the decision to relinquish a child is made without a careful exploration of alternatives. Difficulties can be minimized by competent counseling.[20]
- Unnecessary social or economic poverty, including a lack of medical care for the unmarried mother and her child. Well-developed social services for unmarried mothers exist in many metropolitan areas and offer help that prevents impoverishment and degradation through misfortune.
- Failure to provide and interpret significant medical information to prospective adoptive parents may put both child and parents at a disadvantage. Skilled interpretation of the implications of pertinent medical information for the future life and development of the child is of utmost importance.[21]

If it is decided that the adoption of a child is a desirable and acceptable alternative to institutionalization, whether to prevent placement in an institution or as a postinstitutional placement, the problems just noted must be resolved for that placement to work.

Since a large number of children in our juvenile delinquent or dependent populations come from broken homes, homes with both parents missing, abusive or neglecting homes, and no homes at all, the goal of matching a child with a family that can provide a permanent home, love, and proper care can be beneficial in many ways. Fulfilling this goal could lead to a significant reduction in the number of children who are out on the streets, committing delinquent acts or wandering aimlessly through life with no hope for a secure future and who have a good chance of coming in contact with the juvenile justice system.

Follow-up studies of adopted children tend to indicate that 70 to 80 percent of adoptions are successful. A stable and secure home environment has consistently been shown to be a major factor in forming a child's ego, personality, and social competence. It has also been shown that such an environment is best provided by the parent-child relationships and role exchanges within the traditional family setting. Unfortunately, many children in the United States are denied the love and security of a family of their own, and as a result thousands are forced to spend their entire childhoods in foster homes and/or institutions. As cited earlier in this section, statistics show that there are children to be adopted (the supply). And, partly because of lower birth rates and the increased use in the 1980s of abortions, there is also the demand. Demand has even jumped from once highly coveted "white infants" to now include older, problem, and handicapped children who previously were almost always consigned to foster care.

If you have both supply and demand and still have far too many available children remaining unadopted, then there is obviously a problem with the system. Critics of the system tend to pin this blame on two major types of legislation that seem to be fairly consistent nationwide. The first set of laws tends to preserve the rights of the biological parents and thus prevent the adoption of their children. This is the case even though these children are often the victims of past beatings and other abuses that were the cause for their removal from their parents' home in the first place. This also applies in cases where the biological parents have made no attempt to see their children in several years.

The other set of laws centers around financial aid made available to people whom take in foster children. This aid is taken away from these people as soon as or shortly after the foster children are adopted. For some foster parents this can mean losing over $200 per month in expense allowance per child, and this cutoff of aid can keep those foster parents who have the desire to adopt their foster children from doing so. Even if they could survive the removal of the expense allowance, they probably could not afford to keep up the costly medical, dental, and mental health care that these children typically need; the government in the past has paid for such care only for children under foster care. The cutoff of the aid affects the helping professionals as well and creates a vast conflict of interests among them. It is estimated that more than one-half of the cost per year paid by taxpayers to support foster care is allocated for administrative salaries. Thus, by encouraging adoptions, social service workers and agencies would be putting themselves out of business. And while "working one's self out of a job" may be a noble concept, it is seldom seen in practice.

SUMMARY

In this chapter we have discussed three of the more common alternatives to institutionalization of children. Under ideal conditions any of these alternatives may be the right one for a child, depending upon his or her needs and the circumstances of the individual case. Group home living has been utilized traditionally as a placement for children who have already been in contact with the juvenile system and for whom an alternative to home living is generally mandated.

Ideally, the duration of foster care placement should be as short as possible. It is a temporary solution to the problems of a dysfunctional home, whether the dysfunction is parent or child related. Foster care is often used as an interim placement. Good foster homes may enable some youths to remain outside the institutional experience altogether. For others, it may speed their release by offering them someplace to go.

For the child who should be removed from the influence of adults in parental authority roles, the group home is often a better solution than foster care. Foster care, the reader will recall, is intended mainly for the child who needs the guidance and care of his or her parents but who cannot get that care from the present home situation.

Because it can provide a permanent, loving, caring home that offers the child a substitute family, adoption is actually more of a preventive measure than it is an alternative to institutionalization. By providing such a home to children who may otherwise have none—children who could end up drifting from one foster home to another—adoption helps prevent these children from being exposed to environmental conditions, lifestyles, and experiences that often lead to crime or incorrigibility.

The adopted child can develop a permanent sense of belonging and security about where he or she will be from day to day. The foster child, however, is not quite as fortunate. For example, it is not uncommon to remove a child who has problems from a foster home once these problems appear to be settled and signs of progress are evident. The child then finds himself or herself back in his or her own home where the problems often occur all over again. If this experience is repeated often enough, the child will soon learn that to succeed in a foster placement is a disadvantage. Such frustrating experiences for an already troubled young mind can only jeopardize the chances of the child's having a healthy outlook about himself or herself and society.

Whether the choice is to place the child in a group home, foster home, or adoptive home, the procedures in each of these placements must keep in mind and must be based on pursuing the best interests of the child.

TERMS TO REMEMBER

Adoption	Group homes
Child-related problems	Halfway house
Foster care	Parent-related problems

REVIEW QUESTIONS

1. Define the following terms:
   a. Group home
   b. Foster home
   c. Adoption
   d. Alternative placement.
2. Discuss the following questions:
   a. What types of children are served best by each of the alternatives discussed in this chapter? Why?
   b. What characteristics differentiate these placements from one another?
3. What is the historical background of each of the following childcare alternatives?
   a. Group homes
   b. Foster care
   c. Adoption.
4. What factors cause inappropriate referrals to group homes?
5. What characteristics are generally found in a good foster home?
6. What are some of the problems that may be encountered in the adoption of a child?
7. How does each of the three childcare alternatives discussed in this chapter fit into the present-day juvenile justice system?

NOTES

[1]Gwen A. Holden and Robert A. Kapler, "Deinstitutionalizing Status Offenders: A Record of Progress," *Juvenile Justice* (Office of Juvenile Justice and Delinquency Prevention: Fall/Winter 1995), p. 5.

[2]Edward Eldefonso and Alan R. Coffey, *Process and Impact of the Juvenile Justice System* (Encino, CA: Glencoe Press, 1976), p. 172.

[3]Northwest Regional Council, *State of Washington Group Home Study,* "Comprehensive Analysis of Major Program Components: Specific Finding and Recommendations," Vol. I (Zaring Corporation, October 1973), pp. 19–20.

[4]Robert J. Mutchnick and Margaret Fawcett, "Group Home Environments and Victimization of Resident Juveniles," *International Journal of Offender Therapy and Comparative Criminology,* Vol. 35 (1991), pp. 126–142.

[5]Washington Administrative Code 388-64-055.

[6]*State of Washington Group Home Study,* p. 105.

[7]Alfred Kadushin, "Child Welfare: Adoption and Foster Care," in *Encyclopedia of Social Work, Vol. I* (New York: National Association of Social Workers, 1971), p. 104.

[8]Herbert D. Williams, "Foster Homes for Juvenile Delinquents," *Federal Probation* (September 1949), pp. 46–51.

[9]See Burt Galaway and Richard W. Hudson, "Specialist Foster Care for Delinquent Youth," *Federal Probation,* Vol. 59 (1995), pp. 19–27; Mary I Benedict, Susan Zuravin, Mark Somerfield, et. al., "The Reported Health and Functioning of Children Maltreated While in Family Foster Care," *Child Abuse and Neglect,* Vol. 20 (1996), pp. 561–571.

[10]Leslie W. Hunter, "Foster Homes for Teenagers," *Children* (November/December 1964), p. 234.

[11]S. Robinson, "Remedying Our Foster Care System: Recognizing Children's Voices," *Family Law Quarterly,* Vol. 27 (1993), pp. 395–415.

[12]Shirley Jenkins and Elaine Norman, *Filial Deprivation and Foster Care* (New York: Columbia University Press, 1972), p. v.

[13]See also James W. Davis, Peter J. Pecora, Charley Joyce, et. al., "The Design and Implementation of Family Foster Care Services to High Risk Delinquents Transitioning from Correctional Confinement," *Juvenile and Family Court Journal,* Vol. 48 (1997), pp. 17–32; James M. Gaudin and Richard Sutphen, "Foster Care Versus Extended Family Care for Children of Incarcerated Offenders," *Journal of Offender Rehabilitation,* Vol. 19 (1993), pp. 129–147; Jaana Haapasalo, "Young Offender's Experiences of Child Protection Services," *Journal of Youth and Adolescence,* Vol. 29 (2000), pp. 355–371.

[14]Jenkins and Norman, *Filial Deprivation and Foster Care,* p. 258.

[15]Kadushin, "Child Welfare: Adoption and Foster Care," p. 107.

[16]Albert Kocourck and John C. Wigmore, *Source of Ancient and Primitive Law, Evolution of Law, Select Readings on the Origin and Development of Legal Institutions* (Boston: Little, Brown, 1951), p. 425.

[17]Arthur W. Calhoun, *A Social History of the American Family, Vol. I* (New York: Barnes and Noble, 1960), pp. 306–307.

[18]Charles L. Brace, *The Best Method of Disposing of Pauper and Vagrant Children* (1859), pp. 13–14.

[19]Child Welfare League of America, *Child Welfare League of America Standards for Adoption Service* (New York: 2 CWLA, 1968), p. 17.

[20]See E. V. Meeker, "Termination of Parental Rights: Constitutional Rights, State Interests and the Best Interests of the Child," *Journal of Juvenile Law,* Vol. 17 (1996), pp. 82–93.

[21]Committee on Adoption and Dependent Care, "Adoption of Children," pp. 11–12.

chapter *12*

JUVENILE JUSTICE ASSESSMENT AND CLASSIFICATION

> *Classification refers either to the arrangement or division of entities into groups according to some system or principle or to the placement of entities into groups according to rules already determined. . . . usually it means the allocation of persons into initially undefined classes in a way that the persons in a class are in some way similar or close to each other. . . . the aim is to develop groups whose members are similar to one another and who differ from members of other groups.*
>
> — Don Gottfredson

CHAPTER OVERVIEW

Classification is an arrangement according to some systematic division into classes or groups. In classifying individuals, one separates a group of people into smaller groups, each with something in common. Consider, for example, a situation involving four juveniles—Browne, Greene, Anderson, and Johnson—who are to be classified. Assume that Browne and Greene are in one group (or set) and that Anderson and Johnson are in another. This division of four persons into two groups may be called **classification.** You can say something about Browne and Greene that you cannot say about Anderson and Johnson. For example, Browne and Greene are both males, while Anderson and Johnson are both females.

This is the simplest form of classification based on obvious facts. The student should keep in mind that almost anything suitable for scientific observation is also suitable for classification and the possibilities of classification are almost limitless. It should be noted that, although Browne and Greene in the example may be alike for some classification purposes (e.g., sex), they may also be totally unalike in other categories (e.g., age, crime committed, and so forth). Classification depends on both the available data and the definition of likeness or lack of likeness chosen for the given purpose.

When individuals are classified, they are invariably defined or described by their classification. When the group being observed is comprised of juvenile delinquents, the group is a set of delinquents. This set is called the **initial set.** If one wishes to classify these juveniles, then one divides this initial set into a number of **final sets.**

Observations of differences as the basis of classification must be used cautiously. They must be accurate and objective. If they are not, the grouping in the same final set will not be proof of likeness, but rather the result of observed likeness. For instance, it might appear to a homeowner that two boys seen running from her house were juvenile thieves, when in fact one of them was actually chasing the other in an attempt to recover the woman's property. Mentally, the woman has placed both boys in the same class—thieves—based on what she thought she observed. Observation in this case would wrongly classify both of the boys as delinquents, when one is not. While many systems of classification have been used, the purpose of this chapter in to discuss them in general terms, with a few examples.

CLASSIFICATION IN THE PAST

Previous attempts at classifying offenders were mostly devoted to adult groups, with some recognition given to the fact that children, because of their age, constituted a separate group. Common correctional practices separated adult and juvenile offenders, and there was some limited experimentation with reeducation or retraining of youthful offenders. By separating and assigning prison populations by age, sex, and potential for salvation, correctional administrators in the past were initiating a system of classification that has remained, in large part, with us today.

Ever since the practice of putting people into prisons or jails has existed, there have been various means of separating one type of prisoner from another. Thus, the practice of separation (i.e., simply physically isolating one offender group from another) has become identified with classification.

Most early forms of classification were based primarily on superficial characteristics. For example, men were housed separately from women in Spanish prisons as early as 1518. In the early eighteenth century, the Society of St. Vincent de Paul, which cared for orphans and the poor, realized the necessity of segregating children from adults and instituted separate so-called houses of refuge for children. One of the first houses of refuge for delinquent children was started in Germany in 1824, and a similar refuge was established in New York in 1825.

In the Walnut Street jail, which opened in Philadelphia in 1790, a rudimentary classification of prisoners was practiced. Men were separated from women, and children from adults. In 1797, "the management of the Walnut Street jail actually began a classification that may be regarded as the first attempt to separate prisoners by type."[1]

The first major correctional institution specifically for juveniles was the **New York Reformatory at Elmira** (1876). The founders of the New York Reformatory and others patterned after it reasoned that the separation of young offenders from adult criminals would allow the correctional personnel to more successfully facilitate the treatment of their young charges. These juvenile institutions offered educational programs for their young offenders, as opposed to the industrial programs offered in the adult prisons.

The notion that a system of classification of offenders might lead to better, more effective treatment programs spread to other institutions, juvenile and adult alike. Warden Cassidy of the Eastern Penitentiary (1833) remarked on this type of prison administration called classification:

> . . . after hearing so much of herding and grading, congregation and classification, I am the more fully convinced that the individual treatment for the people that have to be cared for in prisons for punishment of crime, is the simplest and most philosophical and is productive of better results.[2]

During the latter part of the nineteenth century, a slow but discernible trend toward treatment programs was evident. These programs affected both classification and administrative systems. However, progress in treatment was hindered by a lack of money to underwrite such programs.[3]

In the twentieth century, classification of prisoners has moved from the obvious differences among prisoners, such as age and sex, to those related to personality characteristics and to various types of crime. In 1917, for example, New Jersey implemented the first formalized prison classification system in the United States, a system that was the result of the Prison Inquiry Commission of the same year. The commission, among other things, brought clinical experts inside the prison walls to prepare and implement classification systems. Classification in New Jersey prisons was identified as follows:

- The difficult class who are hostile to society and require close custody.
- The better class who are good prisoners with reasonably good prognosis but are serving for long terms and require close custody.

- The simple feeble-minded whose condition is not complicated by psychopathic traits.
- The senile and incapacitated class.
- The psychotic and epileptic class who should be transferred to the hospitals for the mentally ill.
- The defective delinquent class whose low intelligence is combined with high emotional instability and may need long periods of custody and training under an indeterminate sentence.[4]

A congressional act of 1930 provided a program for the classification of federal prisoners. The federal system was similar to New Jersey's and was adopted quickly by other Eastern metropolitan states.[5]

Vernon Fox, who examined the influence of the advent of classification schemes as they relate to the treatment needs of prisoners, concluded that

Classification, in its modern sense, is an administrative vehicle by which treatment resources get to an inmate. Conversely, classification, in its older sense, was a way of getting inmates to the program that would benefit them most and/or hurt them least. A modern classification system serves both functions.[6]

There are three simple ways that youth can be channeled through the juvenile justice system:

- They could all be handled in the same manner, receiving the same dispositions and services (Impractical).
- They could be dealt with randomly, depending on the personal beliefs, skills, and interests of the juvenile justice personnel with whom they come into conflict (Often used).
- They could be assessed, classified, and directed to the programs and services that are most appropriate for them and will provide the level of supervision needed to ensure public safety (Most Desirable).[7]

Juvenile assessment and classification are components of the process of sorting youths into various groups for the purpose of custody, supervision, and treatment (See box 12.1).

In some states, juveniles are assigned to an institution on the basis of their age, sex, and risk potential. One of the shortcomings of such a system is that juveniles, regardless of diagnostic evaluations, are made to fit the institution's needs and limited treatment capabilities and not the other way around.

While classification by management needs has had some good effects at juvenile institutions, it has been implemented at the risk of tailoring

---

Box 12.1 Key Terms in Classification and Assessment

Risk assessment The process of using an empirically based, standardized, objective instrument to evaluate a youth's background and current situation and estimate the likelihood that the youth will continue to be involved in delinquent behavior. In community corrections, the results of risk assessment may be used to specify the level of intensity of supervision needed; in residential settings, risk assessment results determine the security level and living unit.

Prediction A determination of behavior that can be expected in the future based on past behavior. Behavior that occur less frequently, such as violence, are more difficult to predict, because there are fewer data upon which to determine a statistical probability that the behavior will be repeated.

Needs assessment A systematic process of identifying what the offender's needs and problems are, and whether they are chronic or crisis needs and then using the information to determine the specific program interventions to be used for the youth.

Case classification The arrangement or grouping of persons according to a system, principles, or rules. Persons within a class are similar to one another but different from members of other groups.

Override The process of overruling or changing classifications when factors are present that outweigh the category indicated by usual risk and needs assessment instruments. Mandatory overrides provide for automatic changes in classification when certain characteristics are present. Discretionary overrides allow staff to make exceptions in classification when they defer circumstances that are not captured by the risk or needs instruments.

Case management The system by which an organization applies resources to meet client goals. Case management decisions affect allocation of resources, levels of service delivery, and budgetary practices.

Source: Crowe, *Jurisdictional Technical Assistance,* p. 1.

---

the treatment needs of juveniles to fit the institutions, whether or not those needs are in concert with the institution's treatment philosophy. Diagnostic practitioners are often frustrated by this course of events. They see their treatment recommendations being accommodated to a managerial classification system and wonder why they should bother with the diagnostic process in the first place.

CLASSIFICATION TODAY

The development of a method to accurately identify juvenile offenders with a high potential of recidivism or who might be dangerous to themselves or others would be of great benefit today. Such a system could be of help at the time of disposition or sentencing in making the right choice in each case, increasing the cost-effectiveness of correctional programs, and looking after the potential safety to the community. Worth mentioning, however, is the fact that sentencing decisions are not based on risk factors alone or even the desire to protect others from the offender. Courts are also expected to maintain civil liberties, act as deterrent forces to others, maintain a sense of fair play, and punish those who transgress the law, and many of these goals are not altogether compatible with protecting the interests of society and reducing recidivism.

In dealing with juvenile correctional populations, classification systems can be useful and beneficial in several ways. One is as an effective managerial tool for institutional administrators. Managerial in this sense means effective control to prevent the juveniles from returning to delinquency while the agency or institution is still responsible for them. But not all classification systems today are aimed at easing the management of the offenders or at assessing the risks of recurrent delinquent or criminal behavior. For example, classification for treatment purposes has been attempted. One must consider, however, that the true, as contrasted to the actual, function of treatment in a juvenile correctional institution is to modify undesirable personality traits of offenders or the aspects of their environment that are in part responsible for their delinquent behavior. Therefore, it becomes paramount for the survival of the treatment model that juvenile offenders be assigned to treatment programs that will accomplish these goals.

In assessing the utility of classification as it relates to our current juvenile justice system, three major judgment calls by members of officialdom must be considered. First is the *classification of the actor*—the juvenile delinquent himself or herself. There are several schemes, some of which will be examined later in this chapter, that attempt to classify juveniles in some meaningful and useful way. However, it is generally conceded that no valid and applicable system of classification of delinquents now exists. There is agreement within the juvenile correctional field that such a system is desirable, and a number of serious and dedicated social scientist researchers have long sought the development of "treatment-relevant typologies" of delinquents. There is even a possibility that they might reach a consensus regarding the basic components of a classification system and types of delinquents at some future point.

The second major judgment call required of the classifiers is the *classification of the act*—the delinquent behavior. Judging the seriousness of the crime is aimed at accurately assessing the harm caused by the juvenile and what punishment is in order.

The third judgment call is perhaps the most important: it answers the question, "For what *purpose?*" Most juvenile classification schemes in use today are referred to as *classification systems for treatment purposes.* However, even a cursory analysis of these schemes and the ways in which they are used reveals that they could be called more accurately *classification systems for management purposes.* Once those making the decisions determine why a juvenile is to be classified, it will make the how to do it become more logical and self-evident. As mentioned earlier in this chapter, there are two major purposes for the development of juvenile offender typologies: classification for management purposes and classification for treatment purposes. With some variations, the methods of accomplishing these purposes interface quite frequently. We now turn to a more in-depth discussion of classification for management purposes, interspersed with the examination of various classification methods applicable to both management and treatment.

Box 12.2 lists goals and applications caseworkers can employ in analyzing and classifying juvenile cases. As the elements listed in Box 12.3 indicate, classification/assessment instruments typically include:

1. Risk of recidivism
2. Detention decisions
3. Placement considerations
4. Custody levels within facilities
5. Clients' service needs.

The instruments are used at different levels of the juvenile justice system to fit their different decision-making requirements.

Classification for Management

By management, we mean the efficient and effective control of the behavior of the offender in order to curtail further law violations while the offender is the responsibility of a correctional agency. In an institutional setting, for example, efficient and effective management involves (1) protecting the weak delinquent from the strong, (2) separating the hardcore offender from the one with nondelinquent attitudes or background, (3) keeping instigators from those who are easily instigated, (4) separating those who are homosexual from those who are nonhomosexual, and so forth.

Classification for management purposes is intended not only to protect or separate one kind of delinquent from another. It is also intended to protect the community from the offender. Delinquents with high escape or

---

Box 12.2 Goals and Applications for Assessment and Classification

GOAL	POSSIBLE APPLICATIONS
1. To determine case plans for individual youth.	• Conduct an individualized assessment of each youth. • Assess the risk of recidivism. • Channel youth to programs and/or levels of supervision that best meet their needs and control risks. • Ensure youth are receiving equitable and consistent treatment compared with others with similar risks and needs. • Match identified needs with available resources. • Ensure that certain types of problems are considered for all cases. • Provide data for future monitoring of cases. • Identify youth for whom further indepth assessments are needed.
2. To allocate resources appropriately and implement effective supervision policies.	• Direct the most intensive interventions to the most serious, violent, and chronic offenders. • Set priorities for case plans. • Organize staff and other agency resources. • Determine workloads.
3. To provide justification and accountability for case decisions.	• Reassess and evaluate effectiveness of case plans and program strategies. • Provide equal, nondiscriminatory treatment.
4. To enhance other parts of the juvenile justice system.	• Develop formalized procedures, such as sentencing guidelines. • Provide recommendations to juvenile court (i.e., through presentence reports).
5. To gather program data and evaluate programs.	• Collect uniform statistical data on results of assessments and provision of services. • Use data to plan, monitor, and evaluate programs.
6. To conduct research on programs and juveniles.	• Test hypotheses about programs and youth.

Source: Crowe, *Jurisdictional Technical Assistance*, pp. 4–5.

"run" potential, of example, must be identified and placed in the more secure facilities. The classification of delinquents in an institutional setting has a direct bearing on other management decisions. Open or closed settings, single or dormitory rooms, types of job assignment, time in the institution, types of punishment, time spent in isolation, custody security levels, and the use of tranquilizing drugs are among the more common examples.

Most management classification systems have taken on a new responsibility today. That responsibility entails the accurate assessment of the offender's potential risk in terms of danger to both self and the com-

Box 12.3   Classification in Juvenile Corrections

JUVENILE CORRECTIONS COMPONENT	REASONS FOR CLASSIFYING YOUTH	PRIMARY RISK MEASURES	PROCESSES
Detention	•Community safety •Youth's personal safety. •Risk of failing to appear for a court hearing. •Population management. •Program evaluation.	•Seriousness of the offense. •Recency and frequency of prior offenses. •Whether youth was under court supervision at time of current offense. •Stability measures (i.e., a history of escapes or runaways).	•Confinement or release.
Community-based Corrections	•Public safety/risk control (risk of recidivism). •Youth's service needs (for rehabilitation). •Management of resources. •Program evaluation.	•Age at first referral or adjudication •Prior out of home placements •Prior arrests •Academic achievement •School behavior and performance •Substance abuse •Family stability •Parental control •Peer relationships •Needs Assessments are also often included	•Risk and Needs Assessment •Supervision level decided (number & type of contacts) •Case plan decided •Services provided also decided
Residential Placement	•Inmate, staff and community protection (e.g., risk of escape, suicide, and/or assaultive behavior) •Offender treatment needs matched with appropriate programs •Resource and population management •Program Evaluation	•Number and seriousness of prior offenses •Seriousness of the present offense •Age at first jurisdiction •Emotional stability, mental health needs •Family problems, parental control •School problems •Intellectual ability •Substance abuse •Risk assessment	•Risk and Needs Assessment •Assignment of youth to appropriate (and least restrictive) security level, facilities and/or living unit •Selection of programs and services needed by youth

Source: Crowe, *Jurisdictional Technical Assistance,* pp. 6–7.

munity, and the subsequent placement of the offender in a facility capable of assuming that risk and protecting the offender from both himself or herself and other inmates, and the community from the offender.

It is generally accepted that classification for managerial purposes takes place in one of three locales or organizational arrangements:

- Within an existing juvenile institution
- Within a reception and/or diagnostic center
- Within the community itself

The superiority of any of these locales over the others is a widely debated topic. All three types may be found within most state systems. However, with the emphasis on community-based corrections, the community classification center, which often entails a much wider range of personnel and resources than previously supposed, is most favored and potentially effective.

Institutional Classification   Classification within the first locale, an existing juvenile institution, is prevalent in many state correctional systems. There are two basic levels of decisions made at this point: placement and custody assessments.

The placement decision involves the determination of restrictiveness that fits the severity of the juvenile's offense balanced by the desire to protect the community. The aim is to decide whether the juvenile should be

Institutional Counseling Session. (Kentucky Department of Juvenile Justice)

placed in an institution or under community supervision. Balancing the risk to the community and the potential for rehabilitation are the aims of this process. Accordingly, the classification instruments at this level combine items that assess the seriousness of current and past offenses plus the youth's potential for recidivism. Thus, they place great emphasis upon **risk assessment.** These instruments are research based and reflect the probability that a youth with certain characteristics are more likely to reoffend. A list of such categories is presented in Box 12.4, and Box 12.5 is an example of a placement assessment instrument.

The Louisiana instrument is geared toward making a decision on whether to institutionalize the offender or place him or her in a community-based program. Once the decision on institutionalization is made, a **custody assessment** comes into play. This is an instrument meant to

---

Box 12.4 Factors Related to Juvenile Recidivism

HISTORY

- Age at first referral/adjudication.
- Number of prior offenses.
- Type and severity of most recent offense.
- Prior assaults.
- Abuse/neglect victimization.
- Gender.
- Prior adjustment to supervision.

STABILITY

- Substance abuse.
- Number of prior out-of-home placements or commitments.
- Family relationships, stability, and parental control.
- School problems (achievement, behavior, attendance).
- Peer relationships.
- Special education placement.
- Mental health stability.
- Running away from home.

Source: Crowe, *Jurisdictional Technical Assistance*, p. 8.

Box 12.5 Louisiana Office of Juvenile Services Secure Custody Screening Document

		Score
1. Severity of Present Adjudicated Offense		___
Level 0 felony	10	
Level 1 felony	7	
Level 2 felony	5	
Level 3 felony	3	
Level 4 felony	1	
All other	0	
2. If Present Adjudication Involves		___
Possession/use of firearm	2	
Multiple felonies	2	
3. Number of Prior Adjudications		___
Two or more felony adjudications	2	
One felony or two+ misdemeanors	2	
None	0	
4. Most Serious Prior Adjudication		___
Level 0 or Level 1 felony	5	
Level 2 felony	3	
Level 3 or below	0	
5. For Offenders With Prior Adjudications		___
Age at first adjudication		
Age 13 or younger	2	
Age 14	1	
Age 15 or older	0	
6. History of Probation/Parole Supervision		___
Offender currently on probation/parole	2	
Offender with probation/parole revocation	2	
7. History of In-Home/Nonsecure Residential Intervention		___
Three or more prior failures	3	
One or two prior failures	1	
None	0	
8. In the Offender Had a Prior Placement in the OJS	2	___
9. Prior Escapes or Runaways		___
From secure more than once	3	
From secure once or nonsecure 2+	2	
From nonsecure once	0	
	Total Score	___

Recommended Action
    0–6 = Consider nonsecure placement
    7–8 = Consider short-term placement
    9+ = Consider secure placement

Source: Crowe, *Jurisdictional Technical Assistance,* p. 150.

gauge the youth's potential for disruption in the institution, affecting both himself or herself or others. Here, common concerns include assaults on staff or peers, escapes, and suicides.[8]

Custody assessment consists of a number of different decisions, including the following:

- Deciding when, where, and how assessment and classification will be completed and who will take responsibility for the process.
- Selecting cutoff scores that result in appropriate work levels for staff.
- Scores should also establish the least restrictive program placement for youth and the protection of the youth, staff, and the public.
- Make the scoring system simple to complete.
- Deciding how frequently cases will be reassessed and reclassified, if appropriate. With youth, reassessments often take place every ninety days. Here, the adjustment of the youth, not just the risk factors, should be recognized.
- If a different level of supervision, security, or programming is necessary, establish a method where staff can override a youth's assessment score.
- Classification should serve as the basis for the agency's recordkeeping system for monitoring, planning and evaluation services.[9]

Box 12.6 is an example of a custody assessment instrument.

Needs assessment scales are used to match youths with appropriate programs and services. Typically, they assess the problems of the youth with the aim of eliminating or mitigating them through intervention. They often include assessment of the following areas:

- Substance abuse
- Family functioning and relationships
- Emotional stability
- School attendance
- Peer relationships
- Health and hygine issues
- Cognitive/intellectual ability or achievement
- Learning disability
- Parent's problems: substance abuse, mental health, criminality, parenting skills).
- Housing/residential stability
- Financial resources
- Child abuse or neglect
- Sexual adjustment
- Vocational/employment concerns

Box 12.6 Illinois Department of Corrections Juvenile Custody Risk Assessment

Score
_____

1. Prior Aggressive Behaviors

No prior aggressive behavior	0
Aggressive toward peers in school, detention, R and C	2
Aggressive behavior toward staff in school, detention, R and C	6
Aggressive behavior toward peers and staff	8

_____

2. Number of Petitioned Property Offenses

Less than 11	0
More than 11	6

_____

3. Parental Control

Parent has some control over youth	0
Parent has no control or supports antisocial activity or no parental involvement with youth	3

_____

4. Needs Level (Based on clinical evaluation)

No need: no clinical done or no need	0
Minimal: needs 2–4 monthly contacts with MH professional	1
Moderate: needs weekly contact	2
Urgent: needs more than one contact weekly	3

Total score _____

Classification

0–2 Minimum	3–9 Medium	10+ Maximum

Escape/Security/Risk	Minimum	Medium	Maximum
1. Nature of the Offense Comments:	_____	_____	_____
2. Run History Comments:	_____	_____	_____
3. Outstanding Charges/Warrants Comments:	_____	_____	_____
4. Time to Serve Comments:	_____	_____	_____

Source: Crowe, *Jurisdictional Technical Assistance,* p. 152.

- Involvement in structured activities
- Independent living skills
- Communication skills.

Unlike a risk assessment scale, the needs assessment scale lists items that can be treated by corrections professionals. They provide a basis for supervision and intervention. Box 12.7 is an example of a needs assessment scale.

Community Assessment Centers As part of the Comprehensive Strategy for Serious, Violent, and Chronic Juvenile Offenders, the Office of Juvenile Justice and Delinquency Prevention developed the Commmunity Assessment Center (CAC). The hope was that local centers would help agencies identify and serve these types of juvenile offenders. It is based on recognition that risk factors led to chronic delinquency and that they must be dealt with comprehensively at the local level.

The CAC model is based upon four key elements:

1. **Single point of entry.** CACs provide a twenty-four-hour centralized point of intake and assessment for juveniles who have come into contact with the juvenile justice system.

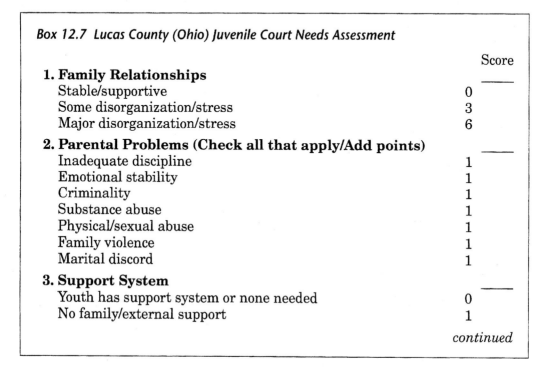

Box 12.7 Lucas County (Ohio) Juvenile Court Needs Assessment

		Score
1. Family Relationships		___
Stable/supportive	0	
Some disorganization/stress	3	
Major disorganization/stress	6	
2. Parental Problems (Check all that apply/Add points)		___
Inadequate discipline	1	
Emotional stability	1	
Criminality	1	
Substance abuse	1	
Physical/sexual abuse	1	
Family violence	1	
Marital discord	1	
3. Support System		___
Youth has support system or none needed	0	
No family/external support	1	

continued

Box 12.7 Lucas County (Ohio) Juvenile Court Needs Assessment (continued)

4. School Attendance _____
No problem   0
Some truancy   1
Major truancy   2

5. School Behavior _____
No problem   0
Some problem   1
Major problem   2

6. Substance Abuse _____
No use   0
Experimenter   1
Former abuse/in recovery   3
Occasional use   4
Abuse   8

7. Emotional Stability _____
No problem   0
Some problem, occasional interference   1
Major problem, serious interference   2

8. Peer Relationships _____
Good support/influence   0
Associations with occasional negative results   1
Associations primarily negative   2

9. Health _____
No problem   0
Some health problems   1
Major handicap/illness   2

10. Sexual Adjustment (Check all that apply, enter highest) _____
No problem   0
Prostitution   1
Sex offense   1
Sexual identity/awareness problems   1
Pregnant/has child   3
Aggressive/assaultive sex offense   4

11. Structured Activities _____
Involvement   0
No involvement   1

Total Score _____

Source: Crowe, *Jurisdictional Technical Assistance,* p. 154.

Institutional vocational program. (Kentucky Department of Juvenile Justice)

2. **Immediate and comprehensive assessment.** Juvenile justice practitioners and community-based youth service providers affiliated with the CAC make initial, broad-based, and, if necessary later, more indepth assessments of juveniles' circumstances and treatment needs.

3. **Management information system (MIS).** Through the use of an MIS, CACs manage and monitor youth, ensuring the provision of appropriate treatment and rehabilitation services and avoiding duplication of services.

4. **Integrated case management.** CAC staff use information from the assessment process and MIS to develop recommendations, facilitate access to services, conduct follow-ups and periodically reassess cases.

In fiscal year 1996, CAC "planning sites" were established in Denver, Colorado, and Lee County, Florida. "Enhancement sites" (JACs) were developed in Jefferson County, Colorado, and Orlando, Florida.[10]

These four demonstration sites set goals for their programs. The following list highlights the purpose of these assessment centers and how they hoped to better coordinate juvenile services.

- Reduce law enforcement time devoted to juveniles.
- Create a central booking and receiving facility specifically for juvenile offenders.
- Collect good, clear information about juveniles' needs.

- Accelerate access to treatment for juveniles.
- Pool resources from different agencies.
- Provide referrals to parents and children.
- Develop a facility to hold dependent juveniles who are awaiting placement.
- Expedite court proceedings by providing better information to defense attorneys and prosecutors.
- Provide early intervention services for troubled services.
- Develop a single point of entry for assessing and referring juveniles.
- Facilitate cooperation and communication among the agencies.
- Expedite processing of juveniles through the system.
- Streamline the current fragmented service delivery system.
- Provide courts with better tools and information.[11]

Clearly, these centers are designed to do more than simple assessment. They are structured to serve as "one-stop shopping" for juvenile services. The centers will streamline services and prevent gaps in the system. They also hope to provide services for all the types of cases that the juvenile justice system receives and prevent the problems that lead to both delinquency and dependency. For example, research on the Hillsborough, Florida, JAC has noted that the center has increased coordination among the various social service agencies that serve youth and improved efficiency in the processing of youths who have been arrested. The center has served youths with substance abuse and mental health problems.[12]

SUMMARY

Classification schemes were devised to serve particular purposes. Some have direct application to the management of offender populations; others have direct application to their treatment; and still others are useful in deducing hypotheses that can be tested. Classification systems are needed for the control of delinquents, for demonstrating treatment effectiveness, and for enumerating possible etiologies.[13]

As noted, a good assessment and classification system should attempt to answer three questions:

1. What caused the juvenile to become a delinquent?
2. What kind of help does the offender need to prevent further law violations? and
3. Where can the juvenile obtain the help needed?

We have examined classification in a general way—its definition, the physical settings of classification systems, and its dual purposes: for management and for treatment. In addition, the Community Assessment Center model offers hope that juvenile problems will be better coordinated and handled more effectively for the benefit of all.

TERMS TO REMEMBER

Classification	Initial set
Community Assessment Center	Needs assessment
Custody assessment	New York Reformatory at Elmira
Final sets	Risk assessment

REVIEW QUESTIONS

1. Define what is meant by classification. Give examples of how you personally have seen a classification system used.
2. What is meant by (a) risk assessment and (b) needs assessment?
3. What are the essential elements of a "good" classification scheme or system?
4. Using the various scales presented in this chapter, classify the following cases using the most appropriate scale for the case.
   a. Kyle is 13 years old and was brought to the detention center with several peers after they were arrested for vandalism. They had defaced signs in a park and deliberately scratched and broken mirrors on vehicles. Kyle has had no previous contact with the juvenile justice system. The school reports that until this year his grades were average, but his work declined in recent months. A urinalysis indicated involved in the incident said they sniff paint on occasion. Kyle's mother reported that she and her husband divorced a year ago, and, as a single mother, she has had increasing difficulties managing Kyle and her other children. Kyle was released to his mother pending further processing of the case to determine the best disposition.
   b. Jennifer is 15 years old and was arrested for prostitution. There is a record at protective services of involvement with the family because a relative sexually abused Jennifer and a sister. During intake at the local detention center, Jennifer's urine screen tested positive for marijuana. She reported that she began smoking cigarettes and using drugs and alcohol around age 11.

   When her family was contacted, they said Jennifer frequently runs away and had not been home for several days. Although Jennifer is enrolled in school, she is often truant and makes very poor grades. Jennifer has never been arrested before, but her parents did arrange for her to spend six months in a private treatment cen-

ter. She claims her best friend is a 21-year-old male who is homeless and has a record of drug-related offensess. Jennifer's parents felt it was not best for her to return home, and she was placed in a nonsecure emergency shelter until her case is arraigned.

c. Brad is 17 years old and was arrested for armed robbery. He was with two other males, ages 19 and 20, when they robbed a gas station attendant at gunpoint. Brad tested positive for amphetamines. His records indicate a lengthy list of juvenile crimes, beginning with status offenses at age 11. His first arrest for a delinquent offense was at age 13. Brad quit school at age 16 but had only completed about half the credits needed for ninth grade work. School reports also indicate frequent disciplinary problems, including fights with other students and one indicent in which he hit a teacher. His mother has had recurring hospitalizations for a mental illness, and Brad was placed on probation, but his record of compliance with court orders was poor.

Source: Crowe, *Jurisdictional Technical Assistance,* p. 1.

NOTES

[1]Harry E. Barnes and Negley K. Teeters, *New Horizons in Criminology* (Englewood Cliffs, NJ: Prentice Hall, 1959), p. 466.

[2]*Annual Report of the Eastern Penitentiary,* 1968, p. 80.

[3]Vernon B. Fox, "Changing Classification Organizational Patterns: 1870–1900," *Correctional Classification and Treatment* (Cincinnati, OH: Anderson Press, 1975), p. 8.

[4]W. J. Ellis, "Classification as the Basis for Rehabilitation of Prisoners," *News Bulletin of the National Society for Penal Information* (February 1931).

[5]Congressional Act of 1930 (C, 339, Section 7, 46 Stat. 390).

[6]Fox, "Changing Classification Organizational Patterns," p. 9.

[7]Ann Crowe, *Jurisdictional Technical Assistance Package for Juvenile Corrections* (Washington, DC: OJJDP National Training and Technical Assistance Center, December 2000), p. 3; http://www.ncjrs.org/html/ojjdp/juris_tap_report/ch5.html.

[8]Ibid., pp. 10–11.

[9]Ibid., p. 13.

[10]Debra Oldenettel and Madeline Wordes, *The Community Assessment Center Concept* (Washington, DC: Office of Juvenile Justice and Delinquency Prevention, 2000), pp. 1–2.

[11]Ibid., p. 4.

[12]Richard Dembo, G. Turner, J. Schmeidler, C. C. Sue, P. Borden, and D. Manning, "Development and Evaluation of a Classification of High Risk Youths Entering a Juvenile Assessment Center," *Substance Abuse and Misuse,* Vol. 31 (1996), pp. 303–322; Richard Dembo, J. Schmeidler, B. Nini-Gough, and D. Manning, "Sociodemographic, Delinquency-Abuse History, and Psychosocial Functioning Differences Among Juvenile Offenders of Various Ages," *Journal of Child and Adolescent Substance Abuse,* Vol. 8 (1998), pp. 63–78; James E. Rivers, Richard Dembo, and Robert S. Anwyl, "The Hillsborough County, Florida Juvenile Assessment Center: A Prototype," *The Prison Journal,* Vol. 78 (1998), pp. 439–450.

[13]See Richard D. Hoge and Donald A. Andrews, *Assessing the Youthful Offender: Issues and Techniques* (New York: Plenum Press, 1996).

PART THREE

JUVENILE JUSTICE IN THE TWENTY-FIRST CENTURY

chapter *13*

DEALING WITH DELINQUENCY: THEORIES, ISSUES, AND PRACTICE

Nothing fails like success.

— Simon Dinitz

CHAPTER OVERVIEW

Theories are attempts to explain events. They have two main functions: (1) they organize existing knowledge about a subject into a coherent framework, and (2) they help provide direction for future research on the topic. Kaplan reminds us that theories often attempt to make sense of a disturbing situation (such as delinquency).[1] Thus, they provide a vehicle to interpret, criticize, and unify existing beliefs. Theories make the comparison of different approaches possible. They allow us to consider the question of causation by specifying the relationships between different social, physical or even economic variables and a phenomenon like crime.

Like all theories, criminological theories have certain attributes. For one thing, they exist at different levels of **generality.** Some theories, called **grand theories,** strive to explain all types of criminal behavior. For example, Charles Tittle contends that a number of different crimes (e.g., theft, burglary, rape, homicide, voyeurism) could be considered as "instances of the same act—intrusion into private domains."[2] Other theories, more limited in their approach and scope, try to explain a specific area or type of crime (e.g., serial murder, white collar crime). They are based on the belief that there is too much variation in human behavior, criminal motives, cultures, economic conditions, and historical contexts to expect a general theory to give an adequate explanation for crime. Merton calls these **middle-range theories** (See box 13.1).[3]

Criminological theories also differ in focus. Some theories highlight the actor (e.g., the criminal or the victim). Others consider the social background (e.g., education) and relationships (e.g., family structure) among all individuals in society as potential crime causing agents.[4]

The primary aim of criminology is to determine the causes of crime. Cressey (1979: 457) defines **criminology** as

> the body of knowledge concerning crime as a social phenomenon. It is the product of systematic studies of the processes of making laws, breaking laws, and reacting to the breaking of laws. The objective of criminology is persistent progress in the development of valid information regarding this set of interactions.[5]

Similarly, Lynch and Groves (1996:89) list several desirable attributes of a "culturally and historically specific" criminological theory:[6]

1. Address multiple levels of causation
2. Demonstrate a connection between structural and subjective factors
3. Include a discussion of opportunity structure as an important (but not the only) dimension for understanding crime
4. Discuss the effects of enforcement policy, the context and construction of law as these elements bear upon the social construction of crime
5. Built theory from the bottom up (from the concrete), keeping in mind the cultural and historical limits of explanation
6. Construct explanations that are grounded in (but not a slave to) empirical research findings.

Box 13.1 Attributes of Theory

Generality   Classification of theories by their scope or level of generality.

Grand theories   Sweeping theories that attempt to explain all types of delinquency.

Middle-range theories   Theories that try to explain a certain type of crime (e.g., serial murder, white-collar crime).

In short, **criminological theory** attempts to explain why crime exists, how it takes place, and what can be done about it.

Theories of delinquency attempt to explain the causes of juvenile criminal behavior. The juvenile laws do not search for the underlying reasons for an individual's actions but simply determine whether in fact that act took place and that individual did it. To understand juvenile delinquents better, however, we must continue to examine the relationship between the actors and the kinds of factors and variables that made them commit the deviant act in the first place. Theories are important for students to review in order to have a larger tool kit with which to work in the field of juvenile justice.

What is the cause of the condition called *delinquency?* Historically, the traditional literature on crime and delinquency has approached this question by examining behavior patterns, sociological influence, and economic factors that might lead a child to be labeled as delinquent.

In part, delinquency is caused by the social judgment process that defines it in the first place. This tenet is exacerbated when one considers that the outcome of most, if not all, delinquency research is predetermined by those whose values have been adopted for the purposes of distinguishing the comparable criterion groups of delinquents and nondelinquents.

The absence of a discriminating scheme for the prediction of who is or is not a delinquent can also lead to a tainting of the targeted delinquents in the treatment population. The use of inconsistent discriminators could result in *false positives* (juveniles labeled as probable delinquents who are not) and *false negatives* (juveniles labeled as nondelinquent who are actually serious delinquents). If juveniles in the false-positive category are faced with intervention strategies (such as *radical nonintervention,* wherein nothing is done to "fix" them), they will never become delinquents anyway and the effort will tell researchers nothing. On the other hand, juveniles in the false-negative category, where serious intervention might be called for, will continue to be delinquent and will therefore also brand the effort a failure.

Students will find many studies that declare that there are observable and predictable differences between delinquents and nondelinquents. These books and articles contain theories from many disciplines, ranging from those based on the medical model to those embracing the "process model" and everything in between. The most valid observable difference between delinquents and nondelinquents is that one gets *caught and labeled,* and the other does not. Apart from this, as mentioned earlier, we do not believe that there is any cut-and-dried difference between the two groups. If such a discernible difference did exist, it would make prediction much easier, it would help to eliminate false positives from target groups, and it would assist the juvenile justice system in achieving one of its most sought-after goals: the prevention of delinquency in the first place.[7]

This chapter will examine some of the better-known definitions of delinquency and will describe some of the theoretical bases of causality.

We will stress the linkage between theory, a serious issue, and the resulting practices that have been developed in the juvenile justice system.

DEFINING DELINQUENCY

Before attempting to discuss conditions or circumstances that appear to cause delinquency, it is important for us to define juvenile delinquency, a term that tends to conjure up a vision of a leather-jacketed thug. However, even the clearly identified delinquent is difficult to categorize. For example, suppose that there are two boys who have nothing in common but the fact that both have violated the law. One was caught engaging in an armed robbery and the other stealing soft drinks from a grocery store. Although they may both fit into the same legal pigeonhole, they do not necessarily share the same or even a common psychological category. In this case, the label *delinquent* cannot be used without qualification, as though it denoted a common set of facts or a specific kind of juvenile. We cannot simply assume that, because a youth was in court, he was *ipso facto* a member of some subspecies of citizenry.

To simplify the process of definition, juvenile delinquency can be divided into two separate areas—legal and social.

Legal Definition

Juveniles in the United States must obey and are subject to the same ordinances and criminal statutes that govern adults. In addition, they are governed by a second set of rules that are applicable because they are specific to juveniles.

Most states continue to include status offenders in the category of delinquents. This is the case despite the major provisions of the Juvenile Justice Act amended in 1977 that called for the deinstitutionalization of status offenders and their eventual removal from the purview of the juvenile court. In fact, even today, according to some guesses, close to one-half of all youths brought before our juvenile courts are involved in acts that, *if committed by an adult,* would not be a crime (See box 13.2).

Box 13.2 Status Offender

A *status offender* is generally accepted as a juvenile who has come into contact with the juvenile authorities based upon conduct that is an offense only when committed by a juvenile. A status offense is conduct that would not be defined as a criminal act when committed by an adult.

Teen boys shoplifting. (Jim Smith)

For example, Substitute House Bill No. 371 of Washington state lists the following conditions that characterize a child as dependent and therefore subject to the jurisdiction of the juvenile courts. A dependent child is one

1. Who has been abandoned; that is, left by his or her parents, guardian, or other custodian without parental care and support.
2. Who is abused or neglected or Who has no parent, guardian, or custodian.
3. Who is in conflict with his or her parent, guardian, or custodian.
4. Who refuses to remain in any nonsecure residential placement ordered by a court.
5. Whose conduct evidences a substantial likelihood of degenerating into serious behavior if not corrected.
6. Who is in need of custodial treatment in a diagnostic and treatment facility.[8]

State codes vary on the legal definition of **juvenile delinquency.** Keeping this in mind, the following definition of delinquency is based upon material developed in Title 11, U.S. Code and therefore facilitates general application at the federal and state level:

Juvenile delinquency is a violation of a law of the United States or its several states committed by a person who is not yet 18, which would

have been a crime if committed by an adult and which is liable to disposition through the juvenile justice system.

A juvenile, also based primarily on the U.S. Code (Title 11), is defined as

> A person who is not yet 18; or, for the purposes of proceedings and
> disposition of such a person for an act of juvenile delinquency or a
> crime committed prior to his/her eighteenth birthday, a person who is
> not yet 21.

The 18-year-old limit is applied in approximately two-thirds of the jurisdictions in the United States. Some states include youths up to age 21 in
their delinquency statutes, and others allow children as young as 12 to be
bound over to adult courts and tried as adults.

Obviously there are many legal definitions of delinquency. Depending
on the source, whether federal statutes, state laws, social commentators,
or textbooks, the definition will vary. A legal definition of delinquency,
even once agreed upon, provides only a partial insight into the delinquency problem. A knowledge of the sociological factors surrounding delinquency becomes equally important in the quest for a solution to the
definition problem. In fact, the term juvenile delinquency was developed
in conjunction with the rise of the juvenile court in Chicago, Illinois, in
1899.[9] The legal definition of delinquency is inadequate for the understanding of the juvenile's position in society, for the public's approval or
disapproval of that child, or for understanding the factors contributing to
the juvenile's becoming labeled as a delinquent. We now turn, therefore, to
a discussion involving the social impact of delinquency.

Social Definition

The social definition of delinquency primarily involves the views of the
family, friends, and community regarding a child's behavior. A child may,
for example, be part of a subculture that could have as norms many behaviors that would be labeled delinquent if exhibited outside that subculture. Thus, a ghetto black child who is bused to a predominantly all-white
suburban school may elicit disapproval from his new temporary community and may be forced to associate with groups and persons who are less
conducive to the transmitting of socially accepted norms.

The social definition of delinquency, therefore, is a subjective reflection of how the youth's parents, friends, neighbors, and community view
him or her as a person. It is also a reflection of how well "they" feel that he
or she is fitting into a socially sanctioned behavioral mold in keeping with
community standards of accepted behavior. This reflection is often quite
different from the way in which the members of officialdom (i.e., the
courts, police, and parole and/or probation officers) might see the youth.

THE CLASSICAL SCHOOL OF CRIMINOLOGY

The "classical" school of criminology was founded in the 1700s by **Cesare Beccaria.** (See Box 13.2). Its emphasis was on the crime committed by the person. Its basic tenet was that humans are rational beings who seek the good things in life (that is, they are pleasure oriented) and avoid the bad (or pain oriented). Assuming, therefore, that people prefer pleasure to pain, Beccaria contended that no one would commit a criminal act unless it could be anticipated that the pleasurable consequences would outweigh the painful ones. The purpose of society was to secure the happiness of the majority. Early laws were quite simple, with punishments administered publicly and aimed primarily at deterrence (see Boxes 13.4 and 13.5 for discussion of deterrence levels and theory).

Beccaria and his contemporaries embraced the doctrine of free will and its correlative that each person is morally responsible for his or her own acts. In keeping with this doctrine, Beccaria's principles about punishment are summarized as follows:

Beccaria put the problem of punishments on a new plane, stating that the purpose of penalties is not retribution, but prevention; justice requires a right proportion between crimes and punishments, but the purpose of penalties is to prevent a criminal from doing more harm and to deter others from doing similar damage. . . . Beccaria wanted a society of kind and civilized people and he believed that the abolition of cruel punishments, including the death penalty, would contribute to the formation of such a society.[10]

Beccaria believed that the function of law was to promote justice. In *On Crimes and Punishments* (1764), he formulated the following principles that were a departure from the criminal law:[11]

Box 13.3 Cesare Bonesana, Marchese di Beccaria (1738–1794)

Beccaria wrote *An Essay on Crimes and Punishment*—published anonymously in 1764—the most exciting essay on law of the eighteenth century. It proposed a reorientation of criminal law toward humanistic goals. Beccaria suggested that judges should not interpret the law but, rather, that the law should be made more specific, as he believed that the real measure of crime was its harm to society. He is regarded as the founder of the classical school of criminology.

Box 13.4 Levels of Deterrence

Deterrence is based upon the idea that persons are free to choose a course of action in a rational manner. They will act in ways that maximize pleasure and minimize pain. It can take place on two levels of deterrence that have different effects:

- **Specific deterrence** focuses on the individual offender. It seeks to teach criminals a lesson so that they will learn from the experience and "go straight" in the future. **Incapacitation** is another feature of specific deterrence. In terms of the death penalty, the executed inmate is prevented from ever committing murder again.

- **General deterrence** is concerned with society as a whole. Punishment is a message aimed at everyone. The punishment of the offender demonstrates what will happen to them if they violate the law. Here, the death penalty is a negative example. Execution of an offender is meant to be a lesson to all.

Box 13.5 Elements of Deterrence Theory

The elements of deterrence theory outlines several aspects of punishment that are predicted to affect the future behavior of the offender or potential offender.

- The primary assumption behind deterrence theory is that individuals have free will and are rational.
- In order for punishments to have the maximum deterrent effect, they should guarantee that the anticipated benefits from a criminal act will not be enjoyed.
- Certainty of punishment (especially of apprehension) is more important that severity of punishment. The level of punishment should reflect the severity of the crime.
- Punishments should be uniform: All persons, regardless of their position, status, or power, convicted of the same crime should receive the same punishment.
- All penalties should be known in order to prevent the rational individual from committing crime.

1. Prevention of crime is more important than punishment for the crime committed. Punishment is desirable only as it helps to prevent crime and does not conflict with the ends of justice.

2. Desirable criminal procedure calls for the open publication of all laws, speedy trials, human treatment of the accused, and the abolition of secret accusations and torture. Moreover, the accused must have every right and facility to bring forward evidence.

3. The purpose of punishment is to deter persons from the commission of crime, not to give society an opportunity for revenge. In addition, punishment must be certain and swift, with penalties determined strictly according to the social damage wrought by the crime. Therefore, celerity—the time span between the crime and punishment—is a key element in deterrence.[12]

Beccaria redefined criminality, prescribed fair treatment for individuals, and temporarily removed revenge and retribution as rationales for punishment. Beccaria was a reformer who was interested in limiting the official abuse of power—both political and judicial. He believed that the primary concern of the judge was the determination of guilt or innocence. He also denounced the use of torture and the death penalty.[13]

Despite Beccaria's liberal views, deterrence has become the centerstone of conservative policy in the fight against crime and delinquency. Foremost among the potential penalties has been the death penalty. It has been called for use against juveniles who commit murder.

Issue: Juvenile Homicides

As we have discussed in this text, a "get tough" movement to fundamentally refocus of the sanctioning capacities of the juvenile justice system beyond child saving and rehabilitation to stress deterrence and incapacitation has been adopted. Accordingly, policy changes have focused upon trying serious juvenile offenders as adults, even sentencing juveniles convicted of murder to death. For example, Kentucky legislation was enacted in 1994 to send juveniles who use a gun to commit felonies to an adult institution.

But are things getting worse? Let's check the data on juvenile homicides. Statistics reveal that the 1999 juvenile murder arrest rate was the lowest in twenty years. Between 1980 and 1999:

1. Juvenile murder victims were predominantly male (83 percent) and white (51 percent).

2. Most of the juvenile murders were male (93 percent) and more than half (56 percent) were black.

3. Male juvenile offenders were most likely to kill someone they know (56 percent), but 37 percent killed a stranger.

4. Female juvenile offenders were most likely to kill a family member (39 percent)—21 percent of them killed young children.

5. 82 percent of the juvenile offenders murdered persons of their own race. This was especially true of female offenders.

6. Older juvenile offenders were more likely to commit murder with adults.[14]

7. In 1999, about 1,800 juveniles (a rate of about 3.0 per 100,000) were victims of homicide in the U.S. This rate is higher than that of any other developed country.

8. Homicides of juveniles in the U.S. are unevenly distributed, both geographically and demographically. Rates are substantially higher for African American juveniles in certain jurisdictions. Yet, 85 percent of all U.S. counties had no homicides of juveniles in 1997.[15]

Studies of juvenile murderers reveal that most juvenile homicides are spontaneous, unpremeditated acts. Emotional stress, lack of experience, irresponsibility, volatility, brain damage, absence of calculation and a lack of consideration for the consequences of their actions. Typically, the murders stemmed from another offense and then the juvenile panicked and killed the victim, often in a most brutal and heinous manner.[16]

In sum, these studies question the effectiveness of deterrence to prevent juvenile homicide. Their roots do not run to the factors that deterrence can reach. Premeditation is markedly absent. In its place are factors that can only be affected by attention to treatment and social problems.

Practice: The Death Penalty for Juveniles

According to the NAACP Legal Defense and Education Fund (2002), a total of 3,718 inmates were under a sentence of death in the United States as of July 1, 2002. Of this total, eighty-three inmates (all male, 2.23 percent of the total) were juveniles when they committed their offenses.

Since the reinstitution of capital punishment in the United States in 1976, 784 persons have been executed for murder. Of this total, twenty inmates (2.6 percent) were juveniles at the time of the offense.[17] A list of these inmates is presented in Table 13.1.

In 1642, the first juvenile execution was conducted—Thomas Graunger, Plymouth Colony, Massachusetts. Throughout American history, Hale presents five periods of time during which juveniles were susceptible to a sentence of death for their crimes. Period One (1642 to 1762) contains the first execution of a juvenile in the United States. Social control was a paramount concern. Juveniles were treated no differently than adults during this period. In Period Two (1762 to 1842), Beccaria's call to abolish capital punishment was taken up by Benjamin Rush and William

TABLE **13.1**   U.S. Inmates Executed for Homicides Committed as Juveniles, 1985–July 1, 2002

YEAR	STATE	NAME
1985	Texas	Charles Rumbaugh
1986	South Carolina	James Terry Roach
1986	Texas	Jay Pinkerton
1990	Louisiana	Dalton Prejean
1992	Texas	Johnny Garrett
1993	Texas	Curtis Paul Harris
1993	Missouri	Frederick Lashley
1993	Missouri	Ruben Cantu
1993	Georgia	Christopher Burger
1998	Texas	Joseph Cannon
1998	Texas	Robert A. Carter
1998	Virginia	Dwayne Allen Wright
1999	Oklahoma	Sean Sellers
2000	Virginia	Douglas C. Thomas
2000	Virginia	Steve Edward Roach
2000	Texas	Glen McGinnis
2000	Texas	Gary Graham
2001	Texas	Gerald Mitchell
2001	Georgia	Jose High
2002	Texas	Napoleon Beazley

Bradford. Period Three (1842 to 1922) marked a transition in attitudes toward juveniles. Child labor laws and the juvenile court were established on the philosophy of *parens patriae*. Period Four (1922 to 1962) introduced the modern view of the juvenile. Juveniles were not executed. Period Five (1962 to the present) marks a return to the death penalty for juveniles.[18]

Since the Graunger execution, approximately 361 persons have been executed for juvenile crimes (1.8 percent of roughly 20,000 confirmed American executions since 1608). Eighteen of these executions have been imposed since the reinstatement of the death penalty in 1976.[19] Sixteen states and the federal government have an age minimum of 18 for capital punishment.[20]

The United States Supreme Court has made several key rulings about the constitutionality of the death penalty for juveniles. Three major decisions have been issued to clarify the Court's position on this matter. In *Eddings v. Oklahoma* (1982), the juvenile defendant was charged with the murder of a state police officer. The Court deferred on the key issue of whether capital punishment for juveniles violated the Eighth Amendment prohibition against cruel and unusual punishment. Instead, it focused on age as a mitigating circumstance in a capital trial and noted that the trial court judge had failed to consider it.[21]

In a second decision on this matter (***Thompson v. Oklahoma,*** 1988), the Court again avoided the Eighth Amendment question and ruled that the Oklahoma statute was unconstitutional because it failed to specify a minimum age for which the commission of a capital crime by juvenile can lead to execution. Defense counsel made some standard arguments on behalf of their juvenile client—that juveniles lack the emotional and mental capacity of adults, that they have rehabilitative potential, and that they can be sentenced to death at an age when they cannot vote, drink, or drive.[22]

The Court finally addressed the Eighth Amendment question in a landmark decision, ***Stanford v. Kentucky*** (1989). Justice Scalia issued the majority opinion that juvenile executions do not constitute cruel and unusual punishment. The majority dismissed the arguments about the diminished capacity of juveniles and noted that no national consensus exists against the death penalty for juveniles. The decision allowed states to determine whether or not to impose the death penalty upon juveniles and at what age.[23] Thus, the Court held that the practice of executing juveniles (aged 16 or 17 at the time of the offense) did not violate the "evolving standards of decency" (ESD) of American society. Their determination was based on legislative authorization of juvenile executions.[24] In effect, the Court drew a line that bans the execution of offenders under the age of 16 but permits execution for crimes committed at the age of 16 or above.

However, several studies indicate that the public sentiment in support of the death penalty for juveniles is waivering. Opinion surveys have revealed that support for capital punishment waivers when the accused is a juvenile, even though they typically commit heinous offenses.[25] The desire to execute juveniles does not appear to be widespread and strong.

It also appears that juvenile cases have not been thoroughly decided in court. A review of ninety-one juvenile death penalty cases (from 1973 to 1991) documented the mitigating circumstances for each offender. They fell into the following categories: (1) "troubled" family history and social background; (2) psychological disturbance; (3) mental retardation; (4) indigence; and (5) substance abuse.[26] These factors were not always noted in the original trial or always fully considered on appeal.

There are more juvenile offenders on death row in the U.S. than in any other country known to Amnesty International. The imposition of death sentences on juvenile offenders is in clear contravention of international human rights standards contained in numerous international instruments. Since 1990, juvenile offenders are known to have been executed in only six countries: Iran, Pakistan, Yemen, Nigeria, Saudi Arabia, and the United States. The death penalty for juvenile offenders has become a uniquely American practice, in that it appears to have been abandoned by nations everywhere else in large part due to the express provisions of the United Nations Convention on the Rights of the Child and of several other international treaties and agreements.[27]

Furthermore, it appears that the U.S. Supreme Court is ready to revisit the Eighth Amendment issue since they have already declared the execution of mentally retarded offenders unconstitutional. It is possible that the death penalty for juveniles will eventually be declared unconstitutional as well. The death penalty for juveniles in the United States may be nearing at an end.

SOCIAL THEORIES OF DELINQUENCY

The social theories of juvenile delinquency are grounded in present-day sociological thought and focus strictly on the *collective* behavior of the individual rather than the individual behavior. Discussion of social theories has caused sociologists to address themselves primarily to two basic questions: (1) How does the juvenile in society acquire criminality? and (2) How does society acquire or produce crime?

The process model, of which social theory is considered to be a part, is meaningful to a present-day discussion of causality. The process model is in direct conflict with the medical model, which contends that criminal behavior is the fault of the individual, caused by some flaw in the individual's psychological, biological, or physiological makeup. The process model holds that criminal behavior is caused by factors external to the individual: economic class, environmental surroundings, delinquent subcultures, lower-class structure, and so forth. The process model, therefore, contends that, as the result of various cultural, economic, sociological, racial and ethnic conditions or influences, criminal behavior is produced, and that changes in these conditions have the potential to influence the incidence of criminal or delinquent behavior.

Social theories state that a child's individuality cannot be separated from his or her interactions in a group. Of special importance in group interaction is motivation. However, social theory concerns itself with those things that determine motivation in social interactions that are external to the juvenile. Internal or psychological motivation are not given as much emphasis. In *Explaining Crime,* Gwynn Nettler emphasizes this point:

> A strictly sociological explanation is concerned with how the structure of a society or its *institutional practices* or its *persisting cultural themes* affect the conduct of its members. Individual differences are denied or ignored, and the explanation of collective behavior is sought in the patterning of social arrangements that is considered to

be both "outside" the actor and "prior" to him. That is, the social patterns of power or of institutions which are held to be determinative of human action are also seen as having been in existence before any particular actor came on the scene. They are "external" to him in the sense that they will persist with or without him. In lay language, *sociological explanations of crime place the blame on something social that is prior to, external, and compelling of a particular person.*[28]

Here, we will examine two explanations of delinquency: (1) subcultural and (2) social disorganization. Both theories relate to and offer explanations for gang behavior.

SUBCULTURAL THEORIES

Richard Cloward and Lloyd Ohlin expanded and applied the theory that delinquent behavior is more likely to be experienced among lower-class juveniles to explain urban gang behavior. Their hypothesis is stated as follows:

> The disparity between what lower-class youth are led to want and what is actually available to them is the source of a major problem of adjustment. Adolescents who form delinquent subcultures, we suggest, have internalized an emphasis upon conventional goals. Faced with limitations on legitimate avenues of access to these goals, and unable to revise their aspirations downward, they experience intense frustrations; the exploration of nonconformist alternatives may be the result.[29]

This explanation characterizes delinquency as being both adaptive and reactive. It is adaptive insofar as it is instrumental in the attainment of goals that most youths generally share, and reactive because it is partly prompted by the resentment of juveniles at being deprived of things that they either believe they should have or have been advised or told they should have.

"Subculture is a term devised by social scientists to refer conveniently to variations within a society on its cultural themes, patterns, artifacts, and traditional ideas, as these are incorporated and expressed within various groups."[30] It is the nature of a community's integration of legitimate and illegitimate means that will normally determine the nature of the subcultural accommodations to goal-achieving criteria. Cloward and Ohlin have identified three types of delinquent subculture: (1) the criminal subculture, (2) the conflict subculture, and (3) the retreatist subculture.

The *criminal subculture,* and criminal gangs, will develop where there is cross-age integration of offenders plus close relations between the carriers of criminal and conventional values. For example, a young boy who grows up in a family where the father and brothers and their associates are all involved in criminal activities may himself be either intrigued or coerced into similar displays of delinquent or criminal behavior. The criminal subculture is comprised of juveniles who are thought to have become delinquent as a result of associations or contacts with persons who are outside the law. Many parole and probation authorities state, as a condition of parole or probation, that the juvenile shall not associate with known felons or persons whose influence may have a negative potential.

Albert Cohen, in *Delinquent Boys*,[31] indicates that the basis of delinquency lies in the variables of social class structure. He theorizes that the delinquent from a lower-class environment lacks self-respect, and in his frustration with his class or social position, he strikes out against middle-class values (called a **reaction formation**) and adopts opposite values. As a result, a delinquent subculture is formed that emerges as a collective attempt to contend with and to solve class-based frustrations and angers.

Within this subculture, the norms of the dominant culture are ridiculed while the—the **norms of the delinquent subculture**—subcultural norms are valued. Thus, for example, physical aggression, toughness, and hedonism are stressed. Members of these delinquent groups do not consider the future consequences of their behavior, but instead focus on immediate gratification of their desires. Gang members are openly hostile to the agents of conformity. Moreover, they oppose other delinquent groups and use force to ensure loyalty and conformity to their own group. In short, it is a culture all its own and of its own making. Box 13.6 discusses key characteristics of such delinquent subcultures.

Walter B. Miller,[32] a principal advocate of the *conflict subculture* explanation of delinquency, rejects Cohen's contention that delinquency is produced by lower-class conflict with or reaction formation to a larger, dominant society. Instead, he contends that the violation of middle-class

---

Box 13.6 Norms of the Delinquent Subculture

- **Nonutilitarianism:** Delinquents are not always rationally motivated and thus may break the law "for the hell of it."
- **Malice:** Delinquents often enjoy tormenting their victims and delight in violating the norms of society.
- **Negativism:** The norms of delinquents tend to be the mirror image or exact opposite of those of society.
- **Short-run hedonism:** The actions of delinquents reveal their emphasis on immediate pleasure. They live for the moment and do not calculate the consequences of their actions.

norms "is a 'by-product of action' primarily oriented to the lower-class culture, and the standards of lower-class culture cannot be seen as merely a reverse function of middle-class culture—as middle-class standards turned upside down'; lower-class culture is a distinctive tradition many centuries old with an integrity of its own."

Miller uses the concept of focal concerns in explaining his interpretation of the conflict subculture approach. *Focal concerns* are areas or issues that command widespread and persistent attention and a high degree of emotional involvement and that Miller feels tend to characterize a lower-class culture—thus named the **six focal concerns of lower-class delinquents.** Some of these focal concerns are trouble, toughness, smartness, excitement, fate, and autonomy. Miller prefers to speak of these focal concerns within a conflict subculture rather than of values, because focal concerns can be observed and examined more readily in direct field investigation. These attributes are listed in Box 13.7.

Lower-class delinquency resulting from a conflict subculture cannot be classified as deviant or aberrant in Miller's view. Rather, it is part of the lower-class culture and, within the group, is highly functional and necessary in preparing youngsters for an adult life that will probably be lived within the confines of that subculture. Therefore, delinquent behavior among lower-class youths can be considered as normal behavior within that class. What causes a lower-class youth's behavior to be considered delinquent is that the youth's focal concerns come in conflict with those roles and norms that constitute the traditional and institutional values of the middle class.

The final type of delinquent subculture to be discussed is the *retreatist subculture.* "A retreatist subculture, and retreatist gangs, will develop among boys locked out of the above two avenues [criminal and

---

Box 13.7 Six Focal Concerns of the Lower-Class Delinquents

- **Trouble:** The underlying goal; the street is where the action is.
- **Toughness:** The need to demonstrate that one can stand up to adversity and "take" whatever the street brings (e.g., run-ins with other gangs and the police).
- **Smartness:** The high value placed on "street smarts"; one must know how to handle oneself on the street.
- **Excitement:** The view of what "life" is all about; the thrill of engaging in conflict and ripping people off.
- **Fate:** The belief that what happens in life is beyond one's control; whatever happens is "meant to be."
- **Autonomy:** The intolerance of challenges to one's personal sphere; the need to stand up to anything or anyone.

conflict subcultures] because of the lack of means for integration and because of 'internalized prohibitions' or 'socially structured barriers' to the use of violence. This 'double failure' leaves only retreat, most specifically through drugs and alcohol."

A retreatist subculture can occur, therefore, almost by default. Youths barred from participation in the criminal or conflict subcultural gangs often find themselves banding together out of commonality, and, thus, as their numbers increase, a gang comes into being. Juveniles constituting a retreatist gang are often typified as being "odd-balls," misfits, or loners in relationship with the larger delinquent subculture around them. Because of rejection by their peers, parents, or others, they may seek out or simply happen to find themselves hanging around with other youth "outsiders." They replace violent or criminal behavior with retreatist behavior, such as drinking, smoking pot, or other activities that, while they may cause trouble with the law, are generally either nonviolent or low-key.

In general, these subcultural theories attempt to explain why lower-class boys become delinquent. The gang offers them an opportunity to "be somebody" and achieve the status that has been denied them by society. One flaw of these theories, however, is that they ignore individual deviance. They assume that subcultural values are strong enough to determine individual behavior. On the other hand, this perspective does provide a framework to study and examine gang activity.

SOCIAL DISORGANIZATION THEORY

At the University of Chicago, a pioneering group of delinquency researchers emerged in the late 1930s. Robert E. Park, a former Chicago news reporter, believed that the city could be used as a laboratory to study

---

Box 13.8 Forms of Delinquent Subcultures

- **Criminal subculture:** Follows the basic organized crime model. Areas where organized crime is firmly established provides a goal for delinquents. Inhabitants of this subculture rationally seek economic gain and view crime as a career.
- **Conflict subculture:** Places high premium on violence. This subculture often occurs in neighborhoods populated with new immigrants, where the delinquent pursues opportunities lacking elsewhere.
- **Retreatist subculture:** Emphasizes drug abuse or other forms of escape. This delinquent is a "double failure" who cannot achieve success in either the criminal or conflict subcultures.

crime. Influenced by prominent sociologists W. I. Thomas, George H. Mead, Erving Goffman, and Georg Simmel, Park saw a connection between how animals live in natural settings and how humans live in urban settings.[33]

Park considered the city a social organism within which neighborhoods either survive, thrive, or fall apart. Why, he asked, is crime and delinquency widespread in certain areas and not in others? To answer this question, Park and his colleague, Ernest Burgess, organized 1920s' Chicago into a series of concentric zones according to residential, occupational, and class characteristics. Specifically, they sought to understand how these urban zones changed over time and what effect this process had on rates of crime.

Park and Burgess identified the **zone in transition** as the major source of urban crime. This suggested that as businesses expand into this area from the central zone and as zoning laws change to accommodate them, those residents who can afford to leave do so. With the stable wage earners gone, housing deteriorates and the zone becomes an undesirable place to live. Those who are left have no economic or political power. They are the poor, the unemployed, and the disenfranchised. Social control mechanisms weaken, and ethnic and racial segregation become a way of life. Given the social disorganization caused by conflicting norms and competing values, the crime rate is bound to soar: residents of this zone are in conflict and competing to survive.[34]

Park and Burgess found that these areas also have the highest rates of delinquency, disease, infant death, and other social problems. In addition, they found that the crime rate declines as one moves from the center of the city to the outer zones.

Other theorists built upon this research foundation. Perhaps the best known are Clifford Shaw and Henry McKay. Shaw and McKay focused their attention on four trends that have come to characterize urban life: crime, poverty, ethnic heterogeneity and residential mobility. These trends, they contend, lead to the disruption of community social organization, and thus to crime and delinquency.[35] In other words, the urban environment spawns criminality: the social conditions in transitional neighborhoods promote deviance.

To study this breakdown of social norms, Shaw and McKay conducted several studies on delinquency in Chicago over a thirty-year period. Their studies confirmed Park's finding that delinquency is highest in the zone in transition. Furthermore, the farther one moved from this zone, the lower the rate of delinquency.

Other key findings include the following:

1. Stable communities have lower rates of delinquency.
2. Communities with higher rates of delinquency have social values that differ from those with lower rates of delinquency.
3. Lower-income areas with a high rate of frustration and deprivation have a higher level of delinquency.

4. Social conditions in a community (such as overcrowding, physical deterioration, and concentrations of foreign-born and black populations) are directly related to the rate of delinquency.

5. In lower-class areas, no stable social values unify the community; therefore, delinquency is seen as a legitimate alternative to a law-abiding posture.[36]

Yablonsky also cites several key concepts about youth gangs that emerged from "Chicago School" research:

1. The youth begins his delinquent career on a thin line of malicious and mischievous play and then becomes more concretely involved in delinquent gang activity.

2. The natural conflict of a youth with the community and its conflicting set of norms and values drives him further into gang activity.

3. The gang emerges as a result of the failure of community forces, particularly the family, to properly integrate many youths into the more constructive, law-abiding society.

4. Loyalty and esprit de corps are strong mobilizing forces in the delinquent gangs, and it becomes a cohesive entity.

5. The gang becomes a kind of street corner family for youth who are detached and disassociated from and in conflict with the law-abiding community.

6. The gang in this context becomes a school for crime that provides both the opportunity, the training, and the motivation for a criminal career in association with others.

7. A youth enmeshed in the delinquent gang as a primary group gets driven further into a delinquent career by the negative effect of society's institutionalized patterns for dealing with the gang youth and his problems.[37]

Thus, faced with the pressures of a community in decline, the youth enters the gang and is emersed in the delinquent subculture.

Taken together, these theories explain the forces that lead to gang formation.

Issue: Juvenile Gangs

Youth involvement in gangs is not a new problem. As early as the nineteenth century, youth gangs roamed the streets of urban America. Early gangs were viewed more as a nuisance than as a problem. However, this perception changed in later years as gang violence began to emerge.

In the early part of the twentieth century, gang activity and violence usually were associated with protecting territory. Gang violence was controlled by, directed toward, and limited to gang members, with rival gangs being the target. Gang activity briefly subsided in the 1960s, but resurfaced in the 1970s with increased vengeance. Gang members no longer were directing their energies solely toward protecting their own turf; drugs and weapons had begun to play a major role in their activities. In fact, large profits from the sale of illegal drugs motivate many youth to join gangs.

Gang expert Lewis Yablonsky offers the following summary of gang attributes based in part on his fifty years of research:

1. Gangs have a fierce involvement with their territory in their hood or barrio and will fight and "gangbang" to protect their turf.
2. Gangsters have different levels of participation—partially based on age—and can be characterized as core or marginalized participants.
3. Different gangs have diverse patterns of leadership.
4. Many gangs and gangsters participate intensely in the commerce and the use of various drugs.
5. Gangs are, in part, generated by their cultural milieu in a response to a society that blocks their opportunity to achieve the success-goals of the larger society.[38]

Yablonsky's conclusions are the result of his review of the previously mentioned theories, research findings, and personal experience. Together, these conclusions stress that a gang is not a singular entity that is easily defined and that gang involvement varies.

A female shows off an electronic tracking device. (John M. Discher/*AP/Wide World Photos*)

Youth participation in gangs has reached dramatic proportions in some communities. An official survey of gang involvement (*The National Youth Gang Survey*) noted the following trends in 1999:

1. Forty-four percent of the respondents reported active youth gangs in their jurisdiction in 1999 (down 4 percent from 1998).

2. A total of 3,911 jurisdictions experienced gang activity in 1999, a 19 percent decline from the high of 4,824 in 1996.

3. More than 26,000 gangs were estimated to be active in 1999, down 9 percent from 1998. However, this pattern varies by location. Since 1998, the number of gangs decreased by 11 percent in suburban areas, 19 percent in small cities, and 23 percent in rural areas. However, large cities (which account for 49 percent of all gangs) registered a one percent increase over this period.

4. More than 840,500 gang members were estimated to be active in 1999—an 8 percent increase over 1998 findings. This increase counteracted the decline noted from 1996 to 1998 and approached the estimated peak of nearly 846,500 members in 1996.

5. Fifty percent of 1999 gang members were aged 18 to 24—an increase from 46 percent in 1998 and 37 percent in 1996. The proportion of gang members aged 15 to 17 decreased to 26 percent, down from a high of 34 percent in 1996.

6. Race/ethnicity composition remained the same as previous years: Hispanic (47 percent), African American (31 percent), Caucasian (13 percent), Asian (7 percent), and other (2 percent).

7. Respondents were also asked to identify gang members by social class in 1999: Underclass (50%), Working Class (35%), Middle Class (12%), and Upper Middle Class (3%).

8. Offense types that were most likely to be committed by gang members included larceny/theft, aggravated assault, and burglary/breaking and entering.

9. Forty-six percent of youth gang members were estimated to be involved in the street drug sales to generate profits for the gang.

10. The percentage of youth gangs that are considered drug gangs increased from 34 percent in 1998 to 40 percent in 1999.

In sum, the results of this survey indicate that the youth gang problem continues to be "widespread and substantial across the United States."[39]

Youth involvement in gangs poses a threat to communities and a challenge for the juvenile justice system. As juveniles' participation in gangs increases, so does the need to develop more effective ways to prevent and suppress gang activity. In spite of the growing magnitude of the problem, until recently only limited programs and resources have been directed against juvenile gangs.

Practice: The Office of Juvenile Justice and Delinquency Prevention's Comprehensive Gang Model

In 1987, the Office of Juvenile Justice and Delinquency Prevention began a project to prevent gang violence and delinquency. It began as a project under the direction of Dr. Irving Spergel at the University of Chicago and is now known as the OJJDP Comprehensive Gang Model.

This model is built on five core strategies and the overall premise that gang prevention must be based upon a team approach by a number of social service agencies acting in conjunction. The five core strategies are

1. **Community Mobilization:** Involvement of local citizens, including former gang youth, community groups and agencies, and the coordination of programs and staff functions within and across agencies.
2. **Provision of Opportunities:** The development of a variety of specific education, training, and employment programs targeted at gang-involved youth.
3. **Social Intervention:** Youth-serving agencies, schools, grass roots groups, faith organizations, police, and other criminal justice organizations "reaching out" and acting as links among gang-involved youth, their families, and the conventional world and needed services.
4. **Suppression:** Formal and informal social control procedures, including close supervision or monitoring of gang youth by agencies of the criminal justice system and also by community-based agencies, schools, and grass roots groups.
5. **Organizational Change and Development:** Development and implementation of policies and procedures that result in the most effective use of available and potential sources within and across agencies to better address the gang problem.

This model is firmly based upon the premise that "long term change would not be achieved without also addressing at-risk youth and the institutions which support and control youth and their families."[40]

The model promotes program strategies that hold gang members accountable for crime but also provide critical services to prevent their further involvement in delinquency. These strategies include

1. Understanding different gang structures, systems, and processes in the neighborhood.
2. Development of an interagency street-level team approach to prevention, intervention, and suppression that is supported by clear policy.
3. Targeting, monitoring, arresting, and incarcerating gang leaders and repeat violent offenders.

4. Targeting, monitoring, arresting, and incarcerating gang leaders and repeat violent offenders.

5. Referring gang members, including fringe members and their parents, to youth and family services for counseling and guidance.

6. Crisis intervention and prevention of gang fights or disputes.

7. Probation and police team patrols of community "hot spots."

8. Close supervision of gang offenders and those at high risk by criminal and juvenile justice and community-based agencies.

9. Remedial education for targeted gang members, especially middle or junior high school youth, and remedial or special education for older gang youth.

10. Job orientation, training, placement and mentoring for older youth gang members, including those with criminal records.[41]

Again, the model stresses the need for a coordinated, integrated approach to dealing with gangs. Punishment and treatment must be combined to be effective.

Since 1995, the model has been implemented in several cities across the country including Bloomington, Illinois; Mesa and Tucson, Arizona; Riverside, California; San Antonio, Texas; and Louisville, Kentucky. Comprehensive research results are not yet available on the effectiveness of the model but the previously cited Youth Gang Survey findings may be indicative of success. The decline in gang involvement in most areas could be due to this model. To obtain up-to-date information on this project, consult the National Youth Gang Center website at http://www.iir.com/nygc.

SOCIAL CONTROL THEORY

The central theme of social control theories is that all youths have the same potential for delinquency. Beyond the influence of personality, the forces in the social environment can pull, pressure, or push individuals toward a life of crime. Society has developed certain control mechanisms to maintain the social order, including values and behavioral norms. Delinquency results when the mechanisms of social control fail.

Standing other criminological theories on their heads, social control theorists ask, "Why aren't we all criminals? Why is it that only certain individuals living in a crime-promoting environment become criminals while others do not?"[42]

Reckless's Containment Theory

An early version of social control theory was developed by Walter Reckless (See box 13.9). He felt that criminological theory had not explained why certain individuals who were exposed to criminal influences did not turn

---

Box 13.9 Walter C. Reckless (1899–1989)

A member of the "Chicago School" of criminology, Reckless developed *containment theory* as another way to explain criminal behavior. His theory stated that the tendency to commit unlawful acts is determined by the type, or quality, of the self-concept the individual has, and the individual's ability to "contain" the act.

---

to crime. Noticing that some youngsters who lived in high-crime areas did not turn to delinquency, Reckless concluded that they were "insulated" (hence the term **insulation**) from crime. The primary insulator he found, was self-concept. A favorable self-concept could lead an individual, even one faced with a crime-promoting environment, away from a life of crime.[43] Thus, his **containment theory** explains both conforming and criminal behavior. Box 13.10 lists his ingredients of inner and outer containment.

Reckless believed that internal containments were stronger, more important, and more effective crime control elements than outer containments. Individuals lacking a high degree of inner containment, Reckless suggested, would be unlikely to be saved by external containment. For example, if unemployment or lack of educational opportunity pressures juveniles toward crime, the last line of defense is the self-concept. If it is strong, the juvenile can resist the lures of delinquency.

However, Reckless did not present containment theory in a causal framework. Rather, he described the forces of containment as buffers or insulators that block the social pressures bearing down on the individual. If these buffers are not in place, the individual confronted with crime-promoting conditions is more likely to deviate. Conversely, the presence of inner and outer forces of containment make an individual less likely to succumb to the temptations of a bad environment.

Reckless's research on self-concept showed that "bad" boys clearly had lower self-esteem than "good" boys.[44] Research showed that the "good" boys avoided delinquency and had a higher self-concept.[45] Yet, an intervention project designed to improve the self-concept of predelinquent boys in Columbus (Ohio) junior high schools had no significant impact.[46]

Moreover, follow-up research on self-concept and delinquency failed to establish a firm link between the two.[47] Yet, Jensen did discover that juveniles with high self-esteem were less likely to engage in delinquent acts.[48] But a positive family environment is viewed as potentially an inhibiting factor in criminal behavior.

In summary, inner containment is most important when aspects of external containment are absent. The self-concept can serve as a buffer when the influence of traditional structures like the family, church, and

---

Box 13.10 Ingredients of Containment

INNER CONTAINMENT

In addition to self-concept, Reckless outlined other forms of "inner containment," including

Self-control
Ego strength
Well-developed super ego (conscience)
High frustration tolerance
High resistance to diversions
High sense of responsibility
Goal orientation
Ability to find substitute satisfactions
Tension-reducing rationalizations
These inner forces enable the individual to resist the lure of criminal behavior.

OUTER CONTAINMENT

These elements represent "the structural buffer in the person's immediate social world" that is able to restrain the individual. They include

Presentation of a consistent moral front
Institutional reinforcement of norms, goals, and expectations
Existence of a reasonable set of social expectations
Alternatives and safety valves
Opportunity for acceptance

These social forces help the family and other groups contain the individual and prevent delinquency.

Source: Based on Walter C. Reckler's, *The Crime Problem* (New York: Appleton-Century-Crofts, 1973).

---

school is weak or ineffective. Resistance is especially great when individuals internalize law-abiding norms and values makes them a part of their self-concept. Containment theory explains why some people who live in high-crime areas do not turn to crime and why some juveniles do not become involved in gang activities. Therefore, it also indirectly prescribes treatment by citing its forces as insulators against crime and delinquency. Prevention efforts must include the traditional elements of society to establish a united front against crime.

Containment theory has been influential. Potential inadequacies of his theory not withstanding. Reckless is cited as "one of the fathers of control theory laying the groundwork for the more sophisticated later versions of scholars like Travis Hirschi."[49]

Hirschi's Social Bond Theory

Travis Hirschi developed a social control theory that modified containment theory. Like Reckless, Hirschi believes that all youths are potential delinquents. The central issue is why some youths do not commit crimes at all.

According to Hirschi, **social controls** are the actual or potential rewards either positive or negative, internal or external, for conformity to social mores. These controls take the form of **social bonds:** the ties that people have to parents, school, peers, and others. When those bonds are weak, a person is freer to engage in criminal activity. Moreover, a person is more apt to learn to be delinquent or criminal when young, and juveniles are more likely to become delinquent when social bonds are weak. Thus, social bonds are essential to the prevention of crime and delinquency. People who strongly believe in conventional norms and values are unlikely to become involved in deviant behavior.

Hirschi's social bonds manifest themselves in conformity, involvement, and respect for social institutions. For example, a conformist has an investment in society. Conventional actions like taking a job and developing a social reputation, build prosocial ties and discourage criminal involvement. In addition, allegiances to norms and legitimate behavior block the formation of ties to deviant subcultures. Seeking success, the conformist will not risk the chance of advancement by committing crimes. Moreover, involvement is a time-consuming process. The more heavily one is involved in conventional activities, the less time available to engage in deviant behavior. Finally, belief in the way the society operates engenders sensitivity to the rights of others and respect for the laws. Box 13.11 summarizes key elements of the social bond.

Hirschi stressed the importance of the family as a sponsor of conventional, conformist behavior. Parents can strongly contribute to conformity by providing supervision for, by building a quality relationship with, and by communicating with their children. The stronger the bonds the individual has with the family, the greater his or her resistance to crime and delinquency.

In two major studies, Hirshi basically confirmed his control theory in two ways. In the first study he showed that a strong attachment to, and good communication with, parents was a strong factor in nondelinquent

---

Box 13.11 Elements of the Social Bond

Attachment   The basic element for the internalization of norms and the values of a society. Attachment reflects effective ties to family, schools, and friends, and affection for and sensitivity to others.

Commitment   The stake an individual has in society and what that person stands to lose by committing a crime.

Involvement   The extent to which one participates in the conventional activities of a society.

Belief   Respect for moral validity of the rules of a society. The extent to which people believe in the laws of a society and what that society stands for.

---

behavior. In the second study he found that the less the subjects of the study felt they should obey the laws, the more likely they were to break them. His theory has its detractors, as Hirshi himself understands, and for which he gives some probable reasons.

> . . . the problem with social control as a concept is that it tends to expand until it becomes synonymous with sociology, and then it dies. It dies because there is nothing unique or distinct about it. This danger is present even when the concept is limited initially to delinquency.[50]

Despite the critics, the concept of social control is a basic theory for delinquent behavior.

Issue: Juvenile Violence

Juvenile violence has become a serious problem. As both victims and perpetrators, certain youths are at risk for violent behavior. Research on juvenile violence in Washington, D.C., and South Carolina has identified the following **risk factors:**

For offending:

1. **Age:** Many juveniles involved in violent behavior (including homicide) begin their involvement by age 15.
2. **Race:** African Americans were somewhat overrepresented in the homicide and assault and battery groups compared with other serious offender groups in these studies. Including Hispanics in the analysis, studies in Denver, Colorado, and Rochester, New York, determined that violence prevalence rates were higher among minority groups than among Causasians at each age and site (except for 18-year-olds in Rochester).

3. **Other Individual Factors:** Hyperactivity, risk taking behavior, aggressiveness, early initiation of violence (by age 12–13), and involvement in other forms of antisocial behavior.[51]

As victims of homicide/violence:

1. Typically, juvenile homicide victims are of the same race and sex as their perpetrators.
2. The most likely victims of juvenile homicide are acquaintances, followed by strangers, and then family members.
3. Most juvenile homicide victims are male.
4. The majority age group for juvenile homicide victims was 16 to 17 (69 percent).

In addition, these studies demonstrated that many violent juvenile offenders live in disruptive and disorganized families and communities.[52]

Practice: The SafeFutures Initiative

The SafeFutures Initiative is an extension of the Office of Juvenile Justice and Delinquency Prevention's Comprehensive Strategy for Serious, Violent, and Chronic Juvenile Offenders. This strategy focuses upon:

1. Youths who are at high risk of future delinquent behavior and
2. Youthful offenders who have already exhibited delinquent behavior and are at risk of, or already are, engaging in serious, violent, or chronic law breaking.[53]

The initiative is based upon the Hawkins and Catalano **Social Development model.** It is a comprehensive approach to preventing youth crime that is based on social control theory.

Consistent with social control theory, the model is based upon the premise that the most important units of socialization (family, schools, peers, and community) influence behavior in a sequential fashion. When youths have the opportunity to engage in conforming behavior within each of them, law abiding behavior is the result. To accomplish this, youths must develop necessary skills and be rewarded for positive behavior. These conditions will sponsor the development of the social bonds listed by Hirschi. These social bonds inhibit association with delinquent peers and prevent delinquent behavior.[54]

The social development model is based upon such research findings. Hawkins and Catalano present data on risk factors associated with a number of problem behaviors, such as violence, drug abuse, teen pregnancy, and school drop-out. In the social development model, these **risk factors** are conditions that increase the likelihood that a child will develop one or more behavior problems in adolescence. The greater the exposure to these factors, the greater the likelihood that juveniles will engage in these negative behaviors.

Community Risk Factors and the behaviors they sponsor include:

- Availability of drugs (substance abuse).
- Availability of firearms (delinquency, violence).
- Community laws and norms favorable toward drug use, firearms, and crime (substance abuse, delinquency, and violence).
- Media portrayals of violence (violence).
- Transitions and mobility (substance abuse, delinquency, and drop-out).
- Extreme economic deprivation (substance abuse, delinquency, violence, teen pregnancy and school drop-out).

Family Risk Factors and the behaviors they sponsor include:

- A family history of high risk behavior (substance abuse, delinquency, violence, teen pregnancy and school drop-out).
- Family management problems (substance abuse, delinquency, violence, teen pregnancy and school drop-out).
- Family conflict (substance abuse, delinquency, violence, teen pregnancy and school drop-out).
- Favorable parental attitudes and involvement in the problem behavior (substance abuse, delinquency, and violence). Children whose parents engage in violent behavior inside or outside the home are at greater risk for exhibiting violent behavior.

School Risk Factors and the behaviors they sponsor include:

- Early and persistent antisocial behavior (substance abuse, delinquency, violence, teen pregnancy and school drop-out).
- Academic failure beginning in elementary school (substance abuse, delinquency, violence, teen pregnancy and school drop-out).
- Lack of commitment to school (substance abuse, delinquency, violence, teen pregnancy and school drop-out).

Individual / Peer Risk Factors and their indicators consist of:

- Alienation and rebelliousness (substance abuse, delinquency and school drop-out). It may be a more significant risk for young people of color. Discrimination may cause these youths to reject the dominant culture and rebel against it.

- Friends who engage in the problem behavior (substance abuse, delinquency, violence, teen pregnancy, and school drop out). This factor has proven to be a consistent predictor of problem behaviors.
- Favorable attitudes toward the problem behavior (substance abuse, delinquency, teen pregnancy, and school drop-out). Here, the middle school years are particularly significant. If youths are involved with peers who demonstrate favorable attitudes to these behaviors, they are more likely to engage in them.
- Early initiation of the problem behavior (substance abuse, delinquency, violence, teen pregnancy and school drop-out). The research review demonstrates that youths who begin to use drugs before age 15 are twice as likely to have drug problems than those who wait until after the age of 19.
- Constitutional factors (substance abuse, delinquency, and violence). These factors are biological or psychological in nature. Youths who have problems with sensation-seeking behavior, low harm-avoidance, and lack of impulse control are more likely to engage in these problem behaviors.[55]

Hawkins and Catalano assert that these risks occur in multiple domains. Therefore, the most effective way to combat them is a multi-faceted approach across the community. Neighborhood residents and community agencies of all types should join together to deal with these problems. The aim is to provide protection against the sponsorship of risk factors and the spread to problem behaviors that result from them. The goal is to use the public health model to prevent crime. Awareness of these factors is the first step in the development of plans and programs to deal with them in an effective manner.

Within demonstration communities, SafeFutures is based upon nine components:

1. Afterschool Programs (Pathways to Success)
2. Juvenile Mentoring Programs (JUMP)
3. Family Strengthening and Support Services
4. Mental Health Services for At-Risk and Adjudicated Youth
5. Delinquency Prevention Programs
6. Comprehensive Community-wide Approaches to Gang Free Schools and Communities
7. Community-based Day Treatment Programs (Bethesda Day Treatment Center model)
8. Continuum-of-care Services for At-Risk and Delinquent Girls and

9. Serious, Violent, and Chronic Juvenile Offender (SVCJO) Programs (with an emphasis on enhancing graduated sanctions).[56]

This program is presently in the implementation stage.[57] But it offers great promise by incorporating the principles of social control theory and bringing them into operation.

LABELING THEORY

Labeling theory emphasizes the influence of powerful groups in society to both define and react to deviant behavior. The general position is that no act is inherently criminal. Rather, the law defines certain acts as criminal. For example, Erickson (1962) claimed that deviance is not inherent in all socially defined deviant acts, but depends on (1) when the act is committed, (2) who commits the act and who is the victim, and (3) what the consequences of the act are.[58] In labeling theory, the crucial dimension is the societal reaction to the act, not the act itself. It attempts to explain all forms of deviant behavior, not just crime and delinquency.

According to Tannenbaum, labeling can be defined as "the process of making the criminal [by] tagging, defining, segregating, describing, emphasizing, making conscious and self-conscious. . . . The person becomes the thing he is described as being."[59] Thus, labeling theory focuses on the process of labeling and on the reasons some persons can commit deviant acts and avoid the consequences while others cannot.

In terms of delinquency, labeling theory is especially applicable to status offenses and offenders.

Juveniles and Secondary Deviance

Edwin Lemert developed the theory of **secondary deviation** to further explain how the legal process can make the crime problem worse through intervention. Box 13.12 lists the steps in this process.[60]

Lemert is not concerned with the motivation behind the initial deviant act. Instead, he focuses on the official reaction to the act and the way in which it causes more damage than the act itself. For example, Schur condemns the sanctioning by juvenile courts of status offenses—acts (e.g., running away, truancy) committed by juveniles that would be considered crimes if committed by adults. Schur maintains that these are moral judgments that make a bad situation worse. A runaway (primary deviation), placed in a juvenile institution, can become a burglar (secondary deviation) because of the labeling process. Like Tannenbaum and Lemert, Schur suggests a policy of **radical nonintervention:** *Leave kids alone whenever possible.*[61]

Box 13.12 From Primary to Secondary Deviance

Phase 1:   A person commits a deviant act.

Phase 2:   Society reacts by instituting repressive measures against the individual.

Phase 3:   The individual responds with more deviation, (secondary deviation), which draws more penalties, which draws still more deviation, in a continuous cycle.

Phase 4:   The labeled individual develops hostilities and resentments toward law enforcers.

Phase 5:   Society reacts by further labeling and stigmatizing the offender.

Phase 6:   The individual's options become so restricted that the deviant status is accepted by both sides and the deviance is strengthened.

Phase 7:   The individual accepts deviant social status.

In sum, Lemert argues that the stigma that society places on the deviant causes more (and possibly worse) criminal behavior. As a result, the stigmatized, labeled deviant organizes his or her self-concept around deviance. Box 13.13 outlines this process.

If labeling theory is right, status offenders will eventually engage in secondary deviance as a result of this process. However, research on status offenders does not appear to support this idea. For example, Murray cites several studies that show that status offenders do not "escalate." In other

Box 13.13 Key Processes of Labeling

Phase 1:   Stereotyping.

Phase 2:   Retrospective Interpretation: Once a person is identified as deviant, he is seen in a totally new light. Reconstituted, he is what he was "all along."

Phase 3:   Negotiation: Depending upon the social status of the individual, the stigma attached to the label can be negotiated and even avoided.

Phase 4:   Official Reaction: Labeled by others as evil, abnormal people, not to be trusted by law-abiding people.

words, they do not engage in secondary deviance and go on to commit more serious offenses.[62]

Issue: Status Offenders in Juvenile Court

We have examined this issue in several other chapters. We revisit it to determine what the nature of the problem is and its linkage to theory and practice. Again, labeling theory asserts that labeling juveniles as status offenders will make the problem worse by tagging them and causing secondary deviance.

In 1974, the U.S. Congress passed the Juvenile Justice and Delinquency Prevention Act. The act provided for the removal of all status offenders from juvenile detention and correctional facilities. States were required to comply with this mandate and report on their progress in achieving it or face the loss of federal funding. There have been a number of amendments to the act in passing years that have continued to address this issue. In 1990, judges were permitted to confine status offenders in secure detention for a limited time, if they had violated a valid court order. A related problem concerns the "chronic status offender"—runaways or juveniles with emotional and behavioral problems who often flood the juvenile justice system. When to intervene and for what purpose? These are the key issues on status offenders.

Practice: Decriminalization, Diversion, and Deinstitutionalization of Status Offenses

Calls to eliminate juvenile justice system involvement in status offenses have specifically called for the decriminalization, diversion, and **deinstitutionalization** of status offenses (known in short as DSO). Sponsored by the JJDP Act, these actions are undertaken with the belief that the juvenile justice system has been ineffective in solving the problems of status offenders, unjust in its treatment of these offenders, and has, through labeling and stigmatization, caused more harm than good.[63] The DSO requirements caused states to examine current practices, abandon the use of detention as the dominant method to deal with status offenders, and to pursue legal, administrative, and physical remedies to achieve the goal of this policy.

Studies have demonstrate that the DSO mandate has been effective. Although implementation was difficult, most states have achieved either full or minimal compliance with the requirements of the JJDP Act. They have reformed their laws, policies and practices for handling status offenders, particularly dependency and neglect cases. In addition, noninstitutional programs and community based services have been developed for these youths.[64]

Of course, the ultimate goal is to act in the best interests of the youth. Treatment of status offenders requires a careful approach that will alleviate, rather than aggravate, harm.

SUMMARY

Obviously there are other theories regarding delinquency causation that are not covered in this chapter. Our selectons were guided by their application within the juvenile justice system. They have resulted in action programs designed combat delinquency. Theory without practice based upon sound research does little but add to the already voluminous rhetoric regarding the causes of delinquency. Great strides are being made in this area.

Sound policy must be based upon theory. Theory serves to guide programs and policies, rather than reliance upon rhetoric and guesswork. Of course, these policies and programs must be thoroughly researched and evaluated to determine if they are being properly implemented and effectively executed.

The practices highlighted in this chapter are based on sound theory. They have several common themes. First is the importance of a community-based approach to delinquency. It cannot be handled by governmental officials alone. The factors that prevent delinquency are centered on the community and its institutions: schools, the family, the neighborhood, and churches. They must sponsor the foundations of self-control and the development of a sound self-concept. Second, treatment does not exclude punishment. Juveniles must be held accountable for their actions but punishments must truly fit both the crime and the offender. Delinquency will not be conquered by treatment or punishment alone or by the community or government officials acting alone. A balanced, cooperative approach is what these various theories promote. The programs that build upon them offer hope for the future.

TERMS TO REMEMBER

Cesare Beccaria
Containment theory
Criminological theory
Criminology
Deinstitutionalization
Elements of deterrence theory
Forms of delinquent subculture
Generality
Grand theories

Insulation
Juvenile delinquency
Labeling theory
Levels of deterrence
Middle-range theories
Norms of the delinquent subculture
Radical nonintervention
Reaction formation
Risk factors

Secondary deviation
Six focal concerns of lower-class
   delinquents
Social bonds
Social controls

Stanford v. Kentucky
Status offender
Thompson v. Oklahoma
Zone in transition

REVIEW QUESTIONS

1. What are the elements of a criminological theory? What is their purpose?

2. Why is deterrence theory so attractive to some people? What are its key premises?

3. The delinquent subculture has many attributes. Choose one and give an example of how it is present in American culture.

4. Why are gangs subcultures? What evidence would you cite to support such a claim?

5. How does containment insulate against delinquency? Why are you a college student instead of a criminal in prison or jail?

6. How does labeling contribute to delinquency?

7. Does the death penalty constitute a sound policy in response to juvenile violence? Why or why not?

8. What are the key features of the social development model? Does it look like an effective way to combat delinquency?

9. Do you think the deinstitutionalization of status offenders is a good policy? Why or why not?

10. Explain why someone you either know personally or know of may have committed a delinquent act.

NOTES

[1]Abraham Kaplan, *The Conduct of Inquiry: Methodology for Behavioral Science* (San Francisco: Chandler, 1964), p. 295.

[2]Charles R. Tittle, "The Assumption That General Theories Are Not Possible." In Richard C. Monk, ed., *Taking Sides: Clashing Views on Controversial Issues in Crime and Criminology* (Guilford, CT: Dushkin, 1996), pp. 76–81.

[3]Robert K. Merton, *On Theoretical Sociology.* (New York: Free Press, 1967).

[4]Clayton A. Hartjen, C. A. (1978). *Crime and Criminalization* (New York: Holt, Rinehart & Winston, 1978), pp. 51–53.

[5]Donald R. Cressey, "Fifty Years of Criminology: From Sociological Theory to Political Control," *Pacific Sociological Review*, Vol. 22 (1979), p. 457.

[6]Michael J. Lynch and W. Byron Groves, "In Defense of Comparative Criminology: A Critique of General Theory and the Rational Man." In Richard C. Monk, ed., *Taking Sides: Clashing Views on Controversial Issues in Crime and Criminology* (Guilford, CT: Dushkin, 1996), p. 89.

[7]See the thirty-five-year study of delinquency by Sheldon and Eleanor Glueck , *Unraveling Juvenile Delinquency* (New York: Commonwealth Fund, 1950).

[8]Engrossed Third Substitute House Bill No. 371, State of Washington, 45th Legislature, 1st Extraordinary Session, April 11, 1977, the Committee on Institutions, pp. 18–19.

[9]Donald J. Shoemaker, *Theories of Delinquency* (New York: Oxford University Press, 2000), p. 3.

[10]Marcello Maestro, *Cesare Beccaria and the Origins of Penal Reform* (Philadelphia: Temple University Press, 1973), pp. 158–159.

[11]George B. Vold, *Theoretical Criminology* (New York: Oxford University Press, 1970), pp. 18–22.

[12]Ernest van den Haag, "The Neoclassical Theory of Crime Control," *Criminal Justice Policy Review,* Vol. 1 (1986), p. 100.

[13]Elio Monachesi, "Cesare Beccaria," in Hermann Mannheim, ed., *Pioneers in Criminology* (Montclair, NJ: Patterson-Smith, 1960), pp. 36–50.

[14]James A. Fox, *Uniform Crime Report: Supplementary Homicide Reports, 1976–1997.* (Boston, MA: Northeastern University, College of Criminal Justice [producer], 1999).

[15]David Finckelhor and Richard Ormrod, *Homicides of Children and Youth—OJJDP Juvenile Justice Bulletin* (Washington DC: Office of Juvenile Justice and Delinquency Prevention, October 2001), p. 1.

[16]Studies of juvenile homicide offenders include: Dewey G. Cornell, "Juvenile Homicide: A Growing National Problem," *Behavioral Sciences & the Law,* Vol. 11 (1993), pp. 389–396; Dewey G. Cornell, D. G., E. P. Benedek and D. M. Benedek, "Characteristics of Adolescents Charged with Homicide: Review of 72 Cases," *Behavioral Sciences & the Law,* Vol. 5 (1987), pp. 11–23; Joel P. Eigen, "Punishing Youth Homicide Offenders in Philadelphia," *Journal of Criminal Law and Criminology,* Vol. 1079 (1981), pp. 867–1924; Dorothy O. Lewis, "Intrinsic and Environmental Characteristics of Juvenile Murderers," *Journal of the American Academy of Child & Adolescent Psychology,* Vol.27 (1988), pp. 582–587; J.R.P. Ogloff, "The Juvenile Death Penalty: A Frustrated Society's Attempt at Control," *Behavioral Sciences & the Law,* Vol. 5 (1987), pp. 447–455; J.C. Rowley, C. P. Ewing and S. I. Singer, "Juvenile Homicide: The Need for an Interdisciplinary Approach," *Behavioral Sciences & the Law,* Vol. 5 (1987), pp. 1–10; and Victor L. Streib, *Death Penalty for Juveniles* (Bloomington, IN: Indiana University Press, 1987).

[17]NAACP Legal Defense and Education Fund, *Death Row U.S.A.—Summer 2002.* http://www.deathpenaltyinfo.org/.

[18]Robert L. Hale, *A Review of Juvenile Executions in America* (Lewiston, NY: Edwin Mellen Press, 1997).

[19]Death Penalty Information Center, "Executions of Juvenile Offenders," http://www.deathpenaltyinfo.org/juvexec.html.

[20]The states are California, Colorado, Connecticut, Illinois, Indiana, Kansas, Maryland, Montana, Nebraska, New Jersey, New Mexico, New York, Ohio, Oregon, Tennessee, and Washington. Death Penalty Information Center, "Juveniles and the Death Penalty," http://www.deathpenaltyinfo.org/juvchar.html\#overview.

[21]*Eddings v. Oklahoma,* 455 U.S. 104 (1982).

[22]*Thompson v. Oklahoma,* 101 L Ed 702 (1988).

[23]*Stanford v. Kentucky,* 45 CrL 3202 (1989). Kevin Stanford has been pardoned by Kentucky Governor Paul Patton. His sentence was commuted to life in prison

[24]Mark C. Seis and Kenneth L. Elbe, "The Death Penalty for Juveniles: Bridging the Gap Between an Evolving Standard of Decency and Legislative Policy," *Justice Quarterly,* Vol. 8 (1991), pp. 465–487.

[25]N. J. Finkel, K. C. Hughes, S. Smith, et al., "Killing Kids: The Juvenile Death Penalty and Community Sentiment," *Behavioral Sciences and the Law,* Vol. 12 (1994), pp. 5–20; Mark S. Hamm, "Legislator Ideology and Capital Punishment: The Special Case for Indiana Juveniles," *Justice Quarterly,* Vol. 6 (1989), pp. 219–232; M. Sandys and E. McGarrell, "Attitudes Toward Capital Punishment: Preference for the Penalty or Mere Acceptance," *Journal of Research in Crime and Delinquency,* Vol. 32 (1995), pp. 191–213; Gennaro F. Vito and Thomas J. Keil, "Selecting Juveniles for Death: The Kentucky Experience, 1976–86," *Journal of Contemporary Criminal Justice,* Vol. 5 (1988), pp. 181–198.

[26]Dinah A. Robinson and Otis H. Stephens, "Patterns of Mitigating Factors in Juvenile Death Penalty Cases," *Criminal Law Bulletin,* Vol. 28 (1992), pp. 246–275.

[27]Death Penalty Information Center, "Juvenile Death Penalty in Other Countries," http://www.deathpenaltyinfo.org/juvintl.html.

[28]Gwynn Nettler, *Explaining Crime* (New York: McGraw-Hill, 1974), p. 138.

[29]Richard A. Cloward and Lloyd E. Ohlin, *Delinquency and Opportunity* (Glencoe, IL: Free Press, 1960), p. 86.

[30]Cloward and Ohlin, *Delinquency and Opportunity,* p. 86.

[31]Albert A. Cohen, *Delinquent Boys* (New York: Free Press, 1955).

[32]Walter B. Miller, "Lower Class Structure and Generating Milieu of Gang Delinquency," *Journal of Social Issues,* Vol. 14 (1958), p. 19.

[33]Robert Park, *Human Communities* (Glencoe, IL: Free Press, 1952); Robert Park, *The Criminal Area* (New York: Humanities Press, 1966).

[34]Randy Martin, Robert Mutchnick and Tim Austin, *Criminological Thought: Pioneers Past and Present.* (New York: Macmillan, 1990), p. 103.

[35]Robert Bursik, "Social Disorganization and Theories of Crime and Delinquency," *Criminology,* Vol. 26 (1988), pp. 519–551.

[36]Rodney Stark, "Deviant Places: A Theory of the Ecology of Crime. *Criminology,* Vol. 25 (1987), pp. 893–909.

[37]Lewis Yablonsky, *Gangsters: Fifty Years of Madness, Drugs, and Death on the Streets of America* (New York: New York University Press, 1997), pp. 37–38.

[38]Ibid., p. 184.

[39]OJJDP Fact Sheet, *Highlights of the 1999 National Youth Gang Survey* (Washington, DC: Office of Juvenile Justice and Delinquency Prevention, November 2000, #20).

[40]OJJDP Comprehensive Gang Model, *A Guide to Assessing Your Community's Youth Gang Problem* (Washington, DC: Office of Juvenile Justice and Delinquency Prevention, March 2001), pp. 8–9.

[41]Ibid., p. 10.

[42]Martin, Mutchnick, and Austin, *Criminological Thought,* p. 183.

[43]Walter C. Reckless, *The Crime Problem* (New York: Appleton Century Crofts, 1973), pp. 55–59.

[44]Walter C. Reckless, Simon Dinitz and E. Murray, "Self Concept as an Insulator Against Delinquency," *American Sociological Review,* Vol. 21 (1956), pp. 744–756.

[45]Frank R. Scarpitti, E. Murray, Simon Dinitz and Walter C. Reckless, (1960). "The "Good Boy" in a High Delinquency Area: 4 Years Later, *American Sociological Review,* Vol. 25 (1960), pp. 555–558.

[46]Walter C. Reckless and Simon Dinitz, *The Prevention of Juvenile Delinquency.* (Columbus, OH: The Ohio State University Press, 1972).

[47]Walter C. Reckless and Thomas G. Enyon, "Companionship at Delinquency Outset," *British Journal of Criminology,* Vol. 2 (1961), pp. 162–170; M. Schwartz and S. S. Taangri, "A Note on Self-Concept as an Insulator Against Delinquency," *American Sociological Review,* Vol. 30 (1965), pp. 922–926; M. Schwartz and S. S. Tangri, "Delinquency Research and the Self-Concept Variable," *Journal of Criminal Law, Criminology, and Police Science,* Vol. 18 (1967), pp. 182–190.

[48]Gary F. Jensen, "Inner Containment and Delinquency," *Criminology,* Vol. 64 (1973), pp. 464–470.

[49]Martin, Mutchnick, and Austin, *Criminological Thought,* pp. 185–186.

[50]Travis Hirschi, *Causes of Delinquency* (Berkeley, CA: University of California, 1969), p. 26.

[51]Office of Juvenile Justice and Delinquency Prevention, *Report to Congress on Juvenile Violence Research* (Washington, DC: Office of Juvenile Justice and Delinquency Prevention), pp. 5–6.

[52]Ibid., pp. 7-9.

[53]Elaine Morley, Shelli B. Rossman, Mary Kopczynski, Janeen Buck, and Caterina Gouvis, *Comprehensive Responses to Youth at Risk: Interim Findings From the SafeFutures Initiative* (Washington, DC: Office of Juvenile Justice and Delinquency Prevention, 2000), p. 3.

[54]J. David Hawkins and Joseph Weis, "The Social Development Model: An Integrated Approach to Delinquency Prevention," *Journal of Primary Prevention,* Vol. 6 (1985), pp. 73–97.

[55]J. David Hawkins and Richard F. Catalano, *Communities That Care* (San Francisco: Jossey-Bass, 1990). See also J. David Hawkins, "Controlling Crime Before It Happens: Risk-Focused Prevention," *National Institute of Justice Journal* (August 1995), pp. 10–18. In addition, see the website for the Hawkins Catalano model at http://www.preventionscience.com/.

[56]Morley, Rossman, Kopczynski, Buck, and Gouvis, *Comprehensive Responses to Youth at Risk: Interim Findings From the SafeFutures Initiative,* p. x.

[57]Kathleen Coolbaugh and Cynthia J. Hansel, *The Comprehensive Strategy: Lessons Learned from the Pilot Sites* (Washington, DC: Office of Juvenile Justice and Delinquency Prevention, 2000).

[58]Kai Erickson, (1962). "Notes on the Sociology of Deviance," *Social Problems,* Vol. 9 (1962), pp. 397–414; Harold K. Becker, *The Outsiders—Studies in the Sociology of Deviancy* (New York: Free Press, 1963).

[59]Frank Tannenbaum, *Crime and the Community.* (Boston: Ginn, 1938).

[60]Edwin M. Lemert, *Human Deviance, Social Problems, and Social Control* (Englewood Cliffs, NJ: Prentice-Hall, 1967).

[61]Edwin M. Schur, *Radical Non-Intervention.* (Englewood Cliffs, NJ: Prentice Hall, 1973).

[62]John P. Murray, "Status Offenders: Roles, Rules, and Reactions," in Ralph A. Weisheit and Robert G. Culbertson, eds., *Juvenile Delinquency: A Justice Perspective* (Prospect Heights, IL: Waveland Press, 1990), pp. 17–26.

[63]Edward J. Latessa, Lawrence F. Travis, and George P. Wilson, "Juvenile Diversion: Factors Related to Decision Making and Outcome," in Scott H. Decker, ed., *Juvenile Justice Policy: Analyzing Trends and Outcomes* (Beverly Hills, CA: Sage, 1984), pp. 145–165.

[64]Gwen A. Holden and Robert A. Kapler, "Deinstitutionalizing Status Offenders: A Record of Progress," *Juvenile Justice,* Vol. 2 (1995), pp. 3–10; National Criminal Justice Association, *Unlocking the Doors for Status Offenders: The State of the States* (Washington, DC: National Criminal Justice Association, 1995).

chapter 14

THE FUTURE
OF JUVENILE JUSTICE

*Even though get-tough political rhetoric and adultification legis-
lation have characterized juvenile justice in the last fifteen years,
the juvenile justice system will continue with its mission to help
youthful offenders and reduce delinquency.*

— Peter J. Benekos & Alida V. Merlo

CHAPTER OVERVIEW

In previous chapters, we have sought to describe the procedures,
processes, and people who make up the juvenile justice system. This final
chapter integrates some of the forces at work in the system and points out
important areas in which change is occurring and will need to occur in the
twenty-first century.

The Model Muddle

Humphrey Osmond first applied the term "model muddle"[1] to the situation
in the field of mental illness; the term applies equally well to the juvenile
justice system and other large systems. Each decision-maker for such systems seems to have a different view and opinion. Like the juvenile justice
system, where there is little consensus as to what is being accomplished
and what it is supposed to be accomplished. Juvenile judges, probation officers, police, juvenile correctional personnel, and parole staff are far from
agreement as to which "model" to use in processing juvenile offenders.

Two of the most prevalent models have been discussed in several previous chapters. The **treatment model** assumes that delinquent behavior has some root cause in a physical, mental, educational, or occupational handicap of the offender. If the underlying problem can be identified and a liberal dose of corrective "medicine" (e.g., therapy, education, or surgery) applied, the patient will be *cured* of any further deviant behavior. This model is under heavy attack at both the adult and juvenile levels of criminal justice, for its efficacy has never been proven. This **medical model** has been attacked as a failure because many jurisdictions do not follow up recommendations by providing the financial and professional resources needed to administer those medically oriented "treatments" for which the individual was confined. Without treatment, there is no justification for confinement, and therefore the model has no validity.

The original philosophy behind the juvenile justice system was the model of *parens patriae.* Although the rhetoric behind these high-sounding words claims *protection* of youths from the harsh realities of broken homes, criminal companions, and other evils, the setting that developed to implement this "protection" has often been worse than the conditions from which youths were being protected. The state has seldom proven to be a *better* parent for juveniles in trouble, only a harsher and stricter one, so the incarceration of juveniles has had to be justified on the basis of a model other than *parens patriae.*

Deterrence, the literal meaning of which is "that which frightens away from," may be either *individual* or *general.* It might be argued that some *individual* deterrence does take place at various points in the juvenile justice system, but there is little evidence of success with *general* deterrence. Juvenile crime rates continued to rise, despite the deterrent efforts of the harsh reform schools of the 1930s and 1940s and the work camps or treatment centers of the 1960s and 1970s. It is generally conceded that deterrence is most effective when punishment is swift, sure, fair, and universally applied. But, in the juvenile justice system it is often delayed, capricious, and applied mainly to the poor and the powerless. Such a model seems clearly doomed to failure. *Reformation and corrections* are different terms for the same model. As noted by Sommer:

> Literally, to reform is "to reshape, form again, or change into a new and improved condition." Its concrete realization, the reformatory, had as its goal the reshaping of a young person's character. Although the term has rather archaic overtones, this is what most advocates of rehabilitation really want. Rather than restoring a person to a former status, either as someone desperately in need of money or full of hatred, the goal of the reformer is to reshape the offender into a new and improved form.

This model is the logical antecedent of today's emphasis on *corrections,* literally "a setting right or on a straight path." John Augustus, the first probation officer, wrote in 1852: "the object of the law is to reform criminals, and to prevent crime and not to punish maliciously, or from a spirit of revenge." This eminently sensible view led Augustus to bail offenders out of prison and keep them in his home. Unfortunately, the term *reform* subsequently became associated with such brutal institutions as the reform school and state reformatory, so it became lost to the criminal justice system and a less useful term (rehabilitation) was substituted. However, the attempt at euphemism was only partial. We still talk about reforming prisons when we want to change them. To rehabilitate prisons, at least in common speech would mean refurbishing or modernizing older facilities. Both reform and corrections emphasize a reshaping, and corrections has the additional connotation of a standard to guide the process of change—setting the person not just on a different path, but on the right path. Most inmates will acknowledge the legitimacy of reform as a social objective, whereas rehabilitation makes no sense to them. Their criticism concerns the practicability of accomplishing positive character change through immersion in a total criminal society; any reforming or reshaping under such circumstances would probably be in a negative direction. Ironically, *reform* today is more often applied to efforts to change institutions than to programs to change prisoners.[2] This warning seems especially applicable to a juvenile justice system that calls its institutions "reform schools" and "reformatories" while inmates and critics refer to them as "schools of crime," where children learn to be tough and aggressive in order to survive.

The *punishment* model is one that American society finds hard to accept in principle, even though it seems to be the most commonly used in practice. Punishment is another form of the "retribution" or "vengeance" model, which seeks an "eye for an eye and a tooth for a tooth." The manner in which much of our institutional "protection" of juvenile offenders is carried out makes it clear that the punishment model, however rejected in principle, is too often the basis for a great deal of juvenile justice practice. The following description of conditions in a juvenile institution of the 1970s illustrates this point.

> Wallace had already prepared me for the worst. The place was jammed. The majority of kids locked up in the place weren't allowed to attend school. Many were being kept months after their sentencing to other institutions, and their months of waiting at Youth House did not count toward their time. Psychotic kids were mingled with lost kids, kids with sexual problems mingled with truants. Big kids awaiting trial for murder sat confined with little kids awaiting trial for glue sniffing. The windows were still stuck closed. For the perversely nostalgic, Youth House has remained free from the surrounding currents of change . . . the *New York Daily News* began another expose

series on the Youth House, calling it by its new name—Spofford Juvenile Center—and headlining drug traffic, sadism and "unnatural sex acts." Two state legislators promised a legislative hearing and the carousel music began again.[3]

It would be difficult to justify or classify these conditions, typical of many jurisdictions today, under the rubric of *parens patriae*. Until society decides what it really wants to do to, as opposed to for, juveniles. . . the model muddle, and the serious lack of direction or purpose, will continue to strangle any progress.

The current trend toward the provision of more *rights* for juveniles constitutes an improvement but poses a new dilemma. This movement attempts to provide at least some of the protections of due process that have become an integral part of the adult criminal justice system. When one examines the adult system, however, it becomes doubtful that society really wants to inflict a similar monstrosity on its juveniles! Torn, between the need for more structural and legal safeguards for youth. While, at the same time, still attempting to maintain the informal atmosphere of *parens patriae,* the juvenile justice system reaches out in every direction for a model to cling to. It will be a long time before the vast gaps between the rhetoric and reality of this haphazard *nonsystem* close enough so that it may be described as having a "model."

Juvenile court judges still favor *parens patriae* as the dominant purpose of the juvenile justice system. A survey of 220 juvenile court judges revealed that they:

- Favored the continued separation of juvenile court from its adult counterpart.
- Did not believe that the waiver to adult court should be expanded.
- Thought that the juvenile court does not intervene in the lives of troubled juveniles quickly and soon enough to prevent problems.
- Strongly believed that treatment should continue to be the dominant philosophy of the juvenile court.[4]

Clearly, we share these beliefs. The juvenile justice system must continue to serve the youths of this country and make the effort to heal the problems that they face.

FRAGMENTATION: A MAJOR PROBLEM

Juvenile justice is meted out at every level of government in the United States, but their differing standards, procedures, and alternatives make these juvenile justice systems a fragmented hodgepodge of contradictory programs that compete for the same limited resources. Under these circumstances, it is less surprising to the authors that juvenile justice is as bad as it rather is than that it is as good as it is!

From the garbage heap detention centers that can be found in major metropolitan areas to the campus-like cottages in some of the more afflu- ent areas, juvenile Justice can be described as *inconsistent*. Fragmenta- tion of resources in the corrections sector of the criminal justice system has been described as a major problem:

> Corrections today lack a clear and coherent mission. Many different constituents demand that their own objectives for corrections be met. The public wants protection and punishment of predatory offenders. Offenders demand fairness, justice, and assistance, while elected offi- cials demand whatever they think the general public might want on a specific issue before them, without consideration for or appreciation of the long-term application of the 'law of unintended consequences' that flows from their actions. Other agencies expect cooperation, col- laboration, and compliance. In the past, correctional administrators have tried to be everything to everyone in a passive effort to satisfy all (and have in fact satisfied none). This helps them avoid making the necessary but hard choices. But correctional administrators can- not pose as ostriches, keeping their heads in the sand and ignoring the need for proactive effort. Some corrections leaders think that stamping out fires and staying within the budget is all that can be expected of their agencies. Conflicting expectations will require choices and leadership[5]

The fragmentation problems of the juvenile justice system are exacer- bated even further by the broad discretionary powers of the juvenile court. When the juvenile correctional system does not seem to meet the needs of the court, it uses one of a number of available alternatives that include private placement at public expense. An almost endless chain of federal, state, and local commissions, panels, ad hoc committees, and the like, have commented on the fragmentation problem. Like most such studies and re- ports, the majority continues to collect dust on shelves and the fragmenta- tion continues.

The specialized court models discussed in this text (See Chapter 6) including drug courts, and teen courts must be maintained and expanded.[6] They are the potential solution to the fragmentation problem. Focusing on the problem and unifying the many social programs and agencies that can be brought to bear on them may offer the best hope of ef- fective treatment.

Status Offenders: An Attempt to Clarify the System

The umbrella of *parens patriae* has been used to cover juveniles in a num- ber of categories. Recently, there has been pressure to eliminate from the system those juveniles whose only offense is a status that requires protection by the state. It has been urged that only juveniles whose acts would result in criminal prosecution if they were adults be handled in the juvenile justice system and that status offenders should be kept from contact with the juvenile justice system entirely and instead be cared for by alternative agencies. This represents a significant portion of the juvenile population.

This elimination of such a large portion of the juvenile population from the juvenile justice system *should* result in a better focus on the problems of those remaining. This legislation appears, at least, to be a move in the right direction and one that is here to stay.

Alternatives to the System: One Solution

Diversion has usually been a turning away from a system that is dysfunctional to satisfy the needs of the juvenile court for some categories of juveniles. Status offenders may be treated by a completely separate system, and other offenders have also been singled out for special programs.

Many alternative programs have been developed by communities to handle specific problems in that particular community. Placing an inner-city juvenile drug addict in a rural juvenile institution, for example, can result in serious problems for the institution and for the juvenile when he or she returns to the urban setting. Community treatment centers for juvenile drug abusers are one alternative response to this specific problem.

Although some reasonable alternatives to the juvenile justice system are necessary and helpful, they cannot proliferate and fracture the system indefinitely. At some point it is necessary to look for better alternatives *within* the juvenile justice system itself, to satisfy the needs of juveniles within the institutional system.

One of the dangers of a proliferation of diversion programs is that it gives rise to a search for dollars instead of answers to the juvenile justice problems. This is outlined in *Hard Cores Don't Come from Apples,* a classic book on juvenile delinquency:

> Diversion, like therapy and counseling, is fast becoming a catchall term to describe various programs for the purpose of obtaining funds. Rossi objects strongly to those people and programs that act under the guise of diversion. Some people are quick to catch onto semantics and use a new term when it's popular and can be used to their monetary advantage. Those who would labor under the mistaken thought that they can be successful and obtain funds by adding a program like ceramics to their appeals are sadly misinformed. They aren't truly exercising a diversion program. Diversion is a total commitment. It is dedication that requires a 24-hour job . . . those misdirected imitative programs that go under the title of diversion must be separated from those programs that are purely diversion. The

tragedies of diversion and the economics of its success form an interesting eye-opening parallel. This strange brotherhood of opposite magnetic poles can be exemplified through the near awesome fact that neither force is well known. By-and-large, hardly a respectable percentage of the population is familiar with diversion. Certainly, a large percentage of the people who should be aware of it are not. Therefore, they are totally unaware of the ramifications of diversion.

It is also disastrous that not enough funds have been extended to expand diversionary programs into private agencies within the communities of the United States. Who can debate the fact that most communities, large and small, could use diversion programs? But that presents another area of insufficient planning. Not enough people have been trained for diversion. Its study is an entirely new field, as it were, and its new perspective of criminal justice needs to be explored and cultivated. Perhaps, it's realistic to say that not enough people care about our youth. Or, it could be that not enough parents care about their own children. There are several methods of dealing with juveniles, but diversion is *the one* coming area that our city, county, and country fathers cannot afford to overlook.[7]

Arthur recommends that status offenders need more than simple diversion. He recommends that efforts must be made to restore the family and making changes to assure that fathers have meaningful visitation and that they make child support payments—if necessary, through community service.[8]

Juvenile Rights: A Solution or Part of the Problem?

The Supreme Court decision *In re Gault* opened the door for procedural rights in juvenile justice. Since that decision there has been a continuing reexamination of procedures resulting in the provision of juvenile rights similar to those of adults in most areas. Guaranteeing these rights, however, has been a mixed blessing. The provision of procedural safeguards has not yet transformed the juvenile justice system into a copy of the adult system. Thus far it seems to have combined some of the less desirable aspects of *both* systems . . . not a very desirable outcome.

The informal nature of juvenile justice was predicated originally on the belief that protective and reformative procedures would follow which would be good for the juvenile. As the juvenile 'Correctional system became less and less *reformative,* and more and more *punitive,* the need for greater procedural safeguards became apparent. It took action by the Supreme Court in the *Gault* decision to bring about action, however. This has been a pattern in both the adult and juvenile systems—to wait until the judiciary makes a major decision before taking action to remedy the ill.

As each of the procedural rights for juveniles has been provided, the juvenile justice process has undergone great change, which has been positive by legalistic standards but hard to measure in human terms. One major change has been from the informal proceedings of the past to the advocacy proceedings of the present.

Advocacy: A New Meaning Since In re Gault

The *Gault* decision has provided new strength to juvenile justice advocacy. The advocacy process between the prosecution and defense was previously conducted without the participation of the juvenile and sometimes without the juvenile's presence. Mistakes and bad decisions in the juvenile court could not be corrected by the juvenile's representative in the courtroom or later on appeal prior to the *Gault* decision.

Advocacy is aimed at the decision maker, in this case the juvenile court judge, to get him or her to adopt the advocate's view of the case. Through this process, facts are brought to light that might otherwise have remained undiscovered. The purposes of the advocacy system, often misunderstood by the public, are legitimate and functional. Without this system of attack and counterattack, one-dimensional decisions would be made and the system (and the accused) would suffer and flounder.

Advocacy is not limited to attorneys for the defense or for the prosecution in the juvenile justice system. At each step of the process, someone is trying to sway decision makers to a different view of the juvenile's situation. All participants in the process seem to adopt a "side" and generally stick to it in attempting to influence the outcome. The police officer that wants to get a "rotten" juvenile off the streets will adopt the prosecution "side." Friends and concerned parents may adopt the defense "side" as their own. Although the practice of providing a specific prosecution and defense in juvenile proceedings was not the rule after *Gault,* they have existed as rough categories all along.

Prosecutors have had a very small part in juvenile proceedings in the past, for most of the process was relatively relaxed and the rules of evidence were seldom followed. Petitioners (complainants) were seldom in need of representation in this informal atmosphere. The court was expected to be there to *protect* the juvenile, and the role of prosecutor seemed to violate this concept. But, as defense counsel was representing more and more juveniles, the scales of justice tipped too far in the direction of the defense. Pretrial investigation and preparation by a strong defense advocate caused many otherwise provable cases to be dismissed.

The function of the judge is to be a referee. Assuming that the prosecution role obviously results in bias on the part of the judge, closing a mind that should be open, Besharov notes that:

> the judge should be "the only disinterested lawyer connected with the proceeding. He has no interest except to see that justice is done, and

he has no more important duty than to see that the facts are properly developed and that their bearing upon the question at issue are clearly understood by the jury." He can intervene in a proceeding only in situations where counsel is inadequately examining a witness, the witness is reluctant, an expert is inarticulate or less than candid, the facts are insufficiently elucidated in a long trial, an issue needs to be clarified or when justice or the orderly progress of the trial requires it.[9]

Attorneys for the petitioners, therefore, have had to become real prosecutors, ready to fight for the rights of their clients instead of assuming a *parens patriae* relationship with the court and the accused juvenile. After proof of their case, they can look toward nonjudicial handling of the case and the use of diversion and other alternatives. Above all, it is the prosecutor advocate's job to seek the truth and *do justice* . . .anything less is unethical and probably illegal.

The defense advocate's role in the juvenile justice process grew during the press for similar advocacy in the adult system during the 1950s and 1960s. *In re Gault* made this role a right, and regular representation of juveniles is now the rule. Juvenile advocates seek to keep their clients from any further contact with the juvenile justice system, if possible. They have generally shown great energy toward getting their clients "off." The lack of proof that treatment, offered under *parens patriae,* is effective in spurring many juvenile defense advocates to use all their skills to keep clients out of the clutches of the system. The defense advocate must be prepared to fight as hard as the prosecution and leave *parens patriae* to the judge.

Advocacy, since *Gault,* has turned the juvenile court proceeding into a true legal proceeding. The advocates on both sides have had problems in developing protocols and procedures in a system that had not previously been a legal battleground. Many of the same tactics—motions, delays, obfuscation, and bluster—that have slowed down the adult system are creeping into juvenile proceedings, for advocacy, like rights for juveniles, is a two-edged sword. As the practice grows, the system becomes more and more cumbersome. Unfortunately, the juveniles are the ones who often suffer by either being denied the treatment needed for their problems (defense wins) or by being placed into a system that does not work (prosecution wins). It is still too early to make judgments on advocacy, but it appears to be leading to another adult system at the juvenile level.

The legal rights of youth have undergone a number of changes during the history of juvenile court. Recent developments include:

1. Increased visibility for the legal rights of children;
2. Improvements in the admissibility of evidence favorable to child victims;
3. More complex characterization of relationships essential to children;

4. Extensive efforts to fund various preventative and ameliorative efforts in child welfare.[10]

Bross asserts that these changes, while not solving all of the problems of juveniles, have helped to protect their interests. Others hope that the juvenile court will strive to protect the rights of both offenders and victims through the use of a combination of rehabilitation, reintegration, and restorative justice.[11]

Screening and Classification: Some Hope

Juveniles whose needs are best met outside the juvenile justice system, by more effective school counseling programs and family therapy, should be screened out as early as possible. In many jurisdictions, screening is combined with classification in an attempt to match juvenile problems with effective solutions.

The promise of treatment has been largely unfulfilled. This is primarily because of society's failure to provide adequate financial support. The newer movement attempts to provide a more effective match between the juvenile's specific custody/treatment combinations of needs to protect society while helping the juvenile to cope. Identification of the deficiencies in the juvenile's ability to handle behavioral problems has become a specific goal of current projects aimed at classification for treatment.

Many classification typologies have been attempted in past juvenile justice systems. The failures of these typologies are more the result of omission than of commission. Too often, the classification diagnostics were ignored or modified by institutional personnel with a vested interest in perpetuation of the status quo. New attempts at classification seem to have promise.

Summary: Where Next?

In this somewhat lengthy text on juvenile justice, it has often been necessary to accentuate the negative, perhaps because there is so much of it to accentuate. Perhaps we have often attempted to apply principles that have failed in other systems to the juvenile justice system, describing intervention strategies and detailing processes for their implementation. Perhaps it is time to reassess our priorities.

The first priority seems to be to provide some kind of a climate where there is hope and incentive for those children who turn to delinquent behavior, often-violent behavior, in the United States. The problems of the homeless, the poor, the ignorant, and those who burn out their future with drugs sometimes seem to be insurmountable. These problems seem to be looked at by most people as separate issues, handled by separate agencies or programs. In fact, the juvenile justice system is where the sum of these issues seems to come together. The juvenile justice system is a *reaction* to the lack of *action* by other segments of society. As we begin to understand some of the dynamics of delinquency, we begin to understand that it is often the reaction to life that strikes out and says, "I'll get what I want any way that I can." The spate of dishonest politicians, religious leaders, teachers, businesspeople, and other persons, who should serve as role models, give mixed messages to the youth of today.

We close by offering a glimpse of the future by reviewing the evolution of the juvenile justice system. As Cohn indicates, the philosophy, operations and processes of the juvenile justice system have been affected by:

1. The adoption of the concept of *parens patriae;*
2. The *Gault* decision that extended due process of law to juveniles;
3. The "get tough" movement that concluded that rehabilitation was impossible and incapacitation should be the aim of juvenile sentencing;
4. Federal intervention requiring the separation of status offenders and delinquents as well as juvenile from adult offenders.
5. The current movement focusing on the politics of fear and increased punishment of juveniles.[12]

The final and possibly "coming" revolution will be in juvenile justice management. Management philosophies like *Reinventing Government* and *Total Quality Management.*[13] These participatory based management philosophies can help develop change within the system and move to multi-modal treatments and less costly sanctioning mechanisms.[14]

This new society must be one that values children more than cars, is willing to provide *quality* education to all youths, does not provide a negative role model for the young, and will be willing to spend the time and money to show that we value our future in our children. It is our hope that the readers of this book will feel motivated to make a difference so that the twenty-first century in the United States will be a time that provides love, safety, and *hope* for our children.

TERMS TO REMEMBER

Deterrence	Treatment model
Model muddle	

REVIEW QUESTIONS

1. What is the "model muddle"? What problem does it represent for the juvenile justice system?
2. Should *parens patriae* be the guiding philosophy of the juvenile justice system? Why or why not?

3. How should the juvenile justice system be operated in the future?

4. What will be the next "revolution" in juvenile justice?

5. Check the World Wide Web for new trends in juvenile justice.

NOTES

[1]M. Siegler and H. Osmond, *Models of Madness, Models of Medicine* (New York: Macmillan, 1974).

[2]Robert Sommer, *The End of Imprisonment* (New York: Oxford University Press, 1976), pp. 24–25.

[3]L. Cole, *Our Children's Keepers* (New York: Grossman, 1972), pp. 26–27.

[4]Ralph A. Weisheit and David M. Alexander, "Juvenile Justice Philosophy and the Demise of Parens Patriae," in Barry W. Hancock and Paul M. Sharp, eds. *Criminal Justice in America: Theory, Practice, and Policy,* (Upper Saddle River, NJ: Prentice-Hall, 1996), pp. 321–332.

[5]Harry E. Allen and Clifford E. Simonsen, *Corrections in America: An Introduction (9th ed.)* (Upper Saddle River, NJ: Prentice-Hall, 2001), p. 668.

[6]Peter J. Benekos and Alida V. Merlo, "Reaffirming Juvenile Justice," in Roslyn Muraskin and Albert R. Roberts, eds. *Visions of Change: Crime and Justice in the Twenty-First Century,* (Upper Saddle River, NJ: Prentice-Hall, 2002), pp. 265–286.

[7]J. Rossi, *Hard Cores Don't Come From Apples* (Pasadena, Calif.: Ward Ritchie, 1976), pp. 124–125.

[8]L. G. Arthur, "Tomorrow's Choices," *Juvenile and Family Court Journal,* Vol. 47 (1996), pp. 39–47.

[9]D. Besharov, *Juvenile Justice Advocacy: Practice in a Unique Court* (New York: Practicing Law Institute, 1974), p. 42.

[10]Donald C. Bross, "Evolution of Independent Legal Representation for Children," *Protecting Children,* Vol. 16 (2000), pp. 20–33.

[11]Michael Cavadino, Ian Crow, and James Dignan, *Criminal Justice 2000: Strategies for a New Century* (Winchester, UK: Waterside Press, 1999).

[12]Alvin W. Cohn, "The Future of Juvenile Justice Administration: Evolution v. Revolution," *Juvenile and Family Court Journal,* Vol. 45 (1994), pp. 51–64.

[13]Paul H. Hahn, *Emerging Criminal Justice: Three Pillars for a Proactive Justice System* (Thousand Oaks, CA: Sage, 1998).

[14]Commission on Behavioral and Social Sciences and Education of the National Research Council, *Losing Generations: Adolescents in High-Risk Settings* (Washington, D.C.: National Academy Press), p.167.

Index